Computers
and
Information Processing

Second Edition

Floyd Fuller

LEES-MCRAE COLLEGE

William Manning

PORTLAND STATE UNIVERSITY

Webmaster materials prepared by

Sue Conger

SOUTHERN METHODIST UNIVERSITY

CREDITS:

Managing Editor	DeVilla Williams	**Text and Cover Design**	Efrat Reis
Product Manager	Lisa Strite	**Marketing Manager**	Susanne Walker
Production Editor	Debbie Masi	**Editorial Assistant**	Samantha Smith
Composition House	TSI Graphics	**Editorial Assistant**	Scott MacDonald

For more information contact:

Course Technology
One Main Street
Cambridge, MA 02142

International Thomson Publishing Europe
Berkshire House 168-173
High Holborn
London WCIV 7AA
England

Thomas Nelson Australia
102 Dodds Street
South Melbourne, 3205
Victoria, Australia

Nelson Canada
1120 Birchmount Road
Scarborough, Ontario
Canada M1K 5G4

International Thomson Editores
Campos Eliseos 385, Piso 7
Col. Polanco
11560 Mexico D.F. Mexico

International Thomson Publishing GmbH
Künigswinterer Strasse 418
53227 Bonn
Germany

International Thomson Publishing Asia
211 Henderson Road
#05-10 Henderson Building
Singapore 0315

International Thomson Publishing Japan
Hirakawacho Kyowa Building, 3F
2-2-1 Hirakawacho
Chiyoda-ku, Tokyo 102
Japan

AIE: 0-7600-4623-9

Student Edition, soft cover: 0-7600-4622-0

Student Edition, hard cover: 0-7600-4932-7

Printed in the United States of America
10   9   8   7   6   5   4   3   2   1

BRIEF TABLE OF CONTENTS

CONTENTS

PART ONE
Introduction xxvi

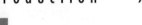

CHAPTER 1

COMPUTERS AND INFORMATION PROCESSING 2

CHAPTER 2

COMPUTERS, SOCIETY, AND YOU 34

PART TWO
Hardware   74

CHAPTER 3

INPUT DEVICES AND MEDIA   76

CHAPTER 4

THE CENTRAL PROCESSING UNIT AND MEMORY   112

CHAPTER 5

OUTPUT DEVICES AND MEDIA   146

CHAPTER 6

SECONDARY STORAGE   178

CHAPTER 7

TELECOMMUNICATIONS AND THE INTERNET 212

PART THREE
Software and Data Management   262

PART FOUR
Systems and Development 340

CHAPTER 10

COMPUTER-BASED PROBLEM SOLVING 342

CHAPTER 11

SOFTWARE DEVELOPMENT AND PROGRAMMING   386

CHAPTER 12

VISUAL SYSTEMS   424

PART FIVE
Computers and Society   460

CHAPTER 13
SECURITY, CRIME, AND ETHICS   462

CHAPTER 14

ENSURING YOUR FUTURE IN AN INFORMATION SOCIETY   496

An Introduction to

COMPUTERS AND INFORMATION PROCESSING Second Edition

Fuller/Manning

No field is more important to the future
success of today's students than computers and
information processing. Whether preparing to
enter the competitive job market for the first
time, working to acquire skills necessary for
advancement in a chosen career path, or setting
off in a new career direction, students will find
that computers will be an integral part of their
experience.

Our goal for the Second Edition of *Computers and Information Processing* is to immerse the student in real-world applications and issues surrounding computers in society today, while expanding and updating our coverage of all aspects of information processing systems.

This book is ideal for undergraduate introductory computer concepts courses. Although tailored in length for courses that include application software labs, the text also works well in courses that focus on concepts alone. This book enables students to understand how computer systems are used today through coverage of basic concepts of both computers and information processing and introductory software skills. A **systems perspective** places concepts and skills in context, raising students' interest and demonstrating the relevance of topics to real-world problems and opportunities.

Three central themes unite the topics covered in the text:

Personal and organizational productivity are critical to ensuring quality goods and services and a successful organization. As global markets expand and competition intensifies, organizations look to information processing systems to make them more efficient, more competitive, and hence more profitable. High quality standards are implemented and enforced through complex information systems. Individuals can also use computers to increase their personal productivity and the quality of their work.

The work environment is dynamic. Creativity. Teamwork. Globalization. Intranets. Trends shift rapidly in the competitive business world. New technologies continue to emerge which shape and reflect the rapid advancements in the global marketplace. This text integrates coverage of emerging trends and related technologies to aid students in preparing to enter today's workplace.

Computers can help students to succeed. The ideas and insights gained from this book will help students to succeed in school, at work, and in every aspect of their lives.

ORGANIZATION

PART ONE: INTRODUCTION

Chapters 1 and 2 provide a general introduction and overview of computers and information processing and how these technologies are changing businesses and society.

PART TWO: HARDWARE

Chapters 3 through 7 cover the details of hardware technology, including input devices, types and properties of processors, memory, output devices, data storage and retrieval systems, telecommunications, and the Internet.

PART THREE: SOFTWARE AND DATA MANAGEMENT

Chapters 8 and 9 describe operating systems, utility programs, data management, and databases.

PART FOUR: SYSTEMS AND DEVELOPMENT

Chapters 10 through 12 describe the evolution of information systems; explain how information systems are used in decision making; and trace the steps of systems analysis, design, and implementation. An all-new chapter takes a look at computer graphics, presentations, and multimedia computer applications.

PART FIVE: COMPUTERS AND SOCIETY

Chapters 13 and 14 focus on the effects computers have on society. Critical issues such as computer crime, security systems, privacy, and ethics in an electronic world are examined, and future impacts of emerging technologies and trends are discussed. Special attention is paid to how coming changes will influence students' lives as we enter the 21st century.

PEDAGOGICAL FEATURES

Chapter Outlines provide an overview of topics covered in each chapter. **Learning Objectives** help students set goals for mastering concepts in each chapter.

Key Terms

Key Terms are listed to aid students in reviewing the large number of new terms and in preparing for exams.

Summary

Chapter Summaries tie together key concepts and provide a synopsis of topics covered in each chapter.

14 Easy steps to being a webmaster

14 Easy steps to being a webmaster projects provide opportunities for students to sharpen their skills by creating and improving their own personal web pages.

Exercises

Exercises, including review questions, fill-in-the-blank questions, matching, and activities for groups and individuals, provide a way for students to test themselves or for instructors to assess the level of student mastery. These exercises are designed to get students used to using the correct terminology and to help them master the concepts.

Skills for Living

Skills for Living, a feature found in each chapter, helps students learn to use the Internet to find a job, buy a car or a computer, research stocks and bonds, find articles to use for other classes, and more. A large **Skills for Living** project appears at the end of each chapter.

CHANGES TO THE SECOND EDITION

The computer and information processing field changes more rapidly than any other field in the world. The importance of staying current when new technologies are developed at break-neck speed is paramount; every year computing speeds typically increase 30 percent, while becoming 30 percent less expensive. Every effort has been made to offer cutting-edge coverage, and expected future trends are identified.

Changes to the text include:

Expanded and updated coverage of the Internet, including new sections on:

- The Internet and accessing the Internet (Chapter 7).

- Issues of privacy and security on the Internet, including the transmission of confidential and/or pornographic materials over the Internet (Chapter 13).

Focused attention on current issues, the latest technology, and recent trends, including:

- The role of computers in society, the growing impact of digital convergence, the increasing popularity of the Internet, health and safety issues, and the proposal of the National Information Infrastructure—a high-speed digital network that makes information and services available to everyone—are now covered in Chapter 2.

- Computer graphics, presentations, multimedia, and virtual reality are now covered in a brand new chapter (Chapter 12).

- The features of Windows 95 are now covered in a new section in Chapter 8.

- Open systems, industry self-governance, more powerful microcomputers, the globalization of the office, and integration of office systems have been added to Chapter 14.

- Nonimpact printers—the most popular printers available today—receive greater focus in Chapter 5.

REORGANIZATION OF TOPICS

- Coverage of systems development and the various types of information systems has been condensed into one chapter (Chapter 10).

- In recognition of the wide acceptance and implementation of Total Quality Management techniques and the expansion of many businesses into the global marketplace, coverage of these issues has been moved from special interest boxes to within the text.

■ Application Modules have been removed to make room for more extensive concepts coverage; these modules are available on CTI's home page on the World Wide Web: **http://www.course.com**.

NEW END-OF-CHAPTER FEATURES

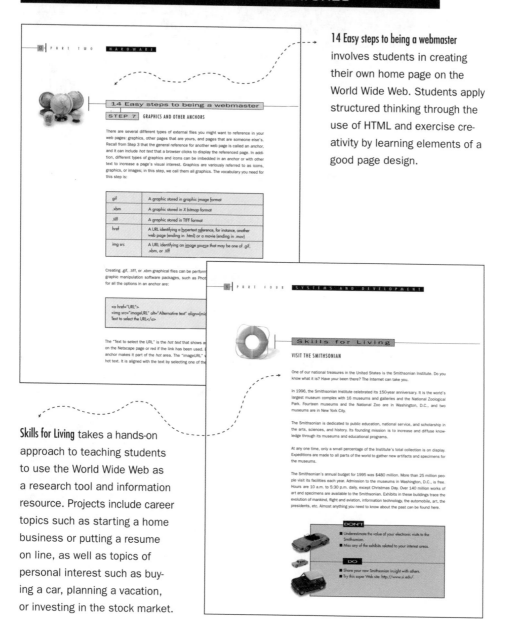

14 Easy steps to being a webmaster involves students in creating their own home page on the World Wide Web. Students apply structured thinking through the use of HTML and exercise creativity by learning elements of a good page design.

Skills for Living takes a hands-on approach to teaching students to use the World Wide Web as a research tool and information resource. Projects include career topics such as starting a home business or putting a resume on line, as well as topics of personal interest such as buying a car, planning a vacation, or investing in the stock market.

SUPPLEMENTAL INTEREST BOXES

In each chapter, special sections capture students' interest, demonstrate application of concepts, and touch on selected topics in the field of information processing.

FOCUS

The World at Your Fingertips

Nowhere in the world of networking have designers had higher hopes—or more troubles—than in constructing computer communications systems for . . .

Focus sections emphasize current applications and selected topics, including international concerns and Internet issues. Each one provides examples of real-life organizations and individuals implementing the newest computer applications and achieving successful results.

COMPUTER CURRENTS

Dear Mr. President

In the course of his 1992 bid for the presidency, Bill Clinton repeatedly relied on so-called "town hall forums" of local citizens who were offered the opportunity to speak directly to the candidate about their concerns and views. In an apparent effort to "stay in touch" after winning the election, the Clinton White House moved quickly to go "on-line" with the nation's computers . . .

Computer Currents boxes provide coverage of cutting-edge technologies, quality issues, and reengineering processes. Examples relate to chapter concepts and are relevant to students, without getting overly and needlessly technical.

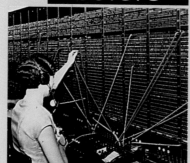

Property of AT&T Archives. Reprinted with permission of AT&T.

Property of AT&T Archives. Reprinted with permission of AT&T.

AT&T uses sophisticated techniques and equipment to monitor the flow of voice and data traffic over its complex communications network.

Telephone communications were rustic at best: poor sound quality, static, and archaic equipment were the norm, with service nonexistent in some areas.

Before Computers/After Computers These boxes are designed to make students aware of the impact computers have had in our society as a result of gradual changes. These sections highlight examples of how computer technology profoundly influences our daily lives.

Spectacular **Spotlights**

At the end of Parts One through Four, fascinating photo essays bring to life the impact of computers in society. The NO BOUNDARIES essay illustrates the pervasiveness of computers in all aspects of our lives; MAKING THE CONNECTION highlights telecommunications issues and the Internet; NOT SO LONG AGO details the evolution of computer technology from the 1950s through the present; and DO THE RIGHT THING examines the many ethical issues faced by an increasingly technological society.

COURSETOOLS

Let you teach the way you want to teach

This text is accompanied by our highly praised CourseTools—technology-based teaching and learning resources that have been carefully integrated with this text to form a system of instruction. Each CourseTool fits into at least one of the four stages of an instructional model with the following framework: **Preparation**, **Instruction**, **Reinforcement**, and **Assessment**. Most importantly, CourseTools enable instructors to teach the way they want to teach, and help students learn faster and easily, and have a little more fun along the way.

Course Test Manager is cutting-edge Windows-based testing software that enables instructors to design and administer pre-tests, practice tests, and actual examinations. The full-featured program provides random test generation of practice tests, immediate on-line feedback, and generation of detailed study guides for questions that are incorrectly answered. On-line pre-tests help instructors assess student skills and plan instruction.

Also, students can take tests at the computer; tests can be automatically graded and can generate statistical information for the instructor on individual and group performance. Instructors can also use Course Test Manager to produce printed tests. A printed test bank is also available to adopters.

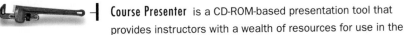

Course Presenter is a CD-ROM-based presentation tool that provides instructors with a wealth of resources for use in the classroom, replacing traditional overhead transparencies with computer-generated screen shows. The presentations integrate closely with the book and other CourseTools and provide instructors with another resource to use so they can teach the way they want to teach.

SUPPLEMENTAL TEACHING RESOURCES

Instructor's Resource Kit, featuring:

- **Solutions Manual** with answers to all review questions, fill-in-the-blanks, matching, and activities.

- **Instructor's Manual** Each chapter contains a statement of the purpose of the chapter, and covers major vocabulary words, learning objectives, and lecture outlines.

- **Teaching Tips**, notes for the special interest boxes, lecture anecdotes, questions for in-class discussion or testing and their answers, and classroom activities.

Annotated Instructor's Edition

In addition to the complete student text, this edition of the text offers instructors marginal annotations. These annotations allow greater flexibility in emphasizing selected concepts in accordance with an individual instructor's goals for his or her course.

There are six categories of annotations:

- **Teaching Tips** provide helpful suggestions on how to convey ideas effectively to your students.

- **Points to Stress** restate or clarify topics of particular importance.

- **Discussion Topics** offer approaches for structuring classroom discussions on selected topics.

- **Current Applications** feature examples of the latest technologies supporting relevant concepts.

- **Common Student Misconceptions** identify concepts which are often misunderstood by students and offer alternative explanations for clarification.

- **Quotations** offer perspectives on critical issues from noteworthy individuals.

Student Study Guide

This material provides an excellent tool for students who are mastering the concepts presented in this text. Featuring review materials, self-tests with answers, and other learning aids, the study guide is an invaluable resource.

ACKNOWLEDGMENTS

Writing or revising a book is a team effort. For this second edition of *Computers and Information Processing*, we had the very best team to work with and we would be remiss without acknowledging individuals who gave so much of themselves to make this book a success. These are the unsung heroes who devoted their untiring efforts toward the successful completion of this work. For those efforts, we are forever grateful.

First, we would like to thank all of the people at Course Technology for their confidence in us as authors. Joe Dougherty, President of CTI, provided us with the resources to make this edition even better than the first. Managing Editor DeVilla Williams was the guiding force whose insight, knowledge and dedication is evident throughout this book. Working with her has been a delight that every author should have an opportunity to experience. Lisa Strite, Product Manager, coordinated the efforts of many people in meeting deadlines and ensured that the final manuscript was in excellent condition. Our special thanks go to Becky Johnson, Developmental Editor, who worked diligently on the organization and content of the chapters. Her ideas and suggestions are reflected throughout the book. Abby Reip, Photo Researcher, deserves praise for selecting and obtaining impressive photographs and illustrations that help bring the information in the chapters to life. Our Production Editor, Debbie Masi, did an outstanding job in preparing the manuscript for production and supervising production of the final product. Congratulations also go to Efrat Reis for her exceptional interior and cover designs and to TSI Graphics for implementing the design and composing the pages in an attractive way. Our sincere appreciation to Sue Conger for her outstanding work in preparing the Webmaster materials that are contained in the book. Susanne Walker, Marketing Manager, developed an impressive plan for marketing the book so that instructors will be knowledgeable about the book and its supplements. Editorial Assistants, Samantha Smith and Scott MacDonald, assisted us in a variety of ways. To each of them, we offer our gratitude.

Our academic institutions and colleagues deserve recognition. Students, faculty, staff, and administrations at both Lees-McRae College and Portland State University have supported our efforts in every way possible. Thank you, all, for your support.

Special acknowledgments are also due to our families. They spent many an evening alone, while we worked frantically to make publication deadlines. Our wives, Edith and Norma, and our children Cindy, Michael, and Jenna; Toni, Kelly, and Andee deserve our love and appreciation for their support and encouragement that helped make our dream of completing this book a reality.

We appreciate and acknowledge the support of colleague reviewers in the field. Often, professors begin to feel they "know it all!" It is a humbling experience to expose your best work to other colleagues in the field, only to have them expose your weaknesses. We were constantly amazed and impressed by the quality and quantity of our reviewers' suggestions for improving this book. This book is better because of them.

Terry Dorsett, Central Arizona College; Steve Drasner, Northern Virginia Community College; Celeste Dubeck-Smith, Northern Virginia Community College; Diane Fischer, Dowling College; Bunny Howard, Florida Community College; Delia Perez Joseph, St. Philips College; Rose Laird, Northern Virginia Community College; Jean Luoma, Great Lakes Junior College; Dennis McNeal, Delta College; J. M. Merrell-Beech, Triton College; Mike Michaelson, Palomar College; James Payne, Kellogg Community College; Mysore Ramaswamy, Grambling State University; Pam Schmidt, Oakton Community College; Gayla Jo Slauson, Mesa State College; Mike Wackerly, Delta College

We feel it's also necessary to acknowledge those who have shaped the book in its prior edition. Their helpful comments and invaluable insight have helped make this book what it is today:

C. T. Cadenhead, Truckee Meadows Community College; Chris Carter, Indiana Technical College; Gena Casas, Florida Community College at Jacksonville; Thomas Case, Georgia Southern University; William Cornette, Southwest Missouri State University; Pat Cude, Tarleton State University; Elaine Daly, Oakton Community College; Mary Garrett, Lansing Community College; Rosemary Gross, Creighton University; Stephen Haag, University of Minnesota; Arlene S. Handy, Wilkes Community College; David Herzog, St. Louis Community College; C. Brian Honess, University of South Carolina; Robert O. Johnson, Frostberg University; Jeanne Massengill, Highland Community College; Matthew McConeghy, Johnson and Wales University; John McKinney, University of Cincinnati; Linda Salchenberger, Loyola University; Janice Sipior, Villanova University; Janet Spears, Central Michigan University; Denis Titchenell, Los Angeles City College; Todd Waymon, Montgomery College; Ken Whitten, Florida Community College at Jacksonville

—Floyd Fuller and William Manning

PART ONE

INTRODUCTION

As the uses and capabilities of computers increase, so too have the ways in which computers influence every aspect of our lives. Continuous education and personal development will be necessary to keep current with new computer technologies.

CHAPTER 1
Computers and Information Processing

CHAPTER 2
Computers, Society, and You

COMPUTERS AND INFORMATION PROCESSING

OBJECTIVES

AFTER STUDYING THIS CHAPTER, YOU SHOULD BE ABLE TO:

1. Discuss the role of computers in bringing about both the computer and the information revolutions.
2. Explain why computers are commonly referred to as productivity tools.
3. Discuss the difference between data and information, and describe the role of knowledge in transforming one into the other.
4. Explain what a computer is and how it is different from a computer system.
5. Explain the difference between a processor and processing.
6. Describe the four components of a computer system.
7. Identify the components of an information processing system and describe how an information processing system differs from a computer system.
8. Distinguish between general-purpose and special-purpose computers.
9. Identify three important components used to describe information processing systems.
10. Classify computer systems into five general categories.

CHAPTER OUTLINE

THE COMPUTER REVOLUTION
    The Computer as a Productivity Tool

THE INFORMATION REVOLUTION
    Data, Knowledge, and Information

INFORMATION PROCESSING

WHAT IS A COMPUTER?
    Components of a Computer System
    Components of an Information
    Processing System

PROCESS CONTROL

INFORMATION PROCESSING SYSTEMS
    Types of Processors
    Processing Power
    Main Memory Storage
    Single-User vs. Multi-User Systems
    Computer System Classifications

INFORMATION PROCESSING SOFTWARE
    System Software
    Application Software

INFORMATION PROCESSING

The plant hums in the darkness as pieces travel down conveyor belts to stations where mechanical arms weld them into completed units. The units are then quickly packaged and shipped off to distant parts of the globe. No human voice breaks the stillness, since no humans are present. It's the factory of the future, and it's already here. A generation ago, no one could have imagined a factory of this kind, one capable of adjusting quickly to changes in demand, and with the ability to produce high-quality goods faster and more efficiently than previously thought possible. Consider the record:

- At General Electric, an undisputed leader in total quality management and successful automation, a computerized assembly unit has taken over the tedious job of installing compressor blades into jet engines. In addition to reducing the installation time by a factor of five to one, the new system inspects its own work. Putting robots to work on its titanium sheet-welding operation cut manufacturing time from 3.5 hours to 57 minutes—with no errors. A computerized assembly line that makes crankshafts for compressors inspects each unit 1,000 times during its production to ensure that tolerance is held to within 50 millionth of an inch, or about 1/100 the thickness of a human hair.

- Electrolux Corporation, makers of "the Cadillac of vacuum cleaners," had trouble selling its basic-model cleaner when priced at $599. Today, thanks to a redesign of the vacuum and the automation of its plants, the same Electrolux model costs just $299—and sales are brisk. Automation and redesign also worked wonders at Whirlpool, boosting sales and enabling the firm to expand its operations by 80 percent and its workforce by over 50 percent.

- Automation dramatically cut costs and production time at Badger Meter, Inc. Formerly, dies and equipment had to be changed for each casting of a particular meter component, forcing the firm to make hundreds of one type of component before moving on to the next type. A complete set of castings took 12 weeks to create. Now, more flexible equipment can make and inspect an entire set of castings in just six minutes.

In Japan, a severe labor shortage has made automation and robotics not only economically desirable, but vitally necessary for firms in many industries. Because of the labor shortage, Japanese firms spend far more on automating their manufacturing operations than they do on the information management systems that are so common in U.S. businesses. In fact, 80 percent of all the robots in the world work in Japan.

Arguably the biggest improvement in manufacturing that can be credited to computers has nothing to do with robots or quality control. It lies in the future of the "paperless office." In the aviation industry, the standing joke has long been that the weight of a new-model airplane generally equals the weight of the paperwork (about 8,000 pounds) involved in creating it. But Northrop Corporation, makers of aircraft for commercial and military use, has instituted a new computerized information system that will reduce the need for much of the paper.

THE COMPUTER REVOLUTION

A revolution is something that causes fundamental change in a society and its economy. Over the past several decades, society has experienced a revolution—the **computer revolution**—sparked by the invention and proliferation of computers. As the uses and capabilities of computers have increased, so too have the ways in which computers influence every aspect of our lives.

THE COMPUTER AS A PRODUCTIVITY TOOL

The foundation for the computer revolution was laid by the **industrial revolution**, which began over a century ago. The industrial revolution introduced society to mechanized ways of manufacturing products. Machines began to perform much of the manufacturing work, replacing or enhancing human labor. Each generation of machines was capable of producing more and better products at lower costs. This increase in productivity (the amount of value produced in a given period of time) led to a rising standard of living throughout the world.

The computer revolution has brought about similar changes. Today, much of the work people do is done by computers. Machines in manufacturing plants, such as those described in our chapter-opening scenario, are now being operated and controlled by computers. Computers have automated difficult, dangerous, and even humanly impossible tasks. **Automation** is the replacement of human observation or effort by mechanical or electronic devices. Some computer-controlled welding devices can join metal parts faster and more accurately than even the most skilled craftsperson. Some manufacturers use computers as part of quality management programs. These ensure that products are consistently produced within tolerances too small for humans to easily determine. Moreover, computers have removed the "drowning in the details" aspect of many jobs, allowing individuals to concentrate more fully on the important aspects of a problem or project. Many automated inventory systems reduce the burden of constantly keeping track of the physical amount of goods available for sale. These computerized systems allow the problem focus to shift from "when to buy" to "what to buy."

Computers are also making it possible for scientists, researchers, and engineers to tackle problems previously considered too difficult and to pioneer new frontiers never before thought possible. Astronomers can measure distances between planets with an accuracy undreamed of just a generation ago. Biologists can map the entire genetic code of an organism as has recently been done with the smallpox virus. Meteorologists are better able to make long-range weather forecasts, and space flights are now commonplace. These and many other scientific advances would have been impossible without the assistance of computers.

FOCUS

Press the Enter Key and Call Me in the Morning

Consider the statistics. In the course of their lifetimes, more than half of all Americans suffer from serious stress and/or relationship problems, and some 60 percent will experience serious depression. Yet most will not seek professional help for one or more reasons. Certainly the cost of psychi-

Courtesy Thought Technology Ltd.

atric help is often high, running over $100 per hour for many doctors. Even more significant is probably the continuing stigma attached to emotional problems. Indeed, many people whose company insurance programs would pay the cost of such treatment refuse to go because they fear the impact on their careers if their employers learned

they were "seeing a shrink."

To help address this dilemma, several companies have developed computer programs that purport to turn your PC into a psychotherapist. For somewhere between $25 and $500 (far below the cost of professional personal therapy), you can select from psychological self-help programs that span an impressive range of problems. Those suffering from stress can take advantage of programs such as ProComp + ™/DOS and FlexComp, Help-Stress, and Relax, which first help users measure their stress levels in terms of physical responses such as forehead muscle tension or electrical charges in the fingertips. These programs then try to help users lower their stress levels using the same types of relaxation techniques that have long been employed by behavioral psychologists. Other programs address everything from lack of assertiveness (Help-Assert) to eating disorders (Foods, Moods, and Willpower) to sexual dysfunction (Sexpert).

By far the most controversial programs, however, are those aimed at overcoming depression. In the eye of the controversy is a recent study of one such program, MORTON, at the University of Wisconsin/Madison. In this study, 36 patients diagnosed as suffering from mild to moderate depression were divided into three groups for a six-week period. The first group received no treatment, a second group received therapy from a human therapist, and the third group got to use MORTON. Only one person who received no treatment reported significant improvement, as opposed to three-quarters of those who met with the human therapist. But to the surprise and concern of many involved, the computer did nearly as well as the human therapist—two-thirds of MORTON's patients reported feeling considerably better.

This report, and a similar one with phobics in Canada that also showed computers to be successful therapists, touched off a firestorm in the psychotherapeutic community. Many professionals decried the study, noting that the human therapist limited his own technique to the computer's capabilities and that the study was too short (6 weeks versus the typical 20-week course of therapy recommended for depressives). They argue, too, that if seriously depressed individuals turn to computers rather than human therapists, they may never get the intensive help they need and may get worse, not better.

Those in charge of the Wisconsin study admit that their study was limited and that their findings are only tentative. However, study director Paulette M. Selmi, a psychologist in private practice, feels that their experiment shows "there's definitely a place for computers in the mental health field." That place may be as a kind of assistant to human therapists, since the computer proved particularly adept at getting people to record their feelings and admit the nature of their problems. Lacking the skills to hold a dialogue with its patients, MORTON had to rely heavily on users' answers to multiple-choice questions in deciding on appropriate therapies.

While computer self-help may not be for everyone (no software company is currently even proposing programs for such highly serious disorders as psychosis, multiple personalities, and schizophrenia), many in the therapeutic community admit that it may at least be "better than nothing" for most individuals. And this "doctor" is always "in."

The way in which individuals go about their daily lives has also changed quite dramatically as a result of computer technology. A simple, computer-controlled automatic coffeemaker allows you to awake to a pot of freshly brewed coffee. Most new-model cars come equipped with antilock brakes, a computer-controlled system which "pumps" the cars' brakes hundreds of times per second, a rate much faster than humanly possible. Many more of the conveniences of modern living are available because of computer technology—from the ability to enjoy compact disk music while jogging, to the flexibility of banking whenever you want through a "cash machine."

Computer technology has allowed both organizations and individuals to achieve greater productivity. In fact, computers are often referred to as **productivity tools**, because people use them to do more in less time. The potential uses of computers have become so numerous, and their value so great, that it is now unusual to find any business organization without one. Moreover, in addition to the computers found in such devices as coffeemakers, TVs, and VCRs, general-purpose computers are entering households as well (see Figure 1.1).

Figure 1.1

Over the next few years, an increasing percentage of America's 97 million households will have general-purpose computers, many of which will feature over-sized screens simular to televisions, built-in telephone answering machines, and communications software.

= 5%

*Projected

92 93 94 95 96* 97* 98*

Experts predict that by the end of this decade personalized computers will replace today's personal computers. **Personalized computers** are computers capable of being intimately customized to the user and can become even more so over time by learning the usage patterns and traits of that individual. You may even be able to communicate with these new-generation personalized computers through facial expressions and voice intonations.

With computers becoming involved with an ever-increasing number of human endeavors, it is safe to say that the computer revolution is still occurring. As with the industrial revolution, society and the economy will continue to experience fundamental changes as a result. Another important similarity between the industrial revolution and the computer revolution is that many people feared the machines brought about by the industrial revolution. Not only did they fear the machines themselves, but they were afraid the machines would make human workers obsolete and, as a result, they would lose their jobs. Likewise, many people today fear not only the computer, a fear called **cyberphobia**, but that computers will replace workers.

Fortunately there is nothing to fear from computers. As you will see, they are completely predictable and are dependent upon human instruction for everything they do. While they have displaced some workers from particular jobs, they have also created many exciting new job opportunities which we will discuss in later chapters. In addition, they have made many jobs more personally fulfilling and rewarding. Moreover, computers have allowed human knowledge to greatly expand and have often provided a higher quality of life along the way.

THE INFORMATION REVOLUTION

The computer revolution has spawned still another revolution, called the **information revolution**. The information revolution refers to the societal and economic changes brought about by greater access to a wider variety of information. In the past, much of this information was either too difficult or too costly to obtain. The information revolution is taking place today as a result of computer technology and the

before	AFTER
Reprinted with permission from Cerulean Technology, Inc., creators of PacketCluster Patrol.	Courtesy of U.S. Public Technologies, Inc., San Diego, CA.

Officers were required to locate and apprehend speeders in residential neighborhoods. Often the case went to trial and became the word of the officer against that of the accused. This system was long, costly, and sometimes unfair.

Now computers have taken over the job of ticketing speeders. Using an unmarked van, computers, radar, and a camera, the system takes photos of all autos exceeding the posted speed limit. A photograph is also taken of the driver behind the wheel as he or she speeds down the road in order to establish guilt. The owner of the auto is identified via the license plate. The violator then receives a ticket and a copy of the photograph in the mail. During the first ten days this system was tested in Portland, Oregon, over 1,400 citations were issued.

importance people place on information. It is now information, rather than a physical product, that is being produced in a new way. But what exactly is information?

DATA, KNOWLEDGE, AND INFORMATION

People use information to make decisions. **Data** are raw, unorganized facts that describe reality. **Knowledge** is the body of rules, guidelines, and procedures used to select, organize, and manipulate data to make it more useful for a specific task. **Information**, therefore, is data that has been selected, organized, refined, or manipulated, and is appropriate for a particular purpose, such as making a decision. Information is data that has been made more useful through the application of knowledge.

All facts can be considered data, including such descriptions of reality as sounds and images. Even facts not suited to a particular purpose are data. The act of selecting or rejecting facts based on their relevancy to a particular task is part of the process of converting data into information.

Figure 1.2

People use their knowledge of the world to convert data into information that is meaningful for a particular purpose.

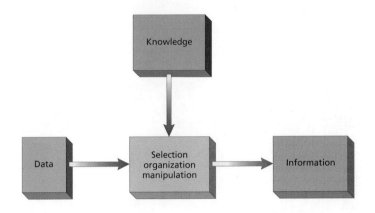

If you could measure it, the amount of information consumed throughout the world every day would be staggering. Each day on a worldwide basis, people make trillions upon trillions of decisions. Some decisions, such as what to eat for lunch, are more or less commonplace. Other decisions, such as whether or not to vote for a particular political candidate, are arguably more important. Many decisions, including which career to pursue and whether or not to buy something, have financial consequences. The basis for these decisions is information. The process of changing or converting data into information is depicted in Figure 1.2.

Computers have changed much about the way people obtain information. In general, computers make accessible information that is more current and more accurate. Do you need to know the latest trading price of a particular stock? That information is available within minutes of the trade. Do you need to know what the weather in Mexico is like in January? That information is available. Do you need to know all of the restaurants in your metropolitan area serving Chinese food, meriting a four-star rating, within walking distance from where you are now, and with entrees averaging under $10? Such a listing, with a map and directions from your current location are also available.

City-Guide information is available showing restaurants, hotels, and other points of interest in most major cities.

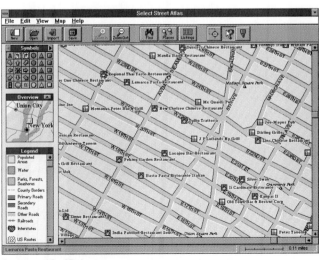

Courtesy of ProCD, Inc.

Frequently updated news and entertainment information is available through the America Online service.

Computers have changed the information-gathering and decision-making behaviors of people throughout the world. These changes continue to occur and affect the very quality of our lives. Let's look at the role of computers in delivering information.

INFORMATION PROCESSING

Computers are useful because they assist operators in the process of changing or converting data into information, **information processing**. In order to assist in this conversion process, a computer must be able to perform four basic functions: input, processing, output, and storage. A computer processes data according to a set of specific instructions, called a **program**. Figure 1.3 illustrates the concept of information processing.

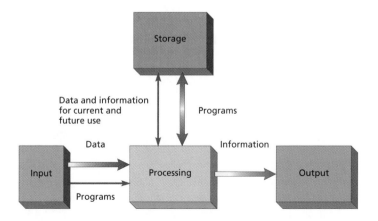

Data and information for current and future use

Programs

Data

Information

Input

Programs

Processing

Output

Storage

Figure 1.3

A computer must perform four basic functions in information processing: input, processing, output, and storage.

During the **input** stage of information processing, data collected from the relevant surrounding environment are entered into the computer. During the **processing** stage the computer selects, organizes, and manipulates the data according to instructions from programs. Programs themselves can be entered into the computer as input. Programs may also be held in storage and accessed later. During the **output** stage, the converted data are either made immediately available for use or are placed in storage for future use. While not considered a stage of information processing, **storage** is nevertheless an important function because it allows the processing activity to occur more efficiently by providing a place to hold input data, programs, and output until they are required.

Note the similarity between the conversion of data into information as shown in Figure 1.2 and information processing as shown in Figure 1.3. In a real sense, the program instructions that tell a computer how to process data perform the same function as human knowledge in converting data into information. Assuming the program works, input data that has been processed into output are defined as information, because the data has been selected, organized, and manipulated for some particular purpose.

When people speak of the power of computers and information processing, they are often referring to the aspect of processing. This is because computers are capable of accepting vast quantities of input data, performing complex selection, organization, and manipulation procedures on this data (processing), and delivering output to any designated location in an extremely rapid fashion. For example, if programmed to do so, a typical microcomputer can access from storage the birthdates of everyone in your class and compute the average student age in much less time than it took for you to read this sentence! While they are indeed extremely fast and powerful, it is important to remember that computers do no more than assist in the processing of data into information, and human beings design that process.

WHAT IS A COMPUTER?

As you have seen, the driving force behind the computer and information revolutions has been the processing power of computers. The processing power of computers is due to many significant advances in the field of micro-electronics. **Micro-electronics** refers to the miniaturization of the components of an electronic circuit. An **electronic circuit** is a series of components that form a pathway capable of carrying an electrical current, the most important component of which is some type of on/off switch. When all of the components

Photos courtesy of Intel Corporation.

of an electronic circuit are placed together on a single piece of semiconducting material, such as silicon, an *integrated circuit (IC)* is formed. Without integrated circuits, computers as they are known today would not exist.

In some ways, any counting device could be called a computer in that it "computes." But today, the term **computer** commonly refers to an electronic device that accepts input, executes program instructions, and delivers output so as to assist in the conversion of data into information. A computer in this sense is a special type of integrated circuit known as a **microprocessor**, **microchip**, or just simply **processor**. A processor consists of thousands of electrical circuits etched onto a very small ("micro") slice ("chip") of silicon (see Figure 1.4). It is through the activity and paths of these circuits that the processor accepts input, executes program instructions, and delivers output.

COMPONENTS OF A COMPUTER SYSTEM

By itself, a computer or processor has no capabilities. An entire computer system is needed to make the computer a useful tool. A **computer system** is a collection of at least four basic components organized for some purpose. Figure 1.5 illustrates the four basic components of a computer system: the computer, input devices, output devices, and storage devices.

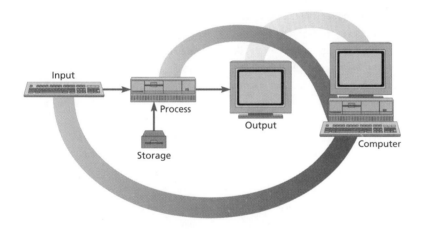

Figure 1.5

The four basic components of a computer system are the computer, input devices, output devices, and storage devices. In a typical microcomputer system, as shown here, storage devices are often contained within the system unit, as is the processor. Note the correlation between the components of the computer system and the stages of information processing.

The Computer   The computer or processor is the "brains" of a computer system. In a typical computer system, the processor is contained within the system unit. The **system unit** is the "box" or case that also contains the power supply, cooling fans, wires, and other assorted devices. The processor does not act upon the actual data. Instead, the processor acts upon electronic representations of the data.

Strictly speaking, a computer is just a processor. Calling a computer system or system unit a computer is incorrect. The computer is the processor chip inside the system unit.

Input Devices   Input devices transmit data to the processor for processing. Each kind of input device is designed to transmit a different type of data. For example, an input device designed to transmit typed characters is configured differently than an input device designed to transmit images. One example of an input device is a keyboard. As will be discussed in Chapter 3, input devices convert data into electrical pulses suitable for the electronic circuitry of the processor.

Output Devices Output devices are those components of a computer system that accept processed data and make this information available for use. A printer is one type of output device. Chapter 5 covers output devices.

Storage Devices Storage devices hold data and programs for current or future use. There are two kinds of storage: primary storage and secondary storage. **Primary storage**, usually called *main memory* or simply *memory,* holds data and instructions for *current* use by the processor.

Like the processor, primary storage devices are themselves microprocessors, capable of accepting electronic input and providing electronic output. The main difference between microprocessors considered to be computers and those considered to be memory devices is that memory microprocessors simply save or hold data and instructions efficiently, while computer microprocessors process the data that is sent back and forth to and from the memory device. Located physically close to the processor (so as to decrease access or travel time), the memory microprocessors rapidly provide data and instructions to the processor for use during processing.

Data and programs held for *future* use are held in **secondary storage**. The most common secondary storage device is the **disk drive**, a piece of equipment capable of retrieving data and programs that have been stored magnetically on thin pieces of circular plastic, called **disks**. Most newer computer systems house one or more disk drives within the system unit.

Although a processor can process large amounts of data very quickly, it can only handle relatively small amounts of data at any one time. In addition, due to the electronic nature of microprocessors, if the power sustaining the microprocessor is turned off, the data and program instructions contained therein are lost. For these two reasons, computer systems require secondary storage devices to keep the data and programs available in electronic form for future use. In addition, secondary storage devices often allow data and programs to be transported from one computer to another by way of a storage medium. A **storage medium** is the material on which data and programs are stored. In the case of a disk drive storage device, the storage medium would be the magnetic plastic material of which the disk is made. The disk can be transported from one computer to another.

COMPONENTS OF AN INFORMATION PROCESSING SYSTEM

Even with a computer system in place, no information processing can occur. An **information processing system** is required. An information processing system, illustrated in Figure 1.6, consists of hardware, software, data, people, and procedures, all organized for a specific purpose.

Hardware The computer, input devices, output devices, and storage devices are all collectively referred to as hardware. **Hardware** consists of those electronic components of an information processing system that you can physically see and touch.

The role of the computer or processor is so important that all other hardware devices are often referred to as peripheral devices. A **peripheral device** is any hardware device not part of the processor. You need to be careful with this term, however, since it is often used to refer to only those hardware devices outside of the system unit. For example, some people may disagree whether a disk drive housed in the system unit is considered a peripheral device. Strictly speaking, an internal disk drive is a peripheral device.

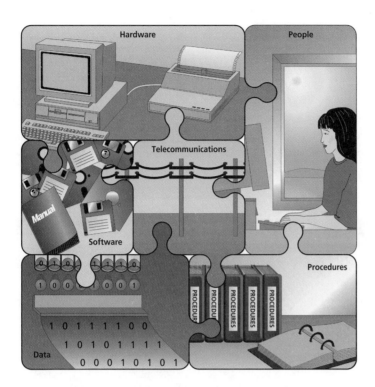

Figure 1.6

Components of an information processing system.

Software   All instructions that direct the operation of the computer system are called **software**. Software includes both programs and the written documentation that explains how to use the programs. For example, when you withdraw money from a bank cash machine, it is a computer program (software) that identifies you as a legitimate customer, checks to see that you have the funds available for withdrawal, and allows you to complete your transaction. While perhaps not as obvious, the written material you received instructing you how to operate the cash machine is also considered part of its software.

Data   As you have seen, without data there would be nothing to process. Data are first input into the information processing system, processed, and then output as useful information. It is important to recognize two important characteristics of data. First, data are reusable. That is, they can be processed over and over again. A single set of data can yield different information depending on the program used to process it. Second, data that has been processed into information through one level of organization can then be reprocessed as data if a second level of organization is desired. For example, your name, bank account number, and current balance are used in the cash machine transaction described previously, and these data items can then be used by the bank as part of its calculations and reports.

People   The single most important component in an information processing system is people. Information is data that has been processed for a purpose, and it is people that bring this purpose to the information processing system. People who need to use an information processing system are often called **end users**, because "in the end" it is the requirements of these people that drives the overall system.

Many people are involved with information processing systems besides the end users. These include people who write the programs that instruct the computer how to process the data, people who instruct end users how to use various software, and people who buy and install entire systems.

Procedures The methods, policies, and rules that govern the use of the information processing system are called **procedures**. Some procedures describe when a certain program can be run. Others describe when a certain group of end users can use the system or how to handle the removal of outdated data from storage. A written notification from your bank informing you that you are only allowed two withdrawals per month from their cash machine is an example of a procedure.

PROCESS CONTROL

Almost any physical activity or task can be considered a sequence of events or a *process*. For our purposes, we can identify a special kind of information processing system. **Process control** is computer automation of real-world events or physical activities by using inputs, programs, and outputs that are set in a fixed way. For example, when vibrations sensed by some automobile antitheft devices surpass a certain threshold for a certain period of time, a computer inside the antitheft device triggers an alarm. In this example, the data (the vibration level) is the only data the system is designed to accept and process, and triggering the alarm is the only output.

While inputs, processing, and outputs are set in a fixed way in process control, it is important to recognize that information processing does occur. To further clarify this, let's consider the example of a potato chip packaging plant. Imagine that after being loaded with potato chips, each bag passes over a scale to be weighed. By way of some input device, the weight of each bag is then electronically communicated to a computer. The computer compares the weight of the loaded bag to a range of acceptable weights. When the weight of a particular loaded bag falls below an acceptable range, the computer triggers a mechanical arm that rejects the bag at this point in the production process. Presumably, if the weight of a loaded bag exceeds the range, the computer will just let it go—to the delight of a hungry customer. Over time, however, if too many loaded bags exceed the range, this information would be fed back to the computer and the computer would signal an operator to adjust the volume of chips being loaded into each bag. It might also be possible to adjust the range of acceptable weights to accommodate those "jumbo bags." While exhibiting a bit more flexibility than the automobile antitheft device, this process control system is still constrained in terms of inputs, processing, and output. Nonetheless, information processing occurs in this process control example. Data (the weights of the loaded bags) are converted into meaningful output and a decision is made (a rejected bag or a signal to an operator).

INFORMATION PROCESSING SYSTEMS

Information processing systems can be classified by the characteristics of each component; that is, the characteristics of the hardware, software, data, people, and procedures that go into making up a particular system. While the attributes of each component are important, at this point it will be easier to concentrate on a few characteristics.

TYPES OF PROCESSORS

Of all the components of an information processing system, the characteristics of the hardware are the easiest to recognize. The processor is usually considered the most important piece of hardware. The two types of processors are special-purpose processors and general-purpose processors.

Special-Purpose Processors A processor designed to accept a limited set of inputs, to process these inputs in a limited set of ways, and to deliver a limited output response is a **special-purpose processor**. Special-purpose processors are the kind most often used in manufacturing or other process control applications. One example is a processor in an automobile factory that controls the operation of a welding robot, as illustrated in Figure 1.7. A **robot** is a computer-controlled device equipped with features for environmental sensing, assessment, and motion. Instructions stored in the computer tell the welding robot when and where to place weld spots on the vehicle being assembled. These instructions are so precise that the locations of the welds are exact to within 1/1,000 of an inch. No human welder could consistently be this accurate.

Courtesy of Chrysler Corporation.

Figure 1.7

Instructions stored in the special-purpose processor tell each robot when and where to place the weld spots on the vehicle being assembled.

One subset of special-purpose computers is known as embedded computers. **Embedded computers** are processors contained within products people use. Embedded computers are an essential component of watches, microwave ovens, fax machines, VCRs, television sets, cameras, telephones, and automobiles. For example, many microwave ovens contain an embedded computer that keeps track of the cooking time. When the input time has elapsed, the computer automatically turns the microwave off and alerts us with a beep.

General-Purpose Processors A **general-purpose processor**, sometimes called a **programmable computer**, is designed to accept a wide variety of inputs, undertake a wide variety of processing activities, and deliver a wide variety of outputs. Unlike special-purpose processors, the program instructions used by general-purpose processors are easily changed. Because of their versatility, general-purpose processors are the kind that individuals and organizations use today for the vast majority of their end-user-oriented information processing systems. For this reason, whenever the term *processor* is used throughout the remainder of the book, it will refer exclusively to general-purpose processors.

Special-purpose processors are often the processors of choice for process control systems, but a general-purpose processor could also do the job. For a specific task, however, a special-purpose processor is almost always more efficient than a general-purpose processor because its circuitry is less complex and it is therefore less expensive. But what if the specific task is no longer needed? The special-purpose processor becomes worthless. A general-purpose processor, on the other hand, can be reprogrammed to do something else. The strength of a general-purpose processor lies in its versatility.

PROCESSING POWER

Information processing systems are often characterized by the speed at which the processor can process data into information. Compared to humans, computers can process data very quickly. During processing the processor selects, organizes, and manipulates data according to program instructions. Think of the processing activity as one which first requires the *accessing* of data and instructions, and then requires the *execution* of the selection, organization, and manipulation operations. **Processing power** is the speed at which this activity can occur. As you shall see, processing power is a result of the interplay of processor speed, primary memory access, time and storage capacity.

Processor Speed Because a processor has no internal moving parts, it can execute instructions almost as fast as electricity can flow through the computer's circuitry. Electricity travels at about the speed of light, which is approximately 186,000 miles per second. The combined length of a computer's circuitry is much less than 186,000 miles, making the computer's processing speeds very quick. For this reason, computer speeds are often expressed in millionths of a second. Most processor speeds are measured in *millions of instructions per second (MIPS)*, though some supercomputers are rated in *billions of instructions per second (BIPS)*. The processor speed of many small computer systems are measured in MIPS.

Imagine the huge amounts of data processed by NASA during a space shuttle mission. The orbital flight pattern must be exact and all on-board systems are monitored carefully. This means that millions of pieces of data are processed each second. Even with these incredible speeds, manufacturers continue to seek ways to make computers faster by manipulating microprocessor circuitry and exploring new semiconducting materials. Recently, computer manufacturers have produced computers that can process trillions of instructions per second.

Processing Memory Primary storage, or main memory, provides the processor with a working area for data and programs. Located physically close to the processor to decrease access time, the memory microchips rapidly provide data and instructions to the processor.

MAIN MEMORY STORAGE

Storage capacity is measured in *bytes.* One byte records one character, number, or special character. One *kilobyte* (abbreviated with the letters KB) is 1,024 bytes. For convenience, most computer users refer to a kilobyte as 1,000 bytes. One *megabyte* (abbreviated with the letters MB) is 1,046,516 bytes. Again, users commonly refer to a megabyte as one million (1,000,000) bytes. One *gigabyte* (abbreviated with the letters GB) is 1,073,741,824. Similarly, users often refer to a gigabyte as being one billion (1,000,000,000) bytes.   Thus, a storage device with a capacity of 640KB (640 kilobytes) can hold 640 X 1,024 (or 655,360) bytes. A storage device with a capacity of 8MB (8 megabytes) can store 8 X 1,046,516 (or 8,372,128) bytes or characters. Some large computers contain many internal memory chips capable of holding the equivalent of a billion or more letters, numbers, and special characters.

SINGLE-USER VS. MULTI-USER SYSTEMS

People bring a purpose or goal to an information processing system. Often the satisfaction of this goal requires that more than one person be able to use the system at the same time. An important characteristic of an information processing system, therefore, is the number of users the system is designed to support. A **single-user system**, as the name implies, is an information processing system primarily designed to support only one end user at a time. A **multi-user system**, on the other hand, is an information processing system designed to support the activities of many end users at the same time. Multi-user systems allow many people in different locations to share the same set of data and programs without these having to be duplicated for each individual. In addition, multi-user systems often allow people to interact with each other in an extremely rapid fashion. Within minutes, data that have been entered into the system by one user can be accessed and even modified by another user.

Courtesy of IBM Corporation.

Courtesy of IBM Corporation.

Businesses use both single- and multi-user systems. A single user (top) is able to use a self-contained micro-computer system for his own individual information processing needs. The computers in the office shown below, by being connected to a larger processor, are part of a multi-user system, allowing each employee to use the same central computer at the same time.

COMPUTER SYSTEM CLASSIFICATIONS

When a processor is combined with input, output, and storage devices, a computer system is created. Over the years, people have developed terms to describe and classify computer systems. These terms include *supercomputer, mainframe, minicomputer, workstation,* and *microcomputer*. Most people have a general understanding of these terms, yet providing precise definitions is difficult. Frequent technological advances will make today's definitions inaccurate tomorrow. In addition, different types of computer systems display a wide range of capabilities. We could use any number of computer system characteristics to help classify the various types of systems. For our purposes, we have chosen those characteristics discussed above: processor size, processing power, memory size, and single- vs. multi-user capability. We have also added the characteristics of cost and physical size. Systems shown in Figure 1.8 on page 20 all feature general-purpose processors.

Figure 1.8

In order to gain an understanding of some of the basic similarities and differences among computer systems, it is helpful to examine the characteristics listed here.

Typical Characteristics	Microcomputer	Workstation	Minicomputer	Mainframe	Supercomputer
Processor Speed	30 million instructions per second	100 million instructions per second	150 million instructions per second	250 million instructions per second	60 billion instructions per second
Processing Memory	4-16MB	16-192MB	32-256MB	64-1,024MB	8,192MB
User Capability	Single-user	Single-user	Multi-user	Multi-user	Single-user priority application
Cost	$1,000 to over $5,000	$5,000 to over $20,000	$25,000 to over $150,000	$250,000 to over $2,000,000	$2,500,000 to $35,000,000+
Size	Desktop	Desktop	Filing-cabinet-sized	Refrigerator-sized	Automobile-sized

Photos courtesy of IBM Corporation.

Figure 1.9

The floor beneath the Cray T3E supercomputer conceals the miles of cabling and wires required to maintain the computer's connections to other on-site devices.

Courtesy of Cray Research, Inc.

Supercomputer Systems As Figure 1.9 makes clear, **supercomputer systems** are the Goliaths of the computer industry. These systems are the largest, fastest, and most expensive available. Only large businesses and government agencies have them. The supercomputers' amazing speed makes them indispensible for complex applications such as weather forecasting, engineering, and other instances where it is necessary to process huge quantities of data quickly.

The Cray T3E is one of the most powerful supercomputer systems in the world. It has a memory capacity of 100 trillion characters (compared to the 2 million character capacity of a personal computer). It can process trillions of instructions per second and costs about $10 million.

COMPUTER CURRENTS

Cray Computers

Cray Research, Inc. has launched the powerful new CRAY T90 series of large-scale supercomputer systems, the world's first wireless supercomputers. Cray Research holds a two-thirds global marketshare in supercomputers.

The CRAY T90 series has from 1 to 32 processors (CPUs) and provides up to 60 billion calculations per second of peak computing power. The new series also features innovative connectors that eliminate all internal wires—older CRAY systems contain more than 36 miles of wires.

Courtesy of Cray Research, Inc.

U.S. prices range from $2.5 million to $35 million for the new CRAY T90 series. The CRAY T932 models feature: from 16 to 32 CPUs that can perform from 30 billion to 60 billion calculations per second; 4,096–8,192MB of memory; the machines are liquid-cooled. U.S. list prices start at $22 million

for a system with 16 processors and 4,096MB of memory, and go up to $30 million for a system with 32 processors and 4,096MB of memory. A system with 32 processors and 8,192MB of memory lists at $35 million.

The high end production supercomputing sector includes government, industrial, and university customers who often support hundreds or thousands of users running tens or hundreds of third-party and proprietary applications.

Because of new technologies and increased operating efficiencies, development costs for the CRAY T90 series were lower than for the preceding CRAY C90 product line, noted Cray Research president and chief operating officer Robert H. Ewald. "The new systems are also easier to manufacture and maintain, and we've boosted reliability and availability as well." New features include wireless connectors called eZIF (electrically activated, zero-insertion-force) connectors and 52-layer printed circuit boards developed exclusively by Cray Research. Each board, smaller than a standard sheet of paper, can contain over one mile of interconnected circuitry.

"The North Carolina Supercomputing Center (NCSC) used a current generation Cray Research supercomputer and air-quality decision support software to help the state develop clean-air policies required by the 1990 Clean Air Act," said NCSC executive director Jeffrey Huskamp. "This pioneering approach substantially shortened the policymaking process and vastly improved its quality by allowing us to evaluate many scenarios quickly." NCSC plans to use the CRAY T90 system's increased power to evaluate the entire ecosystem.

"Chrysler Corporation has realized a substantial return-on-investment by utilizing Cray Research's most advanced supercomputer system in our vehicle design process," according to Choon T. Chon, executive engineer, Simulation and Computer Aided Engineering at Chrysler. "The timely simulation of future vehicles, and their manufacturing processes, is essential to guide the design to optimize product features, address safety and environmental issues, while reducing the design and development cycle time and cost." If you can't afford the T90, CRAY makes smaller computers, such as the CRAY J90, that sell for as little as $225,000! Who wants one?

Mainframe Systems Large computer systems accommodating hundreds of users doing different computing tasks are called **mainframe systems**. Their main memory can store hundreds of millions of characters. Typical applications are large and complex. Mainframe systems are useful for dealing with large, ever-changing collections of data that are accessed by many users simultaneously. Organizations such as government agencies, banks, universities, and insurance companies use mainframes to handle millions of transactions.

Minicomputer Systems Over the past two decades, smaller systems have become more popular than large mainframe systems. The trend began in the early 1970s with **minicomputer systems**, or "minis" for short. Minicomputer systems, often called **midrange systems**, are physically smaller and less expensive than mainframe systems. Newer minicomputer systems are even faster and more powerful than some of their older mainframe counterparts.

The trend toward smaller computer systems has accelerated over the years. This acceleration is due to two factors: the processing power of smaller computer systems has dramatically increased, and telecommunication technologies that allow smaller computers to communicate with each other have become available.

Workstation Systems Some tasks, such as complex mathematical computations, sophisticated product design, and the development of high quality graphics, require an exceptional amount of processing power. **Workstation systems** are single-user systems providing a large amount of processing power and typified by high quality display devices.

Microcomputer Systems Primarily designed for single users, **microcomputer systems**, or **personal computer (PC) systems**, are the most popular. While often used by themselves, PCs can also be connected to larger systems. Today many individuals and small businesses use microcomputer systems to perform the bulk of their information processing and decision support activities. Microcomputer systems are also commonly referred to as *desktop computer systems* because they are appropriately sized for use on the average desk.

Even smaller than desktop computer systems are *portables* (any computer you can easily carry around), *laptops* (they fit on your lap), *notebooks* (they try to be as small and as portable as a typical notebook), *palm-sized computer systems* (they fit into the palm of your hand), and *personal digital assistants* (special-purpose record keepers). These types of systems are illustrated in Figure 1.10. Continuous improvements in computer technology and micro-electronics promise to deliver ever greater processing power in ever smaller units.

Courtesy of IBM Corporation.   Courtesy of AST.   Courtesy of Apple Computer, Inc.

Figure 1.10

All microcomputer systems that are smaller in size than desktop units are considered to be portable.

INFORMATION PROCESSING SOFTWARE

Computers do only what they are instructed to do by people. These instructions are provided by computer programs or software. Two types of software are system software and applications software.

SYSTEM SOFTWARE

System software, tells the computer how to operate itself. As we will discuss more fully in Chapter 8, the principal component of system software is the **operating system**. At one time, operating systems were called *executive programs*. As these names imply, operating systems run the computer in which they reside. The operating system retrieves lists of jobs and then sets up computer devices to handle the work. A sophisticated operating system can even order storage disks or disks needed for jobs.

System software has another important function. System programs support the programs that process the data. In this role, system software helps to eliminate duplication of functions among application programs. Duplication occurs due to common requirements among virtually all programs that process data. For example, all application programs have input and output functions, and they retrieve and store data on secondary storage devices. The management of data residing in memory is another common requirement of application programs. These and other universal processing needs can be handled by operating systems programs.

APPLICATION SOFTWARE

Application software are software programs designed to meet specific processing needs for users. **Application software** programs *apply* the power of information processing to a specific tasks.

As previously indicated, application software program instructions are usually written in higher-level programming languages rather than in machine language. These languages make use of English-like words and phrases to create instructions. Such instructions can be understood by people but not by computers. Another level of system software is needed to convert application programs to computer instructions. This type of system software includes *compiler* and *interpreter* programs. Compilers and interpreters translate application software program instructions into machine language for computer execution. Figure 1.11 shows the relationship of the end user to application software, system software, and system hardware. This relationship and the function of compilers and interpreters is discussed in detail in Chapter 8.

Figure 1.11

An end user interacts with a computer system through levels of supporting system and application software.

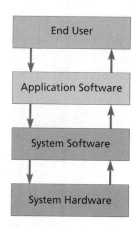

Application software programs provide instructions for handling and transforming data. These programs can be written to perform accounting tasks, to organize large files of data, to process words, and much more.

Many people and organizations share common information processing needs. For example, many organizations share the need to prepare printed documents. For such common needs, it is not necessary to write individualized application software programs. Prewritten application software programs are readily available. Some of the more popular prewritten application software include programs for word processing, spreadsheets, database management, and graphics. In addition, application software has been developed for such personal tasks as preparing and submitting tax documents, organizing recipes and compiling a shopping list, and designing a new floor plan for your home.

INFORMATION PROCESSING

Information processing systems use computer systems to assist in the selection, organization, and manipulation of data, transforming them into more useful information for end users. The tasks most easily automated with information processing systems are those that are routine and repetitive. An information processing system can perform these routine tasks quickly and accurately.

Information processing systems are also used for complex or unique purposes, such as forecasting sales estimates, designing new products, and monitoring energy consumption. The limits of information processing are the limits of one's financial resources and imagination.

Key Terms

application software

automation

computer

computer revolution

computer system

cyberphobia

data

disk drive

disks

information revolution

input

knowledge

mainframe systems

microchip

microcomputer systems

micro-electronics

microprocessor

midrange systems

minicomputer systems

multi-user system

operating system

output

peripheral device

personal computer (PC) systems

personalized computers

primary storage

procedures

electronic circuit

embedded computers

end users

general-purpose processor

hardware

industrial revolution

information

information processing

information processing system

process control

processing

processing power

processor

productivity tools

program

programmable computer

robot

secondary storage

single-user system

software

special-purpose processor

storage

storage medium

supercomputer systems

system software

system unit

workstation systems

Summary

The advent of computers ushered in a revolution—the **computer revolution**—that changed the way business and organizations operate, and the way people lead their lives. Most of these changes are due to computers being used as **productivity tools**, increasing human productivity through the **automation** of tasks.

An **information revolution**, caused by an ability to rapidly access information that was hitherto too expensive or too difficult to obtain, is presently changing our society and our behavior.

Data are raw, unorganized facts. People use their **knowledge** to select, organize, and manipulate data for a specific purpose. Data that have been selected, organized, and manipulated, and are appropriate for a specific purpose, are called **information**. People use information to make decisions.

Using a computer to assist in the conversion of data into meaningful information is called **information processing**. In order to participate in information processing, a computer system must be able to perform four functions: **input**, **processing**, **output**, and **storage**.

A computer quickly processes large amounts of data according to a set of instructions, called a **program**. A **computer** is a **microprocessor**, or simply **processor**, consisting of millions of **electronic circuits** etched onto a small piece of semiconducting material.

A computer is not the same thing as a **computer system**. A computer system includes the computer, input devices, output devices, and storage devices. A computer system uses two kinds of storage: **primary storage** or **memory** and **secondary storage**. Memory holds data and instructions for current use by the processor. Secondary storage holds data and instruction for future use.

A complete **information processing system** is required to process information. An information processing system consists of **hardware**, **software**, **data**, **people**, and **procedures**. Hardware includes the computer system and peripherals. Software consists of programs that instruct the processor and direct the processing activity, as well as the documentation supporting those programs. An **end user** is a person seeking information from the system. Procedures are the rules that govern the overall use of the system.

Process control systems are specialized information processing systems where inputs, programs, and outputs are set in a more or less fixed way, usually by employing a **special-purpose processor**. **General-purpose processors**, in contrast, can accept a wide variety of inputs, do various processing tasks, and produce a variety of outputs.

Information processing systems can be characterized by the attributes of the components that make up the system. Three important characteristics of an information processing system are: type of processor, processing power, and single-user vs. multi-user design.

A convenient classification scheme for computer systems is one that considers all of these characteristics, as well as the size and cost of the computer system. Using this classification scheme, computer systems can be classified into five general categories for descriptive purposes: **supercomputer systems**, **mainframe computer systems**, **minicomputer systems**, **workstations**, and **microcomputer systems**.

Routine and repetitive tasks are most easily automated by information processing systems. However, information processing systems are also used for complex or unique purposes.

14 Easy steps to being a webmaster

STEP 1 | GENERATE IDEAS

There are three stages to building World Wide Web (web) applications.

1. The idea stage, during which the information owners choose the goals, audiences, and content of their intended web application.
2. The analysis stage during which individual information objects and their relationships are identified, and specific contents of each information object are decided.
3. Several development stages during which the information objects are implemented in repeated steps:
   a. Creation of text-only presentation
   b. Imbedding graphics, photos, and icons
   c. Adding links to other web locations to provide complementary and supplementary information
   d. Including applets to provide for interactive or action sequences in the pages.

During the 14 steps, we will develop these ideas in small stages so you can easily follow and do the actions described. Keep in mind that these steps are only a subset of possible actions you might take in designing web applications.

Web pages begin with ideas and structured thinking. In the idea stage, you envision and define the message(s) that each web page should convey. If you are creating pages about yourself, what is it that you want everyone in the world to know about you? What about you is interesting and makes you unique?

When companies develop web pages, they begin by defining the web user to whom they want to appeal. Users might be customers, vendors, or stockholders, who are each interested in a different aspect of the company. For instance, customers are interested in products and orders. Vendors are interested in inventory for their products. Stockholders are interested in financial reporting information.

Each type of information, whether developed by a student, entrepreneur, or company, requires structured thinking about the audience and information content. The average web user looks at a web page for about 6.8 seconds in the process of deciding what to do next. This means that you, as a web page developer, have just seven seconds to get your message across! Therefore, it is important to know both the intended audience(s) and the message(s) that will appeal to them.

The message should be short, complete, unique, and valuable to the user, enticing him or her into continued viewing of the page. While structured thinking does not have a fixed starting point, the two most common are the web user and the main idea(s), or content, of the subject web pages. The process of defining content and audience is iterative, that is, the process repeats as many times as needed to define all audiences and the message contents for each.

Clarity is a component of both content and audience definition. Each audience and message should be defined as narrowly as possible. For instance, if you are developing a web resume to appeal to prospective employers, you would want to define who might those employers be, including industry, department, and maybe even job type.

Clarity is important because the eventual design of page contents will differ depending on your definitions of content and audience. Just think what information might appeal to web users looking for video game programmers vs. bank programmers. A video game resume page might be judged on liveliness, animation, bold use of color, and the author's understanding of how to use the page space. A bank resume page might be judged on how stable, serious, and business-like the author appears. Keep in mind that the same person would develop both of these pages, but each page would reflect a different personality perspective to best appeal to the intended audience.

The less clear the definitions of audience and content, the less likely the pages are to appeal to the desired audience. Being clear is not easy for the first definition of anything, including web page audience and content. Therefore, we can get ideas from others, in this case, other web pages.

Web search engines allow searching of web page topics using keyword queries. One engine, AltaVista from Digital Equipment Corporation, indexes over 40,000,000 web pages. Queries are of the form: keyword1 + keyword2 + (keyword3 keyword4 keyword5). A keyword is some word in the document that is used for the search. Keywords in parentheses require the same order and proximity (closeness) of the words. A real-world example might be: (systems + analysis) + web + page + design.

This example is looking for systems analysis as a single term, with web, page, and design someplace else in the same document. AltaVista returns a count of the number of occurrences for each term, a count of the combination of all terms, and the web addresses resulting from the search, ten addresses at a time. More complex queries are also supported.

There are two assignments for this step that can be done in any order.

ASSIGNMENT 1: List and define between two and five audiences for your pages. Define the main message content for each audience. Try for overlap in some information to be provided. The final list and all definitions should be no longer than a single, typed sheet of paper.

ASSIGNMENT 2: Browse the Web to look at other pages with content or audiences similar to yours. To do the browsing step:

1.   Activate Netscape or other graphical browser.

2.   From the file menu, select the open URL[1] option.

3.   Enter the address of a search engine. Several popular ones are AltaVista at Digital Equipment Corporation at: http//www.altavista.com, Yahoo at: http//www. yahoo.com, and WebCrawler at: http//webcrawler.cs.washington.edu/WebCrawler.

4.   Enter your query and perform the search.

5.   Browse the web addresses returned by the search engine, deciding for yourself the intended audience and content. Create bookmarks for pages you want to revisit.

1.   URL stands for uniform resource locator and is the name for all Internet addresses, including web pages as well as file transfer sites (ftp addresses), gopher sites, and others. All web pages begin with the URL code http// and is followed by an organization identifier, one or more directory names, and the html page name.

Exercises

 REVIEW QUESTIONS

1.   Why are computer systems commonly referred to as productivity tools?

2.   What is the difference between data and information?

3.   What is a computer and how does it differ from a computer system?

4.   Is a processor the same as processing? Why or why not?

5.   What are the four basic components of a computer system?

6.   What are the components of an information processing system?

7.   What are two important characteristics of data you should remember in terms of information processing systems?

8.   Which is more flexible, a special-purpose processor or general-purpose processor? Why?

9.   Why is it difficult to classify computer systems?

10. What are the five general classifications of computer systems used in this book? Into which classification would you expect the largest number of new computers to be introduced? Why?

 **FILL IN THE BLANKS**

1.   _____ is the replacement of human observation or effort by mechanical or electronic devices.

2. The computer revolution has sparked another revolution called the _____ revolution.

3. _____ are raw, unorganized facts used to describe reality.

4. _____ is the body of rules, guidelines, and procedures used by humans to select, organize, and manipulate data to make it more useful for a specific purpose.

5. A _____ is a tiny computer contained in another product, such as a television or a microwave oven.

6. A _____ is an electronic device that can be programmed to accept data and process it into useful information.

7. A _____ consists of input devices, the processor, output devices, and storage devices.

8. A type of computer designed to accept a wide variety of inputs and perform a wide variety of different tasks is known as a _____ processor.

9. A type of computer designed to perform one or a few tasks is called a _____ processor.

10. The capabilities of main memory are measured in access time and _____.

MATCHING

Match each term with its description.

a. computer system

b. embedded

c. cyberphobia

d. peripheral

e. versatility

f. computer

g. people

h. special-purpose processing

i. process control

j. programmable computer

____ 1. Another word for processor.

____ 2. Automation of real-world events using limited inputs, fixed programs, and limited outputs.

____ 3. Collection of components including a processor, input devices, output devices, and storage devices.

____ 4. Computer limited to one, or a few, tasks.

____ 5. Processors contained with everyday products such as TVs, VCRs, and cameras.

____ 6. Computer that operates under control of program instructions that are easily changed.

___ 7. Most important component of an information processing system.

___ 8. Fear of computers.

___ 9. Primary advantage of general-purpose processors as compared to special-purpose processors.

___ 10. Term used to describe all devices except the processor.

ACTIVITIES

1. Contact an official or computer teacher at your school and request a tour of the computer facility. If you have an opportunity to tour the facility, determine the various purposes for which these computer systems are used.

2. Contact someone who works at a hospital in your area. Ask them to explain how computers are used for routine clerical tasks and in patient health care. Ask the person to tell you about any special computers that are used for special purposes, such as those used to monitor a patient's vital signs.

3. Visit a manufacturing firm to learn how the firm uses computers in manufacturing and production.

4. If your school uses computers to teach students to design objects such as a floor plan for a house, ask the instructor to display a finished design on a computer screen.

5. On paper, prepare a comprehensive list of possible uses for a personal computer in your home. Your list should contain a minimum of ten applications.

Skills for Living

WELCOME TO THE INTERNET AND THE WORLD WIDE WEB

If information is power and if time is the new currency of the nineties, think of the Internet as your own vast treasure chest containing unlimited quantities of both information and time. The Internet is your personal on-line library, home shopping guide, entertainment center, connection to the world, personal travel agent, etc. As you begin to use this rich personal resource, you will work smarter and faster than ever before.

The Internet and the World Wide Web are changing the way we work, learn, and do business. At the end of each chapter, we have included Internet material and exercises for your review. We hope they serve to guide you through the Web and show you the value of understanding its application.

What is the Internet and the Web?

The Internet began as a research effort by the U.S. Department of Defense in 1969. During the Cold War years (1974–1979), the strategy was to have dispersed national computing with no overall reliance on one computer in case of attack or national emergency. In 1990, the network was opened for public use. In June 1993, there were estimated to be 130 web sites in the world. One year later, in 1994, this number had grown to 2,700 sites. Today, there are over 200,000 sites. More than half of these sites are commercial. There are estimated to be 65 million users worldwide and 25 million e-mail users on the system.

How It Works

In 1994, universal communication standards were adopted for text, pictures, sound, and video. This network became known as the World Wide Web, or WWW, or Web.

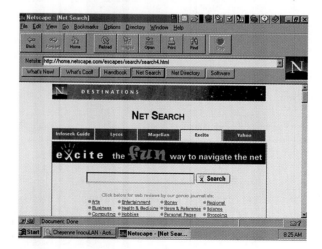

Information in a web page (standard format) is retrieved and transferred from its host site, where it is stored and maintained, to another user's location somewhere in the Internet. The requesting user uses a browser to perform the search. A standard formatting language for the page is called Hypertext Markup Language or HTTP. Each web page site has a unique address (much like a mailing address) called a Universal Resource Locator or URL. Once a useful site is found, its URL can be stored and reused at a later date. This is called a bookmark. A collection of bookmarks is called a webliography (functioning much like a library bibliography, only the reference sources are located on the WWW).

The Internet and the Web were initially developed by individuals and organizations to do personal research and communications. But, as web technologies and services have grown, it has become obvious that this system can do more to facilitate business activities. The pioneers created the right-of-ways for the information superhighway. As big companies such as Microsoft, Intel, MCI, AT&T, and the entertainment giants join forces, they will supply new products and services to link customers and companies together in the exchange of products and services. The newcomers will pave this highway and supply the vehicles needed to navigate its unfolding opportunities. We hope our Internet activities will help you prepare for your role in this exciting process.

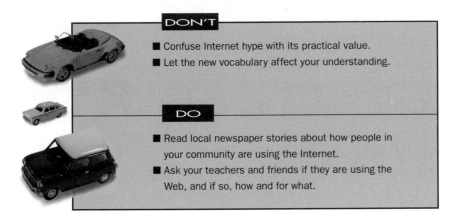

DON'T
- Confuse Internet hype with its practical value.
- Let the new vocabulary affect your understanding.

DO
- Read local newspaper stories about how people in your community are using the Internet.
- Ask your teachers and friends if they are using the Web, and if so, how and for what.

Student Activities

1. Ask five of your fellow students, not in this class, to define the terms the *Internet* and the *World Wide Web*. What do they know about them? Have they ever used them? Record and evaluate their answers.

2. Ask older family members the same questions as in #1. Do you feel there is any significant difference in the level of understanding between these two groups? Do you think age or work experiences affect these differences? What else might account for the differences?

3. Find one current article in your local newspaper about the Internet or the Web. How was it used and why? What were the benefits of this application? Can you personally use any of the insights gained from this application or article? How?

CHAPTER 2

COMPUTERS, SOCIETY, AND YOU

OBJECTIVES

AFTER STUDYING THIS CHAPTER, YOU SHOULD BE ABLE TO:

1. Explain the roles of computers in today's society.
2. Explain the evolution of computers since the ENIAC.
3. Explain how digital convergence will affect the communications, entertainment, and publishing industries.
4. Explain how multimedia differs from text-based documents.
5. Describe the objectives of the plans to build the digital highway.
6. Identify health and safety issues about which computer users should be aware.
7. Describe some of the key features of a well-designed computer work area.
8. List three types of artificial intelligence and explain how each supports normal human activities.
9. Explain the three major components of the national information infrastructure.
10. Explain what computer skills and knowledge employers require of new employees.
11. Explain what information appliances are and how they are used.
12. Explain how computers have affected our lives, work, and education.

CHAPTER OUTLINE

OUR CHANGING WORLD
The Forces Driving Change
How to Be Prepared

COMPUTER EVOLUTION
The ENIAC
Apple and IBM
Microsoft and Intel
Today, Computers Are Everywhere

CURRENT COMPUTER ISSUES
Digital Convergence
Computers and the Environment—
 "Green Computing"
Artificial Intelligence

INFRASTRUCTURE OF THE NATION
Computing Power
Digital Technologies and Networks
Information Appliances

IMPACT OF COMPUTER APPLICATIONS
Where We Work
Where We Live
Where We Learn
Where We Play

Computers are everywhere. They are used by businesses, government agencies, schools, and individuals for a seemingly limitless variety of applications. For many organizations, computers are essential for normal operations. Businesses use computers to maintain up-to-date inventories, to process payrolls, and to keep track of customers, suppliers, and sales. Manufacturers use them to order raw materials, to design and build new products, to prepare catalogs and brochures, and to monitor assembly lines. Banks use them to process customer accounts, to keep track of current interest rates, and to transfer funds between banks and branches. The Internal Revenue Service uses computers to keep track of taxpayers, to audit income tax returns, and to process tax refunds.

Many computers are now linked together in networks. Computer networks make it possible for information to be sent back and forth among computers throughout the world.

Computers touch the lives of everyone. We use them in our jobs to work more productively and efficiently. We have them in our homes and in our schools. The popularity of computers continues to increase each year. It is estimated that annual world sales of PCs in 1998 will exceed 100 million units. In that same year, for the first time, annual PC sales are expected to exceed the sales of color television sets.

OUR CHANGING WORLD

Today's organizations appear to be in a constant state of change, evolving to new and higher performance levels. But, changing the way people work during business operations is like rebuilding your automobile engine while you're driving down the freeway. Hopefully nothing will go wrong. Process and product improvements are being made through a combination of employee empowerment and group problem solving supported by new computing tools and computer-based technologies.

THE FORCES DRIVING CHANGE

To be both competitive and profitable, organizations must be efficient. Employees must learn to work hard, smart, and use the latest problem-solving technologies and systems for support. Information technologies save time and money, improve the problem-solving process, and help the organization maintain its competitive advantage in the marketplace. To be competitive, an organization must be electronically connected to its suppliers, its customers, and its information sources—wherever they may be located.

HOW TO BE PREPARED

What will work be like for the 21st-century manager? What computer skills will be needed? Statistics show the average person will change careers three or four times. Continuous learning and personal development will be necessary to keep current with new computer technologies. Today, organizations expect basic computer competency from new employees. This includes a good understanding of software basics such as word processing, electronic spreadsheets, and databases. Advanced skills in graphics, e-mail, and the Internet add to an employee's value.

In this chapter, we introduce a framework for understanding computer applications and their evolving impact on our work, home, education, and play.

COMPUTER EVOLUTION

The last ten years have shown dramatic growth in the computer industry. Some key companies and milestones are described below. Figure 2.1 illustrates the evolution of computing.

Some significant computing events of the past 50 years

Year	Event
1946	First public demonstration of the ENIAC.
1949	First fully functional computer capable of executing a stored program.
1951	First commercially available stored program computer.
1957	First commercially available computer using transistors rather than vacuum tubes.
1959	First minicomputer (smaller than a refrigerator).
1961	First integrated circuit, which has transistors etched directly onto a piece of silicon rather than mounted on a board.
1964	First "mouse."
1970	First e-mail.
1971	First floppy disk; first pocket calculator.
1973	First personal computer with monitor.
1975	First microchip.
1977	First commercially successful personal computer (Apple II).
1978	First commercially available hard drive.
1979	First commercially available spreadsheet program.
1981	First portable microcomputer, the Osborne 1; IBM introduces its PC.
1982	First laser printer.
1984	First Macintosh.
1991	First "pen-top" computer capable of reading handwriting.
1992	First international computer virus scare. The virus was known as Michelangelo because it struck on March 6, the artist's birthday. It did little damage.
1993	First personal digital assistants, such as Apple's Newton.

Figure 2.1

Significant computing events.

Sources: *Engines of the Mind* by Joel Shurkin; Isaac Asimov's *Chronology of Science & Discovery; World Book Encyclopedia*—The Dallas Morning News

THE ENIAC

Just over 50 years ago, computer engineers at the University of Pennsylvania turned off the lights in their lab and turned on their newest invention, the first general-purpose computer, called the Electronic Numerical Integrator and Computer (ENIAC). Funded by the U.S. military, the huge computer (30 tons, 8 feet high, 17,500 vacuum tubes, and costing almost $500,000) was used to track artillery shell paths. For the first time, a computer could determine a shell's trajectory faster than the shell could travel. It took 30 seconds for the shell to reach its target, and the computer determined the trajectory in 24 seconds!

Today, scientists are on the verge of building computers that can run 100 billion times faster than the ENIAC. Nevertheless, the ENIAC was a major breakthrough that helped launch the computer industry.

The ENIAC weighed 30 tons and filled a room two stories high at the University of Pennsylvania.

Courtesy of IBM Archives.

ENIAC FACTS

WHAT:	Electronic Numerical Integrator and Computer
WHEN:	Feb. 14, 1946
WHERE:	Moore School of Electrical Engineering, University of Pennsylvania
WHO:	John W. Mauchly and J. Presper Eckert, Army Capt. Herman Goldstine
COST:	$486,800
SPACE:	A 30-by-50 foot room
POWER CONSUMPTION:	174 kilowatts a second—enough to power a typical home at the time for 1½ weeks
WEIGHT:	30 tons
HEIGHT:	8 feet
NUMBER OF VACUUM TUBES:	17,468
AVERAGE RUNNING TIME BETWEEN BREAKDOWNS:	5.6 hours
LIFESPAN:	Retired in 1955
QUOTE:	"It was like fighting the Battle of the Bulge to get it going."—*Goldstine*
WHERE IS IT NOW:	Parts of it are at the Smithsonian Institution, the Computer Museum in Boston, the University of Pennsylvania and Maryland's Aberdeen Proving Ground

Source: *From wire Reports*

APPLE AND IBM

In 1977, Steve Jobs and Steve Wozniak formed Apple Computer Company. Two years later, the company introduced the commercially successful Apple II computer and launched the era of personal computing. For the next two years, "Big Blue" (IBM's

a)

Courtesy of Apple Computer, Inc.

b)
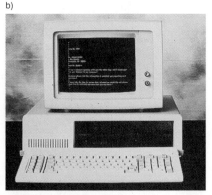
Courtesy of IBM Corporation.

a) The Apple II family.

b) The first IBM PC, 1981.

nickname) watched Apple's progress. Finally, when IBM was sure that there was a market for "toy" computers, it introduced the IBM PC in 1981. Equipped with two floppy disk drives, a keyboard, and monitor screen, the new IBM PC sold for approximately $3,500.

MICROSOFT AND INTEL

Two other companies have made major contributions to the personal computer industry. Computers cannot run without software programs that tell them what to do. Today, the dominant software producer for the personal computer is Microsoft, a computer software giant founded by Bill Gates in Bellevue, Washington, in 1980. In that year, IBM asked Microsoft to develop an operating system for its new PC. Gates seized this major opportunity and developed MS-DOS (Microsoft Disk Operating System). Its subsequent success launched Microsoft's explosive growth. Its latest operating system, Windows 95, is the developing standard for the industry.

Courtesy of Microsoft Corporation.

Bill Gates founded Microsoft Corporation in Bellevue, Washington in 1980.

Microsoft has developed families or "suites" of application programs that work together. Microsoft Works and Microsoft Office combine word processing, spreadsheets, database management systems, and graphics software into integrated and easy-to-use packages. The company has recently moved into multimedia, on-line communications, home banking and shopping, and even movie delivery systems. Currently, Microsoft is the largest software provider.

Intel, founded in July 1968, is the second major contributor to the computer industry. In 1971, the company introduced the Intel 4004 microprocessor, the first "computer on a chip." The size of a postage stamp, it consisted of 2,300 transistors and contained as much computing power as the mammoth ENIAC. In the mid-1970s, the company toyed with the idea of combining a keyboard, screen, and a microprocessor chip and building a "home computer." The company concluded that the computer's only use would be to keep track of recipes. The idea was dropped.

Today, Intel has defined current digital electronics with its microprocessor chips, memories, and controllers. It is the world's largest semiconductor supplier with over 30,000 employees and annual revenues exceeding $16 billion. Its current Pentium and

The Pentium® Pro microprocessor.

Courtesy of Intel Corporation.

newer Pentium Pro processor chips come in a variety of speeds and prices. In the future, the company will work to integrate interactive entertainment, networked information services, and real-time multimedia communications into one place—your PC! Figure 2.2 shows the evolution of the personal computer.

Figure 2.2

The evolution of the personal computer.

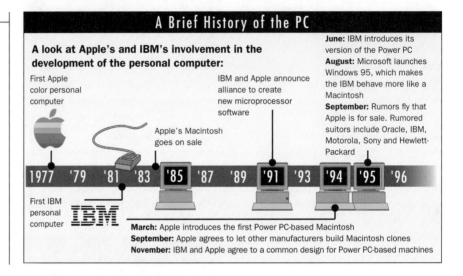

A Brief History of the PC

A look at Apple's and IBM's involvement in the development of the personal computer:

First Apple color personal computer

Apple's Macintosh goes on sale

IBM and Apple announce alliance to create new microprocessor software

June: IBM introduces its version of the Power PC
August: Microsoft launches Windows 95, which makes the IBM behave more like a Macintosh
September: Rumors fly that Apple is for sale. Rumored suitors include Oracle, IBM, Motorola, Sony and Hewlett-Packard

1977 '79 '81 '83 '85 '87 '89 '91 '93 '94 '95 '96

First IBM personal computer

IBM

March: Apple introduces the first Power PC-based Macintosh
September: Apple agrees to let other manufacturers build Macintosh clones
November: IBM and Apple agree to a common design for Power PC-based machines

TODAY, COMPUTERS ARE EVERYWHERE

This year, a new car will have an average of 500 computers on board. Computers help us make coffee, cook breakfast, and earn a living. They are at work in dishwashers, VCRs, cameras, TVs, grocery stores, schools, and hospitals. Some experts estimate that over half of today's bank branches will close as home banking and ATM machines pick up the load. You can even buy clothing, concert tickets, and a pizza with your computer. Quietly, but systematically, the computer is invading almost every aspect of our daily lives—work, home, education, and play.

CURRENT COMPUTER ISSUES

Evolving computer technologies have created a wealth of opportunities. However, some important concerns have also emerged. Issues such as the impact of computers on the environment, computer-related health issues, and computers designed to replicate human behavior and human activities have captured our attention.

DIGITAL CONVERGENCE

Digital convergence refers to the merger and integration, or convergence, of technologies and products from the communications, entertainment, publishing, and computer industries. Conversion of the information transmitted by each of these industries into a digital form that can be processed, stored, and distributed by computers is making this merger possible. Formerly, the conversion of non-computer information into a digital form has been limited by hardware and software. For example, digital phone service has been available for a number of years, but digitized video, which consists of tremendous amounts of data, has not been widely implemented. Recent advances in both hardware and software will soon make practical high quality digitized video and audio in areas such as communications, entertainment, and publishing.

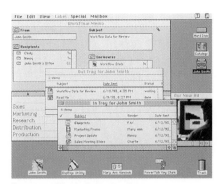

Courtesy of Apple Computer, Inc.

Figure 2.3

The use of fiber optic cable and other more powerful communications channels allows users to include intensive applications such as video clips in something as commonplace as e-mail transmissions.

In the field of communications, a more widespread use of fiber optic cabling will allow data to be transmitted at higher speeds. The higher-volume transmission will enable data-intensive applications such as video and graphics to be transmitted over phone equipment. Video will also become a more common component of transmitted information such as electronic mail, as illustrated in Figure 2.3. Video transmissions over phone lines will also allow customer service representatives to show customers how to use or repair products while they are talking to them.

Wireless communications will also become more common. Personal digital assistants (PDAs), small hand-held computing devices used by mobile workers, usually have a wireless capability to send and receive data (see Figure 2.4). Some also have fax capabilities.

In entertainment, digitization will enable products such as movies and television programming to be distributed in new ways. For example, a user could choose a personalized selection of previously recorded shows, movies, or events, and have them downloaded into their digital entertainment system to be viewed later (see Figure 2.5).

Significant changes in the field of publishing are already under way. Several major newspapers and magazines now

Courtesy of AT&T Archives. Reprinted with permission.

Figure 2.4

The AT&T EO is one of the several personal digital assistants (PDAs) that have wireless communications capabilities. With its built-in cellular phone, the EO can transmit voice, data, and fax images.

Photos courtesy of Your Choice TV.

Figure 2.5

Interactive TV is one of the technologies currently in development for bringing television programming under the control of the home viewer.

offer readers the option of downloading the most recent issue into their computers. Information service companies help users reduce the amount of time spent doing library research. The service company, which reviews and classifies articles from numerous sources, provides the user with a summary of the articles that meet the user's criteria. Full versions of the articles are also available. Digitized electronic versions of books are becoming popular.

Multimedia The combination of text, graphics, video, and sound is called **multimedia**. Some describe multimedia as a combination of traditional text-based computers and television, but it is more than a combination of these previously separate information elements. Multimedia provides the user with options for the amount and the sequence in which material will be reviewed. For example, a typical multimedia presentation displays text material along with one or more photos or graphic images. Some sound or voice narration may also be provided. In addition, the screen usually shows icons that represent additional material, such as pictures, sounds, animation, or maps, which the user can choose to review. Most multimedia presentations use a technique called **hypermedia** that allows users to move quickly to related subject areas.

Figure 2.6 shows a screen from Microsoft's multimedia encyclopedia, Encarta. It shows text information about the composer Ludwig van Beethoven. The small icons at the top of the text material indicate there is a sound item (represented by the speaker-shaped icon) and an image item (represented by the camera-shaped icon) that can also be reviewed. To hear or see these items, the user double-clicks on the icons with the mouse. To see related topics, the user can choose the "See Also" button at the bottom of the screen. When this is done, a list of related topics is presented. The user can move directly to any of these topics by choosing one with the mouse.

Like most multimedia products available today, the Microsoft Encarta multimedia encyclopedia is stored on a CD-ROM disk. This type of storage device is necessary because of the large amounts of memory that most multimedia applications require. For example,

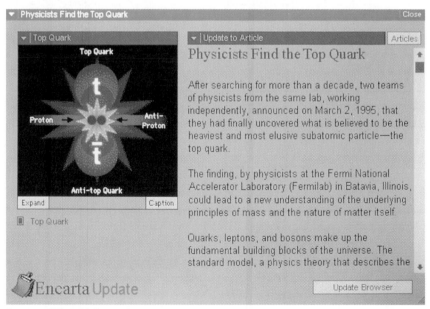

Figure 2.6

Microsoft Encarta is a multimedia encyclopedia. Text, graphics, sound, and animation are all available.

Courtesy of Microsoft Corporation.

the Encarta encyclopedia takes up over 550MB of storage space. Full-motion video, which is used sparingly in most multimedia presentations, requires over two *gigabytes* of storage for each minute of video. In the future, data compression techniques will reduce storage requirements.

Currently, multimedia applications are used primarily in four areas: education, training, entertainment, and multimedia kiosks typically located in shopping malls, museums, airports, and hotels. A shopping mall multimedia kiosk contains a monitor screen on which categories are displayed. Touching the category "department stores" on the screen quickly pulls up a list of stores in that mall. Touching a particular department store brings up information about that store and its location. Multimedia techniques may eventually be incorporated into most software applications.

Virtual Reality Computer-generated three-dimensional environments that simulate sight, touch, and sound are known as **virtual reality (VR)**. VR equipment includes a headset that tracks head movements and changes vantage points accordingly; gloves that track hand movements and initiate commands; eyeware that simulates a three-dimensional environment; and speakers that broadcast sound. VR software applications include flight simulation and surgical procedures. VR is also used by architects to help their clients envision floor plans. Being able to walk through the design before it is implemented allows clients to make changes, such as enlarging windows to take advantage of the morning sun or changing the height of a kitchen counter, before it is too late.

Figure 2.7

Virtual reality equipment includes a headset, gloves, eyewear, and speakers to simulate sight, touch, and sound.

Courtesy of NASA.

In more advanced forms, VR software requires the user to wear specialized headgear, gloves, and body suits to enhance the experience of the artificial location (see Figure 2.7). Eventually, experts predict, the body suits will provide tactile feedback so the wearer can experience the touch and feel of the virtual world.

Most experts agree that VR is still in its early stages and that practical applications are just now becoming available. The potential applications of VR, however, have interested many people and kept millions of dollars flowing into VR research.

The general public's first encounter with VR will likely be three-dimensional electronic games such as Dactyl Nightmare, Battle Tech, or Martian Death Race on the Red Planet. Special visors allow the player to "see" the computer-generated environment. Sensors in the surrounding game machine record movement and direction as the player "walks" around the game's electronic landscape. Because of their relatively high cost (over $50,000) and the special equipment required, VR games are not spreading across the land as fast as pinball machines once did. But most major metropolitan U.S. cities have VR arcades installed or planned for the near future.

Medical science is also working to adapt VR technology to its needs. Stanford University Medical School has created a virtual patient complete with internal organs and bodily fluids. Using VR gloves and headsets, medical students can practice surgery on a simulated patient instead of using live patients or cadavers. The National Library of Medicine has also created an electronic body for medical use, but theirs is a digital representation of a real human, a 5-foot-11-inch, 180-pound, 39-year-old Texan who willed his body to science. The body was frozen in foam and gelatin and sliced into one millimeter sections. Each slice was photographed and digitized. The digitized images, over 20 billion bytes of data, were combined to create a three-dimensional representation of the body. Using VR software, the digitized body can be inspected, dissected, and toured as if it were a building.

Commercial applications of VR include virtual showrooms and a virtual office. The showroom lets customers wander among available products and inspect those they find interesting. In the virtual office, created for an office furniture company, clients can see what their selected furniture will look like and can experiment with different furniture arrangements.

FOCUS

Virtually There

It's Tuesday, and Morris Bettor, the owner of a large investment firm, is meeting with Crystal Cleary, the architect for his firm's new building, to go over the plans. But Ms. Cleary lays no plans on her desk. In fact, there is no desk in the room . . . only some strange-looking, oversized goggles and two pairs of bulky gloves. Asking Mr. Bettor to don one set of goggles and

San Diego Supercomputer Center/Alan Decker.

gloves while she puts on the other, the architect speaks briefly into the microphone attached to her goggles. Suddenly, standing before them

appears to be the building itself. Reaching out, Ms. Cleary opens the door, and they enter the building, moving slowly from room to room and floor to floor to give Mr. Bettor a chance to comment on the structure. When he complains that the windows in his office won't let in enough light, Ms. Cleary again speaks into her microphone, and newer, larger windows appear.

A scene from some futuristic scenario? Far from it. All across the nation, architects and scientists, games players and doctors are taking advantage of the fast-developing technology known as "virtual reality."

Virtual reality uses computers to simulate environments in three dimensions and to "move" through these environments with the help of special equipment. For example, typical virtual reality gear includes goggles known as "eyephones." These devices put a small video monitor in front of each eye. The sophisticated program in the computer generates images that appear on these monitors, with each eye receiving a slightly different picture, just as your two eyes receive slightly different information in real life. It is in reconciling these differences that you perceive depth, distance, and other qualities that make the world appear in three dimensions. The goggles also contain electronic sensors that track movements of the user's head and adjust the "picture" accordingly. A microphone attached to the goggles or built into a helmet containing such goggles allows the user to command the voice-activated computer, while specially placed speakers provide virtual sound.

Gloves are another crucial element of virtual reality systems. Fiber-optically wired, they give the illusion that the user is manipulating objects in the environment by telling the computer that the user has reached out and grabbed the area corresponding to the door knob in the environment, for example. The computer receives this information and makes the door appear to open.

San Diego Supercomputer Center.

With devices like these (attached to high-powered computers), virtual reality offers users attractions far beyond the architect's office. For example:

■ Surgeons in California have conducted a gall bladder operation on a computer-generated image of a human body in a test of a system that may soon be used by medical students as part of their training. (Virtual bodies develop no scars and never sue for malpractice.)

■ Engineers at Boeing Aircraft had trouble reading the pressure gauge through the maintenance hatch of a virtual plane they were developing. By finding this out before making an actual prototype, they avoided spending time and money on redesign and reengineering.

■ The U.S. Army has developed a virtual Gulf War that leaves young trainees in the tank corps sweating, cursing, and experienced in battle, but with no real wounds.

What lies ahead? The options are virtually unlimited in the opinion of Jaron Lanier, coiner of the term "virtual reality" and pioneer in its development. Indeed, attempts to use virtual reality are proceeding in many directions

Much work remains to be done, however. Chief among the problems are the limited abilities of current virtual reality equipment and its high cost. At up to $50,000 per headset and over $300,000 for the necessary computer equipment to run an architectural virtual reality, for example, few individuals are rushing out to buy such a setup for the fun of it. And except for the most expensive units, existing goggles are usually too slow and sound systems too tinny for users to feel they have really entered another world. Indeed, poor goggle speed can create nausea in users after a while. And that's a bit too much reality for most.

As computing power increases, VR applications will be run on lower cost computers. This in turn will increase the number of commercial VR applications and make VR technology available for a wider number of users.

COMPUTERS AND THE ENVIRONMENT — "GREEN COMPUTING"

Working with computers in a way that does not harm the environment or endanger the health of users is called **green computing**. These issues are gaining attention due to the increasing amount of time people spend working with computers on the job, at school, and at home. The major concerns of green computing are threefold: power consumption, the use of consumable supplies, and health issues.

Power Consumption　Computers are considered a leading cause of the increased demand for electrical power. Today, it is estimated that computers account for five percent of all commercial energy consumption. By the year 2000, this figure could be as high as ten percent. Manufacturers are combating this problem by designing computer components that require less electricity. Low-voltage designs, first developed for portable computers, are now being incorporated into desktop systems. Manufacturers are also designing systems that automatically switch to reduced power when the system has not been used for some period of time, say three to five minutes. The reduced power state is often referred to as a "sleep" mode. Some systems are already designed with two levels of sleep mode: a "standby" mode in which the system can instantly return to action, and a "suspend" mode in which the maximum amount of energy is saved, but the system will take longer, perhaps a minute or more, to return to operation.

The U.S. government, through the Environmental Protection Agency (EPA), has formally endorsed the power management approach through its Energy Star program. Backed by major computer systems and parts manufacturers, the goal of the **Energy Star program** is to design major system components (CPUs, monitors, and printers) that use no more than 30 watts of power when they are turned on but not in use. Current sleep mode energy expenditures are 100 to 200 watts of power used by conventional CPUs, 50 to 150 watts used by color monitors, and 50 to 150 watts used by laser printers. Manufacturers that meet the EPA guidelines can display the Energy Star logo (see Figure 2.8) on their products for marketing purposes. To further encourage manufacturers, the U.S. government, the largest buyer of computers in the world, has directed all its agencies to purchase only computers that meet the Energy Star guidelines.

Can reduced-power components and power management techniques really make a difference in total energy consumption? Most experts think they can. Currently, it's estimated that there are over 60 million personal computers in use, with approximately two-thirds in businesses and one-third in homes. As much as 25 percent of these systems are left on 24 hours a day, 365 days a year. According to one study, if all computers in the United States met the Energy Star guidelines, enough energy could be saved to power a city of six million people for a year. In terms of money, it is estimated that the Energy Star guidelines could result in an

US EPA.

average savings of over $100 per computer per year. For a corporation running 1,000 computers, that would mean savings of over $100,000.

Consumable Supplies Another area of environmental concern regarding computers (and related office equipment) is the amount and type of supplies they consume. At the top of this list is paper. Although computers have eliminated paper in some applications, they have substantially increased its use in most areas. One reason for increased paper use is that with today's software, documents are much easier to change. This encourages users to make a series of small changes as they strive to produce perfect letters, spreadsheets, or overhead slides. The result is many pages of wasted paper.

Many commercial and home offices have recycling bins to collect unwanted paper from printers and copiers. For internal documents, some organizations reuse unwanted copies by printing on the reverse side. Caution must be used however, to avoid the confusion caused by a report on twice-printed paper falling on the floor! One copier company has designed a system that removes the ink from previously used pages. The company claims that a single sheet of paper can be used up to ten times. Because the components of page printers are similar to copying machines, this technique for reusing paper may someday be applied to computer printers.

Another consumable supply issue concerns toner cartridges used in page printers and copiers. Approximately 12 million cartridges are disposed of each year. One option is to recycle the cartridge with the manufacturer. Hewlett-Packard, Canon, and IBM each provide postage-paid mailers so users can return their cartridges. Another option is to have cartridges remanufactured. Numerous companies provide this service, refilling cartridges with toner and replacing worn parts, if necessary. Remanufactured cartridges cost about one-half the price of new cartridges. One laser printer manufacturer, Kyocera, has developed a page printer that does not use a disposable cartridge. Instead, toner is added directly to a permanent storage compartment. Although the initial cost of the printer is higher, the company claims that the per-page operating cost is lower than that of any competitor. Recycling options also exist for ink-jet and ribbon printers. Users can purchase a kit to re-ink these cartridges, or pay an independent business to do the work.

Other computer supplies that can be recycled include batteries from portable computers, disks, user's manuals, and shipping materials such as cardboard boxes and styrofoam packing. Two major manufacturers, Hewlett-Packard and IBM, have programs to accept obsolete or unwanted equipment. Hewlett-Packard's program recycles over 500,000 pounds of products each month. After the removal of parts that can be used for maintenance support, the products are sold to recyclers that remove the integrated circuits, gold, and other usable metals. According to Hewlett-Packard, about 90 percent of these products is salvaged, and only ten percent winds up in landfills.

Computer Health Issues Computer health issues are not new. They were first reported over 20 years ago when people began spending long hours using keyboards and sitting in front of computer screens. Today, even more people work with computers; according to the U.S. census, over one-third of Americans use computers at work, and a large percentage of those have another computer at home. With increased computer use have come increased reports of health problems. These can be serious and should be understood by every computer user.

One of the most commonly reported problems goes by several names: **repetitive strain (or stress) injury (RSI)**, **repetitive motion injury (RMI)**, and **cumulative trauma disorder (CTD)**. The injury is usually to a hand or arm and results from repeating the same motion over and over. According to government statistics, this category of injury accounts for more than half of all work-related illnesses. With computer users, the injury is usually caused by working long hours at a keyboard. A specific type of repetitive stress injury is **carpal tunnel syndrome (CTS)**. CTS sufferers experience pain and weakness in their hands and lower arms. These symptoms are caused by swelling and pressure on the median nerve in the wrist. CTS injuries are serious and can be permanently disabling. In order to prevent CTS, some manufacturers have developed alternative keyboards that incorporate redesigned key layouts and built-in wrist rests. As shown in Figure 2.9, some manufacturers have even split the keyboard into separate pieces. The manufacturers claim that these keyboards allow the hands to maintain a more natural position and thereby reduce the likelihood of RSI injuries.

| Figure 2.9 |

In order to prevent repetitive strain injuries such as carpal tunnel syndrome, some manufacturers have designed keyboards that are significantly different from the traditional flat style. These keyboards allow the hands to be placed at angles that manufacturers claim are more natural.

Courtesy of Apple Computer, Inc.

Another computer-related health issue concerns the amount of electromagnetic radiation (EMR) generated by computer monitors. At one time, it was thought that EMR might be responsible for an increase in miscarriages among pregnant women using computer terminals. However, a seven-year study by the National Institute for Occupational Safety and Health found no statistical relationship. In recent years, many monitor manufacturers have modified their designs to meet the strict MPR II monitor radiation standards developed by Sweden. For older monitors that do not meet these standards, a number of companies offer add-on products they claim can significantly reduce EMR.

Addressing computer-related health issues is best done by considering the needs of the worker, the job to be performed, and the condition of the workplace. The science of ergonomics is often involved. **Ergonomics**, sometimes called *human engineering*, addresses people's job performance and well-being, the equipment they use, and the environment in which they work. Ergonomically designed work areas, an example of which is shown in Figure 2.10, help to minimize fatigue, increase worker satisfaction, and contribute to higher productivity.

In addition to well-designed work areas, health considerations should also include the type and volume of work. For example, people in more stressful jobs, such as telephone customer service representatives, need more frequent breaks. Jobs that require high volumes of data entry should also include regularly scheduled breaks and hand and wrist exercises to reduce the chances of repetitive strain injuries. People in all computer-related jobs should follow these guidelines:

Work in a well-designed area. Alternate work activities to prevent physical and mental fatigue. If possible, change the order of your work to provide some variety.

Take frequent breaks. At least once per hour, get out of your chair and move around. Every two hours, take at least a 15-minute break. Incorporate hand, arm, and body

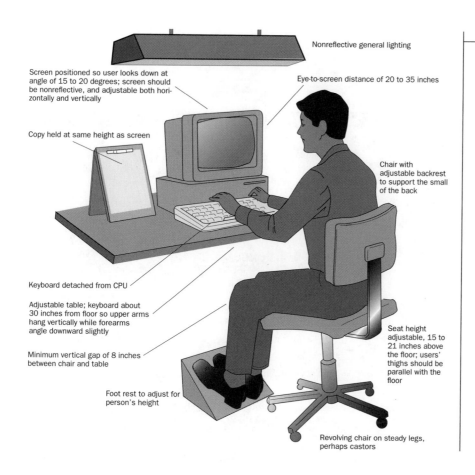

Nonreflective general lighting

Screen positioned so user looks down at angle of 15 to 20 degrees; screen should be nonreflective, and adjustable both horizontally and vertically

Eye-to-screen distance of 20 to 35 inches

Copy held at same height as screen

Chair with adjustable backrest to support the small of the back

Keyboard detached from CPU

Adjustable table; keyboard about 30 inches from floor so upper arms hang vertically while forearms angle downward slightly

Minimum vertical gap of 8 inches between chair and table

Seat height adjustable, 15 to 21 inches above the floor; users' thighs should be parallel with the floor

Foot rest to adjust for person's height

Revolving chair on steady legs, perhaps castors

Figure 2.10

Ergonomic work areas help to minimize fatigue and contribute to higher productivity.

stretching exercises into your breaks. At lunch, try to get outside and walk. Make sure that your computer monitor is designed to minimize EMR. If it is an older model, consider adding EMR-reducing accessories.

Try to eliminate or minimize surrounding noise. Noisy environments contribute to stress and tension. If you frequently use the phone and the computer at the same time, consider using a telephone headset. Cradling the phone between your head and shoulder can cause muscle strain.

Be aware of symptoms of repetitive strain injuries. Soreness, pain, numbness, or weakness in neck, shoulders, arms, wrists, and hands may be a symptom of a repetitive strain injury. Don't ignore early signs; seek medical advice.

ARTIFICIAL INTELLIGENCE

Can computers think? The COMPUTER CURRENTS feature box on the next page highlights a 1996 chess tournament between "Deep Blue," an IBM supercomputer, and Garry Kasparov, a human world chess champion. The computer won the first game, but Kasparov won the series. The computer had the colossal ability to analyze billions of alternative moves, but Kasparov used his intelligence to recognize the futility of 99 percent of those moves and quickly focus on the best option.

Although "Deep Blue" was beaten handily in chess, research in artificial intelligence continues unabated. **Artificial intelligence (AI)** is the science of enabling computers to perform tasks that would require intelligence if performed by a person.

COMPUTER CURRENTS

Supercomputer Challenges Man to a Battle of Wits

February 1996, Philadelphia, PA: World-champion chess player Gerry Kasparov and "Deep Blue," the most powerful supercomputer ever built, went "head-to-head" in a best-of-five chess tournament. Sponsored by the Association for Computing and Machinery (ACM), the tournament celebrated the fiftieth anniversary of computing. IBM engineers worked for six years on "Deep Blue" (a reference to "Big Blue," the nickname of IBM). The computer's strength was its ability to calculate up to 100 billion possible moves with the three minutes allotted each player for every move. The computer's logic system was built specifically to calculate the ramifications of various chess maneuvers.

"Another obvious strength of a supercomputer is that it is immune to the psychological rigors of the game," said IBM research scientist Murray Campell. "It doesn't become tired or distracted."

"Deep Blue" won the first match of the series and became the first computer to defeat a human world-champion. Kasparov won the second and third matches. In an interview after the third match, Kasperov said he was not impressed by the computer's strength and had no opinion of its strength as an opponent. Kasparov went on to win the tournament and "Deep Blue" went back to the drawing board.

Courtesy of Association for Computing Machinery.

AI takes advantage of the speed at which computers process data. Early systems, developed in the 1950s and 1960s, concentrated on having the computer calculate several moves ahead in complex games such as chess. Today's systems integrate even more complex information into the computer's calculations, making the computer appear to act intelligently. Three key elements support artificial intelligence efforts: natural languages, vision systems, and robotics.

Natural Languages A **natural language** is a type of query language that allows a user to enter a question in conversational rather than in computer language. For example, a user can retrieve stored information by asking a question such as "tell me the names of all employees who have been absent from work more than five days during the month of July." The use of natural languages allows for greater ease of use. Although a few natural languages are currently available, they are not widely used. Programming a computer to interpret and then respond to ordinary speech is the challenge of natural language programs. Every spoken language has its own set of colloquial phrases and jargon that make literal interpretations extremely difficult, but advances in the development of natural languages are being made.

Vision Systems The linking of camera devices to computer systems has made possible the development of vision systems. **Vision systems** enable computer-controlled devices to take digital photographs of items placed before them, analyze the components of the photograph against program-specified criteria, and make conclusions based on the criteria. For example, the Eyegaze Response Interface Computer Aid (ERICA) is designed to track eye movement with the use of a video camera. When a user looks at a command on a monitor set up with this system, the computer will activate that command. And, as you will recall from Chapter 1, developers are taking these systems one step further. Soon, by combining vision systems and natural languages, your PC will turn into a "personalized" computer that responds to your verbal commands through natural language technology and your facial expressions through vision systems.

Robotics The study, design, and use of robots is called **robotics**. Robots were originally used for jobs that were considered too dangerous, demanding, monotonous, or expensive for people to perform, such as welding large car parts in automobile plants. With the development of vision systems and physical sensory devices, robots can accomplish sophisticated tasks, such as navigating through warehouses or testing the temperatures and the solidity of metals and other materials. A new type of miniaturized robot may someday aid in diagnostic surgery by entering the human body. Robots do not require sick leave, health benefits, vacation pay, or overtime, and therefore have the potential to save corporations a great deal of money. Examples of robots in action are shown in Figure 2.11.

Courtesy of ABB Flexible Automation, Inc.

Figure 2.11

Robots are often used for tasks considered too dangerous or difficult for people to perform. Sophisticated robots have been developed for research and development.

INFRASTRUCTURE OF THE NATION

Government sponsorship of a nationwide communications network was first proposed in 1991 as part of the High Performance Computing and Communications (HPCC) initiative. As originally proposed, the network, sometimes referred to as a

digital highway, was intended to provide high-speed links between government research centers. The HPCC initiative was sponsored by then-U.S. Senator Al Gore.

When Gore was sworn in as Vice President of the United States in 1993, the scope of the network project was significantly expanded. Based on input from computer and business leaders, a **National Information Infrastructure (NII)** was proposed. An infrastructure is the underlying foundation needed for the continuance and growth of a community. The NII was envisioned as a high-speed digital network that would make information services, job training, education, medical services, and government data available to everyone.

Some of the preliminary work on a nationwide network is already being accomplished by private organizations such as cable TV and telephone companies. This is consistent with the NII plan to allow private companies to construct and operate much of the network. The government's challenge is to provide guidelines, standards, and incentives to make sure that the separately constructed parts of the network can communicate with each other and that all individuals have access to the network at a reasonable price. The three main elements of the NII are computing power, digital technologies and networks, and personal information appliances (see Figure 2.12).

Figure 2.12

The three main components of the NII are computing power, digital technologies and networks, and personal information appliances.

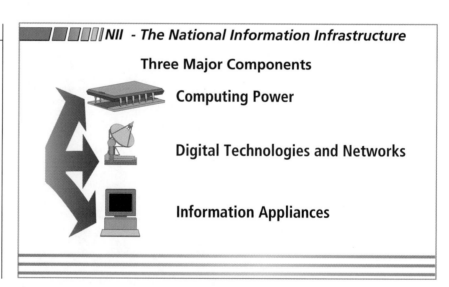

NII - The National Information Infrastructure

Three Major Components

Computing Power

Digital Technologies and Networks

Information Appliances

COMPUTING POWER

Improved computing power is an important part of the NII. For the last ten years, the computing industry has been referred to as the "30/30 industry." Each year computer technology gets 30 percent faster and 30 percent less expensive. With lower costs come more users and more application opportunities. The market grows and sales increase. More research funds become available and the improvement cycle continues. With more processing power, programs become bigger and more powerful. Program documentation is now included in the program for easy and immediate user access, rather than in cumbersome, external, printed manuals. By using icons and picture-based **graphical user interfaces (GUIs)** for instructions, programs become more user-friendly, thus lowering education and training costs.

Increased computing power also improves the speed and ease of software development. With increased processing speeds, old programming instructions or code used in previous operating systems and application programs can be reused in new applications. Improved self-checking development software makes newly written code almost error-free, thus reducing program debugging and production time. Using modular design principles, hardware and software maintenance is easier and faster. Figure 2.13 shows the major computer power elements.

 NII - The National Information Infrastructure

1. Computing Power ("30/30" Growth Industry)

Hardware
Processing Speeds
64-bit processors
"Free computing"

Software
Ease of development/use - GUI's
Code reuse/recycling
Zero-defect code development

Ease of hardware/software maintenance

#1

DIGITAL TECHNOLOGIES AND NETWORKS

Connections between points in the NII will be made through networks that send primarily digital signals. Data-intensive multimedia, including voice, sound, data, images, and video, will pass from one location in the network to another on demand. Because normal, voice-grade phone lines cannot handle the data volume required by some of these mediums, fiber optic cable and special-purpose digital lines will be used to transmit and receive the signals. Wireless communication systems will be used wherever feasible (see Figure 2.14). In some cases, lines will

NII - The National Information Infrastructure

2. Digital Technologies and Networks

Wireless communications
Xerox - "Virtual Office"
Custom publishing – Laserquick – Digital copying/storage
Combine data/tele/video communications
Holograms/virtual reality – shopping/design/"Catia Man"– Boeing 777
"Open Computing Systems" – IBM/MAC
Earth data systems – GIS – Siting/Census/Transport/Construction

#2

PIM's

be required to carry two or more media signals at once (for example, images, sound, and numeric data).

Networks require pathways and right-of-ways. Most businesses have phone systems and computer networks. Most homes have cable TV access. Because of its load capabilities, many communities are now being wired with fiber optic cable in anticipation of future needs and services. Rewiring every home with fiber optic cable will be expensive. Some estimates range up to $1,000 per household. It still has not been determined who will foot the bill—the homeowner or the service provider.

Wireless communication providers must buy land and build multiple local send/receive transmission towers to ensure seamless communication coverage for their customers. Once outside the provider's range of coverage, customers are automatically passed to other area service providers.

<table>
<tr><td>

Figure 2.15

Information appliances provide access to networks for police officers to check an individual's name, license plate number, and vehicle registration number from any jurisdiction.

</td><td>

Photo reprinted with permission from Cerulean Technology, Inc., creators of PacketCluster Patrol.

</td></tr>
</table>

INFORMATION APPLIANCES

Information appliances are personal input/output devices that can access networks. Examples of information appliances include: mainframe and personal computers, mobile and stationary telephones, television sets, and special purpose connection devices such as pagers, credit card terminals, or specialized wristwatches.

Many new information appliances will be application-specific devices. They will be mobile, small, personalized, and specialized to occupational needs. They can be used in the office, at home, in the field, or in the car or airplane. Because they are specialized, the appliances will be easy to use and require little training. Figure 2.15 shows the specialized information appliances a police officer might use in the line of duty.

IMPACT OF COMPUTER APPLICATIONS

Computer applications enable us to accomplish things that were not possible before and affect every aspect of our lives—how we work, live, learn, and play (see Figure 2.16).

It would be impossible to list every influence computers have on our lives. We have simply highlighted a very few and ask that you use your personal experiences to add even more. As technology improves, your list will continue to grow.

In an organization, computer applications can be divided into two categories: intra-system computer applications and inter-system computer applications. **Intra-system computer applications** connect various internal applications, streamlining communication among departments, and enabling the organization to run more efficiently. **Inter-system computer applications** enable systems to communicate with systems in other organizations—allowing a business system to link-up with the systems of suppliers, customers, competitors, and even regulatory agencies.

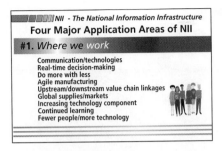

NII - *The National Information Infrastructure*
Four Major Application Areas of NII

#1. *Where we work*

Communication/technologies
Real-time decision-making
Do more with less
Agile manufacturing
Upstream/downstream value chain linkages
Global supplies/markets
Increasing technology component
Continued learning
Fewer people/more technology

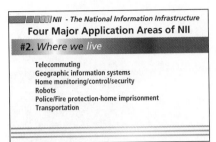

NII - *The National Information Infrastructure*
Four Major Application Areas of NII

#2. *Where we live*

Telecommuting
Geographic information systems
Home monitoring/control/security
Robots
Police/Fire protection-home imprisonment
Transportation

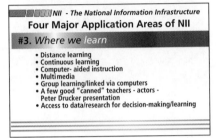

NII - *The National Information Infrastructure*
Four Major Application Areas of NII

#3. *Where we learn*

• Distance learning
• Continuous learning
• Computer- aided instruction
• Multimedia
• Group learning/linked via computers
• A few good "canned" teachers - actors -
  Peter Drucker presentation
• Access to data/research for decision-making/learning

NII - *The National Information Infrastructure*
Four Major Application Areas of NII

#4. *Where we play*

• Interactive
• Holograms
• Shopping
• Travel
• Sports
• Excercise
• Health

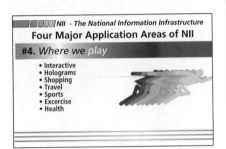

Figure 2.16

Computer applications affect how we work, live, learn, and play.

The primary pathway for inter-system computing applications is the Internet. The **Internet** is a vast, international web of interconnected computers and networks that allows users to access and exchange audio, video, and text data. The Internet is discussed in detail in Chapter 7.

WHERE WE WORK

Competition in business is fierce. To remain competitive, businesses must take advantage of new technologies in order to increase production and efficiency and lower costs. Two companies in particular have successfully integrated advanced computer technology: Chrysler and McKesson.

Most new-model cars take five or six years to be transformed from a sketch in research and development to

Courtesy of the Chrysler Corporation.

The Dodge Viper, designed and produced in only three years, boasts a 400-horse-power V-10 engine, and a top speed of more than 180 miles per hour.

a product on the assembly line. Using Cray Research Company's largest supercomputer, Chrysler was able to take the Dodge Viper from design to production in just three years. The company made the creation of a new-model car more efficient by using the supercomputer to simulate Viper performance specifications, production design, and assembly processes.

McKesson, a pharmaceutical supply company, used computers to streamline ordering. McKesson supplies each of its retail customers with a computer terminal linked to McKesson's mainframe computer. Pharmacists and store owners can now check prices and the availability of products, and order these directly from McKesson using the provided terminal. Other pharmaceutical supply companies have had difficulty competing with McKesson's efficient new system.

before	AFTER

Shelly R. Harrison.	Courtesy of Winnebago Software Company.
Students working on class projects had to ruffle through card catalogs and dusty reference works to find the most recent research on any particular topic. Often the appropriate magazine or book was missing or checked out by another student.	Students can now use their computers to access the most recent theories and research, using the Internet. Students can even correspond with others interested in the same topic, using bulletin boards and electronic mail. When the right research material has been found, it can be downloaded and printed out. Computers have made the research process much more efficient.

A number of other companies have used computer technology in ingenious ways to become more competitive. Levi-Strauss, the jeans manufacturer, has tried to personalize mass-production. For an additional charge, customers can send in their measurements, and Levi's will custom-make a pair of pants and ship them to the customer's home.

Some department stores and boutiques entice customers by projecting three-dimensional holographic images of clothing onto sidewalks. Passers-by "try on" the featured ensemble as they pass through the image.

WHERE WE LIVE

Computers have transformed the home environment. Many people are now able to work part- or full-time from their homes, using their computers to contact customers, place orders, communicate with fellow employees, and conduct banking. In the future, PCs will link applications software with phones, home entertainment systems, thermostats, security, and other systems, creating an automated household.

Currently, Intel Corporation, in cooperation with NBC, CNN, QVC, Netscape, and Packard Bell, is developing a technology called "Intercast." This service combines the accessibility of the PC, the variety of television, and the dynamic world of the Internet to create a completely interactive telecommunications experience. Imagine that you are watching television and a commercial for your favorite restaurant is broadcast. Simply press a highlighted word on your screen, and immediately you are connected to the restaurant's home page for more information and home delivery. This system is now being tested in a small number of homes throughout the United States.

Additional home applications allow you to order groceries over your computer and have them delivered to your home within three hours. Geographical information systems on CD-ROM are used as guidance systems for automobile travel. Monitors display maps and warn you of traffic troublespots to speed you on your way.

On a different note, the judicial system uses home confinement systems to combat the problem of prison overcrowding. An electronic surveillance bracelet is attached to the prisoner's wrist or ankle. Periodically a signal is sent through the telephone to verify the person's location or presence in the home.

WHERE WE LEARN

The importance of education will only increase and may necessarily become a lifelong endeavor. The brisk pace of technological change forces us to learn many new skills in order to remain valuable workers. To support this increased need for education, virtual universities have begun to appear on the Internet. These cyber-schools offer education on almost any topic, available wherever and whenever you can connect to the Internet.

Conventional physical universities are also taking advantage of computer technology. Students in different colleges, and even in different countries, can collaborate on projects by utilizing chat sessions and bulletin boards. Worldwide databases and on-line libraries give students immediate access to the most current articles and research data.

WHERE WE PLAY

With every other facet of our lives being impacted by computers, why should our free time be any different? Multimedia and virtual reality will transport you to exotic locales, though you never leave your room. A computer can even become your personal fitness trainer. Computers will help us learn a language, play an instrument, or plan a vacation. You can even view the works housed in the Louvre art museum in Paris from the comfort of your own office.

Fingers aren't the only part of your body that can get a workout from a computer. The Precor C544 allows you to simulate walking, running, hiking, or cycling, in forward and

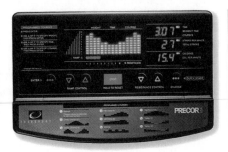

The Precor C544 Transport.

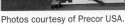
Photos courtesy of Precor USA.

reverse motion, on one piece of equipment. An electronic course profice lets you view your progression through preprogrammed hill and valley courses.

With the convergence of the computer and entertainment industries, new full-motion CDs will replace videotape. You don't like Hollywood tear-jerkers? With interactive movies, you can choose your own endings. Other possible computer-based leisure-time applications include the following:

■ Use virtual reality to practice your putt. The cyber-caddie can give you advice on your form.

■ Play virtual one-on-one basketball against a life-sized Michael Jordan.

■ Monitor your physical and emotional health. Consult with experts about health concerns or symptoms.

In this chapter, we have discussed the impact of computers on our lives and stressed the importance of staying on top of technological change. The remainder of this book will help you understand the basics of the computer industry and how to integrate computer technology into your personal and professional life.

Key Terms

artificial intelligence (AI)

carpal tunnel syndrome (CTS)

cumulative trauma disorder (CTD)

digital convergence

digital highway

Energy Star program

ergonomics

graphical user interfaces (GUIs)

green computing

hypermedia

Internet

inter-system computer applications

intra-system computer applications

multimedia

National Information Infrastructure (NII)

natural language

repetitive motion injury (RMI)

repetitive strain (or stress) injury (RSI)

robotics

virtual reality (VR)

vision system

Summary

Digital convergence describes the merging of technologies and products from the communications, entertainment, publishing, and computing industries. Digital convergence is the source of radical change in these industries.

Multimedia is the combination of text, graphics, video, and sound, often in an interactive format. Most multimedia presentations use a technique called **hypermedia** that allows users to control the sequence in which topics are presented.

Virtual reality (VR) refers to the use of a computer to create an artificial environment that can be experienced by the computer user. Applications of virtual reality are currently used in the fields of architecture, medicine, and entertainment. As computing power increases and cost decreases, VR applications will become more widely available.

The **National Information Infrastructure (NII)**, sometimes called the **digital highway**, is envisioned by the federal government as a high-speed digital network that will make information services, job training, education, medical services, and government data available to everyone.

Green computing means working with computers in a way that does not harm the environment or endanger the health of users. Power consumption, consumable supplies, and health issues are the main concerns.

An increasingly common health problem is **repetitive strain (or stress) injury (RSI)**, also called **repetitive motion injury (RMI)** and **cumulative trauma disorder (CTD)**. Working long hours at a keyboard can cause this type of injury. **Carpal tunnel syndrome (CTS)** is a particular form of RSI.

Ergonomics is the science that addresses workers' performance and well-being, and how workers respond to their equipment and work environment. Advances in ergonomics have increased productivity and overall employee health.

Artificial intelligence (AI) is the science of enabling computers to perform tasks that would require intelligence if performed by a person. AI systems include natural languages, vision systems, and robotics. **Natural language** makes it possible to communicate with a computer in colloquial, conversational speech. **Vision systems** link photographic devices to computers so that they may process visual data. **Robotics** is the study, design, and use of robots.

14 Easy steps to being a webmaster

STEP 2   DOCUMENT FORMAT

In this step, we build on the message and audience definitions from Step 1 to do a first-cut format of your web page(s). The three design issues in this step are chunking, proximity, and clarity. Chunks are identifiable objects of information. The number of "chunks" a person can keep in his or her head at one time ranges from five to nine. So, before you analyze the individual words, you organize the information content for your web pages into chunks by audience to ease web user understanding. This step describes how to chunk resume information and arrange it by importance as an example of more general information chunking. Keep in mind that your information chunks may be different, may have different content, and may be in a different order because of their importance to you. While we go through this exercise, analyze your information and apply the ideas to your own resume.

The principle of proximity means simply that ideas or information that belong together should be grouped or otherwise physically referenced together. While you define chunks, also try to identify related chunks. For instance, if you have several past jobs, they all relate to each other as comprising your job history. As you identify chunks, begin to outline them, keeping information that is related together and forming a hierarchy of information that moves from general to specific. If you have several audiences, develop a hierarchy for each audience, then combine those hierarchies into a single one that identifies all information chunks in a single structure. Analyze the outline and all information contained in each list to determine if it is presented as clearly as possible.

In the undergraduate paper resume example in Figure 2.17, we find information chunks about job search goals, education, job history, skills, and extracurricular activities. The chunks are easy to find because the headers for the sections are in boldface type. Other information might not be so easy to chunk; for instance, Cheryl wants information about her choir's concert schedule and worldwide reputation, pets, hobbies, and favorite web sites on her pages, too. A partial outline of Cheryl's information is in Figure 2.18. There are no obvious links between the choir reputation and extracurricular activities, so if a web user were to look at these chunks, they would not make much sense. This means that in the writing process, linkages that are not obvious need some explanation and maybe their own web pages.

Notice that the outline omits personal contact information. NEVER put your address or phone information on web pages. You can include an e-mail address, a post office box, or campus phone.

Once the chunks are identified and outlined, make sure that list groupings provide a clear presentation of the information. For instance, skill information could be subgrouped by type of computer skill for greater clarity as shown in Figure 2.19. In a grouping, items should be listed in descending order of skill level. A web user, looking at skills in Figure 2.19, would assume that Cheryl knows Windows NT, html 3.0, and MS/Office better than the other items in each list.

This shows that grouping is important, and that ordering within a group is important. After all information chunks have been examined, sub-grouped, and improved for clarity, create a page layout, in outline format, just as you would for a paper document, that contains your resume ideas. If you have many ideas on a single topic, as Cheryl does for the choir, create a second page for that information. If you have information that does not really fit with the other information (i.e., lacks proximity), such as Cheryl's hobby and pet information, create another page for that information.

Next, compose text for each information object. Each lowest level entry in the outline may have one or more sentences created to define it. The principle of clarity in page design is that clear, precise ideas should be conveyed with as few words as possible. Do not use adjectives or adverbs. Short, to-the-point writing is paramount because words comprise about 60 percent of all web content. Clear writing requires conscious examination of every word and its purpose. Clarity and brevity do not mean bad writing. Use whole sentences and express whole thoughts. Just express them using simple declarative sentences as much as possible.

Reexamine your page definitions. If there are more than two pages of text, create a menu page that has entries summarizing the lower level details. Then, recompose the details on another page.

Cheryl Ann Hardesty
1234 Hillcrest Dr., Apt. 123
Phone (214) 723-1234
Dallas, TX 75275
e-mail CAHardesty@post.cis.smu.edu

Goal   A challenging position using my MIS skills and experience.
Education
B.B.A., Southern Methodist University, expected May, 1997 MIS Major, Finance Minor, GPA 3.45.
Work Experience
September 1995 Consultant, Center for Non-Profit Management, Dallas, TX Conducted a technology audit of XYZ Center for Children.
May 1994–August 1994 Programmer Intern, Fidelity Resources, Los Colinas, TX Coded and tested four client/server, Visual Basic programs.
Skills
VM/CMS, MS/DOS, MS/Office, Windows NT, MS/Visual Basic, MS/Access, html 3.0, Windows 3.1, MS/C++, Java, Powerbuilder Novell, UNIX
Extracurricular Activities
Mortarboard, Information Systems Organization (President, 1994–1996), Alpha Omega Delta (Secretary, 1995–1996), Metrocrest Church Youth Choir

Figure 2.17

Sample paper resume.

Cheryl Hardesty—Resume and Home Page
Job Search Goal
Job History
Center for Non-Profit Management
Fidelity Resources
Skills—list of skills
Education History—BBA
Extracurricular Activities—list
choir worldwide reputation
choir concert schedule
Hobbies
Piano
N. Dallas Food Bank
Reading
Computers
Pets
dogs—Rusty, Max   cats—Celeste

Figure 2.18

Chunks of desired web information.

Operating Systems
Windows NT, UNIX, Windows 3.1, Novell, VM/CMS, MS/DOS
Languages
html 3.0, MS/Visual Basic, MS/C++, MS/Access, Java
Software
MS/Office, Powerbuilder

Figure 2.19

Sub-grouping for greater clarity.

ASSIGNMENT: Create an outline of the information for your resume page. Begin by chunking the information, grouping for proximity. Write the text to be included for each chunk. Reword as needed for clarity.

Have a friend review your work when you think it is complete. Ask their interpretation of your writing. If their interpretation is not exactly as you intended, rewrite your message.

Exercises

REVIEW QUESTIONS

1. Describe digital convergence.
2. What will the U.S. government's role be in the creation and operation of the digital highway?
3. Define green computing. Describe the three main concerns of green computing.
4. What is the goal of the Energy Star program?
5. What are the symptoms of carpal tunnel syndrome?
6. Define artificial intelligence (AI). List three types of AI systems.

FILL IN THE BLANKS

1. _____ is the combination of text, graphics, video, and sound.
2. Most multimedia presentations use a technique called _____ that enables users to move quickly to related subject areas.
3. _____ is the use of a computer to create an artificial environment experienced by the computer user.
4. The high-speed network planned by the government to link all individuals, businesses, and organizations is the _____.
5. Working with computers in a way that does not harm the environment or endanger the health of the user is _____.
6. _____ is the science that addresses people's job performance, well-being, the equipment they use, and the environment in which they work.
7. Three areas of _____ are natural languages, vision systems, and robotics.

MATCHING

Match each term with its description.

a. multimedia
b. digital highway
c. robots

d. artificial intelligence
e. natural languages

____ 1. Systems first used to remove people from jobs that were considered dangerous or monotonous.

____ 2. Ability of computers to perform tasks that simulate human reasoning.

____ 3. Systems that process the spoken word.

____ 4. Presentation that combines text, graphics, video, and sound.

____ 5. High-speed digital network nickname.

ACTIVITIES

1. Interview a newspaper or magazine reporter. Ask them to explain why they do or do not believe virtual periodicals will replace printed news.

2. List and briefly describe possible future applications of virtual reality technology.

3. Visit the workplace of someone you know who uses computers and analyze the work environment. What concessions have been made for worker comfort and safety? What improvements can still be made?

4. Support or refute the following statement: "In the next five years, everyone seeking employment will need to know about computers." Use what you have learned in this chapter to support your viewpoint.

5. Prepare a one-page resume. Emphasize technological skills you have that employers may find attractive. Use this document to identify areas in which you need more experience.

Skills for Living

SEARCHING THE INTERNET — COMMON WEB SEARCH SERVICES

There are a number of search services available to navigate the Web. These browsers are specialized software provided by an Internet provider. A browser lets you type in key words and then locates specific web pages that contain those words. Different browsers use different search/match methods. Five of the most common ones are described below. Before you select one, ask yourself:

- What information do I need when a match is found?
- How well can I define the topic?
- How many references do I need?
- How do I capture and use the information I have found?
- Do I want to search only web page contents or do I want to search all stored site documents?

Excite

Excite reviews the entire content of all the sites inventoried. Excite provides two different types of searches: concept-based searching and keyword searching.

Most people use keyword searching. The search software will find references containing some of the words in your search phrase. There may be other references about careers that do not use your exact words, but may still be great references. Using key words, these references will be missed. If you choose concept-based searching, Excite will return all references dealing with the topic, even if the topic contains none of the words used in the search phase.

InfoSeek

InfoSeek searches individual web pages, rather than the entire site. It also displays a short quote from each page that agrees with your search criteria. Using as few words as possible, describe what you want to find. If you are looking for a particular place or person, spell out the words, using capital letters where appropriate.

Lycos

Like InfoSeek, Lycos searches only web pages. A Lycos search will return a list of pages that meet your search criteria with hypertext links to those pages, the World Wide Web address (or URL), and a short summary of the pages that it has found.

Magellan

In the spirit of exploring uncharted territory, Magellan is named after Ferdinand Magellan, a Portuguese explorer who discovered the Strait of Magellan in 1520. You can explore the Web using Magellan in either of two ways—by using 23 predefined major topical lists or by key word searches. For either method, Magellan prints a list of sites, a partial or full description of the site's contents, and a rating. Magellan's rating system is based on depth, ease of exploration, and net appeal; each site is given an overall rating of from one to four stars.

Yahoo

Yahoo sorts matched sites into categories. When Yahoo finds a match, it prints a site summary, then supplies a link to the site in question.

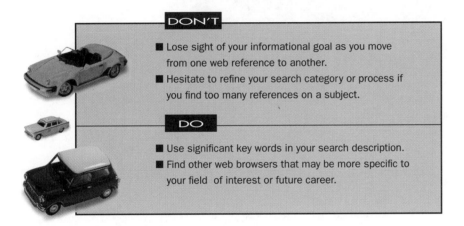

DON'T
- Lose sight of your informational goal as you move from one web reference to another.
- Hesitate to refine your search category or process if you find too many references on a subject.

DO
- Use significant key words in your search description.
- Find other web browsers that may be more specific to your field of interest or future career.

Student Activities

1. Using each of the five browsers discussed above, search for references related to "Future Careers in Information Technology." How are the results reported? Which browser format do you like the best? Why?

2. There are many other browsers than the ones we discussed. See if you can find another browser and compare its format and use to the five used above. Why are there so many different browsers?

3. Try "hopping" from one web page reference to another. Using your favorite browser, follow the topic, "Future Careers in Information Technology." Bring up the first reference it found related to the topic. Then, move to that reference. Review this reference, then move to another reference in that web page. Review this reference. What did you learn about information technology careers using all of these references?

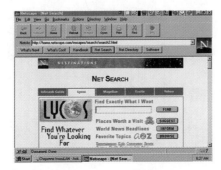

NO BOUNDARIES

As the uses and capabilities of computers and computer technology have increased, so too have the ways in which computers influence our lives. Computers are making it possible for scientists, researchers, and engineers to tackle problems previously considered too difficult and to pioneer new frontiers never before thought possible. The way in which we go about our daily lives has also changed quite dramatically as a result of computer technology. Computers enable us to accomplish things that were not possible before and affect every aspect of our lives—how we work, live, learn, and play. When it comes to computer technologies, there are no boundaries.

Courtesy of NASA.

Spotlights

Courtesy of IBM Corporation.

David Young Wolff/Tony Stone Worldwide.

Courtesy of Precor USA.

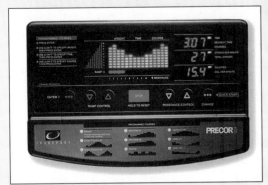

Courtesy of Precor USA.

Courtesy of Virtual i-O, Inc., Seattle, WA.

Courtesy of IBM Corporation.

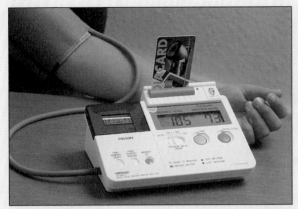

Courtesy of GEMPLUS Card International.

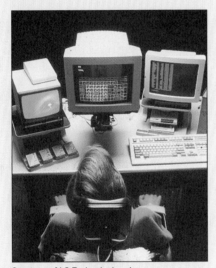

Courtesy of LC Technologies, Inc.

©1996 Harris Corporation.

Courtesy of Berklee College of Music/Photo: Bob Kramer.

Courtesy of Microsoft Corporation.

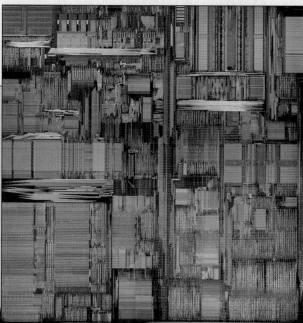

Courtesy of Intel Corporation.

Courtesy of Apple Computer, Inc.

Courtesy of AST.

Courtesy of B.A.A.

Courtesy of Bank of Boston.

Courtesy of ABB Flexible Automation, Inc.

Courtesy of PAR Technology Corporation.

Courtesy of Epson America, Inc.

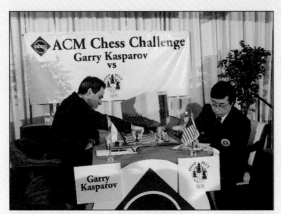

Courtesy of Association for Computing Machinery.

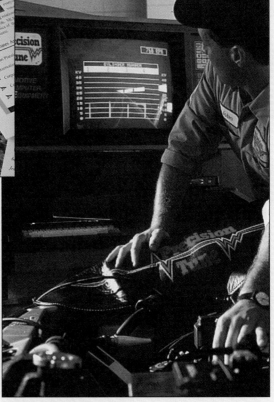

Courtesy of Precision Tune, Inc.

PART TWO

HARDWARE

As the physical part of the computer system, hardware consists of those electronic devices we can actually see and touch. Hardware consists of the computer itself and its input, output, storage, and telecommunications devices.

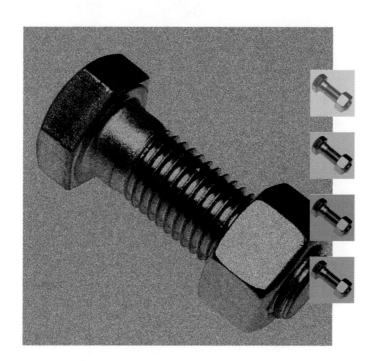

INPUT DEVICES AND MEDIA

OBJECTIVES

AFTER STUDYING THIS CHAPTER, YOU SHOULD BE ABLE TO:

1. Explain the difference between input and input device.
2. Describe the common characteristic of all input devices.
3. Explain how input devices can be categorized and classified.
4. Explain the importance of input accuracy in the information processing cycle and why interactive input devices have some degree of input error risk associated with them.
5. Explain what a keyboard is and how it is used to enter data into a computer.
6. Describe how point and click devices provide additional input capability beyond that available with the keyboard.
7. List applications for pen-based computers.
8. Differentiate between smart and dumb terminals.
9. Describe how source data automation differs from other forms of input.
10. Explain the advantages and disadvantages of voice recognition systems.

CHAPTER OUTLINE

OVERVIEW OF THE INPUT PROCESS
Getting the World into the
Computer System
The Importance of Input Accuracy

THE KEYBOARD
Keyboard Keys
Keyboard Variations
How a Keyboard Works

POINT AND CLICK DEVICES
Mouse
Trackball
Joystick
Touchscreen
Light Pen
Digitizer Tablet

OTHER INTERACTIVE INPUT DEVICES
Pen-Based Computers
Terminals
Point-of-Sale Terminals
Financial Transaction Terminals

SOURCE DATA AUTOMATION
Scanners
Optical Character Recognition (OCR)
Magnetic Ink Character Recognition
Magnetic-Strip Card Readers
Smart Cards

MULTIMEDIA INPUT DEVICES
Sound Input Devices
Voice Input Devices
Digital Cameras
Video Input Devices

Not so long ago, a process as simple as buying groceries at the local supermarket could take twice the time it does today, and sometimes cause twice the aggravation if the checkout clerk had to stop to determine a price for an unmarked item. You probably realize that checkout scanners and bar code readers, two kinds of *input devices,* have something to do with speeding this process. But do you know that those readers and scanners also help the store manage its inventory and make sure prices are raised or lowered uniformly?

Consider a shipment of canned peas. On the cans' labels and the box they are shipped in, the manufacturer has printed a bar code. A bar code is the set of vertical black and white stripes you see on everything from magazines to TV dinners, and every bar code represents a number. The store uses its bar code scanners to read this number directly into the store's computerized inventory system, where it is stored along with data about that particular item, such as price, date of receipt, and weight.

With this system, if the store management decides to have a sale on peas, the price change can be made simply, using a keyboard or other input device to change the price data in the computerized inventory, instead of physically changing the price on each can. When you pull a can of peas off the shelf and take it to the checkout, the cashier scans the code with the laser. The code's dark bars absorb light and its white spaces bounce it back, creating a pattern of electrical pulses that are translated into the item's number. The number calls up the specific product information in the cash register's computer or in a centralized database. The computer determines the correct price and displays it on the cash register, and deducts the items from the store's inventory, so store management knows they have one fewer can of peas in stock.

Scanners aren't the only input devices you'll find at today's checkout counters. The process of buying groceries is further speeded by the recent installation of debit card readers at cash registers. A debit card, which is a type of *input media*, contains information about a customer's current bank account. Customers carry these cards instead of cash or checks. When the debit card is slid through a card reader linked to the store's cash register, the amount of the sale is automatically deducted from the customer's bank account, thus further speeding the payment process and allowing customers to whisk their cans of peas home in record time.

You'll learn more about these and other input devices and media in this chapter.

OVERVIEW OF THE INPUT PROCESS

Recall that **input** is the first stage of information processing. Input consists of data and programs that are fed into a computer system. **Input devices**, such as keyboards or scanners, are hardware components that capture, collect, and transmit data and programs to the computer in a form that the computer can understand. Input devices transmit the input to the computer in a series of electronic pulses representing bits, or digits, of the binary code.

GETTING THE WORLD INTO THE COMPUTER SYSTEM

As we have seen, the word *data* is used to describe "things." And because "things" are all around you—so are data! Anything that can be used to describe the world around you can be considered data. For example, the temperature in a room at any given point in time is a piece of data. The words in a letter to a friend are data. Even the colors of the clothes you are now wearing are items of data.

The primary purpose of any input device is to send digital code to a computer that accurately represents some kind of real-world state or activity. It is this binary representation of the data, rather than the data itself, upon which the computer acts.

It is important to recognize that the computer is unable to directly understand data from the outside world. This is the role of input devices: to communicate data about the real world to the computer in a way the computer can understand. While the common characteristic of input devices is that they all transmit electronic digital impulses to a computer, how this is accomplished is dependent upon the type of real-world data each is designed to represent. These differences are discussed in the following sections and are illustrated in Figure 3.1.

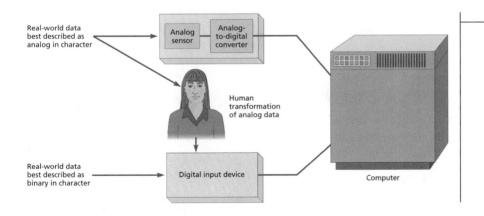

Real-world data best described as analog in character

Analog sensor

Analog-to-digital converter

Human transformation of analog data

Real-world data best described as binary in character

Digital input device

Computer

Figure 3.1

Converting real-world data into computer-readable data. The character of the real-world data determines the type of input device.

As discussed in Chapter 1, computer systems can be used for many purposes. A computer system can, for example, be used to monitor the atmospheric controls of a building. Computer systems are also often used to enter and format text, such as with a word processing application. In both instances, the input devices feed the computer system with bits intended to represent a real-world state or activity that is exterior to the computer system itself. In the first example, the computer system responds to digital signals that represent the building temperature. In the second example, the computer system responds to digital signals that correspond to letters created by the person entering the text.

Input devices can be categorized by the type of data they are designed to communicate to a computer. Moreover, input devices can be classified according to the degree of human interaction required to effectively transmit data to a computer. Let's first consider a class of input devices that generally provides an adequate representation of reality with little or no human interaction.

Input Devices for Analog Activity Real-world activities can be described as either analog or binary in character. The temperature in a building, for example, is constantly changing over time and thus can best be described as analog in character. The device that begins the input process for an analog activity, such as an infinite number of temperature gradations, is called an **analog sensor**. An analog sensor converts analog data into electronic signals of varying voltage. These signals, called **analog signals** because they are analogies of the real world, are translated into digital code through a device known as an **analog-to-digital converter**. **Digital code** is the code used by computers for storing and processing information. An analog-to-digital converter transforms the analog signal into a series of rapid on-off electronic pulses—the binary code of the computer. The transformation of an analog activity into digital code through an analog input device is depicted in Figure 3.2.

Figure 3.2

An analog-to-digital converter transforms the analog signal into a series of rapid on-off electronic pulses—the binary code of the computer.

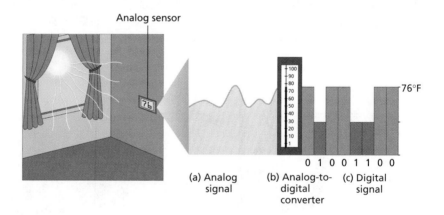

Analog sensor

(a) Analog signal (b) Analog-to-digital converter (c) Digital signal

0 1 0 0 1 1 0 0

76°F

Analog sensors and analog-to-digital converters are used in a variety of special-purpose computer systems for such applications as manufacturing process control and monitoring medical patients. In addition, many general-purpose computer systems use such devices to enable them to communicate with other computer systems whenever the method of communication requires the use of analog signals (as is the case with many standard telephone lines).

A primary characteristic of many input devices used to collect and transmit representations of analog data is that they often require little or no human interaction to be able to do so with adequate accuracy. This accuracy is due more to the sensitivity of the analog sensor and the sample time intervals of the analog-to-digital converter than to the form of human interaction.

Certain storage devices, which we shall explore more fully in Chapter 6, can also act as input devices and require little or no human interaction. With these devices, data are stored in digital form and, when transmitted, are represented to the computer with a high degree of accuracy.

Interactive Input Devices Although many real-world activities are analog in character, analog sensors and analog-to-digital converters are not found in the majority of input devices used with general-purpose computer systems today. Most input devices require some form of human interaction. This is because humans most often take the initial steps in transforming real-world analog activity into binary form.

Suppose you are interested in determining the most popular color of socks found on people in a certain room. Suppose also that a program or set of instructions has been provided to the computer to allow you to do this. All that you need to do is to enter the color or colors found on the stockinged feet of each person in the room. Chances are you or someone else would visually identify the colors and then transmit them to a computer by entering the name of each color via a keyboard. In this activity, you must first mentally transform the visual images into names (language symbols for the visual images), then transform the names into their composite letters, and again transform the letters into physical keystrokes on the keyboard. These keystrokes cause certain individual keys to be pressed while other keys remain as they were. The pressed/not-pressed state of individual keyboard keys is easily translated into the binary code required by a computer.

In the example, you interacted with the input device (the keyboard) by first performing a number of mental transformations of the data and then pressing keyboard keys that corresponded to letter symbols of your language. A keyboard is an example of an **interactive input device**. An interactive input device is a hardware component that provides for human interaction as it captures, collects, and transmits data and programs to the computer in a form that the computer can understand. Human interaction in this sense includes touching, moving, manipulating, or speaking to the interactive input device, as well as the reasoning required to perform this interaction correctly.

Interactive input devices require some human interaction in order for the digital signals they transmit to the computer to accurately represent real-world activity. This accuracy obviously depends on the accuracy of the human input. In the sock color example, human interaction was critical at each transformation. What if the person who transformed the colors into names was colorblind? What if the person who transformed the names into their composite letters could not spell? Or, what if the person who pressed the keys corresponding to the composite letters accidentally pressed the wrong key? If any of these transformation errors were to occur, it is likely that the binary signals transmitted to the computer by the keyboard would not offer an accurate representation of reality.

As with input devices in general, interactive input devices can be classified by the degree of human interactivity required to use them effectively. A keyboard requires a high degree of human interaction. In contrast, a *digital scanner* requires little more human interaction than the proper selection of the item to be scanned and the proper positioning of the scanner device.

THE IMPORTANCE OF INPUT ACCURACY

Input is the most critical stage of information processing. The computer can only process the data it's given; it can't detect human errors. If you want accurate output, you must start with accurate input. Data manually entered into a computer by an operator using a keyboard averages approximately one keyboard error for every 300 characters. Data entered more directly (through a scanning device, for instance) averages only one error for every three million characters.

THE KEYBOARD

Despite these statistics, the keyboard is the most common input device and will probably remain so for a long time. A **keyboard** is an electronically controlled device used to enter **alphanumeric data** (letters, numbers, and special characters) into the computer. As previously discussed, the keyboard converts the alphanumeric data into a binary code the computer can process. The keys on most keyboards are arranged similarly to those on a typewriter. Some of the most popular keyboards today are the original IBM-compatible keyboard, the enhanced IBM-compatible keyboard, and the Macintosh keyboard, all shown in Figure 3.3.

a)

b)

c)

Figure 3.3

a) The Apple II keyboard and Apple Extended keyboard. b) The original (80 key) IBM keyboard. c) The Enhanced (101 key) IBM keyboard.

Courtesy of Apple Computer, Inc.

Courtesy of IBM Corporation.

Courtesy of IBM Corporation.

A variety of keyboards are available. Some contain one or more special keys, such as a "Start" key which, when pressed, automatically activates the computer's operating system. Some keyboards are ergonomically designed to provide greater comfort to the user. A few IBM laptop computers contain a keyboard that extends outward when opened (similar to a butterfly extending its wings).

KEYBOARD KEYS

Although the number and placement of keys on the keyboard vary among manufacturers, most keyboards contain function keys, special-purpose keys, cursor-control keys, and a numeric keypad. Figure 3.4 shows the layout of a 101-key enhanced keyboard sold with the IBM PS/2 computer and describes the purpose of many of the keys.

Figure 3.4

The IBM 102-key enhanced keyboard. Like keys are indicated according to function.

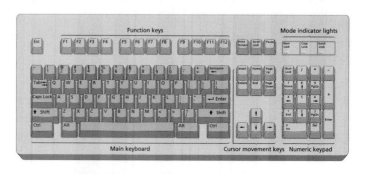

Function Keys Labeled F1, F2, F3, and so on, **function keys**, also called **programmable keys**, allow an end user to quickly access commands and functions, such as saving a document or calling up a program's Help feature. The specific purpose of each function key is determined by the software being used. Many software manufacturers, however, have attempted to standardize use of the function keys. For example, many have set aside the F1 key to initiate a Help feature.

Cursor-Control Keys A **cursor** is the symbol that shows where the next character typed will be displayed on the computer screen. **Cursor-control keys** govern the movement of the cursor on the screen and include the Up Arrow, Down Arrow, Right Arrow, and Left Arrow keys on enhanced keyboards. These keys are also found on keys 8, 2, 6, and 4 on the numeric keypad portion of the keyboard. The arrow keys on the numeric keypad are active when the Num Lock key is off. Home and End are also cursor-control keys. The exact movements of all the cursor-control keys are dependent on the software package you are using.

Special-Purpose Keys Some keys, such as the Control, Alternate, and Delete keys, are used in conjunction with other keys to enter commands into the computer. These keys are called **special-purpose keys** because when they are pressed in conjunction with another key, they cause the other key to perform a task not normally associated with that key.

Toggle Keys The Num Lock key, the Caps Lock key, and the Scroll Lock key are all examples of toggle keys. A **toggle key** is one that, when pressed, activates a certain mode or condition, and when pressed again deactivates the condition. Pressing the Caps Lock key, for example, would cause all the alphabetic characters to appear in capitals without having to press the Shift key. Pressing Caps Lock again would remove this condition. Depending on the particular program in use, the Delete key and Insert keys also act as toggle keys.

Numeric Keypad Located in the far right portion of the IBM enhanced keyboard, the **numeric keypad** is used for entering numbers quickly and for performing the same operations as a calculator. It is activated by toggling on the Num Lock key, which will turn on the Num Lock status light on the keyboard.

KEYBOARD VARIATIONS

The number and placement of keys is not the only difference among types of keyboards. The amount of space between keys also varies. One type of keyboard may feel cramped to you while another may feel just right. Keys also vary in shape and design. Some are flat, others contoured. Some require a strong depression, others are very sensitive to the touch. Some keys make a clicking noise when depressed, while others are completely silent.

Courtesy of Hooleon Corporation.

One variation on the traditional keyboard features Braille key-caps for the visually impaired.

Finally, not all keyboards have the same design or layout. Most keyboards have adopted the so-called QWERTY layout for the alphanumeric keys. It is called QWERTY because those are the first six keys across the top row of letters. Other keyboards have adopted the more progressive Dvorak layout. The Dvorak layout places the most commonly used letters, which are the vowels plus d, h, t, n, and s, on the home row (the middle row of letters). With minimal finger movement, trained keyboardists can enter 40 times as many words from the home row as they can with a QWERTY keyboard, increasing their productivity. However, most training continues to be done on QWERTY keyboards and they remain popular.

HOW A KEYBOARD WORKS

A computer keyboard transforms physical actions (the pressing of a key or sequence of keys) into signals that indicate to the computer which key or sequence of keys has been pressed. Within the keyboard is a grid of circuits, the intersections of which are directly below each key. The microprocessor in every keyboard continually scans this grid thousands of times per second. If the microprocessor detects the circuits associated with a particular key are closed, it transmits a "scan code" to the computer (see Figure 3.5). The computer then translates the scan code into ASCII code which is the format in which information is interpreted inside a personal computer. How the ASCII code, is interpreted depends upon the particular application program in use.

Figure 3.5

If you remove the cover from a keyboard, you will find a network of circuitry which senses the contact of a keystroke and sends the data corresponding to that key on to the computer for processing.

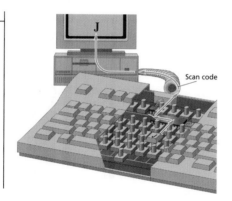

Scan code

POINT AND CLICK DEVICES

Point and click devices offer alternatives to the keyboard. Some control the movements of a **graphics cursor** (also called a **pointer**) on screen as shown in Figure 3.6 on page 86. The graphics cursor is separate from the text cursor controlled by keyboards. The graphics cursor can appear as a straight line (I), an arrow (→), a cross-hair (+), or a variety of other symbols, depending on the software application you are using and where the graphics cursor is positioned on screen. This graphics cursor, along with special buttons built into point and click devices, allows you to enter commands and select options by pointing at them on screen and pressing or clicking the appropriate button.

Point and click devices also add capabilities not found in traditional keyboard input devices. These capabilities allow for precision drawing and design. These devices come in a variety of shapes and sizes.

MOUSE

A **mouse** is a hand-held point and click input device whose movement across a flat surface causes a corresponding movement of a graphics cursor on the screen (see

COMPUTER CURRENTS

Have you ever wondered about the strange arrangement of the alphabet on your computer keyboard? Why don't the letters just appear in alphabetical order? The history of the keyboard, though relatively short (the typewriter has only been around since the mid 1800s), is sprinkled with controversy. Since the advent of the QWERTY keyboard (so named for the first six letters of the first alphabetic row), experts have disagreed over the most efficient organization of letters and characters for the average typist.

Strangely enough, the QWERTY keyboard, invented by Christopher Sholes in the 1800s, was designed to slow typists down. His original typewriter keyboard was arranged alphabetically, but when typists pressed keys too quickly, he found, it jammed the old-fashioned wooden bars holding the characters that struck the typewriter ribbon. Sholes discovered that, by placing the most frequently used characters—E, T, A, O, N, and I—in positions that were not easily reached by the hunt-and-peck typist's index fingers, the typist slowed down considerably, thus preventing the type bars from jamming. This layout, with few alterations, is still the most popular keyboard layout.

However, there are a number of alternatives. One of the most common is the Dvorak keyboard, which places the most commonly typed letters in the "home" row (the row where the typists rests his or her fingers when pausing). Its inventor, August Dvorak, reasoned that, with these 10 letters alone, a typist can produce some 3,000 common English words, compared to the 100 that can be produced on the keys found in the QWERTY home row. Dvorak devotees claim their typing speed increases up to 50 percent compared to using the QWERTY keyboard.

Another keyboard gaining favor in today's ergonomics-conscious workplace is the Maltron electronic keyboard, created by Lillian Malt and Stephen Hobday. This keyboard is split and contoured to fit each hand, with keys raised to different heights to accommodate the differing lengths of fingers. The most

Dvorak keyboard

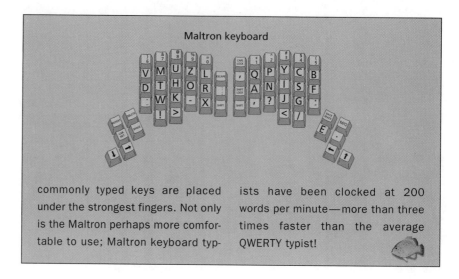

Maltron keyboard

commonly typed keys are placed under the strongest fingers. Not only is the Maltron perhaps more comfortable to use; Maltron keyboard typists have been clocked at 200 words per minute—more than three times faster than the average QWERTY typist!

Figure 3.6

When the small ball at the base of the mouse makes contact with a surface, it sends signals to the computer to move the cursor accordingly. After moving the mouse and positioning the cursor where desired, you can click on one or more buttons on top of the mouse to signal commands to the computer.

Figure 3.6). When you use a mouse, usually both the text and graphics cursors will appear on screen. Again, this depends on the application you are using.

There are several types of mouse devices. The **electromechanical mouse** contains a small ball at its base. When the ball makes contact with a surface, it sends signals to the computer to move the graphics cursor accordingly. The **optical mouse** contains a minicamera that, when moved along the surface of a special grid, relays that position to the computer. The optical mouse doesn't collect dirt and "gum up" like the mechanical mouse, but it does require the special grid which can get lost or scratched.

After moving the mouse and positioning the graphics cursor where desired, you can click one or more buttons on top of the mouse to signal commands to the computer. For example, doing so might cause the repositioning of the text cursor from one paragraph to another. This repositioning often occurs much faster and efficiently than it would if you used the cursor-control keys.

When used in conjunction with a **graphical user interface (GUI)**, the mouse is able to initiate more complicated commands. A GUI uses pictures, called **icons**, to represent actions such as opening, saving, or printing a file. With applications that use GUIs, you can point at an icon of a printer, for instance, click the appropriate mouse button, and thereby send the file shown on screen to the printer. These actions replace typing commands on a keyboard. GUIs have become increasingly popular with software manufactures and users, in turn increasing the popularity of the

Courtesy of Fellowes Corporation.   Used by permission © Logitech 1996.   Used by permission © Logitech 1996.

A recent development in mouse design is the mouse pen which, as shown on the far left, utilizes the same mechanics as the traditional mouse but in a pen-grip-like casing instead of a palm-grip case. Other developments include three-button and novelty mice.

mouse. Most manufacturers of microcomputer software have made using the mouse an essential part of their programs.

TRACKBALL

Another input device similar to a mouse is the trackball. A **trackball** is a plastic sphere sitting on rollers, inset in a small external case, or in many portable computers, in the same unit as the keyboard (see Figure 3.7). The trackball is often described as an upside-down mouse. Like the mouse, a trackball is used to move the graphics cursor on the screen and to issue commands. Using your palm or finger to rotate the ball in a particular direction moves the graphics cursor in the same direction on the screen. Buttons on the trackball allow you to initiate commands.

Courtesy of Apple Computer, Inc.   Courtesy of Fellowes Corporation.

Figure 3.7

The trackball point and click input device is available in a variety of sizes either as a part of the keyboard or as a separate unit.

The main advantage of using a trackball is that it requires less desk space than a mouse, and is therefore good for people working in confined areas. The trackball also requires less arm movement than the mouse, making it a valuable resource for those with limited arm mobility.

Trackballs are often used with portable computers. Some are made to mount on the side of a portable computer so you can use the device while sitting in an airplane seat or other confined area. Other portable computers now come with built-in miniature trackballs. In either case, you can install a regular desktop mouse if you find the trackball inconvenient or hard to use.

JOYSTICK

The **joystick** (named after the control lever used to fly older fighter planes) is a small box that contains a vertical lever that, when pushed in a certain direction, moves the graphics cursor in the same direction on the screen (see Figure 3.8). It is often used for computer games. Some joysticks have a button in the tip near the user's thumb. Pressing this button often performs such actions as firing a game weapon at an object on the screen.

Figure 3.8

The joystick, originally designed for controlling airplanes, is an input device frequently used for playing computer games.

Gravis Analog Pro courtesy of Advanced Gravis Computer Technology.

Recently, portable and laptop users have become accustomed to a new type of joystick, often called a "pointing device" or simply a "pointer." It is small (about the size of a pencil eraser), and as shown in Figure 3.9, fits between the G and H keys of the keyboard. By placing the index finger on top of the joystick, slight pushing or pulling movements adjust the pointer on the screen. This type of joystick eliminates a bulky external mouse or joystick and allows the hand to remain close to the keyboard.

Figure 3.9

The IBM ThinkPad comes with a tiny "joystick" called a trackpoint.

Courtesy of IBM Corporation.

TOUCHSCREEN

A **touchscreen** is an electronic display screen that allows you to make selections by touching specific locations on the screen (see Figure 3.10). When touched, the input device sends electronic signals to the computer for processing. Large amounts of data cannot be entered using a touchscreen. You can only issue a command or choose from among the options displayed on the screen. Special software applications designed for touchscreens determine the selection choices you have.

Applications developed for touchscreens are usually **menu driven**, meaning you choose an option from a menu on the screen, and this menu selection calls forth another menu, and so on, "driving" your progression through the application program. You continue to choose from the options on the menus until you receive the information you are looking for, or until your choice causes some other processing activity to occur. You have probably seen touchscreens in airports, where applications are installed to help travelers find restaurants, lodging, and transportation. If you are shopping for an engaged couple, you might even find their registry in the touchscreen kiosk in a local department store.

Figure 3.10

Touchscreens provide a hands-on method for data input. They are commonly found in the hospitality industry for order entry.

Courtesy of Squirrel Companies, Inc.

Touchscreens have become popular in restaurants and fast food chains such as McDonalds. The plastic membranes on the cash registers are preprinted with all of the menu items. When an item is pressed, it appears on the screen along with pricing information. The order is transmitted to the kitchen, a receipt is issued, and the data stored for inventory tracking purposes.

The advantage of touchscreens is that they are easy to learn and easy to use. They also allow you to make choices and enter data quickly. For these reasons, touchscreens are installed in places where having a computer speeds up the information processing cycle, but employees and customers are not necessarily computer literate.

LIGHT PEN

A **light pen**, resembling a writing pen, is used to write on, draw on, or select menu items on a computer screen. The tip of a light pen contains a highly sensitive photoelectric cell. When the light pen is pointed close to the screen, the photoelectric cell detects the light emitted from the exact spot the pen is touching. This accuracy makes light pens, like the one shown in Figure 3.11, very popular among engineers and draftsmen who use computer-aided design (CAD) software to create blueprints and drawings of products or construction projects.

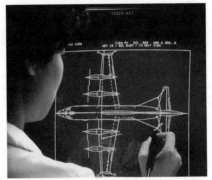

The Stock Market.

Figure 3.11

The light pen is used to make selections or draw directly on the computer screen, making it particularly beneficial for computer assisted design (CAD) applications.

A light pen is versatile. By touching it to the screen, you can draw images, make changes to an object, erase parts of a drawing, or select different colors. Light pens allow you to choose menu selections on a screen by touching the pen to the choice on the screen and clicking the pen's button.

DIGITIZER TABLET

A **digitizer tablet** is a flat tablet used in conjunction with a pen-like stylus or a cross-hair cursor. The tablet, which comes in a variety of sizes and is crisscrossed with thousands of tiny wires, is the working surface. You can place drawings on top of the tablet and trace them with either the stylus or the cursor (see Figure 3.12 on page 90). As these two devices pass over the tablet, the electronic circuitry in the grid of wires opens and closes, recording 0s and 1s. This information is sent to the computer where it is stored in memory as points on a large grid. Images can be called up later and edited from the keyboard or with other point and click devices.

Mapmakers find the precision tracing capabilities of digitizer tablets very helpful. After tracing in streets, parks, and highways, they can then use the keyboard to label the locations with names. Their ease of use and versatility also make digitizer tablets popular with architects and engineers working with blueprints.

You can also create precise freehand drawings with digitizer tablets. They provide a "natural" drawing surface and a convenient working environment. Drawing on a digitizer tablet is similar to drawing on paper with a pen or pencil.

Digitizer tablets have also become popular as mouse replacements when using graphical user interfaces. Moving the pen over the surface of a digitizer tablet moves a pointer on the screen in the same way a mouse moves a pointer on the screen. Menu options and check boxes can be selected with the digitizer pen.

Figure 3.12

The digitized tablet is used in conjunction with either a pen-like stylus or a palm-held cross-hair device.

Reprinted with permission of Wacom Technology Corporation.

OTHER INTERACTIVE INPUT DEVICES

Many manufacturers of input devices have developed variations on the devices just discussed. For example, there are **cordless mouse** devices that control input through the use of radio signals. Some manufacturers have designed "ergonomically correct" mouse devices that fit the human hand in interesting and unique ways. Some mouse devices are held like pens and often called styluses.

PEN-BASED COMPUTERS

Pen-based computers provide another way for users to not only input information into computers, but also quickly edit information and make selections from menus in GUI environments. The screen of a pen-based computer (often called a tablet) is sensitive to the touch of a stylus device. Users actually write on the surface of the screen in their own handwriting, or make gestures that execute specific commands. Typical gestures are pictured in Figure 3.13.

Figure 3.13

Typical gestures used in pen-based computing.

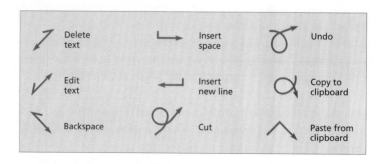

FOCUS

Enabling the Disabled

Virtually every computer maker today touts its products as "user friendly." But for a handful of companies making specialized equipment for people with disabilities, being "user friendly" takes on special meaning—and special challenges.

For some individuals with disabilities, oversized keyboards with one-inch square keys or keyboards that tolerate a trembling touch are a sufficient modification. For more severe disabilities, however, more dramatic changes in input devices are necessary.

Courtesy of LC Technologies, Inc.

Many of these special input devices are essentially on-off switches. One group of special computer programs scans through an array of characters or commands. The user turns on a switch when the desired letter or command is highlighted. In the most common of these programs, the computer displays blocks of five letters.

When a block has been selected, the computer displays each letter in that block until the user selects a particular letter. The computer displays the chosen letter and then begins to scroll through the five-letter blocks until another block is chosen, another letter is added, and so on. As computers increase in speed and storage capacity, an increasing number of input devices are offering not just blocks of letters, but large selections of complete words.

Switch-operating devices for people with disabilities come in a variety of forms to accommodate individual abilities and limitations. Among the most common are:

■ **"Puff-sip" plastic tubes.** This switch-operating input device has a tube into which a user blows to select a particular command or character. The tube contains a switch sensitive enough to respond to an air pressure change of just 0.02 pounds per square inch, or the equivalent of half an inch of water across a flat surface. Thus, almost any individual who does not require a respirator can operate a "puff-sip" tube.

■ **Switch button input device.** These buttons come in many forms and can be mounted on a wheelchair. They are placed near the part of the user's body with the greatest range of movement, such as on the headrest, armrest, or footrest of the wheelchair.

■ **Switches mounted to Morse code software.** A person with the ability to activate two types of switches can use them to send "short" and "long" signals in Morse code, which the computer translates into words.

Some devices used by people with disabilities require only minor modifications of common input devices. Chin-operated "joysticks" allow adults and children with severe disabilities to play a wide variety of computer games. Voice synthesizers, which many analysts predict will someday be the way in which virtually everyone inputs data and gives commands to a computer, are already helping many people with disabilities. In addition, people with a limited range of movement can now use a voice-activated robot arm capable of activating switches and appliances and grasping objects such as books, food, and telephones.

A very small percentage of people with disabilities are unable to use any of the devices mentioned above. These individuals are completely paralyzed, lacking the ability to move and to speak, relying on respirators to help them breathe. Fortunately, scientists have made considerable progress in developing computer links to help these individuals communicate. The Eyegaze System, developed in Fairfax, Virginia, by LC Technologies, Inc., enables people with severe motor disabilities to operate a computer with their eyes. By looking at control keys displayed on a computer monitor, a user can synthesize speech, control his or her environment(lights, appliances, television, etc.), type, operate a telephone, and run computer software.

Seated in front of the computer monitor, the user operates the system by looking at rectangular Eyegaze keys that are displayed on the monitor. To "press" an Eyegaze key, the user looks at the key for a specified period of time, typically a fraction of a second. A specialized video camera mounted below the computer monitor observes one of the user's eyes. Sophisticated image-processing software in the computer continuously analyzes the video image of the eye and determines where on the screen the user is looking. Initially, a main menu is displayed on the monitor with options such as Lights & Appliances, Phrases, Read Text, Telephone, TV/VCR Control, Typewriter, Games, DOS Mode, and Re-Calibrate. Once a selection is made from the main menu, another menu is displayed from which a more refined selection can be made.

Thanks to Eyegaze and other devices large and small, people with severe disabilities have more opportunities for greater self-sufficiency. These new tools help them to work, play, learn, and communicate in ways that would have been impossible a few years ago.

The operating system of a pen-based computer must have built-in handwriting and gesture-recognition software. Some pen-based operating systems such as Microsoft Windows for Pen Computing will work with digitizing tablets attached to regular desktop computers so that users can take advantage of handwriting recognition, gestures, and other pen-based capabilities without the need for a tablet-type computer. Users write on the digitizing tablet instead of on the computer screen itself. However, it is important to recognize that most pen-based computers are portable because they are designed for field use by sales representatives, nurses and doctors, inventory takers, and other people who don't need to input (type) a lot of information (see Figure 3.14). Typically, pertinent information is already displayed on the screen and the operator gestures with the pen to make choices or select items. Because there is no keyboard, the devices are often quite small. For example, a doctor interviewing a patient might ask questions read from the screen, then make check marks in "yes" or "no" boxes.

© 1996 Harris Corporation.

Figure 3.14

Pen-based computers offer flexibility to users who need to take their computers out with them and might not need a full keyboard for input of their specialized data.

Pen-based computers have some interesting features. For example, you can replace text by simply writing over it with the pen. This is useful if you are editing a document that has already been input. You can also "train" the pen-based operating system to recognize characters the way you normally write them. For example, if the pen computer consistently does not recognize the way you write the letter *S*, you can include several versions of the way you normally write the letter in the character library of the computer so it is recognized in the future. The gestures listed in Figure 3.13 are somewhat standardized. However, you can create your own gestures to execute commands you use often. For example, you might create a gesture that executes the command to save the document you are working on. In this way, you don't have to go through the series of steps to choose the Save command from a menu.

One type of a small pen-based computer is called a **personal digital assistant (PDA)**. PDAs are hand-held devices designed for employees working outside, such as salespeople or workers who read electricity meters. PDAs often have built-in communications capabilities that allow the device to use voice, fax, or data communications. For example, PDAs can contain a built-in cellular phone that enables wireless transmission of faxes, electronic mail, and voice mail. Their small size allows them to be carried in pockets, purses, and briefcases, or strapped to arms or legs. A technician might rely on a PDA to obtain information on how to make a particular repair. PDAs can store the equivalent of thousands of pages of technical and repair manuals.

TERMINALS

Terminals are special input devices that contain communications links to a remotely located mini- or mainframe computer system. Terminals are either "smart," meaning they can do some processing on their own, or they are "dumb," in which case they can only input and output data. Dumb terminals are completely dependent on a central

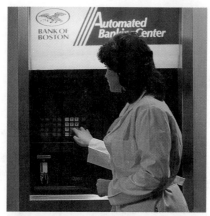

ATMs are smart terminals linked directly to the host bank's mainframe.

Courtesy of Bank of Boston.

A credit card swipe used in department stores is an example of a dumb terminal.

Courtesy of NCR Corporation.

computer system for all their processing capabilities (see Figure 3.15). Unlike a microcomputer, they do not contain a processor. Employees in the financial services industry, for instance, use dumb terminals to check on market prices of various financial instruments such as stocks and bonds.

Terminals often don't look like normal computers since they are used mainly to gather information from credit cards or other devices. For example, the credit card "swipes" in department stores are dumb terminals. They get the card information, then call a main computer and verify credit.

POINT-OF-SALE TERMINALS

A variety of terminals are used to enter data, including **point-of-sale (POS) terminals**, which are smart terminals. Point-of-sale terminals are similar to cash registers, except that they capture sales and inventory data at the time of the customer transaction and send it to the main computer system for processing. These terminals usually contain a keyboard like those found on cash registers. They also contain a cash drawer, a display that shows a description of the product, the product number, and price, and a printer to print a receipt.

FINANCIAL TRANSACTION TERMINALS

Financial transaction terminals are used to perform banking-related activities. The most familiar financial transaction terminal is the **automated teller machine (ATM)** found outside most banks and in commercial areas. These are smart terminals that allow you to make deposits, withdrawals, and inquiries. ATM keyboards are highly specialized with keys that allow you to enter your personal identification number (PIN), the account you're accessing, and dollar amounts.

SOURCE DATA AUTOMATION

Collecting data at the source and sending it directly to the computer system without an intermediate keystroke process is called **source data automation**. Source data automation makes use of many of the technologies already discussed in this chapter. The difference is that it requires not only an input device, but also specially marked, standardized input, such as bar codes on grocery items, preprinted numbers on checks, magnetic strips on credit and bank cards, and microprocessor chips on health care cards. Direct data entry is used to speed up the processing in places that record thousands of transactions every day, such as grocery stores and banks.

For example, when you use a department store charge card, your account information can be updated at the point of sale to include your purchase at the time of the sales transaction. This eliminates any errors that might be introduced by a salesclerk handwriting a receipt or making carbon copies of your charge card number on a sales slip that will be processed by someone else later. This transaction information is then communicated to a centralized computer (often a mainframe) that holds customer information, credit information, and other historical information. It is usually possible to access a particular customer's record by running the credit card through a card reader or to recall records by typing in the customer's name or telephone number.

Source data automation eliminates much of the duplicated effort involved with traditional data processing systems. Aware of the likelihood of human error, companies that rely on keyboard entry take steps to verify data. This adds more people and time to the input process, but the input stage is the least expensive time to detect errors. As more and better input devices are developed, the trend will continue toward source data automation as a means of capturing correct data, saving time, and curbing cost.

SCANNERS

A **scanner** is a device that converts photographs, drawings, forms, text, or any combination of these items into digital form. The scanned material is stored in the computer's memory for further processing or for movement into another document. The scanned image can be edited, printed, enlarged, or reduced.

The two types of scanners in use today: hand-held scanners and full-page scanners.

Used by permission © Logitech 1996.　　Courtesy of Hewlett-Packard Company.

Two popular types of scanners are **hand-held scanners** and **page scanners** (also called **flatbed scanners**). Hand-held scanners are used for scanning small or curved areas. Because they rely on steady hand movement, quality can suffer when scanning large objects: if you accidentally jerk the scanner over the same area twice, that area is recorded twice. Page scanners look similar to tabletop copy machines. Pages are either laid face down on the scanner's glass surface or fed through the scanner by means of a side-feed device. The automated mechanisms of page scanners make them more steady and accurate in their recording of images than hand-held scanners. High-quality laser scanners are used by newspapers, publishers, and service bureaus because of the laser's accuracy.

OPTICAL CHARACTER RECOGNITION (OCR)

Optical character recognition (OCR) is a system of producing machine-readable code on a data source item and reading that code by means of optical scanning devices. The underlying concept of OCR technology is the input device's ability to recognize pattern forms. Special characters and symbols have been developed for OCR code, along with scanning equipment to recognize and translate the code into digital form. Most of the devices contain either a light-sensing component or a laser beam for reading and interpreting the data.

OCR is a highly specialized area. Scanners that read one sort of symbol may be incapable of reading another: the laser scanner at the grocery store probably would not be able to read the optical characters found on clothing tags. OCR technology is rapidly improving to include a larger variety of characters, symbols, and even handwriting.

Figures 3.16

OCR codes appear on everything from canned goods to clothing tags. Whenever pricing, inventory, or tracking is a concern, OCR codes facilitate quick entry and all but eliminate human error.

Courtesy of Norand Corporation.

Optical mark readers detect filled-in shapes on scan sheets.

Courtesy of Scantron Corporation.

Optical Marks If you've ever taken a test for which you had to use a lead pencil to fill in shapes that corresponded with multiple-choice answers, you are already familiar with **optical marks**. The forms on which you made your marks are called optical scan sheets. Optical marks are the filled-in shapes, usually ovals or rectangles, on scan sheets. The data collected on scan sheets are translated into binary form by an **optical mark reader (OMR)**, shown in Figure 3.16. The OMR contains a light beam that passes over the scan sheet and detects the filled-in ovals. In the test example, an answer sheet is also fed into the OMR and the answers are compared and tallied by the computer.

Optical Codes Very popular for identifying a variety of products ranging from groceries to automobiles, **optical codes** are characters or symbols placed on a data source item so as to be suitable for optical character recognition input devices. Optical codes are also popular with package delivery services such as Federal Express and UPS, where they are used to identify, sort, and track packages throughout the delivery process.

The most common type of optical code is the bar code. **Bar codes** are a series of vertical lines manufacturers print on their products to represent alphanumeric data. Bar code data are differentiated by the width of the bars and the amount of space between them. Often, the alphanumeric information is printed below the code, making the data readable by both machines and humans.

There are a variety of bar code schemes. The scheme developed by the supermarket industry for identifying products and manufacturers uses a ten-digit system and is called the Universal Product Code (UPC). The publishing industry uses another coding scheme. It converts the International Standard Book Number (ISBN) to bar code form. This is illustrated in Figure 3.17.

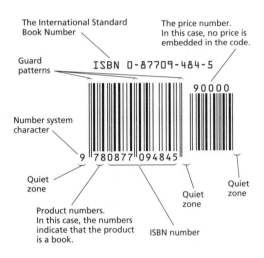

The International Standard Book Number

The price number. In this case, no price is embedded in the code.

Guard patterns

ISBN 0-87709-484-5

90000

Number system character

9 780877 094845

Quiet zone

Quiet zone

Quiet zone

Product numbers. In this case, the numbers indicate that the product is a book.

ISBN number

Figure 3.17

The bars on optical bar codes are suitable for optical character recognition input devices.

There are two types of scanning devices for reading bar codes. One is a **hand-held scanning wand** that uses either magnetic or laser technology. An example of a hand-held scanning wand is depicted in Figure 3.18. As the hand-held scanning wand passes over the bar code, it detects the width of the bars as well as the spacing between them and translates this data into binary code for the computer. The other type is the **stationary scanner,** most often found built into checkout lanes at supermarkets. Instead of passing the scanner over bar codes, bar codes are passed over the scanner. The stationary scanner relies on laser technology.

Bar codes and bar code readers not only save time and help minimize inputting errors, they also automate other parts of the processing cycle. Supermarkets, department stores, and discount stores connect bar code readers to POS terminals which contain store inventory data and allow for immediate updating. Each time a unit of product is sold, the sales transaction is sent to the central computer for processing. One unit of the product is automatically subtracted from the current inventory balance. When the

The Stock Market.

Figure 3.18

The hand-held scanning wand uses laser or magnetic technology to "read" the thickness and spacing of lines in bar codes.

inventory level falls below the item's minimum level, the computer automatically creates a reorder request for that item. Presently, about 80 percent of the information needed by retailers can be captured at the point of sale. Once sales data are captured, they can be used not only for controlling inventory and purchasing new stock, but for evaluating worker productivity and forecasting future sales volume.

In the delivery service industry, bar codes are linked with the package's source and destination information and are used to provide tracking capabilities.

Optical Characters Another kind of OCR system is comprised of **optical characters**. Optical characters usually conform to a standard font called OCR-A (see Figure 3.19), which is readable by both people and optical character scanning devices, called optical readers. An optical reader reflects light off the characters and converts the reflections into a digital pattern. Retail stores print item descriptions and price tags using optical characters. The scanner, hooked up to a POS terminal, directly records the information from the tag to the terminal.

Figure 3.19

The OCR-A typeface.

ABCDEFGHIJKLMN
OPQRSTUVWXYZ,.
$/-1234567890

Though OCR-A is the most common optical character set used, the computer industry is continuing to develop devices that allow for recognition of a greater number of characters and even handwriting. For example, the EZ version of the federal tax form displays the numbers 0 through 9 at the top of the form and requests that you follow that standard when you print your dollar amounts. The IRS runs these forms through an optical scanner, shown in Figure 3.20, saving a great amount of processing time during tax season.

Figure 3.20

Utility companies increase their transactions per hour and minimize entry errors by having their operators run monthly payments stubs through an optical character reader.

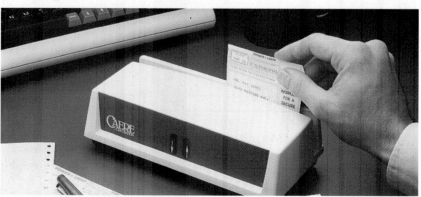

Courtesy of Caere Corporation.

Superstock.

Courtesy of McKesson Corporation.

Manufacturers and distributors of goods had to keep manual records of their stock and of the materials it took to manufacture their goods. This could be extremely cumbersome, time consuming, and inaccurate in industries that dealt in a high volume of goods.

Even the contents of large warehouses can be inventoried easily with the help of scanners and other input devices. Not only do employees and managers know exactly how much stock the warehouse contains, they can locate particular items easily.

MAGNETIC INK CHARACTER RECOGNITION

You have probably noticed a group of unique characters printed along the bottom edge of personal checks. These characters are printed with a special magnetic ink that is read using a process known as **magnetic ink character recognition (MICR)**. MICR is used by the banking industry as a means of processing the millions of checks it receives every day.

The MICR font, adopted by the American Banking Association (ABA) in the 1950s and used as the standard throughout the banking industry, consists of the decimal numbers 0 through 9, and four special codes, illustrated in Figure 3.21 on page 100. The MICR coding scheme includes a check routing number, an ABA transit number, a bank identification number, and an account number. After a check is written and presented at a bank for payment, a clerk uses an MICR inscriber to encode the amount of the check in magnetic characters in the lower right corner. The check is sorted and routed to the customer's bank where it, along with thousands of other checks, is inserted into a machine called an MICR reader. The machine reads the data from each check and enters the data into a computer for processing. Occasionally, the magnetic ink on the check is damaged and can't be read by the MICR reader. When this happens, someone must manually key in the data.

Figure 3.21

The E13-B font provides a standard of ten decimal numbers and four special characters for processing checks.

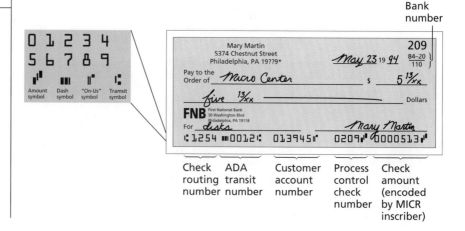

Bank number

| Amount symbol | Dash symbol | "On-Us" symbol | Tramsit symbol |

Check routing number | ADA transit number | Customer account number | Process control check number | Check amount (encoded by MICR inscriber)

MAGNETIC-STRIP CARD READERS

Some cards people use for routine business transactions, such as credit cards, automated teller machine (ATM) cards, and identification cards, are called **magnetic-strip cards** because they contain a magnetic strip on one side. The magnetic strips store information about the card owner. For example, a magnetic strip on a bank credit card may contain encoded data that includes the owner's account number, the expiration date, and the date the card was issued.

Magnetic strip cards contain encoded information. They can be used not only for routine business transactions, but also to restrict entry and for other security applications.

Courtesy of Card Key Systems, Inc.

The cards are sometimes used in conjunction with financial transaction terminals that automate banking activities. The ATM is a smart financial transaction terminal that can not only retrieve account information, but also process transactions. Credit card readers at retail stores are another example. If the amount of the current purchase is within the customer's credit limit, the amount of the purchase price is immediately transferred and credited to the store's account and then added to the customer's credit card balance.

Cards with magnetic strips are used for a variety of other applications. Some hotels issue guests a magnetic-strip card instead of a regular key to open doors to their rooms. Computer center employees are often issued this kind of card to gain access to restricted computer facilities.

SMART CARDS

A **smart card**, often the size of a credit card, contains a built-in microprocessor and memory that identify the card (and its owner) and assists in financial and other transactions. Its primary advantage is increased security: the information can only be read by an authorized user with the appropriate password. The card can also be designed to self-destruct if necessary, such as when someone attempts access with the wrong password more than a few times.

MULTIMEDIA INPUT DEVICES

Multimedia is any combination of text, graphics, sound, and video that is programmed into and delivered by the computer. Multimedia adds a new dimension to computer systems, capturing the attention of those who come in contact with this emerging technology. Sound and video are especially effective tools for engaging an audience. Sound captures participants' attention and viewers tend to retain more of what they see.

Computers with multimedia capabilities typically contain one or more special components, called cards or boards, installed inside the computer. A sound card allows for the capture of sound, such as speech and music. A video card makes it possible to record images of people, documents, and scenery.

SOUND INPUT DEVICES

Devices connected to a computer, including microphones and electronic music keyboards, enable a computer to capture speech and music sounds. An electronic music keyboard, when used with special sound-editing software, enables a user to change the sounds produced by the keyboard.

VOICE INPUT DEVICES

A **voice input device** has two functions. First, it can record a human voice, then with appropriate voice recognition software, convert the voice input to ASCII characters. Second, a voice input device can simply record and play back the voice input as if it were a tape recorder. In the second example, the voice data are converted to digital information so they can be stored in the computer's memory or on a disk storage device for later playback. Voice recording has become popular as more and more users have added sound boards to their personal computers, and as more computers connect together into networks (discussed in Chapter 7) in which computers (and their users) can communicate with one another. Every user on a computer network typically has a specific electronic mail address. Electronic mail systems let you send typewritten messages to other users. If voice systems are installed, these messages can be sent as an audio file.

Voice recognition systems make it possible for a user to speak to a computer through a microphone. A voice recognition system contains an audio digitizer that converts sounds, including spoken words, into ASCII characters. A computer program then recognizes the voice and if so instructed, executes an appropriate command.

Once it has been digitized, human voice, as with any sound, can also be stored for later playback. Currently, many of the long-distance telephone companies are using voice recognition system input devices to identify "person-to-person" or "collect" calls. A recorded message requests that the caller say whether the call is "person-to-person" or "collect." Once the caller states which type of call is being made, it is registered into the computer and the computer then repeats the caller's response and completes the appropriate type of call.

Voice recognition system input devices do experience problems in recognizing a user's voice and converting words to commands. One problem has been the poor reliability of most systems due to the inability to consistently recognize the same word. However, such devices can be trained to recognize the way a user says certain words. Another drawback has been that most devices can recognize only a limited number of words. In addition, many systems have difficulty with homophones, spoken words that

Used by permission © Logitech 1996.

Figure 3.22

Programmers have developed computer software that turns spoken commands into digital instructions. This is just one example of people's imaginations sparking creative solutions.

sound similar, such as "there" and "their," or "pair" and "pear."

Despite these problems, voice recognition systems are gaining in popularity. You can simply speak the entire text of a letter or document into a computer, rather than type it (see Figure 3.22). In addition, some systems offer immediate voice playback verification as you type text or numbers. For example, as you enter monthly sales figures, the computer repeats the numbers back for verification. Likewise, the computer could "read aloud" the contents of a typewritten letter or document.

DIGITAL CAMERAS

Unlike traditional cameras that record images on a chemical based film, digital cameras record images in a form that can be stored by a computer (see Figure 3.23). Some digi-

Courtesy of Epson America, Inc.

Figure 3.23

Digital cameras do not require traditional film. Instead, they store images in digital form. The digital images are transmitted directly to the computer where they can be viewed and manipulated by the user.

tal cameras resemble traditional cameras and are portable. Others are stationary and are connected directly to a computer. When connected directly to a computer, recorded images can be altered, cropped, enlarged, or reduced.

A variety of images can be captured by a digital camera, including people, documents, and products. Some companies use digital cameras to record pictures of products for catalogs and to record employee images that are placed on identification cards or badges.

VIDEO INPUT DEVICES

As the power and storage capacity of desktop computers increase, it has become feasible to record, digitally store, and play back video with computers. Because of the amount of memory and disk space required to store video, video segments are usually limited to a few seconds or minutes on desktop computers. However, computers with much larger processing and storage capabilities are being used as an essential part of the video production process. In all cases, compression algorithms help squeeze video data down to manageable size, but space requirements are still large if segments are over a minute. Video may require large amounts of memory and space, but can be a valuable tool. A product manufacturer could store video presentations of its products, then recall them at any time for reference. In addition, a real estate agent might store a video "walk-through" of a house so that a client could "browse" properties from the agent's office.

Key Terms

alphanumeric data

analog sensor

analog signals

analog-to-digital converter

automated teller machine (ATM)

bar codes

cordless mouse

cursor

cursor-control keys

digital camera

digital code

digitizer tablet

electromechanical mouse

financial transaction terminals

flatbed scanner

function keys

graphical user interface (GUI)

graphics cursor

hand-held scanners

hand-held scanning wand

icons

input

input devices

interactive input device

joystick

keyboard

light pen

magnetic ink character recognition (MICR)

magnetic-strip cards

menu driven

mouse

multimedia

numeric keypad

optical character recognition (OCR)

optical characters

optical codes

optical mark reader (OMR)

optical marks

optical mouse

page scanners

pen-based computer

personal digital assistant (PDA)

point and click devices

pointer

point-of-sale (POS) terminals

programmable keys

scanner

smart card

source data automation

special-purpose keys

stationary scanner

terminals

toggle key

touchscreen

trackball

voice input device

voice recognition systems

S u m m a r y

An **input device** converts programs and data into binary codes the computer can process. The most common type of input device is the **keyboard**. Keyboards contain keys representing letters, numbers, and special characters, and most have a **numeric keypad** for entering numbers quickly. Keyboards also contain **cursor-control keys**. **Special-purpose keys** are used in combination with other keys to perform a wide range of functions.

A **mouse** is a small hand-held input device used to move a cursor or pointer around on the screen. A **trackball** is basically an "upside-down" mouse and is used for the same purposes. A **joystick** is a small box that contains a lever for moving objects or a cursor about on the screen.

A **touchscreen** is an electronic display screen that allows you to make selections by touching the screen. A light pen can be used to write or draw on a display screen, enter data into a computer, or to edit images created on the screen. A **digitizer tablet** usually includes a flat tablet and stylus for drawing on the tablet surface.

Pen-based computers have flat screens that are written on with a stylus-like device. A special type of pen-based computer is **personal digital assistants (PDAs)** that provide communication capabilities to persons working outside.

Source data automation technologies require specially marked, standardized data source items and use input devices capable of reading data in the form of special characters, codes, or symbols.

A **scanner** can read text and images directly into a computer. Two kinds of scanners for use with microcomputers are hand-held scanners and page scanners.

Optical character recognition (OCR) systems can read and interpret printed, typed, and handwritten data from a source document. **Optical mark readers** convert data in the form of marks (such as pencil marks in ovals) in specific locations on a source document into a form the computer can process. **Optical code readers** are widely used in retailing for reading and interpreting coded data for entry into a computer. Optical **bar code readers** are designed to read bars, such as the universal product code (UPC) that identifies a product and the manufacturer.

Magnetic ink character recognition (MICR) is an input system designed to read a set of unique characters or numbers printed with magnetic ink on a document (such as a bank check) for immediate entry into a computer system for processing.

A **magnetic-strip card** is a plastic card with a thin magnetic strip on one side. The strip is used to store coded information about the card owner.

Smart cards contain a microprocessor with memory and can protect its owner by restricting access with passwords.

Multimedia is any combination of text, graphics, sound, and video that is programmed into and delivered by the computer. **Voice input devices** can either convert sounds into digital sounds, or they can simply record and play back the voice input like a tape recorder. **Video input devices** can record, digitally store, and play back short video clips.

14 Easy steps to being a webmaster

STEP 3 | INSERT BASIC HTML

In the previous step, you formatted your first page(s) based on clarity and proximity, and information chunks. In this step, you will imbed the basic html code to format your World Wide Web pages following the design elements of proximity, the 7-second rule, alignment, and white space. In general, html code comes in pairs. An opening code command <code> and a close code command </code>. Codes are enclosed in less than (<) and greater than (>) signs. Basic codes and their meanings are explained below.

Code	Meaning
<html> </html>	The beginning <html> and end </html> of the html code.
<title> </title>	The beginning and end of title information.
<header> </header>	The beginning and end of header information.
<body> </body>	The beginning and end of the body of the page.
<h1> </h1> through <h6> </h6>	Header size information. The larger the size, the smaller the number.
<p>	Skip a line and begin a paragraph.
<hr>	Draw a horizontal ruled line.
 	Line break; go immediately to the next line.
<ul> </ul> <ol> </ol>	<ul> codes identify the beginning and end of unordered lists. <ol> codes identify the beginning and end of ordered lists.
<li> </li>	Identifies the beginning and end of list items. Within <ul> lists, each list item is preceded by a bullet. Within <ol> lists, each list item is preceded by a consecutively assigned number.
<a href=> </a>	The beginning and end of an anchor command to reference another web page.
	Identifies the beginning and end of a passage that is center aligned on the web page.

Figure 3.24 shows a typical text format. There is no standard for where the commands begin and end as long as the elements are described properly. One alternative is to put all html at the beginning of lines; another is html code imbedded in text. Whichever you choose, use a single method so you can train your eye to identify html.

Figure 3.24

Html in text format.

```
<html>
<title><header>C. A. Hardesty Resume</header></title>
<body><center><h1>Cheryl A. Hardesty</h1>
<h2>Goal A job that uses my MIS skills</h2>
<h3>email CAHardesty@post.cis.smu.edu</h3></center>
<hr><h4>Work Experience</h4><ul>
        <li>8/95-9/95
        Consultant, Center for Non-Profit Management, Dallas, TX
        </li><li>5/94-8/94
        Programmer Intern, Fidelity Resources, Los Colinas, TX</li>
</ul></ol><hr>
</body>
</html>
```

Space lines can show where information chunks change. Spacing makes the source code, which is code that you as the html creator see, much easier to read and it is not interpreted by browser software. The html in Figure 3.24 is shown in its Netscape version in Figure 3.25.

Figure 3.25

Sample html in Netscape.

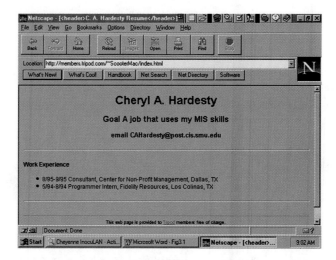

Now, let's discuss how to insert html and design your web pages. Remember that proximity says that information and items that go together should be arranged together. And, conversely, information and items that are different should be separated or easily recognized as different. For instance, job history differs from skills which differs from hobbies, and so on. One design is to separate the different items by blank lines, using different header sizes to identify levels of headers.

The 7-second rule says that whenever you have more information than can be digested in 7 seconds, you design web pages to show a summary on one page with details on one or more other pages. The detail page(s) are accessed by clicking on some text on the first page, for example, your title at the company. This type of reference is called an anchor for a hypertext reference, and the command is an <a href=> </a> command. A URL, enclosed in quotes, follows the href= part of the command. Between the <a . . .> and </a>, you include the hot text that the user clicks.

The design principle of alignment identifies web page elements that follow the same line, either on the left side, on the right side, or both. Centering is considered boring and difficult to read. U.S. custom is to center headers and to left-align resume contents. Another page composition design principle is to include white or blank space. White space makes a page more readable. Notice in Figure 3.25 there is between 40 percent and 60 percent white space, the desired amount. With too much white space, the page looks like there is not enough content. With too little white space the page becomes difficult to read.

ASSIGNMENT: Apply the principles of proximity, white space, and alignment to design your pages. Create a word processed file of your text and the imbedded html commands. Save the word processed file on a disk with an .htm extension as a text-only with breaks file. To test your design, activate the browser, go to the file menu and select the open file option. Type the name of your diskette file and press the Enter key. You will see what your page looks like. Until you feel comfortable typing, saving, and checking, do small sections of the html code at a time.

Exercises

REVIEW QUESTIONS

1. Define *input* and *input device*.
2. What is the common characteristic of all input devices?
3. What is a keyboard, and what role does it play as part of a computer system? Identify specific keys and groups of keys and describe what they are used for.
4. Why is accurate input important? Give an example of a situation in which a business firm might experience a serious problem as a result of processing inaccurate data.
5. What is a mouse? How is a mouse used? How do a mouse and a trackball differ?
6. How are touchscreens used to improve the information processing cycle?
7. How are pen-based computers similar to digitizer tablets? Why are pen-based computers helpful in fields such as medicine and delivery services?
8. How do dumb and smart terminals differ? Give two examples of each type of terminal.

9. What are some of the innovations taking place in optical character recognition systems?

10. How do magnetic cards and smart cards differ?

11. Why might you want to include voice or video input in a presentation?

FILL IN THE BLANKS

1. A _____ is a typewriter-like device used to enter data into a computer.

2. A _____ is a hand-held input device whose rolling movement on a flat surface causes a corresponding movement of the cursor on the screen.

3. A small picture on a computer screen that represents an activity or action that can be taken by a user is called a(n) _____. It is used with applications that make use of _____ technology.

4. A device resembling a writing pen, used to write or draw on a screen is a _____. It is very popular among engineers and draftsmen who use _____ software.

5. _____ are special input devices that contain communications links to a remotely located mini- or mainframe computer system.

6. _____ systems translate characters, marks, and patterns into binary code for the computer.

7. A _____ is a device that can read text and images directly into a computer.

8. A _____ contains a microprocessor for added security.

MATCHING

Match each term with its description.

a. smart terminal
b. smart card
c. numeric keypad
d. touchscreen
e. keyboard
f. pen-based computers
g. scanner
h. trackball
i. stylus
j. mouse
k. cursor

____ 1. Technology popular with industries that don't enter a lot of data, but fill out multiple forms.

____ 2. "First cousin" of a mouse.

____ 3. Blinking symbol that shows where the next character typed will be displayed on the screen.

___ 4.   Microprocessor built into a small plastic card.

___ 5.   Hand-held device rolled about on a desktop to move a cursor.

___ 6.   Contains a communications link to a remotely located mini- or mainframe computer system, but can also do some processing on its own.

___ 7.   Special section of the computer keyboard used for number input.

___ 8.   Device resembling a writing pen and used to draw on a screen or provide input to the computer.

___ 9.   Device that can read text and images directly into a computer.

___ 10.   Allows a user to enter data by touching a location on the surface of the screen.

ACTIVITIES

1.   Visit a school, business, or organization in your area that uses computers. Talk with the person in charge of computer operations to find out the kinds of input devices and media the organization uses. Make a list of the different kinds of input devices being used and how each is being used.

2.   While you are at the firm or organization (in #1 above), ask the person in charge of computer operations whether the business or organization has ever experienced any problems resulting from inaccurate data being entered into and processed by the computer. What were the consequences, and how was the problem corrected?

3.   Visit a computer store in your area. Select a particular microcomputer displayed in the store. Ask the salesperson to list all the different input devices that could be used with that particular microcomputer system.

4.   Examine a personal check. Look at the MICR characters at the bottom of the check to see if you can determine what the code represents. Then, the next time you're at a bank, ask a bank employee to explain the meaning of the code.

5.   Visit a supermarket or another store in your area. Select a product and examine the UPC symbol on the label. Find out what the bar code (UPC) represents.

6.   Write a description of an input device you would like to be able to use with a microcomputer. Be sure the device you choose is one that is not yet available for purchase.

Skills for Living

Starting Your Own Home Business

Today, it is important to develop multiple income sources. With permanent employment always in question, it is smart for you to strive to create a number of additional revenue streams. This can include hobbies, collectibles, investments, second jobs, etc. Another alternative might be to establish a home business. Now, many people are conducting business in their homes as well as pursuing excellent traditional careers at the office. With new communication technologies such as the Internet, teleconferencing, fax, and e-mail, people are earning excellent second incomes at home. Estimates are that these home businesses currently generate over $400 billion per year. Every 11 seconds, someone starts a new home-based business! Many become very successful. Think of the benefits—no commute, no dress code, no 8–5 hours, no boss, and relatively low overhead and risk.

The Internet can help in two ways. First, it is an excellent tool to research home-based marketing opportunities. Second, it can help you market and sell your product or service once you have chosen it.

One search browser revealed over 900,000 references to home businesses. Topics included: Internet access and presence providers, how to publish your web page, home business books explaining best businesses for the 90's, how to use credit cards for payment on the Web, and yellow pages for advertising your web page.

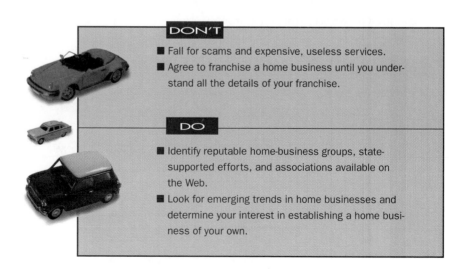

DON'T
- Fall for scams and expensive, useless services.
- Agree to franchise a home business until you understand all the details of your franchise.

DO
- Identify reputable home-business groups, state-supported efforts, and associations available on the Web.
- Look for emerging trends in home businesses and determine your interest in establishing a home business of your own.

The National Association of Home-Based Businesses, (NAHBB) publishes a catalog listing of all types of home-based business. Network · Marketing · Yellow · Pages,™ another reference source, promotes wealth accumulation and time freedom by working with them as a team. These Internet lists will stimulate your creativity and thought processes related to home business opportunities.

1. Use the Internet to find out more about home-based businesses and the opportunities available. What are people doing? How successful have they been? What made them successful? How did they do it? What does it take to create a home business? What are the problems?

2. Think about what you might like to do. Identify your personal interests and skills. What do you think would work for you as a home business? Then use the Web again to investigate the status of this area as a home business. Who is currently doing it? How are they doing it? What do their web pages look like? How are they selling their products and services? How might you do it differently and better?

3. Document your research in #1 and #2 above in a two-page report. Discuss your results with your class, your professor, or your friends. Have a class discussion about home-based business using the Internet and other new or emerging computer technologies.

CHAPTER 4

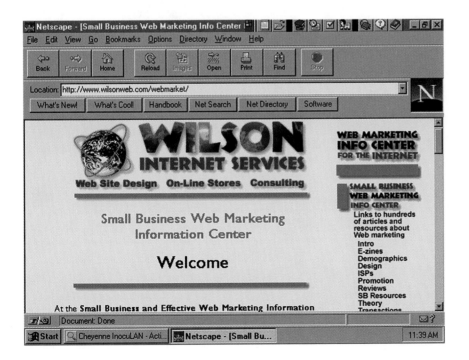

THE CENTRAL PROCESSING UNIT AND MEMORY

OBJECTIVES

AFTER STUDYING THIS CHAPTER, YOU SHOULD BE ABLE TO:

1. Explain the importance of integrated circuit chips in the development of computers.
2. List the components of the CPU.
3. Explain the functions of the control unit.
4. Explain the functions of the arithmetic/logic unit.
5. Explain the purpose of registers.
6. Identify two important characteristics of RAM.
7. Distinguish between RAM and ROM.
8. Describe a machine cycle and identify the three steps in the cycle.
9. Identify three technological approaches to processing that improve processing speed.
10. Describe multiprocessing.

CHAPTER OUTLINE

INTEGRATED CIRCUIT CHIPS
Functions of ICC

THE CENTRAL PROCESSING UNIT
Control Unit
Arithmetic/Logic Unit
Registers
Buses
Clock

DIGITAL DATA REPRESENTATION
From Binary Code to Circuit States
From Real-World Data to Binary Code

MAIN MEMORY
Storage Locations
Storage Capacity
RAM
ROM

THE COMPUTER IN ACTION
The Machine Cycle
An Example of the Machine Cycle

ADVANCES IN MICROPROCESSORS
Technological Advances
Multiprocessor Systems
The Development of Intel Processors
Other Advanced Processors

PROCESSORS OF THE FUTURE

ong before "user-friendly" was a common term, the creators of the world's first computer struggled to make a machine capable of even the simplest mathematical functions. Funded at the height of World War II by a U.S. War Department eager for a device to calculate ballistic firing tables, these early pioneers had two advantages over most researchers; they had virtually no cost or size constraints. Perhaps it is little wonder, then, that the first electronic digital computer, the Electronic Numerical Integrator and Computer (ENIAC), was the size of a football field and kept one worker busy just changing burnt-out vacuum tubes.

No one but the U.S. government could afford to house and "feed" the ENIAC; its successor, the UNIVAC I, was only slightly better. Tipping the scales at a hefty 16,000 pounds, and including over 5,000 vacuum tubes, the UNIVAC was capable of performing the then re-markable feat of 1,000 calculations per minute. Again, the U.S. government, this time in the form of the Census Bureau, footed the bill. Though General Electric Company subsequently bought a UNIVAC, the machine went into retirement in 1957. Only six units were ever sold.

As vacuum tubes gave way to transistors and circuit boards, computers became smaller, lighter, and faster. But the true revolution in computer technology came with a breakthrough its inventor credits to his own laziness. Rather than being bothered with connecting wires on a circuit board, Robert Noyce conceived of connecting transistors on a piece of silicon and wound up creating the first integrated circuit, patented in 1960. Today, progress in integrating more and more transistors on one chip has produced laptop computers with greater capabilities than the developers of the old ENIAC ever dreamed of. Indeed, the first commercially produced microprocessor included 2,300 transistors on a single silicon chip.

Today's computers seem to defy the rule that higher quality equals higher price by consistently getting smaller, faster, *and* cheaper. From 1981 to 1991, the PC's first decade, the power of the typical desktop PC increased by a factor of ten. Computers are often compared in terms of millions of instructions per second, or MIPS. Experts predict that the PC's second decade will see a *hundredfold* increase in speed, resulting in desktop computers whose speeds will be measured in *billions* of instructions per second (BIPS). While the smallest computers now available are about 4 by 6 by 1 inches, we might not be too far from owning wristwatch computers like those worn by characters in the classic 1967 film *2001: A Space Odyssey.*

How have we come so far, so fast? The answer lies in several technological improvements. First, the size of the components integrated on chips has decreased. Many chips now in use are only 0.85 microns or even 0.5 microns wide, and scientists are currently testing chips only 0.1 microns wide. (One micron is a millionth of a meter, just slightly bigger than a virus cell. A human hair is 70 microns wide.) Also, manufacturers have become more proficient at creating chips. As a result, more components can fit on one chip. Most speed barriers in computer technology involve the transmittal of information between chips, not within a chip, so the more one chip can do, the faster it can do it.

INTEGRATED CIRCUIT CHIPS

While calculating machines have been around for over a century, the story of the modern "personal" or desktop computer starts with the invention of the transistor by John Bardeen, Walter Brattain, and William Shockley at AT&T's Bell Labs in the late 1940s. A **transistor** is a semiconductor device that acts as an electronic switch in digital circuits. A **semiconductor** is a combination of natural substances (typically silicon and other elements) that can either conduct electricity or prevent its flow, depending on whether it is charged (with electricity or light) or not. You can think of a transistor as a sort of electronic "valve." Applying a charge to the base, as shown in Figure 4.1, "opens the valve" and allows electricity to flow. Each transistor controls whether electricity flows down one path or another, thus determining how an electronic device acts in a particular situation.

Originally, transistors were stand-alone components, about the size of a pencil eraser, that were individually mounted on circuit boards. A **circuit board** has electrically conductive pathways between each transistor and the other electronic components mounted to it.

As technology improved, it became possible to manufacture a circuit board and its components (such as transistors) in one process. In the early 1960s, **integrated circuit (IC) chips**, or simply **chips**, were mass-produced using a photolithographic process similar to contact printing (see Figure 4.2). An IC chip typically contains electrical components such as transistors and resistors, and the electrically conductive pathways that connect them.

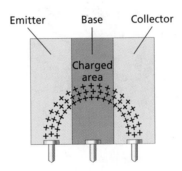

Emitter   Base   Collector

Charged area

Figure 4.1

A charged transistor.

Courtesy of NovaSensor Corporation.

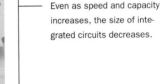
Even as speed and capacity increases, the size of integrated circuits decreases.

Courtesy of IBM Corporation.

Figure 4.2

Microchip production requires clinically sterile conditions and microscopic accuracy.

The process of creating the chips in large batches basically sandwiches layers of silicon and other semiconductor materials one on top of the other. Pathways for conducting electricity are then etched into the materials. Today, a typical IC chip contains anywhere from a few dozen to millions of electronic components on a single chip. The latest microprocessor from Intel, the Pentium, contains three million transistors. Compare that to the Intel 8080, one of the first general-purpose microprocessors, which contained 4,500 transistors.

Chips are typically mounted on a large circuit board, often referred to as a **motherboard** (see Figure 4.3). A typical desktop computer motherboard contains a processor chip, a bank of memory chips, and several controller chips that manage peripheral devices like disk drives. The motherboard also provides the electrical pathways among the chips.

Figure 4.3

The motherboard provides the platform by which chips can communicate via etched conductive pathways. All of these items, fueled by the power supply, interact to collect, process, store, and relay data and information.

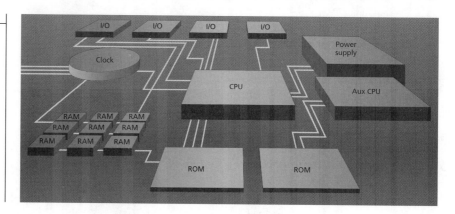

FUNCTIONS OF ICC

Chips are designed to perform many different functions, as described below.

Processor Chips A single **processor chip**, often referred to as the *central processing unit (CPU)*, *microprocessor*, or simply *processor*, contains all the components necessary for computer processing. Desktop computers usually contain a single microprocessor, but new systems may contain multiple microprocessors that work together to improve performance.

Memory Chips Thousands or millions of transistors for the storage of bit values are built into **memory chips**. If power to the chip is lost, the charge is lost, and thus the values in memory are lost. Some memory chips, however, are written with permanent or reprogrammable memory so that power is not required to retain the contents.

Special-Purpose Chips Some chips have specific functions, such as the control of video, sound, input devices, or storage devices. While advances in integrated circuit design now make it possible to combine these controllers directly on a single microprocessor chip, keeping them separate reduces the size and price of the chip. System designers can create custom computers that use special-purpose controllers rather than those that might be built into the chip.

The increasing miniaturization of circuits allows the integration of more and more transistors and other components onto chips of smaller and smaller size. In the late 1970s, companies such as Intel, Zilog, Motorola, and Rockwell began designing and manufacturing microprocessors. Pioneers such as Steve Jobs and Steve Wozniak (founders of Apple Computer) took advantage of the new breed of small chips to develop the first desktop personal computer systems.

Today, when we speak of a CPU, we are often referring to the processor chip within a computer system. Of course, this single CPU is supported by other chips, such as memory chips, disk controllers, and video controllers. For example, IBM mainframes, similar to those shown in Figure 4.4, contain a separate control unit chip that handles input and output between the CPU and the hundreds or thousands of video display terminals that can attach to it.

Courtesy of Apple Computer, Inc.

The first Apple desktop computer was developed by Steve Wozniak and Steve Jobs.

Courtesy of IBM Corporation.

Figure 4.4

Mainframe computer systems contain a separate control unit chip that handles input and output between the computer and peripheral devices.

THE CENTRAL PROCESSING UNIT

The "brain" of a computer system is the central processing unit (CPU). The CPU:

- ■ Receives input
- ■ Interprets instructions provided by programs
- ■ Processes data
- ■ Directs other components of the system to act
- ■ Controls output

The CPU is organized into several discrete elements, shown in Figure 4.5. The elements are:

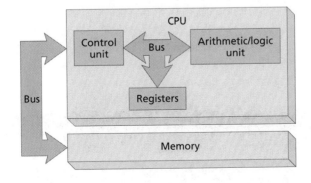

Figure 4.5

All parts of the CPU work to accept data from an input device, process the data into information, and then transfer the information to an output or secondary storage device.

- ■ **Control Unit:** coordinates the flow of data and instructions. Contains a clock that generates a uniform stream of electrical pulses that synchronize the operation of the CPU and other computer components.
- ■ **Arithmetic/Logic Unit (ALU):** performs calculations and comparisons of data.

- **Registers:** hold program instructions, data values, and memory locations as the processor executes a program.
- **Buses:** carry bits between a CPU's components and outside devices.

CONTROL UNIT

The **control unit**, also called the *instruction unit* or *execution unit*, contains a block of circuits that controls the flow of data and program instructions into, out of, and within the CPU. The control unit also issues commands to external control chips such as video and disk controllers so they can display information on the monitor or read files at the appropriate time.

In a general sense, a control unit directs and coordinates the overall operation of the computer system. It acts as a traffic officer, signaling to other parts of the computer system what they are to do. The control unit contains a built-in set of permanent instructions, called **microcode** or *instruction sets*. You can think of microcode as the predefined, elementary circuits in the computer from which come the logical operations that the processor performs when it executes an instruction. Think of microcode as the operator of a train-switching yard. The switch operator opens some tracks and closes others to send freight cars to their destination. Likewise, the microcode determines which transistor switches are open and which are closed to perform a specific operation.

Microcode varies among the different categories of computers, depending on the processor's design, of **architecture**. The architecture of an IBM-compatible system, for instance, is completely different from that of an Apple system, and their microcodes are, therefore, completely different, as well.

ARITHMETIC/LOGIC UNIT

The **arithmetic/logic unit (ALU)** is the part of the CPU that performs the actual arithmetic and logical operations on the data. It carries out instructions specified by the control unit.

Mathematically, the ALU can only add. Through addition it also performs three other operations: subtraction, multiplication, and division. Multiplication is performed through repetitive additions. Subtraction and division are performed with the *complement* of a number. A complement of a binary number is obtained by reversing all of its bits and adding 1. To subtract, you then *add* the complement. For example, to subtract 5 (binary 0101) from 8 (binary 1000), you convert 0101 to 1010, and then add 1 to arrive at 1011. You then add this to 1000 to arrive at 0011, which is binary 3. This operation is shown in Figure 4.6.

Figure 4.6

The arithmetic/logic unit (ALU) uses variations on addition to solve all operations. Here, how the addition of the binary code of a complementary number results in subtraction.

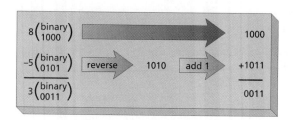

In addition to arithmetic operations, the ALU compares values to determine their logical relationship. Values may be "greater than," "less than," "equal to," or combinations of these, such as "less than or equal to." The results of comparisons are often used to determine the flow of programs. For example, a point-of-sale program in a department store can perform a logical operation to determine if a sale is over $100, then branch to a portion of the program that applies a discount if this is true.

REGISTERS

Immediately before processing, the control unit and the ALU temporarily store the data values and memory locations of the currently executing operation in special areas called registers. **Registers** are special memory locations built into the CPU. The CPU contains several different types of registers that are used to fetch, decode, and execute instructions, hold and transfer information, or perform arithmetic operations. Registers are accessed much faster than memory locations outside the CPU. Therefore, all CPU operations first involve moving data from main memory into CPU registers. To improve performance, instructions are often *prefetched*, or moved into registers before they are ready to execute. Prefetching is often handled as a separate background task so that the processor can work on its current operation without interruption. Some processors contain a separate code prefetch unit designed specifically to handle this process.

Just how quickly registers perform their tasks depends upon their size. Since a 16-bit register is twice the size of an 8-bit register, it can handle twice the number of bits and, therefore, is twice as fast.

BUSES

A **bus** forms an electrical pathway that carries signals among the components of a computer. Typically, there are an address bus and a data bus. The *address bus* carries the location of data in memory. The *data bus* transfers the data between components. Buses exist at all levels in a computer system, as shown in Figure 4.7. At the microprocessor level, buses interconnect the various circuit components, such as the control unit, ALU, and register units. Some of the mounting pins of an IC (shown in Figure 4.7 on the CPU) are connected to the motherboard bus and provide address and data pathways to other motherboard components. A *peripheral interface bus* provides a way to mount additional controller cards and adapters to a computer. When these cards are inserted into the bus slots, they make a connection with the motherboard bus and ultimately to the CPU and its internal bus.

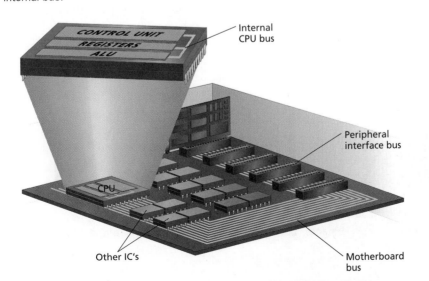

Internal CPU bus

Peripheral interface bus

Other IC's

Motherboard bus

CPU

CONTROL UNIT
REGISTERS
ALU

Figure 4.7

Buses exist at all levels in a computer system.

As with register size, the size of the bus, called **wordsize**, affects processing speed—the wider the bus, the more data it can transfer at one time. The width of the data bus in the Intel 8088 (the chip used in the original IBM PC introduced in 1981) is 8 bits. In contrast, the data bus wordsize of the Intel Pentium (introduced in 1993) is 64 bits.

Ideally, data buses should be wide enough to fully utilize the processing power of registers, meaning wordsize and register size should be the same. This isn't always the case. To cut down on costs, some microprocessors are built with 32-bit registers, but with 16-bit data or address buses, causing a bottleneck when data are transferred. The table below compares register, data bus, and address bus configurations of Intel microprocessors.

Intel Processor Configurations				
Processor	Register Size (bits)	Data Bus Wordsize (bits)	Address Bus Wordsize (bits)	Clock Speed
Intel 8088	16	8	20	8MHz
Intel 8086	16	16	20	8MHz
Intel 80286	16	16	24	8–12MHz
Intel 80386	32	32	32	16–33MHz
Intel 80486	32	32	32	33–66MHz
Intel Pentium	64	64	32	66–100MHz
Intel Pentium P6	64	64	32	100–133MHz
Intel Pentium Pro	64	64	32	133–200MHz

CLOCK

The **clock** portion of the control unit provides a fixed stream of quartz-crystal-generated electrical pulses that the CPU and other components use for synchronization. CPU instructions are executed or "triggered" at the pulse of the clock. Since an instruction may direct the execution of other events either internal or external to the CPU, the clock pulse provides a way for these events to occur in harmony.

The faster the clock rate, the faster a CPU processes information. Clock rates are usually quoted in cycles per second, and the usual rating is in millions of cycles per second, or **megahertz (MHz)**. Intel-based desktop computers have clock rates of 8MHz to 100MHz, depending on the processor type (see the table above). Keep in mind that these ratings don't mean that a CPU will execute millions of instruction codes per second. Several clock cycles are usually required to complete a single instruction. Thus, clock speeds are only useful when comparing processors within the same family (competitive processors might execute more or fewer instructions per cycle).

Another way of rating processor speed is in millions of instructions per second, or **MIPS**. A MIPS measurement can provide a rough method of comparing processors produced by different vendors, but keep in mind that vendors tend to overstate their processor's performance. In addition, some processors require fewer instructions to perform a task in the first place (see the section on reduced instruction set computers, or RISC, later in this chapter). The table below provides a comparison of MIPS ratings for several personal computers and processors.

MIPS Ratings of Computers and Processors	
Processor	**MIPS Rating**
Apple II computer (1979)	.04
IBM PC computer (1981)	.25
Apple Macintosh computer (1984)	.40
Intel 80386 processor (16MHz)	4
Intel 80386 processor (25MHz)	7
DEC Microvax computer	2–3
Intel 80486 processor (25MHz)	8–40
Motorola 68060 processor (50MHz)	77
Intel Pentium pentium processor (66MHz)	100
DEC Alpha RIXC processor (200MHz)	400

DIGITAL DATA REPRESENTATION

In Chapter 1, we defined *data* as raw, unorganized facts that describe reality. These facts describe or represent features or details about the world around you—people, objects, places, ideas, or events.

For example, data can be used to tell about and describe you. Your height, age, and shoe size might begin the list. These facts and others, as well as the things you do, the items you buy, and virtually all of the elements in your life, represent you. In order to develop an adequate description of you, however, a large and complex collection of facts would be required.

In Chapter 1, we also defined a *computer*, or *processor*, as thousands of electronic circuits etched onto a very small slice of silicon. Each circuit in a processor is capable of carrying an electrical current. In addition, each circuit contains some sort of on/off switch. When the switch is "off," there is no flow of electricity through the circuit. When the switch is "on," an electrical current flows through the circuit.

A device that is capable of assuming only one of two states is called **bi-stable**. An electronic circuit, therefore, is a bi-stable device. At any one time electricity either is or is not flowing through each of the electronic circuits of a processor. How then are simple, two-state computer circuits capable of processing descriptions of an often extremely complex reality? The answer to this question lies in a method of representing real-world data to a processor in a form that can turn each of its circuits on or off. That is, a system of symbols and rules is required to represent real-world data to the processor.

Figure 4.8

A simple code must uniquely
map the elements of one set
with the elements of another.

A – 1	N – 14
B – 2	O – 15
C – 3	P – 16
D – 4	Q – 17
E – 5	R – 18
F – 6	S – 19
G – 7	T – 20
H – 8	U – 21
I – 9	V – 22
J – 10	W– 23
K – 11	X – 24
L – 12	Y – 25
M– 13	Z – 26

FROM BINARY CODE TO CIRCUIT STATES

A system of rules that correlates the elements of one set with the elements of another is called a **code**. For example, a simple code that correlates the set of letters in the alphabet with a set of numbers might look like that in Figure 4.8. In this simple coding scheme, each letter of the alphabet is correlated with one, and only one, number. Since there are 26 possible letters in the English alphabet, each letter can be uniquely correlated to the numbers 1 through 26.

Now let's reconsider the circuits of a processor: these circuits either have electricity flowing through them or they do not. If we were to assign one number to every possible circuit state, we might get a code like this:

0 = no electricity flow

1 = electricity flow

Conveniently enough, the digits 0 and 1 comprise the binary numbering system. The binary numbering system has 2 as its base, rather than the more familiar base 10 of the decimal system (see Figure 4.9). The binary numbering system is useful for coding the activity of circuits within the processor.

Figure 4.9

In the familiar decimal number system (top), the decimal number 125 is represented by putting the digit 1 in the hundreds place, the digit 2 in the tens place, and the digit 5 in the ones place. In the binary number system (bottom), the decimal number 125 is represented by the binary number 1111101.

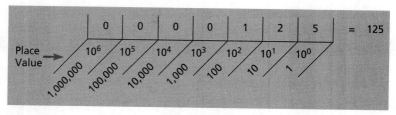

Decimal System

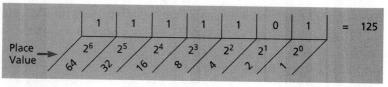

Binary System

The "on" and "off" states of each of the many thousands or millions of circuits within a processor are represented by binary digits, or **bits**, for short. Since there are only two binary digits (0 and 1), a bit can have only one of two values (0 or 1) as illustrated in Figure 4.10.

Bits are used to turn each electronic circuit within a processor on or off. The same principle applies to magnetic storage devices. When a given spot on the storage medium is magnetized, the value is 1. When a spot is unmagnetized, the value is 0.

Figure 4.10

An "off" bit has the value of 0.
An "on" bit has the value 1.

"OFF" $\boxed{\bigcirc}$ = 0   "ON" $\boxed{\bullet}$ = 1

The term **digital** refers to anything pertaining to bits. Thus, a device that accesses data and instructions in the form of bits, as does a processor, can be called a digital device. In addition, binary code is often referred to as digital code.

FROM REAL-WORLD DATA TO BINARY CODE

Bits are used to represent reality. Hence it is bits that form the bridge between descriptive data and the digital circuits within a computer chip. For bits to be useful in representing real-world data, they must represent the symbols people use to describe reality.

When people describe the world around them, they already use a form of *symbolic code*—human language. Human language is comprised of words, which in turn are comprised of letter, number, or character symbols. These symbols, such as A, a, B, b, ?, !, 1, 6, =, and >, are combined and manipulated to communicate and describe reality. For simplicity's sake, all of the symbols are called *characters*. Bits are used to represent these characters.

To accomplish this representation, bits are arranged in series. Codes are assigned to each combination of "on" and "off" bits. The various combinations represent characters. Each individual series of bits used to represent a character is called a **byte**.

ASCII Code One of the most widely used coding schemes to represent data is the **American Standard Code for Information Interchange (ASCII)**. ASCII code uses either a series of 7 bits (ASCII-7 notation) or 8 bits (ASCII-8 notation) to represent characters. Since most computer hardware typically handles data in 8-bit bytes, this discussion will focus on ASCII-8 notation. ASCII is a popular coding scheme for microcomputers and digital telecommunications.

EBCDIC Code While ASCII code is widely used for microcomputers and computer communications, it is not the only coding format available. A commonly used coding scheme for mainframe computer systems is called **Extended Binary Coded Decimal Interchange Code (EBCDIC)**. With EBCDIC, each 8-bit byte is divided into two portions— the zone portion and the digit portion. The bits in both the zone portion and the digit portion are assigned numeric values based upon the binary number system and form the basis for a logical representation of data.

Digitizing Images Not all data are stored or processed in coding schemes like ASCII and EBCDIC. Pictures, for example, are digitized. **Digitization** is the process of converting black and white or color data to digital information. In the simplest form of digitization, a picture is converted into a grid of dots. Each dot is a **pixel**, a contraction of the words *picture element*.

For black-and-white pictures, a black pixel is represented by an "on" bit, while an empty, or white pixel, is represented by an "off" bit. You can see the pixels in black-and-white pictures if you look at photos in a newspaper or on a computer screen through a magnifying glass (see Figure 4.11 on page 124).

Obviously, not all pictures are black and white. Many photographs have color or gradations of black (grays). When these photographs are converted to pixels, each pixel must be coded with a value that represents its particular color or shade of gray (called a *gray scale*). To store and manipulate a color or gray-scale value in a computer system, a combination of bits is required to represent values higher than 1.

Figure 4.11

Pixels on a
computer monitor.

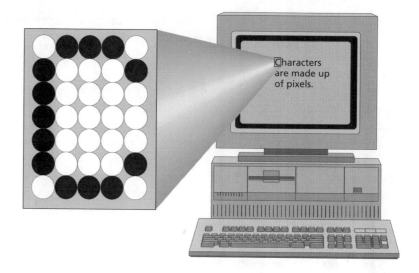

Characters
are made up
of pixels.

MAIN MEMORY

Before programs are executed or data processed, they must first enter into **main memory** (also called *primary storage, random access memory (RAM),* or just plain *memory*). Main memory holds information read from disk or captured by input devices. The CPU then moves information from main memory into its registers for processing. In summary, main memory:

- Accepts and holds program instructions and data.
- Acts as the CPU's source for data and instructions and as a destination for operation results.
- Holds the final processed information until it can be sent to the desired output or storage devices, such as a printer or disk drive.

STORAGE LOCATIONS

Once programs and data are stored in main memory, the CPU must be able to find them. Program instructions and data reside in a memory location known as an **address**. Each location in a computer's memory has its own unique address, just as each individual has a personal mailbox at a post office (see Figure 4.12). When the CPU or other controlling device needs instructions or data from memory, the appropriate address is sent over the address bus. The contents of that location are then transferred on the data bus from memory to CPU registers.

Figure 4.12

Data are stored in individual, unique locations in memory known as addresses, much like the individual addresses assigned to boxes at a post office.

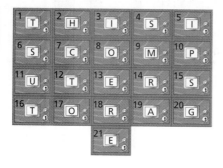

STORAGE CAPACITY

While each memory location can represent a binary bit, memory size is measured in bytes. Since most computers have enough memory to store thousands or millions of bits, it is common to refer to storage capacity in terms of *bytes* (one byte represents one alphabet letter, a number, or a special character), *kilobytes* (one thousand bytes), *megabytes* (one million bytes), and even *gigabytes* (one billion bytes).

RAM

Main memory is often referred to as **RAM**, an acronym for random access memory. Random access means that, because each memory location has an individual address, the computer can go directly to the instructions and data it wants, using that address, rather than searching each individual location one after another (sequentially). RAM memory is both *readable* and *writable*, meaning that the contents of any memory location can be changed and/or read at any time. You might think a better acronym for this type of memory would be "RWM" for "Read-Write Memory," but "RAM" has become the standard term.

One way to think of RAM is to imagine several thousand tiny light bulbs, with each light bulb being controlled by its own switch. The lights are arranged in groups of eight. When a letter, number, or special character is entered into the computer, the computer turns individual switches in each group on or off to represent the character that was entered.

RAM memory is **volatile**, meaning that it requires a constant charge to keep its contents intact. If a computer loses power, the contents of its memory are lost. Therefore, it is important to frequently save any valuable work to secondary disk storage.

The temporary nature of RAM is its most important characteristic. When the computer is finished with one set of instructions and data, it can store another set in the first set's place. RAM works similarly to a chalkboard, chalk, and eraser. You can write any instructions and data on a chalkboard, and then erase and write new instructions and data on the same space. Like a chalkboard, you can use RAM over and over again.

Not all microcomputers come with the same amount of RAM. In most, additional RAM can be installed by plugging a memory-expansion board into an expansion slot on the motherboard. Some computer programs require more RAM than others. For this reason, having enough RAM is critical. Before buying a particular software package, users should read carefully the memory requirements printed on the package.

ROM

Most of the memory in desktop computers is made up of RAM. Many computers also have memory chips on which special instructions are permanently stored. These chips are called **read-only memory (ROM)** chips because the computer can read predefined instructions from the chips but cannot store (write) instructions on them. ROM is permanently stored, nonvolatile memory. When power is interrupted, the memory content of ROM is not lost. In some systems, the operating system program is stored on ROM chips to facilitate faster startup and eliminate the need to load the system from floppy disk or hard disk every time the computer is started.

Some computer software programs, such as word processors and spreadsheets, are supplied on ROM chips. These programs are usually referred to as **firmware**. The firmware is mounted on a cartridge that the user inserts in a slot on the computer. The computer can then immediately access the program without the need to load it from disk. Firmware is popular in the video game market.

PROM   Another type of ROM is **programmable read-only memory (PROM)**, which allows users to write their own program on ROM memory chips. Users must purchase a blank chip and, using special equipment, write and store programs on the chips. Once the program is stored on the chip, it cannot be erased, and it does not lose its contents if the power is lost.

EPROM   Similar in concept to PROM, **erasable programmable read-only memory (EPROM)** differs in that it can be erased and rewritten with new information, assuming the user has the appropriate equipment to do so. The chips are typically erased by exposing them to ultraviolet light. Once erased, the user can write a new program to the chip. EPROM chips are widely used in electronic cash registers to store item prices.

THE COMPUTER IN ACTION

Programs include a set of instructions that direct the computer to perform specific operations. Once a program is written, it is stored on disk for later use. When a program is *run*, it is read, transferred from secondary storage to memory, and each instruction in the program is then transferred from memory to CPU registers, then decoded and executed.

THE MACHINE CYCLE

When a CPU executes a program, it reads each instruction, interprets it, and executes it to complete the operation. This process of executing a single instruction is often referred to as the *fetch*, *decode*, and *execute* cycle, or the **machine cycle**. The three steps (fetch, decode, and execute) are broken down into two phases, the instruction cycle (I-cycle) and the execution cycle (E-cycle). During the **I-cycle**, the control unit retrieves, or *fetches*, the next instruction it is to execute from a main memory location. The control unit then interprets, or *decodes*, the instruction. This phase tells the computer what needs to be done. During the **E-cycle**, the decoded instruction is *executed* by the ALU, and the final results are *stored* temporarily in the registers. The machine cycle is illustrated in Figure 4.13. After these three steps are completed, the computer is ready to begin the next machine cycle.

Figure 4.13

The machine cycle comprises an instruction phase (Steps 1 and 2) and an execution phase (Step 3). The instruction phase is called I-time. The execution phase is called E-time. I-time plus E-time equals the speed at which the complete execution of an instruction occurs.

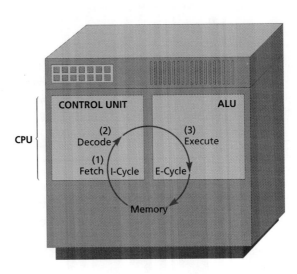

AN EXAMPLE OF THE MACHINE CYCLE

Let's consider an imaginary program and watch the processor work through a few machine cycles.

1. A program is loaded from disk into main memory.
2. When the program is activated by a user, the address of the memory location for the first instruction is placed on the address bus and, at the appropriate clock pulse, sent to memory.
3. The memory chips then retrieve the contents of that memory location and place it on the data bus where it is sent to the register.
4. The instruction in the register is decoded and the control unit sends the appropriate operation instruction and the relevant data to the ALU. Now the address register is incremented so that it points to the next instruction in main memory.
5. The result of the operation is sent to the registers and then on to main memory by the control unit.
6. The next instruction is retrieved and moved into the register and the process is repeated.

ADVANCES IN MICROPROCESSORS

Microprocessors are presently the dominant computing technology. This section reviews advances in this technology and discusses some common commercially available microprocessors used in microcomputers and advanced computing workstations.

David Parker/Science Photo Library/Photo Researchers, Inc.

Increased processing capabilities have automated work in fields such as architecture and design. Now architects and engineers can easily alter the blueprints they have created on computer and analyze the effects of those changes.

TECHNOLOGICAL ADVANCES

Advances in microprocessor technology have resulted in desktop systems utilizing increased processing capabilities.

Parallel Pipelining In its basic form, **parallel pipelining** increases performance by allowing execution of one instruction while another instruction is fetched.

Superscalar Architecture A processor with **superscalar architecture** is designed to execute multiple instructions per clock cycle. A scheduler looks at pending instructions in a queue, determines if they can be executed simultaneously, and if so, sends them to the execution unit.

Branch Prediction Another method used to speed up processing is called branch prediction. A branch occurs when the program can choose among different paths, based on existing conditions. **Branch prediction** provides a sort of intelligence to the processor that can predict with a certain percentage of accuracy in which way a program will branch. If the prediction is correct, the branch is executed without delay and performance is improved.

CISC and RISC Most processors for desktop systems are of **complex instruction set computing (CISC)** design. CISC chips contain a large set of microcode, which requires a large number of instructions to be executed before an operation can be completed. In recent years, processor manufacturers have discovered that a relatively small percentage (about 15 percent) of the microcode instructions are actually needed for most computer operations. As a result, some manufacturers have developed **reduced instruction set computing (RISC)** designs, in which many unnecessary microcode instructions are eliminated. IBM, Apple, and DEC now offer microcomputer systems based on RISC microprocessors. Though some computer programs must be modified for use with RISC computer systems, RISC-based microcomputers operate up to 15 times faster than CISC-based microcomputers.

MULTIPROCESSOR SYSTEMS

Microprocessors are now used in a variety of systems. While desktop computers for word processing and spreadsheets have a single microprocessor, new systems with two, four, or more microprocessors are gaining popularity as operating systems and software are developed to take advantage of their increased computing power. These **multiprocessor systems** were originally designed for high-end engineering/graphics workstations. In recent years, their use has spread to commercial companies processing huge amounts of operational data, often through network server systems. A **network server** is a computer that enables users connected to it to access shared files and resources (discussed in Chapter 7). A *resource* in this case might be printer, a CD-ROM drive, or a disk that holds a very large database of information.

Massively Parallel Processing Systems Hundreds, and sometimes thousands of processors are contained in a single computer in **massively parallel processing (MPP)** systems illustrated in Figure 4.14. Using so many processors, a computer can separate a

Figure 4.14

In a massively parallel processing system, the problem is broken into separate parts, each part is routed to a different processor, and the results from each processor are put together to form the comprehensive final result.

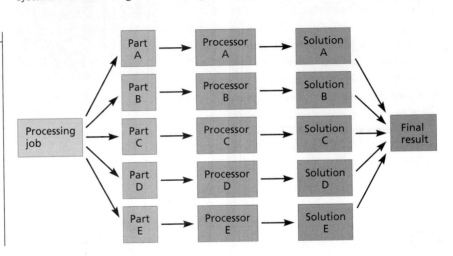

large job into many smaller ones that are executed simultaneously, greatly increasing efficiency. Originally, MPPs were used exclusively for scientific and engineering applications. For instance, oil companies used them for seismic data analysis. Today, however, they are used increasingly in companies that depend on enormous amounts of on-line transaction processing in their day-to-day operations. MPPs are becoming popular in insurance companies, banks, credit card companies, and other organizations that handle large amounts of data and transactions hourly.

Asymmetric and Symmetric Multiprocessing Systems These multiprocessor systems contain two or more processors that operate in parallel. They provide a way to execute more than one instruction per clock cycle. In **asymmetric multiprocessing** systems, each processor handles a different task. For example, one processor might handle input/output while another handles general processing. In **symmetric multiprocessing**, any processor can handle any task. Operating systems such as Microsoft Windows NT are specifically designed to distribute processing tasks to any processor that is available. Symmetric multiprocessing is more powerful and efficient, but the operating system and programs that run on it are more difficult to design and create and have only recently come on the market. Operating systems are discussed in detail in Chapter 8.

THE DEVELOPMENT OF INTEL PROCESSORS

The IBM Personal Computer (PC), introduced in 1981, set the standard for microcomputers. The system was relatively inexpensive and expandable, and it had a large business following. Many third-party developers created hardware and software for use with the PC, thus increasing its market potential. The IBM PC used the Intel 8088 microprocessor. This chip had a 20-bit address bus capability, allowing it to access up to 1MB of RAM. IBM and Microsoft also co-marketed the operating system known as DOS (Disk Operating System) for use on the IBM PC, thus establishing DOS as a standard that is still in use today.

In 1983, IBM announced the IBM PC AT (Advanced Technology) computer, which used the Intel 80286 processor. This processor provided a 24-bit address bus, allowing the IBM PC AT (and compatible systems manufactured by other vendors) to address up to 16MB of memory. IBM and other compatible system manufacturers eventually designed systems that used the Intel 80386, 80486, and Pentium chips. These systems were compatible with previous systems and could run DOS and the software written for DOS.

However, the DOS operating system was designed for the original Intel 8088 and could not take advantage of advanced features of the newer Intel processors. In particular, DOS was unable to directly address as much memory as the processors could. Various "kludges" or fix-up techniques were used to allow applications to access more memory, and some became industry-wide standards, such as the **Expanded Memory Specification (EMS)** created by Lotus, Intel, and Microsoft. However, it wasn't until operating system enhancements like Microsoft Windows, or entirely new operating systems like OS/2 and Microsoft Windows NT, that the features of the newer chips could be used properly. Some of these enhancement features are described on page 131.

FOCUS

Micro-Missions in Space

Advances in chip technology have allowed us to develop smaller and smaller machines that will assist us in exploring the human body and improving manufacturing techniques. Microtechnology will also help us conquer the last great frontier: space.

craft. A small rocket would boost a cluster of four 290-pound egg-shaped craft that would separate in Mars's orbit, heading for different targets on the planet's surface. Two of the probes would land on Mars's north and south poles to sample ice and frozen gases.

Courtesy of NASA.

At NASA's Jet Propulsion Laboratory (JPL) in Pasadena, California, engineers are striving to develop a force of tiny, unmanned spacecraft that they hope will invade Mars and scour the planet for signs of ancient life. Because a proposed manned mission to the red planet by the year 2025 would cost U.S. taxpayers about $500 billion, the JPL staff hopes that their unmanned minimarauders will gain acceptance and funding due to their less costly launching capabilities and their more powerful research capabilities.

JPL's tiny craft would deploy equipment 1,000 times smaller, yet hundreds of times more sensitive, than instruments used on today's space-

Once on the ground, the probes' tops would fold out to unleash a pair of rovers that resemble radio-controlled toy cars. As they explore the planet's surface, the rovers' light-sensitive chips and microprocessors would help them avoid obstructions. Seismometers smaller than a Walkman would measure movements beneath the planet's crust. Tiny spectrometers would analyze the planet's surface composition.

While NASA and earth spectators still may prefer the drama of manned missions, the mini-space travelers proposed by the JPL have another big advantage: if anything should go wrong on the mission, no loss of human life would occur.

Courtesy of IBM Corporation.

Courtesy of IBM Corporation.

In 1981, IBM introduced the IBM PC, which used the Intel 8088 processor. Barely a decade later, the 80486 processor was introduced, greatly increasing processing capabilities.

32-Bit Addressing and Data Transfer The Intel 80386 and its successors have a full 32-bit register size and bus wordsize. Moreover, these chips have 32-bit address bus widths. Therefore, memory transfers are twice as fast as those on Intel 80286-based systems, and four times faster than Intel 8088-based systems.

Courtesy of Intel Corporation.

Faster Clock Cycles Each successive microprocessor in the Intel line has offered higher clock speeds than previous chips. Even when running DOS software programs, which don't take advantage of some of the new chip features, improved clock speeds help speed up processing.

Pipelined Instructions The Intel 80386 processor added the **pipelined instruction** execution feature, which allows the chip to address memory one clock cycle earlier than previous processors, thus increasing processing speed.

Virtual 8086 Mode The Intel 80386 and higher processors provide the **virtual 8086 mode**, which allows the processor to *simulate* one or more computers (technically, a simulation of the Intel 8086 processor). This simulation or "virtualization" provides a way to run multiple applications at the same time on different "virtual processors" within the same microprocessor, without the risk that an application running in one virtual machine will corrupt the memory area of an

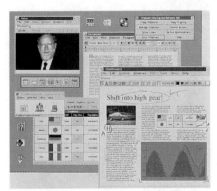

Courtesy of IBM Corporation.

Multiple software applications can run at one time on processors with virtual 8086 mode capabilities.

application running in another virtual machine. Basically, virtual 8086 mode allows one computer to run multiple software programs, called *multitasking*, safely and efficiently.

Virtual Memory The Intel 80286 and its successors provide **virtual memory** capabilities, or the ability to simulate RAM memory on a disk drive in systems that don't have enough physical RAM memory to execute large programs or handle large amounts of data (such as graphic images). In other words, if you need 16MB of memory to run a graphics application, but your system has only 8MB of memory, you can take advantage of virtual memory to simulate the additional 8MB on disk. While somewhat slower than RAM memory, virtual memory does allow users to run applications even if sufficient physical RAM is not available.

The Intel 80386 and 80486 processors were the workhorses of the Intel line in the late 1980s and early 1990s. They provided 32-bit register size, data bus wordsize, and address bus wordsize. The Intel 80386 had clock speeds of 16MHz to 33MHz, while the Intel 80486 has clock speeds of 33MHz to 66MHz.

While the 80386 introduced many new features such as virtual 8086 mode, the 80486 provides improved execution speeds, faster clock rates, and integrated components. For example, the 80486 has a built-in complex math coprocessor. Previous to the 80486, mathematical operations were performed by a separate and optional add-on chip. The 80486 also includes a built-in 8KB *memory cache* unit that improves memory access times. The cache stores recently used data in anticipation of future accesses. In this way, the processor can access the built-in cache, rather than external memory, vastly improving performance speed.

Figure 4.15

The Intel Pentium Pro processor contains 5.5 million transistors and is organized into functional components.

Courtesy of Intel Corporation.

The DEC Alpha chip.

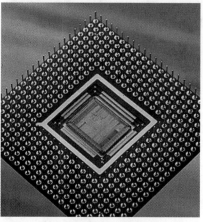

Courtesy of Digital Equipment Corporation.

The Intel Pentium Pro processor, shown in Figure 4.15, was introduced in 1995 as the successor to the earlier Pentium introduced in 1993. The Pentium Pro contains approximately 5.5 million transistors and runs at a clock speed of 150MHz. The processor has a 64-bit register size and data bus. The Pentium Pro can provide several times the performance of the first Pentium processor chip. It is *tri-pipelined*, which means it can execute three instructions at once, but the software must be compiled specifically to take advantage of this feature.

OTHER ADVANCED PROCESSORS

The DEC Alpha Chip Digital Equipment Corporation, or DEC, pioneered the minicomputer industry and has recently moved into desktop microcomputer systems. Its strategy for the 1990s centers around the RISC-based Alpha architecture, which Digital builds into its own chips and licenses to other chip manufacturers.

The Alpha has a 64-bit register size, data bus wordsize, and address bus wordsize. Memory is accessed 64 bits

before

Courtesy of the B.A.A.

AFTER

Courtesy of the B.A.A.

Imagine what the first Boston Marathon, run in 1896, was like. There were no specially-designed running shoes or fancy running garb. There was also no accurate timing mechanism.

When the signal for the beginning of the race was given, the judge at the starting line would note the time on a clock. As the winner crossed the finish line, another judge recorded the time. The two judges then compared their times to determine how long it took the winner to run the marathon. Individual times for other runners were not recorded.

For the 100th running of the Boston Marathon in 1996, an ingenious new timing mechanism was used. Each runner was issued a tiny computer chip that tied onto a shoelace and electronically recorded the time the runner steps over the starting and finish lines. This enabled Boston Marathon officials to know the official time of every competitor.

The two-inch diameter chip, called the Champion Chip, was issued to each runner the week before the race. Each chip's serial number was the same as the runner's bib number. When the runner's foot passed over the starting line, an antenna sent a radio signal to the chip. The chip sent a signal back to the antenna and the time was recorded on a computer disk. The information on the disk was then transported to the finish line. When the runner crossed the finish line, the process was repeated and the running time computed.

at a time. The Alpha is designed for a range of systems, from palmtop computers to parallel-processing supercomputers. The current Alpha processors run at 200MHz and have a consistent peak performance of 400 MIPS. Alpha has multi-instruction capability, and DEC is planning Alpha chips that execute up to ten instructions per cycle. DEC has worked closely with Microsoft to ensure that multiprocessor Alpha systems take advantage of the symmetric multiprocessing capabilities of Microsoft Windows NT.

PowerPC 604 Jointly developed by Apple, IBM, and Motorola in 1991, the PowerPC 604 microprocessor is based on a Reduced Instruction Set Computing (RISC) architecture and incorporates leading technologies and processes from IBM and Motorola.

The Motorola PowerPC 604.

Courtesy of Motorola.

Its enhanced RISC architecture uses streamlined code and optimized chip design to achieve outstanding processing speeds. The PowerPC 604 is capable of executing multiple operations in each clock cycle.

This chip is designed to power portable and desktop systems and provides the type of processing associated with graphic workstations. The joint design of the PowerPC family of chips is intended to enable IBM and Apple to create a product line that takes advantage of each other's applications.

The AMD$_k$86™ microprocessor.

Courtesy of AMD.

MIPS Technologies R10000 Microprocessor Chip In 1996, MIPS Technologies, Inc. introduced a 275MHz version of its powerful R10000™ MIPS® RISC microprocessor. Designed for use with powerful workstations, the microprocessor chip is two to three times faster than the company's earlier R4400™ chip. These processors are true 64-bit chips with fast clock speeds designed for high-end graphics workstations, database, or other sophisticated uses. One of the major advantages of the R10000 processor is that it runs both UNIX and Microsoft Windows NT operating systems and therefore will run the applications already designed for these operating systems. This chip is among the fastest and most powerful microprocessor chips currently available.

The MIPS R10000.

Courtesy of MIPS Technologies, Inc.

Sun Microsystems UltraSPARC™ Processor Sun Microsystems, a manufacturer of high-end graphics and engineering workstations, has developed a new RISC

The Sun Microsystems UltraSPARC.

Courtesy of Sun Microsystems.

processor for computer workstations. The processor, called the UltraSPARC, is a revolutionary new 64-bit processor designed for very high clock speeds (upwards of 200MHz). Its design enables up to four instructions to be executed per clock cycle. The 5.2 million-transistor microprocessor chip is among the fastest in the computer industry.

COMPUTER CURRENTS

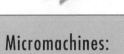

Micromachines: Pint-Sized Wonders

In the world of nanotechnology (molecular-level technology), there's more than meets the eye. Eric Drexler, an independent researcher and visiting lecturer at Stanford University, predicts that by the early twenty-first century, we will be manufacturing entire molecule-sized factories that will in turn be capable of producing thousands of specialized nanomachines. Together these machines will construct everything from bridges and office buildings, to tiny robots for mining and cleaning up toxic waste.

Drexler says the benefits of nanotechnology will include improved products that can be made more cheaply and more quickly, and an opportunity to avoid environmental crises because building molecule by molecule will produce no waste.

In their search for a way to design the molecules that will be necessary to produce sensors, actuators, or motors, nanotechnology researchers are turning to the human body as a model—in particular, to the proteins that perform a stunning array of functions in our bodies.

They fight disease, aid in movement, and digest food. Cells, in fact, contain tiny "nanotech" factories for manufacturing proteins—called ribosomes—as well as the biological equivalent of protein shipping and receiving centers, mass transit, and inventory control. Researchers are looking for a way to tailor these "nanomachines" to our needs, making them suitable for repairing damaged organs, for instance.

Other researchers are looking to diamonds as the component for nanomachines: they're extremely hard and durable, with good heat conduction.

Nanotechnological breakthroughs may be just around the corner.

Courtesy of Lucas NovaSensor.

PROCESSORS OF THE FUTURE

The major trend anticipated in microprocessor development is the integration of more and more transistors per chip. In 1975, Intel predicted that the number of transistors per chip would double every two years, and this has proved accurate. Intel envisions chips in the near future with 50 million transistors, executing up to a billion instructions per second at 250MHz clock speeds. Cramming more transistors on chips will require new processing techniques and semiconductor materials. One technique is to create multiple layers of transistors on a chip, rather than a single layer, as illustrated in Figure 4.16.

Figure 4.16

In an effort to integrate more transistors per chip, the single-layer chip will be replaced with a chip bearing multiple layers of transistors.

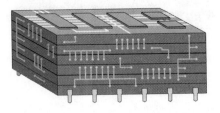

These new "super microprocessors" will include multiple processing units and replace those multiple processors that need to be run in parallel. They will also include integrated voice recognition units, as well as video control units that can handle full-motion graphics and video compression. Other built-in control units will include disk, networking, and communications control units.

Key Terms

address

American Standard Code for
   Information Interchange (ASCII)

architecture

arithmetic/logic unit (ALU)

asymmetric multiprocessing

bi-stable

bits

branch prediction

bus

byte

chips

circuit board

clock

code

complex instruction set computing
   (CISC) design

control unit

digital

digitization

erasable programmable read-only
   memory (EPROM)

execution cycle (E-cycle)

expanded memory specification (EMS)

Extended Binary Coded Decimal
   Interchange Code (EBCDIC)

firmware

instruction cycle (I-cycle)

machine cycle

main memory

massively parallel processing (MPP)

megahertz (MHz)

memory chips

microcode

millions of instructions per second (MIPS)

motherboard

multiprocessor systems

network server

parallel pipelining

pipelined instructions

pixel

processor chip

programmable read-only memory (PROM)

random access memory (RAM)

read-only memory (ROM)

reduced instruction set computing
   (RISC) design

registers

semiconductor

superscalar architecture

symmetric multiprocessing

transistor

virtual 8086 mode

virtual memory

volatile

wordsize

Summary

An **integrated circuit (IC) chip** typically contains electrical components such as transistors and resistors, and the electrically conductive pathways that connect them. A typical microcomputer contains a **motherboard** on which are mounted a processor chip, a bank of memory chips, and several controller chips.

The **central processing unit (CPU)** receives input, interprets instructions provided by programs, processes data, directs other components of the system to act, and controls output. The CPU consists of the control unit, arithmetic/logic unit, registers, and buses. A **microprocessor** contains all of the components of the CPU on a miniaturized chip.

The **control unit** executes program instructions. The **arithmetic/logic unit (ALU)** is the part of the CPU that performs the actual arithmetic and logical operations on the data. **Registers** are storage locations that hold program instructions, values, and memory addresses as the processor executes a program. A **bus** forms an electrical pathway that carries signals among the components of a computer. The **clock** circuit provides electrical pulses that the CPU and other components use for synchronization. Clock rates are usually quoted in millions of cycles (pulses) per second, or **MHz (megahertz)**.

A processor contains electronic circuits that are **bi-stable**, or capable of assuming only one of two states. Each electronic circuit state can be represented by a **bit**.

The term **digital** refers to anything pertaining to binary digits or bits. A series of bits used to represent a character is called a **byte**.

ASCII code is one of the most widely used coding schemes to represent data. The ASCII code uses either a series of 7 bits (ASCII-7 notation) or 8 bits (ASCII-8 notation) to represent characters.

EBCDIC code is a commonly used coding scheme for mainframe computer systems. EBCDIC uses 8-bit bytes to represent characters.

Digitization is the process of converting black-and-white or color data to digital information through the use of **pixels**.

Main memory is often referred to as **random access memory (RAM)**. Random access memory means that the computer can go directly to the instructions and data it wants, using the memory **address**, rather than searching one location after another. RAM is temporary, **volatile memory**.

The computer can read predefined instructions from **read-only memory (ROM)** chips but cannot store instructions on them. ROM is permanently stored, **nonvolatile**

memory. Programs supplied on ROM chips are usually referred to as **firmware**. **Programmable read-only memory (PROM)** allows users to write their own program on ROM memory chips. **Erasable programmable read-only memory (EPROM)** chips can be erased and rewritten with new information.

When a CPU executes a program, it reads each instruction, interprets it, and executes it. This process is referred to as the **machine cycle**.

Parallel pipelining increases performance by allowing execution of an instruction while another instruction is fetched. A processor with **superscalar architecture** is designed to execute multiple instructions per clock cycle. **Branch prediction** allows the processor to predict which way a program will branch, thus improving performance. **Complex Instruction Set Computing (CISC)** chips contain a large set of microcode. **Reduced Instruction Set Computing (RISC)** chips provide fewer built-in microcode instructions, decreasing processing time.

Multiprocessor systems are designed for use as high-end engineering/graphics workstations or as network server systems. In **asymmetric multiprocessing systems**, each processor handles a different task. In **symmetric multiprocessing systems**, any processor can handle any task.

Pipelined instructions allow a chip to address memory one clock cycle earlier than previous processors. **Virtual 8086 mode** allows the processor to simulate one or more 8086 processors. **Virtual memory** enables simulation of RAM memory on a disk drive in systems that don't have enough physical RAM memory to execute large programs or handle large amounts of data.

14 Easy steps to being a webmaster

STEP 4 TEXT SIZE

In this step, we modify the size and format of text to add to the page's visual interest. This is the first step relating to visual interest, based on the principle of contrast to identify important information, such as page or chunk headers. The html codes in this step are:

html Command(s)	Text Function
color="rrggbb" where r=red, g=green, and b=blue intensity.	Color description, part of other commands to define background, links, and text
body	Specifies attributes of the body of a web page
bgcolor="#RRGGBB	Color of background, part of BODY tag
text="#RRGGBB"	Color of text, part of BODY tag
link="#RRGGBB"	Color of hot text, part of BODY tag
vlink="#RRGGBB"	Color of already accessed link, part of BODY tag
alink="#RRGGBB"	Color of active link, part of BODY tag
background="xxx.gif"	Color of background, part of BODY tag
<font size= [1 to 7]>	Changes size of type or font

Font-size differences should be noticeable to provide contrast. There are two types of change that identify the range of contrasts—incremental and radical. An incremental change is small relative to the starting position. A change from font size 4 (the default) to size 5 is incremental. A radical change is a large difference relative to the starting position. A change from font size 3 to font size 7 is radical. According to the principle of contrast, information that is important should be radically different from other text.

Color of text on web pages can be varied for the regular text, hot-button text that shows linkages to other web pages, hot text that has been accessed in the current session, and background. The defaults are a white background, black text, blue for hot text linkages, and red for accessed hot text. If you want all of these customized, it can be done in a single line of html code at the beginning of your document. The basic format for defining text colors is

```
<BODY BGCOLOR="0000FF" TEXT="FFFFFF" LINK="FF7F00"
VLINK=9F9F5F" ALINK="FFFF00">
```

By playing with color combinations, you will soon get the idea behind the combinations. If you used all possible combinations, there are roughly 16 million colors. Keep in mind that most people only have computers which can display 512 colors. Therefore, keep color choices simple, using mostly primary colors.

Adding color to the resume page shows how different this one single change can make the page. In Figure 4.17, a segment of the 'banker' version of a resume page (top screen) contrasts with a segment of the 'video game' version of the resume page (bottom screen). Do you think they sell their message?

Figure 4.17

Applying background colors to resume pages.

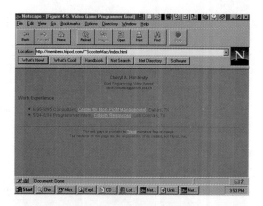

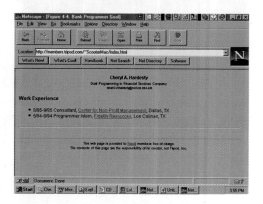

ASSIGNMENT: Imbed html commands in your pages for visual interest by varying the size of font and colors.

Exercises

REVIEW QUESTIONS

1. How did microprocessor chips develop?
2. What are the components of the CPU?
3. What is the function of the control unit and how does it do its job?
4. Explain the process of subtracting one number from another in binary code.
5. What are registers? How is their performance measured?
6. How do an address bus, a data bus, and a peripheral interface bus differ?
7. How is the clock important to the operation of the CPU? How are clock speeds measured?
8. What is a bi-stable device?
9. How is digital code used to represent circuit states?
10. How is digital code used to describe real-world data? What are two common digital coding schemes for representing data?
11. How is main memory different from register memory?
12. How are data located in main memory?
13. What are the three steps in the machine cycle?

FILL IN THE BLANKS

1. The _Control Unit_ oversees the CPU's many operations and contains a set of permanent instructions called _Microcode_
2. _Registers_ are temporary, special-purpose, high-speed staging areas for storing instructions and data inside the CPU.
3. The part of the CPU that performs arithmetic and logical operations is the _ALU (arithmetic/logic unit)_
4. The two phases of a machine cycle are the _I-cycle_ and _E-cycle_.
5. _RISC_ chips allow for fewer built-in microcode instructions.
6. To fully utilize the processing power of registers, _meaning word size_ _register size_, and _____ should be the same.
7. _Buses_ provide electronic highways among all of the components of a computer system.

8. Integrated circuits are mounted on _motherboard_

9. The _architecture_ of processors currently used by Apple and IBM is different.

10. Data are raw, unorganized facts that describe or _represent_ reality.

11. A device that is capable of assuming only one of two states is called _bi-stable_

12. A _code_ is a system of rules that correlates the elements of one set with the elements of another.

13. _Digital_ refers to anything pertaining to the binary digits 1 and 0.

14. ASCII codes use either a series of 7 bits or _8_ bits to represent characters.

15. RAM memory is _volatile_ meaning that it requires a constant charge to keep its contents intact.

MATCHING

Match each term with its description.

a. control unit

b. ROM

c. RAM

d. motherboard

e. CPU

f. register size

g. machine cycle

h. ALU

i. megahertz

j. processor

k. addresses

l. I-cycle

m. bit

n. byte

o. ASCII

p. pixel

____ 1. "Brain" of a computer system.

____ 2. Refers to how many bits a register can hold at one time.

____ 3. Memory that stores permanent instructions.

____ 4. Contains CPU, memory, and other chips, as well as electrical pathways between these components.

____ 5. Part of the CPU that performs arithmetic and logical operations.

____ 6. Tells the ALU what operation to perform next.

____ 7. Memory inside a computer that can be used again and again.

____ 8. Fetching and interpreting an instruction.

____ 9. Synonym for CPU.

____ 10. Three phases for executing a single instruction.

____ 11. Equals a million cycles per second.

____ 12.   Storage locations.

____ 13.   Picture element.

____ 14.   Binary digit.

____ 15.   Popular coding scheme for microcomputers.

____ 16.   Series of bits used to represent a character.

 **ACTIVITIES**

1. Visit a store in your area that sells microcomputers. Ask a salesperson to explain
    the main differences between the store's most expensive and least expensive
    microcomputer. Make a list of specific features included in the most expensive
    computer (such as amount of main memory and type of microprocessor) that
    may account for difference in price.

2. Find copies of current computer magazines. Investigate the latest advances in
    processor chip technology. Write a two- to three-page report on how these latest
    technologies could change the way computers are used in work and at home.

3. Browse through some computer magazines and journals in your school library.
    Find an advertisement for a computer that contains an Intel Pentium processor.
    Prepare a written list of all the computer's features, including processor speed
    and size of busses. Identify the features you consider to be most important if you
    are going to purchase a computer.

4. Over the course of the next month or so, scan as many magazines as possible.
    Try to identify 25 product advertisements that specifically refer to the use of digi-
    tal technology. List these products, and draw generalizations about them.

Skills for Living

INVESTING IN THE STOCK MARKET

Besides employment and home businesses, another major source of income for you could be your investments. Remember, our goal is to work both hard and smart. Investments can include real estate, stocks, bonds, precious metals, even collectibles such as stamps and coins. In this section, we focus on the stock market. But realize that any of these other investment vehicles could also be studied using the Web.

The goal in the stock market is for you to "buy low, sell high." Everyone would like to do this, but not everyone does. We have all heard stories about a new stock offering that doubled in the first day of trading. Overall, the stock market has performed relatively well. Technology-related stocks are fascinating to watch and the Web supplies us with the window.

Using the browsers you have available, see what you can find out about the stock market and about individual stocks. Find sources that will supply you with economic and industry data as well as current stock quotes for individual companies. Search for information about individual companies. Many companies have their own home page on the Web filled with material about their organization, products, services, and future plans. In the exercises below, you will actually track the prices and performances of different stocks using the World Wide Web.

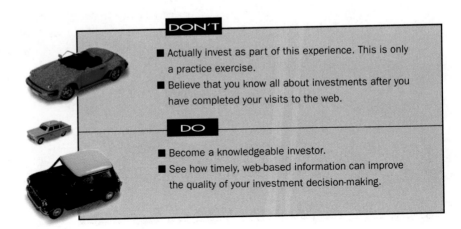

DON'T
- Actually invest as part of this experience. This is only a practice exercise.
- Believe that you know all about investments after you have completed your visits to the web.

DO
- Become a knowledgeable investor.
- See how timely, web-based information can improve the quality of your investment decision-making.

Student Activities

1. Assume you have just inherited $25,000 from your favorite uncle. You decide to invest these funds in the stock market. You are especially interested in high-technology stocks. You review your choices and decide on IBM, Microsoft, Intel, and AT&T. Using the Internet, look at the home pages of each of these companies. Then, pretend to invest all of your money by buying stock in some combination among these four companies. You may choose to invest all of your funds in one company, or different amounts in two, three, or even four companies.

   For the next 20 business days (four weeks), record the price of your stock at the end of each day. Use the Internet or your local newspaper to get the day's closing stock prices. You can even buy and sell your stocks, but charge yourself a brokerage commission of 1/2 percent of the total amount of each transaction (buying or selling). If you are familiar with electronic spreadsheets, enter your data in a spreadsheet and plot the stock prices.

2. At the end of the 20 days, compute the value of your final stock portfolio and your total gain or loss. Write up a one-page report of your project and include your spreadsheet and graph. Discuss the final results with your professor and class. What would you do differently if you were actually investing these funds in the future? What did you learn from this exercise? How did the computer help you?

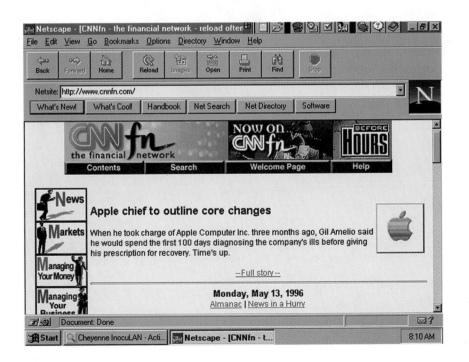

CHAPTER 5

OBJECTIVES

AFTER STUDYING THIS CHAPTER, YOU SHOULD BE ABLE TO:
1. Explain the meaning of the term *output*.
2. Describe the difference between soft copy and hard copy, and give an example of each.
3. Explain what a monitor is and how it is used.
4. Contrast the differences between impact and nonimpact printers.
5. Describe the usefulness of spooling and buffers.
6. Explain how plotters work.
7. Describe the development of presentation graphics and screen image projectors.
8. Describe several uses of voice output.
9. Explain the purpose of computer output microfilm (COM).

CHAPTER OUTLINE

THE BASICS OF OUTPUT

MONITORS
Variables in Graphics Display
Monochrome Monitors
Color Monitors
Flat-Panel Monitors
Monitor Ergonomics

PRINTERS

IMPACT PRINTERS
Dot-Matrix Printer

NONIMPACT PRINTERS
Laser Printers
Ink-Jet Printers
Thermal Transfer Printers
Solid Ink Printers
Dye Sublimation Printers

MULTIFUNCTION DEVICES

SPOOLING AND BUFFER MEMORY

OTHER OUTPUT DEVICES AND MEDIA
Plotters
Presentation Graphics
Sound Output
Voice Output
Music Synthesis
Computer Output Microfilm (COM)

Every workday, Frank Langione, a marketing consultant, enters his office in downtown Cincinnati. After flicking on his overhead lights, he flips the power switch on his personal computer, turns on the video monitor, and powers up his printer. Frank's job involves creating, editing, and printing large volumes of paper documents: letters to clients, drafts of ad pieces, reports to his managers, and the like. As a result, Frank spends a hefty chunk of each workday seated in front of his computer, several components of which are output devices.

For instance, Frank's laser printer is an output device that allows Frank to produce hard-copy printouts of the documents he creates. His video monitor can be considered an output device because it displays the results of Frank's actions on the keyboard and with the mouse. When Frank is asked to give presentations to clients, he uses specialized software to create his entire presentation, then delivers the presentation at other sites, using the software, the computer, and a screen image projector.

When clients wish to see the latest versions of ad pieces, Frank sends his files to the graphics department, where the images are output on dye-sublimation printers which deliver near photo-quality work. As you will see in this chapter, there are many more types of output devices, some geared to specific sorts of tasks and occupations. The continuously developing technology, including monitors with extremely high pixel densities and printers that can produce 800 characters per second, is making the work of everyone who comes in contact with computers much easier and faster. It is also pleasing clients, such as Frank Langione's, by giving them samples that look much closer to final output at an earlier stage in the process—at a much lower cost.

THE BASICS OF OUTPUT

Output is processed data, usually text, graphics, or sound, that can be used immediately by people, or stored in computer-usable form for later use. There are many types of computer output, falling in two general categories: hard copy and soft copy. **Hard copy** is a permanent version of output, typically recorded on a tangible medium such as paper or microfilm. A computer printout is an example of hard copy. **Soft copy** is a temporary version of output and, typically, output displayed on a computer screen. The information displayed on a bank teller's computer terminal screen when he or she checks your savings account balance is an example of soft copy. Voice output is another form of soft copy, since soft copy includes any output that cannot be physically handled. The telephone company often uses computer-generated voice output to perform tasks such as providing directory assistance. Output that is stored in computer-usable form for later use, such as information saved on a computer disk, is generally considered soft copy.

When selecting the type of output that is best for you, consider the quantity and quality of output your applications need, the time required to produce those outputs, and the hardware cost. Your equipment choices range from slow and inexpensive to fast and very expensive. You must compare the cost of the output system to the value it will generate during its lifetime. The rest of this chapter outlines the various types of output devices and media.

MONITORS

Monitors are peripheral devices that contain viewing, or display, screens. They come in various shapes, sizes, costs, and capabilities, and are the most common form of soft-copy output. Figure 5.1 shows some examples. The most common type of monitor uses a **cathode ray tube (CRT)** to display images, similar to the technology used in televisions. A monitor displays data and instructions as they are input and it also displays processed output.

Courtesy of Radius, Inc.

Courtesy of IBM Corporation.

Courtesy of NEC America, Inc.

Courtesy of Radius, Inc.

Figure 5.1

While 15-inch monitors are the standard, 17-inch, 21-inch, and page-length screens are becoming popular. Smaller, flat-panel displays are necessary on most laptop computers.

Monitors are a fundamental component of every single-user computer system. In addition, a monitor is also often paired with an input device, such as a keyboard, to form a special unit called a **video display terminal (VDT)**. A number of VDTs can be connected to multi-user computer systems.

VARIABLES IN GRAPHICS DISPLAY

Early personal computer systems could output only text (letters, numbers, and special characters) on the monitor. But, with time and technological improvements, graphics capabilities were added. Graphics capability allows complex picture images to be displayed.

Bit-Mapping Bit-mapped text characters are formed on-screen using patterns of lighted dots. With the earliest computers, every character was the same size and was placed in a standardized matrix of illuminated dots, or *picture elements*, called **pixels**. Graphics display screens also use a pattern of tiny dots. In these display systems, each dot, which equals a bit, can be "addressed" or illuminated individually by a combination of graphics hardware and software. These screens are called bit-mapped displays. A **bit-mapped display** device makes it possible for the user to manipulate each dot individually, adding, deleting, or coloring specific dots to form or edit the image on the screen.

Most newer microcomputers come with built-in graphics display capability. This is achieved through a device called a **graphics card** or a **graphics adapter board**. To display colorful screen images, the computer must have a color monitor and this type of graphics circuitry.

The dazzling graphics and animation you see on video arcade screens or in video games are the result of data entered into a computer and processed by graphics programs. There are also graphics systems that allow a user to scan text, pictures, and images from one document (magazine, photo, drawing), and then insert them into another computer-generated document, such as a report or electronic publication.

Resolution The clarity of images displayed on the monitor screen is called **resolution**. The resolution quality is directly related to *pixel density* and *dot pitch*. The **pixel**

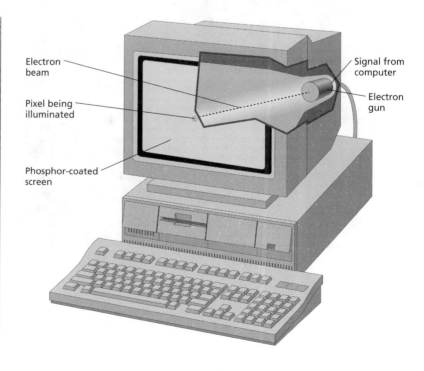

Figure 5.2

In cathode ray tube monitors, an electron gun strikes a phosphor-coated screen, causing pixels to illuminate.

Electron beam

Pixel being illuminated

Phosphor-coated screen

Signal from computer

Electron gun

density is measured by the number of pixel locations across the screen times the number of pixel locations down the screen. Current color monitors have pixel densities ranging from 720 X 350 (252,000) addressable points up to 1,024 X 768 (786,432) addressable points. A monitor used for graphics or computer-aided design can have up to 16 million addressable points. The distance between one phosphor dot on the screen and the next nearest dot of the same color is known as **dot pitch**. Greater pixel densities and smaller dot pitches yield sharper images of higher resolution.

Pixels are electronically maintained, as illustrated in Figure 5.2. An electron beam moves back and forth across a phosphor-coated screen. As the electron beam contacts a phosphor dot, it lights up. As it starts to fade, the beam strikes it again. The process is known as *refreshing* the screen. If the *refresh rate* is too slow, the image on the screen may flash or oscillate. This is known as *flickering*. The combined rate at which horizontal and vertical lines are redrawn is known as the *scan frequency*. The amount and speed of output that the monitor can accept and translate to its maximum resolution is called its *bandwidth*. Both the scan frequency and the bandwidth affect a monitor's refresh rate.

MONOCHROME MONITORS

Monochrome monitors display pixels in a single color on a black screen. The most common colors are green, amber, and white. It is also possible to reverse the color of the pixels, creating, for example, black type on a white screen. Although limited to one color, monochrome monitors can display shades of the color, called **gray-scaling**. This is accomplished by illuminating fewer or more pixels for each character, depending on the intensity of the desired illumination.

Courtesy of Apple Computer, Inc.

A monochrome monitor can display only a single color, typically white, amber, or green. By using this single color in different intensities, called gray-shading, the monitor can represent different "colored" areas.

COLOR MONITORS

Color monitors display characters and graphics using a combination of the colors red, green, and blue, and are therefore called **RGB monitors**. Users are able to display anywhere from eight to upwards of millions of colors, depending on the quality of the monitor, the capability of the graphics adapter card, and the amount of RAM available in the computer system. Color monitors are especially

Courtesy of Apple Computer, Inc.

Color monitors blend red, green, and blue pixels in combinations resulting in upwards of millions of possible colors.

useful for displaying graphics. Detailed images result from illuminating pixels using different color combinations, intensities, and patterns. Through the years, a number of color monitor standards have developed. They vary by dot pitch and density of the pixel pattern used. The table below lists color graphics adapter card standards and their pixel densities. The most common are:

- The original **Color Graphics Adapter (CGA)** standard provides low resolution graphics. Characters displayed in text mode can be difficult to read.
- The **Enhanced Graphics Adapter (EGA)** standard provides four to sixteen colors at a higher resolution than CGA, which makes characters displayed in text mode more legible.
- The **Video Graphics Array (VGA)** standard can handle up to 256 colors. Its resolution is slightly better than the EGA standard.
- The **Super Video Graphics Array (SVGA)** standard provides a high resolution up to 800 X 600 pixels.
- The **Extended Graphics Array (XGA)** can support up to 16.7 million colors at a resolution of 1,024 X 768 pixels.

Video display adapters enable a monitor screen to display information. An adapter may be built into the motherboard, or added as an expansion card to an expansion slot inside the computer.

Adapter type	Explanation
MDA (**M**onochrome **D**isplay **A**dapter)	Designed for monochrome monitors. Does not display color or graphics. Introduced in 1981.
CGA (**C**olor **G**raphics **A**dapter)	Displays information in monochrome at a pixel resolution of 320 x 300 pixels. Also displays color at a low resolution.
EGA (**E**nhanced **G**raphics **A**dapter)	Displays 16 colors at a pixel resolution of 640 x 350 pixels. Introduced in 1984.
VGA (**V**ideo **G**raphics **A**rray)	Displays 16 colors at a pixel resolution of 640 x 480 pixels and displays 256 colors at 320 x 200 pixels. Introduced in 1987.
SVGA (**S**uper **V**ideo **G**raphics **A**rray)	Displays 256 colors at a pixel resolution of 800 x 600 pixels and displays 256 colors at a pixel resolution of 1024 x 768 pixels.
XGA (**E**xtended **G**raphics **A**rray)	Displays up to 16,777,216 colors at a pixel resolution up t 1024 x 768 pixels.

Often the application software you use determines the type of color monitor you need. For instance, if a software program can access the available pixels in a VGA or SVGA monitor/graphics card combination, then your computer system should have that type of color graphics capability to get the maximum performance from that software program. Fortunately, due to the concept of *backward compatibility*, any graphics card that is capable of a higher resolution can run programs that require lower resolution levels. **Backward compatibility** provides that computer system hardware and software developed for a standard of higher sophistication is nevertheless capable of operating at a standard of lower sophistication.

FLAT-PANEL MONITORS

Portable and notebook computers require small, lightweight, low-powered monitors called **flat-panel monitors**. Flat-panel monitors can display text and graphics in either monochrome or color. Two display technologies are used in flat-panel monitors—liquid crystal and gas plasma.

Liquid Crystal Display (LCD)

Both laptop and notebook computers, shown in Figure 5.3, use **liquid crystal displays (LCDs)**. An LCD screen is made of two "sandwiched" sheets of polarizing material with pneumatic liquid crystal solution between them. Electrical currents cause the liquid crystals to align so that light shining through the screen will create characters and images. Small LCD screens are found on electronic calculators with just enough room to display one row of numbers at a time. One benefit of LCDs is that they use relatively little power. However, LCD displays are usually smaller than CRTs and are not as bright.

There are two main kinds of LCD screens, **active matrix** and **passive matrix**. Active matrix screens contain individual transistors that control each pixel on the screen. Passive matrix screens contain fewer transistors. A single transistor controls all pixels in an entire row or column. Active matrix displays are more expensive but display a sharper and brighter picture. When viewed from an angle, active matrix displays are more clearly visible than are passive matrix displays.

Courtesy of AST.

> **Figure 5.3**
>
> Liquid crystal displays are small, lightweight, and low powered, making them ideal for notebook computers.

MONITOR ERGONOMICS

The science of studying the interaction of humans and their office equipment is called *ergonomics*. There has been some concern that electromagnetic emissions from computer monitors might cause cancer or adversely affect pregnancies. Studies of these issues are incomplete and inconclusive (see Focus box, on page 154). The main concern is emissions at the low-end frequencies of 5Hz to 400KHz. Most emissions come from the sides and back of the monitor. Because these emissions dissipate quickly, keeping an appropriate distance from the monitor is important. If possible, keep at least three feet from the rear and sides of the closest monitor and at least two feet from the front of the monitor. Physical barriers (radiation filters) can be used to block electromagnetic emissions; and several low-emission monitors are available. When using monitors, it is important to have adequate lighting, ergonomically comfortable seating, and efficient keyboard location and layout. Glare-reduction devices mounted in front of the screen can also help. Figure 5.4 on page 152 diagrams the ideal positioning of you and your computer equipment. Ergonomics is discussed in more detail in Chapter 13.

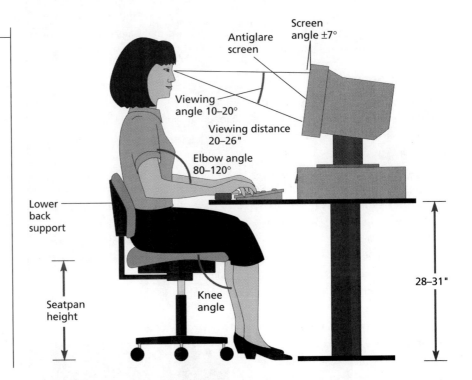

FOCUS

Warning: Offices May Be a Health Hazard

Recent statistics from the Occupational Safety and Health Administration indicate that offices have become the setting for the most common workplace injuries, repetitive strain injuries (RSIs).

Formerly seen primarily among line workers in poultry-processing plants, RSI, particularly in the form of carpal tunnel syndrome, is now a leading complaint among computer workers. Workers ranging from journalists to order-entry clerks have developed RSIs severe enough to permanently disable them.

At fault, say ergonomics experts, is the failure of computer designers to construct safe equipment, especially keyboards. By failing to adjust for the different needs of computer operations, as opposed to earlier forms of office work, companies have compounded the problem. Lawsuits against companies across the nation—and rapid rises in insurance premiums—have U.S. businesses looking for ways to prevent such injuries.

Fortunately, many companies have developed equipment to make computing safer. For example, installing any of the many wrist supports now on the market can keep computer users' hands in the proper position—elbows at 90 degrees and hands even with the keyboard—not arched upward as is common. In addition, some computer peripheral makers have developed specially shaped keyboards that include such safety features as concave keypads and separate keyboards for each hand. Comfortable chairs with good back support, set to a height that puts the feet flat on the floor, can likewise minimize back injuries among office workers. Similarly, positioning video terminals so that the top of the screen is at or just below eye level, and minimizing screen glare with filters and indirect lighting can prevent eye and neck strain. Frequent short breaks in which operators move around and stretch have reduced computer-linked injuries of virtually all kinds.

More controversial is the question of whether display monitors are inherently dangerous because of the very low frequency (VLF) electromagnetic radiation they emit. Recent studies indicate that there may be a link between ELF (extremely low frequency) radiation—most commonly associated with utility power lines—and cancer and pregnancy problems.

In Europe, which has traditionally been far more conscious of office ergonomics than the United States, concern over VLF and ELF emissions has prompted a series of new guidelines. (Because of the power of labor unions in much of Europe, guidelines often have

Courtesy of NoRad Corporation.

the effect of law, since few firms would dare to violate them or to purchase equipment that did.) The strictest of these guidelines come from Sweden, whose 1991 limits on ELF and VLF emissions are expected to become the standard throughout the European Community (EC). As the United States government has undertaken no studies into the health effects of display monitors, the Swedish guidelines may well become the standard here, too.

While the major computer makers all deny that their products present any health hazard, most have rushed to comply with Swedish guidelines, fearful of losing at least the European market if they do not. Indeed, the Japanese are reported to be pouring money into the development of low-emission computer products. And with the extra costs of low-emission monitors ranging from nothing to $200 per unit, American businesses may find such purchases lower not only emissions but their financial risks.

PRINTERS

Printers are the most common type of hard-copy output devices. Printers are separated into two main categories: impact and nonimpact. **Impact printers** print much like a typewriter, by striking an inked ribbon against the paper. **Nonimpact printers** use electricity, heat, laser technology, or photographic techniques to produce output. As we look at the individual printers in each group, you will learn the method used by that printer to create text and images on the paper or other output medium. Some of the methods include:

- Printing solid characters vs. printing characters formed by dots.
- Printing one character at a time vs. printing rows or pages at a time.
- Printing quickly vs. printing slowly.
- Printing capability limited to alphanumeric symbols vs. unlimited graphic content.

IMPACT PRINTERS

Impact printers were the first commercially available printers. Like typewriters, these printers create text and graphics by physically striking a ribbon to deposit ink on paper. An important advantage of impact printers to businesses is their ability to produce carbon copies of documents and forms. For example, some business forms, such as customer order forms, consist of multiple copies. Only impact printers can print multiple-copy forms. The force of the impact is transferred through each carbon to the next layer of copies. Nonimpact printers use very little force when printing and, therefore, do not have this capability.

Although impact printers are still used in many computer facilities and by some individuals, their popularity is decreasing. Many are being replaced with newer types of printers that offer greater capabilities, including ink-jet and laser printers.

DOT-MATRIX PRINTER

Characters are printed on **dot-matrix printers** (also called *pin printers*) in a manner similar to the way numbers appear on a football scoreboard. If you look closely at a scoreboard, you will see that each number consists of a pattern of lighted bulbs. By observing print produced on a dot-matrix printer, you can see that each letter or number consists of a series of tiny dots arranged to represent that letter or number. For example, on a dot-matrix printer, the letter A is printed by activating a matrix of small pins (or wires) that sequentially produces the shape of the letter (see Figure 5.5).

Each letter (both upper- and lowercase), number, and symbol has a unique representation using a matrix of dots, similar to the matrix of pixels used on monitors. A typical matrix is 5 X 7, which means the matrix is five dots wide and seven dots high. When a 5 X 7 matrix is used, the printer has seven pins arranged vertically in the printer's printhead mechanism. Two additional rows of dots are necessary in the matrix to represent the letters and symbols that must be formed below the normal printing line, giving the printhead a total of nine pins.

Dot-matrix printers offer the following advantages:

- They can be used with both mainframes and microcomputers.
- They are economical.
- They can print graphics, such as line graphs and bar graphs.
- They can print at speeds ranging from 100 to 800 characters per second.
- They can print multiple copies using carbon paper sandwiched between sheets of output.
- They can print large amounts of output on continuous, fan-folded paper.

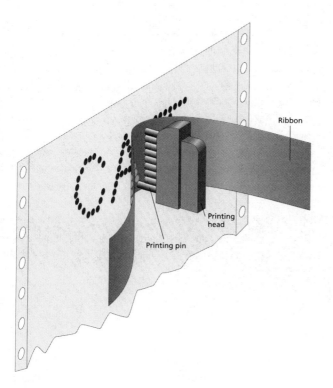

Figure 5.5

A matrix of pins form the characters on dot-matrix printers. A main advantage of dot-matrix and other impact printers is their ability to print multiple-copy documents.

Ribbon

Printing head

Printing pin

The disadvantages of dot-matrix printers are the following:

- Because the characters are not solid, the quality of output is reduced, making them unsuitable for some applications, such as desktop publishing.
- They are noisy.
- Because they print a single character at a time, they are slower than printers that print a line or a page at a time.

NONIMPACT PRINTERS

Nonimpact printers, which represent the fastest-growing segment of the printer market, use heat, electricity, or laser technology to print output. With these printers, no physical contact occurs between the printing mechanism and the paper. Nonimpact printers offer three main advantages over impact printers:

- They are fast.
- They are quiet.
- They have high-quality output.
- They can output a document that uses multiple typefaces.

Nonimpact printers have fewer moving parts than impact printers, which accounts for their faster speed. Their quiet operation results from the absence of the hammering necessary for impact printers.

Nonimpact printers have the ability to change fonts automatically. A **font** is a set of characters of a particular typeface, such as Times Roman or Helvetica. Some machines are available with different fonts permanently stored on ROM chips inside the printer. Others have a slot into which a firmware cartridge containing a variety of fonts can be inserted. When inserted, fonts contained in the cartridge are automatically available to the printer. Thus, nonimpact printers can produce a document with multiple typefaces. Another important feature of nonimpact printers is their ability to produce attractive and detailed graphics.

The two main nonimpact printer technologies are *laser* and *ink-jet*. Higher-quality nonimpact printers include the thermal transfer printer and the dye sublimation printer. Some of these printers are capable of producing output in color, similar to the color illustrations in this book.

LASER PRINTERS

Laser printers are one of the latest and fastest growing segments of the printer market. The primary reason for their popularity is their ability to produce text and graphics with clear, crisp quality.

Laser printers are nonimpact printers that create text and graphics on a rotating metal drum by using a laser beam. During printing, characters are read by a mechanism inside the printer and relayed to the laser mechanism. Then, the laser mechanism sends light impulses through a series of reflective mirrors to the drum. The impulses, in the form of tiny dots, produce tiny magnetic fields on the drum in the shape of characters or graphics. As the drum rotates, the magnetic fields attract an ink-like powder called *toner* (like that used in copy machines). Toner ink is stored in a removable cartridge inside the printer. The toner on the drum is pressed onto and dried on the paper, forming the characters or graphics. The circumference of the drum is approximately the same as the length of a standard sheet of paper. With one revolution of the drum, an entire page is printed. For this reason, laser printers are called "page" printers. The printing process is illustrated in Figure 5.6.

The earliest laser printers, appearing in the early 1980s and printing only with black ink, were large machines used by businesses to print several hundred pages per hour. Their initial cost was several thousand dollars, which limited their use to

Figure 5.6

With laser printers, a small laser beam bounces off a mirror onto a positively charged drum millions of times per second. The ink toner sticks to the neutralized spots touched by the laser beam. Heat and pressure cause the toner to stick to the paper. The drum is then recharged for the next page.

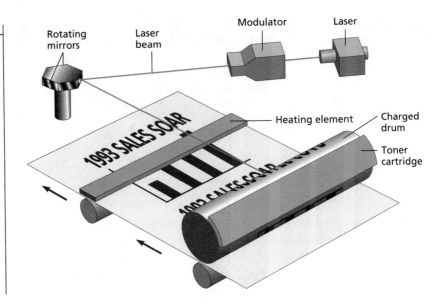

organizations whose need for speed and volume made them cost-effective. However, in recent years, technological advances have significantly reduced manufacturing costs to where small laser printers, using only black ink, can now be purchased at a reasonable price. As a result, even individual personal computer users can take advantage of these top-quality printing devices (see Figure 5.7).

Several laser printer manufacturers now offer new models of laser printers capable of printing characters and images in color. These printers are available for large and small computer systems. However, compared to black-ink laser printers, the price of a color laser printer is still relatively high. As prices decline, color laser printers are likely to become the printers of choice among many microcomputer users, especially those in desktop publishing.

Figure 5.7

High quality and decreasing costs make laser printers an attractive alternative for PC users.

Courtesy of Hewlett-Packard Company.

INK-JET PRINTERS

Ink-jet printers spray tiny drops of ink through a jet nozzle onto the paper to create images in dot-matrix form. With ink-jet technology, the ink is forced out of the nozzle because the nozzle no longer has room for it. There are two methods that produce this effect: thermal and mechanical.

Thermal Ink-Jet Printers

The nozzle in thermal ink-jet printers contains a resistive heater. The heater is part of a long, ink-filled tube connected to an ink reservoir. As the ink heats, gas bubbles form at the opening of the nozzle. When the bubble is fully formed, it leaves the nozzle and more ink is drawn from the reservoir, as illustrated in Figure 5.8.

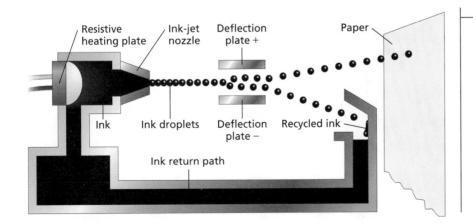

Figure 5.8

The mechanics of thermal ink-jet printing. The diagram shows the printing mechanism that sprays tiny drops of ink onto the paper.

Mechanical Ink-Jet Printers The nozzle in a mechanical ink-jet printer contains a vibrating plate. As the plate pushes into the nozzle, it decreases the volume inside the cavity. The pressure forces ink out. When the vibrating plate returns to its resting position, ink is drawn into the cavity to fill the void. Since mechanical printers don't use heat, their nozzles tend to last longer.

Color ink-jet printers can produce attractive text and graphics, as shown in Figure 5.9. Newer ink-jet models can print four or more pages per minute, compared to ten or more pages per minute printed by black-and-white ink-jet printers.

Figure 5.9

Ink-jet printers are an affordable way to produce attractive, though not complex, color images.

Courtesy of Epson America, Inc.

Ink-jet printers will not render images of photographic quality, but they are able to blend colors and images of some complexity. They are suitable for reports circulated within departments or companies rather than reports meant to impress prospective clients. They are also capable of producing fair quality transparencies for presentations. Their reasonable price makes them a popular tool.

Figure 5.10

Thermal transfer printers produce images of high quality.

Photo provided by Tektronix, Inc.

THERMAL TRANSFER PRINTERS

Thermal transfer printers, such as the one shown in Figure 5.10, heat cyan, magenta, yellow, and black wax onto the page. The waxes are contained on rolls that look similar to plastic kitchen wrap. As the paper passes over the rolls, the waxes are heated, picked up, and blended to form full-color pictures of a very high quality. Their output is suitable for photographic-quality images for professional presentations and color publishing. The initial cost of thermal transfer printers is several thousand dollars more than ink-jet printers.

before

Superstock.

AFTER

Courtesy of Digital Equipment Corporation.

Until the advent of office computers, clerical workers used manual or electric typewriters to create all paper documents. When they made mistakes or when changes were necessary, they either retyped the entire document, or used messy correction fluid to "white out" the mistake, typing in the correct information. How frustrating to be a secretary in a document-sensitive organization such as a law firm, where paper documents are the very lifeblood of the company!

Compared with typewriters, computers and printers, used in conjunction with word-processing and desktop-publishing software, make document production a piece of cake. Not only are changes easier to implement, but the finished product is of a much higher quality and can be produced in a fraction of the time.

Modern printers enable a computer user to produce documents containing both text and pictures in a variety of formats and colors.

SOLID INK PRINTERS

Solid ink printers are capable of producing color text and images that are remarkably clear and detailed. One such printer, Tektronix's Phaser 340 printer (see Figure 5.11), combines the attributes of solid-ink (also referred to as wax-jet) and laser-printing technologies to produce impressive photo-quality color output. Instead of liquid ink cartridges, solid ink printers use colored wax sticks that, when heated by the printer, become liquified colored wax. Some solid ink printers spray the melted wax directly onto paper. The Phaser 340 sprays the

Photo provided by Tekronix, Inc.

Figure 5.11

Solid ink printers are capable of producing color text and images that are remarkably clear and detailed.

Figure 5.12

Dye sublimation printers provide a full range of colors and continuous-tone images for an output that rivals color photos.

Photo provided by Tektronix, Inc.

melted wax directly onto a drum, which then transfers the image onto paper. The Phaser 340 can print nearly four pages per minute at 600 dots per inch. Output can be printed on plain office paper or on transparency film in a variety of fonts and colors.

DYE SUBLIMATION PRINTERS

Dye sublimation printers are the top of the line in color printing. They produce continuous-tone images by vaporizing colored inks onto specially treated, heat-sensitive paper, as shown in Figure 5.12. Dye sublimation printers do not use dot patterns. They heat dyes to a gaseous state and fuse them to special paper, consistently yielding a full range of colors and true continuous-tone images. The output quality of dye sublimation printers rivals that of color photos. These printers are used by organizations looking for the highest quality in their presentations and reports. Desktop publishing companies and graphics departments purchase dye sublimation printers in order to print proofs of their works before sending them to press for final production.

COMPUTER CURRENTS

Slashing Red Tape at Hewlett-Packard

In a series of personal meetings with Hewlett-Packard employees across the nation, William Hewlett and David Packard heard again and again the frustrations of company engineers, marketers, and others who felt stymied by the system of committee review panels that had arisen at HP in the mid-1980s. One vice-president reported needing 19 signatures to discount a software package and approval from 38 committees to release a new networking product. As a result of "trial by committee," many new ideas were shot down as too unorthodox, while those approved took precious extra months to reach the market. Because of this

Courtesy of the Hewlett-Packard Company.

and virtually owns the ink-jet market—despite powerful competition from Apple Computer and virtually every Japanese printer maker.

Yet HP almost didn't get into the desktop printer business at all. Initially it offered only a $100,000 printer designed largely to help the firm sell its large computers. But in 1981, Rick Hackborn, a manager at HP, stumbled onto an early laser printer being made—but not sold successfully—by Canon. Free of the constraints that later committees would impose, Hackborn was able to convince his superiors that HP should market the device. As a result, in 1992, the latest version of this Canon printer, now heavily reworked by HP engineers, accounted for nearly 40 percent of HP's gross income.

Today Rick Hackborn heads HP's PC division, which includes both computers and peripherals such as printers. Since the demise of the committee system, products of all kinds have been flowing out of this division, earning HP the kinds of kudos for marketing savvy that were once reserved for its engineering expertise.

feedback, committees are few and far between at HP, banished in favor of highly autonomous divisions committed to reducing "breakeven time" in half (the time from the conception of a product until it becomes profitable).

To see the effects of these changes, consider HP's printer sales. Hewlett-Packard has an enviable position in the computer printer market. With its line of constantly upgraded and competitively priced laser and ink-jet printers, the company has managed to hold onto a staggering 60 percent of the desktop laser printer market

MULTIFUNCTION DEVICES

Many output devices presently available can perform more than one function. These **multifunction devices** offer users several capabilities. For example, Xerox sells a printer/copier/scanner that can be connected to computer networks. Some multifunction devices also provide faxing capabilities. A single multifunction device capable of replacing four or more single-function devices typically costs less than the separate devices and requires less desktop space.

S P O O L I N G   A N D   B U F F E R   M E M O R Y

The speed at which the CPU performs its actions is extremely fast when compared to the speeds at which peripheral devices, such as printers, operate. This speed imbalance can be bothersome. For example, suppose you have finished a lengthy word-processing document or large spreadsheet and are now ready to print it. Unless your computer system has *spooling* capabilities, the entire document will remain in your computer's RAM memory until it is finished printing. **Spooling** software allows data, such as a block of text, to be stored temporarily in a magnetic storage medium until the printer is ready to print it. Suppose the CPU has just completed a program that created 30 pages of output for the printer. It took the CPU just one minute to complete. Now, if the printer prints ten pages per minute, the job would take three minutes to print. If the computer has to wait until the printer finishes, the user would have to wait three minutes before the computer is free to do another job.

Spooling increases productivity. The spooling program instructs the computer to transfer and store the data in a magnetic storage medium. When the data are transferred to the medium, the spooling process is completed. The program then instructs the computer to transfer the data from the storage medium to the printer, thereby freeing the computer for another application. Figure 5.13 diagrams the steps in the spooling process.

Figure 5.13

With print spooling devices, the data that are destined for the printer are first stored on a magnetic medium and then sent to an output device.

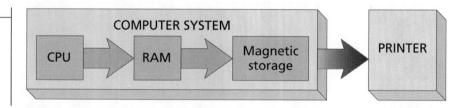

Another way to overcome the difference between fast computer speed and slower printer speed is to use a printer that contains *buffer memory*. **Buffers**, like the CPU's RAM memory, are temporary holding areas inside the output device that compensate for the difference in CPU and output device speeds. Printer buffers absorb and hold output that has just been processed in the CPU and delivered to the printer, until the printer is free. Figure 5.14 shows how buffers work. Buffers can either be installed inside the computer or in the peripheral device.

Figure 5.14

The data destined for the printer are first stored in buffers inside the printer, allowing the CPU to go on to other tasks. When free, the printer retrieves and prints the data.

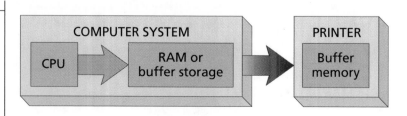

OTHER OUTPUT DEVICES AND MEDIA

There are other kinds of output devices and media besides printed and screen output. In these sections we examine four additional categories. Some output devices and media are used for general output applications; others are used for specialized applications.

PLOTTERS

Plotters are hard-copy devices used for producing graphics on paper or on overhead transparency material. Plotters are available for personal computers and larger computer systems and are used extensively for mapping and design. Mapping applications might include housing subdivision plans, traffic patterns, topographical terrains, or demographics (for example, average age, family incomes, or education level of people in a certain area). Plotters can also be used to create engineering drawings for machinery parts and equipment. The drawings are then taken to the shop where the parts are made.

Some plotters use pens to draw and are therefore commonly called *pen plotters*. Although some plotters use a single color, such as black, most plotters use multiple pens for drawing graphics in

Courtesy of the Hewlett-Packard Company.

various colors. The pens are usually stored in a rack to one side of the page. Software that comes with the plotter instructs the plotter to select a specific color when it is needed.

The most popular type of plotters are ink-jet plotters. **Ink-jet plotters** produce attractive and detailed drawings by spraying tiny drops of ink onto sheets or rolls of paper or plastic (see Figure 5.15). Some use black ink to produce drawings in various shades of black on lighter colored paper or plastic. These plotters produce crisp, sharp images with up to 600 dots per inch. Color ink-jet plotters are capable of producing full-color output. In addition to black, they use color ink cartridges that make it possible to produce more than 16 million colors at 300 dots per inch.

PRESENTATION GRAPHICS

Today, much of a manager's time is spent in meetings, listening to or giving presentations and briefings. Research shows that information is more easily understood and communicated when both speech and images are combined in effective presentations. Today, computers play a major role in the generation and display of visual aids,

Figure 5.16

In a photographic slide
device, a cone fits around
the camera lens and holds
the camera the correct
distance from the screen,
resulting in a sharp image.

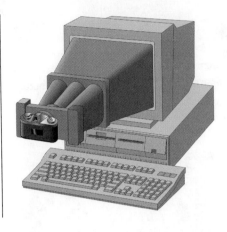

called **presentation graphics**. Specialized hardware such as photographic
slide devices and screen image projectors have been developed to support
this activity.

Photographic Slide Device Special
output devices can produce 35-millimeter
slides. A 35-millimeter slide consists of
images stored on small pieces of photographic film for viewing with an ordinary
slide projector. Various **photographic
slide devices** allow a user to produce
35-millimeter slides from computer output. One device consists of a camera and a
cone, shown in Figure 5.16. The smaller end of the cone fits over the camera lens.
The larger end of the cone is rectangular and fits over a computer screen. Just by
clicking the camera, a user can capture a screen image, such as a graphic, on photographic film.

Screen Image Projectors Visual aids are often created using a computer, graphics
software, and a monitor. The final version is then printed on an overhead transparency for
use with a projector. Often, the computer version is in color on the screen, but the transparency can be printed in black and white.

    Screen image projectors are clear-screened devices that rest on top of an
overhead projector, connect directly to the computer, and duplicate the screen
image exactly as it appears on the monitor, as shown in Figure 5.17. The projected image

Figure 5.17

By using a screen image projector in conjunction with an
overhead projector, clear
screen images are dupli-
cated on a large surface.

Courtesy of TRW, Inc.

fills the screen, making it easily readable in a large room. You can save images for a complete presentation, including transitions between images and sound effects. You can even save complete presentations on diskette, transport the projector to other sites, and deliver the presentation, using the host's computer. These systems are excellent for demonstrating software applications and screen displays to students in a classroom.

SOUND OUTPUT

Sound output devices produce a variety of sounds ranging from beeps to music. Multimedia computer systems containing speakers and a sound adapter card plugged into an expansion slot inside the computer are capable of producing amazingly clear, high-quality sounds.

VOICE OUTPUT

In Chapter 3, you learned that you can "talk" to a computer. But did you know that computers can also talk to you? The following examples are probably familiar to you. You dial a telephone number and hear a voice say, "The number you dialed has been changed, the new number is. . . ." Or, you receive a computerized telephone message describing a new product or service. Or, upon entering your recently purchased new-model automobile, you hear a voice telling you to "please fasten your seatbelt." Each of these messages is computer output translated into voice messages, or **voice output**.

Voice output systems permit a computer to deliver messages via the spoken word. Spoken messages can be produced by computers of almost any size, from large computer systems to tiny embedded computer chips in your automobile. Voice output includes recorded messages, such as solicitations for new products. In the case of the changed telephone number, a computer accesses the new telephone number from an electronically stored directory of numbers and converts the new number to a *digitized voice message* for the caller. A digitized voice message is an intelligible spoken message that a computer system composes (and stores) from words and phrases. Although voice output systems have been available since the late 1970s, some people do not like the "robotic" voice produced by them.

MUSIC SYNTHESIS

A special application in which a computer converts electronic signal data into sound is called *music synthesis*. With special software, you can use a computer to compose music and play existing arrangements of musical works. A **music synthesizer** (see Figure 5.18 on page 168) is a specialized output device that converts electronic signals into sounds. Synthesizers can produce a variety of high-quality musical sounds by imitating musical instruments, the human voice, or even animal sounds.

COMPUTER OUTPUT MICROFILM (COM)

Have you ever wondered how many magazines, journals, and periodicals a university receives, and how much space would be needed if the library kept all of these items in their original form? To save space, libraries store publications on *microfilm* or *microfiche*. Microfilm is a continuous roll of acetate film, similar to movie film.

Figure 5.18

Students at Berklee College
of Music in Boston learn how
to write and record music
using a music synthesizer.
Sounds can be created and
stored on a magnetic medium
and played over again.

Courtesy of Berklee College of Music/Photo: Bob Kramer.

Microfiche are 4 X 6-inch sheets of film, often called *fiche*. Both are the result of a technology called **computer output microfilm**, usually referred to by the acronym **COM**.

With computer output microfilm, a camera is used to photograph images (such as documents or pages). The images are sent to a special device that records the information as microscopic images on roll or sheet film. A special magnifying device, such as a microfilm reader or microfiche reader, is required for reading these microscopic images.

COM technologies are used by companies and organizations that need to preserve and store a huge volume of information, such as libraries, insurance companies, banks, and government agencies.

Key Terms

active matrix

backward compatibility

bit-mapped display

buffers

cathode ray tube (CRT)

color graphics adapter (CGA)

computer output microfilm (COM)

dot pitch

dot-matrix printers

dye sublimation printers

enhanced graphics adapter (EGA)

extended graphics array (XGA)

lat-panel monitors

font

graphics adapter board

graphics card

gray-scaling

hard copy

impact printers

ink-jet plotters

ink-jet printers

laser printers

liquid crystal display (LCD)

monitors

monochrome	RGB monitors
multifunction devices	screen image projectors
music synthesizer	soft copy
nonimpact printers	solid ink printers
output	sound output
passive matrix	spooling
photographic slide devices	super video graphics array (SVGA)
pixel density	thermal transfer printers
pixels	video display terminal (VDT)
plotters	video graphics array (VGA)
presentation graphics	voice output
resolution	

Summary

Output is processed data, usually text, graphics, or sound, that can be used immediately by people, or stored for later use. Output can be produced as **hard copy** or **soft copy** by a wide variety of output devices and media.

Monitors create temporary visual displays on screens. Monitors using cathode ray tube technology are called **CRTs**. When monitors are part of a terminal system, the system is called a visual display terminal, or **VDT**. The resolution of monitors is measured by the number of pixels the screen contains. **Bit-mapped displays** and **graphics cards** allow monitors to display graphic images. Monitors may produce **monochrome** or color displays. The common standards for color graphics adapter cards and displays are **CGA**, **EGA**, **VGA**, **SVGA**, and **XGA** (in order of increasing clarity or resolution). **Flat-panel monitors** used with laptop and notebook computers contain **liquid crystal displays (LCD)**.

Printers are the most common hard-copy output devices. One way to classify printers is by whether they are impact or nonimpact. **Impact printers** create text and other images on paper by striking a ribbon to deposit ink on a page. **Nonimpact printers** use heat, electricity, or laser technology to print output.

Dot-matrix printers create characters in the form of small dots arranged in matrix format. **Ink-jet printers** spray tiny drops of ink from jet nozzles onto the paper to create characters in dot-matrix form. **Laser printers** print an entire page at a time using a magnetically-charged drum. **Thermal transfer printers** contain heating devices that when used on chemically treated paper form high-quality images. **Solid ink printers** use solid ink (wax) to produce photo-quality output. **Dye sublimation printers** produce continuous-tone images by vaporizing colored inks onto specially treated, heat-sensitive paper.

The CPU is much faster than peripheral devices. To equalize the imbalance, **spooling** software allows temporary data storage in a magnetic storage device until the printer is ready to print. **Printer buffers** are another means of absorbing and holding output until the printer is ready.

Though monitors and printers are most common, there are various other output devices. **Plotters** are hard-copy devices for producing graphics on paper. The most popular plotters are **ink-jet plotters**.

Voice output systems convert data into digitized voice messages that are sent to the user. A **music synthesizer** can transform electronics signal data into high-quality musical sounds.

Photographic slide devices are available for producing 35-millimeter slides of data that are then displayed on a computer screen. **Screen image projectors** rest on top of an overhead projector, connect to the computer, and duplicate the screen image exactly as it appears on the monitor.

Many large organizations, libraries, and businesses use **computer output microfilm (COM)** for miniaturizing and saving documents on microfilm and microfiche.

14 Easy steps to being a webmaster

STEP 5 | ADDITIONAL TEXT FORMATTING

In this step, we discuss typeface, the use of special characters and the design tenet of repetition. In addition, we develop your artistic sense of page design by discussing two key characteristics of page design—effectiveness and affectiveness. First, the html codes in this step are:

html Command(s)	Text Function
&quot	Represents a double quote mark (")
&amp	Represents an ampersand (&)
&copy	Replaces the symbol name with a copyright symbol ©
<b> </b>	Presents text in boldface
<big> </big>	Identifies text to be presented at about three points larger than the default
<i> </i>	Presents text in italics
<pre> </pre>	Uses user-defined preformatting
<small> </small>	Identifies text to be presented at about three points smaller than the default
<tt> </tt>	Presents teletype-style text, fixed width characters
<u> </u>	Identifies text to be underlined

The above commands change the look of text, thus providing contrast and, perhaps, repetition. A short example of each of the codes is shown in Figure 5.19. The special character codes allow use of characters that would otherwise be either unprintable or replaced with a local browser software version of the character. The commands for high-lighting text provide more ways to show emotion in ideas and to separate sub-header or other identifying information from details.

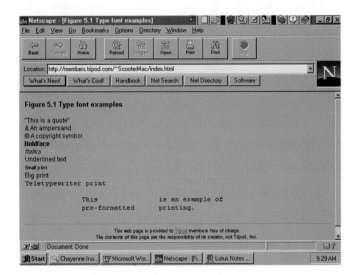

Figure 5.19

Examples of text codes.

These formatting commands, along with the commands you have already learned, allow you to improve your web pages by using repetition to tie the them together. The principle of repetition, recommends that information that is the same and that appears in more than one place should be formatted identically in every location, thus providing design consistency. Consistent design that includes judicious repetition simplifies user under-standing of your pages. If the user's interpretation is correct, he or she is more likely to make a good decision about whether or not to continue looking at your pages.

Repetition and the desirability for the user's mental model to match the author's mental model both apply to all of the design ideas we have discussed so far—contrast, align-ment, clarity, chunking, and proximity.

Other design elements should be present on every page—a disclaimer, date of last page update, contact name and contact information (see Figure 5.20). Disclaimers are standard to absolve you, your school or a company of legal liability in the event that hackers (or others) might change your pages.

This page was last updated on June 12, 1996. Any comments or errors should be reported to Sue Conger at SConger@mail.cox.smu.edu. Although we make every attempt to ensure the accuracy of these pages, we cannot be responsible for their content.

Figure 5.20

Disclaimer, date, and contact information

Much information on the web is date-sensitive, and must be maintained to remain useful. Web pages are only as useful as they are current. Pages should be reviewed monthly to determine which pages will be going out of date in the next four to six weeks. Then, a schedule for updates can be developed and followed. Contact information lends credibility to the page in that its contents are no longer anonymous. Contact information allows page users to ask questions, clarify date-related issues, or report bad information when it occurs. The contact information might be a work phone or an e-mail address. Remember, NEVER put a home phone number on the web!

The key criteria for good web pages are effectiveness and affectiveness. Effectiveness requires that the content of pages be accurate, complete and convey the message intended. Each of these characteristics contributes to the pages doing the job you intend them to do whether it is getting a job, selling services, or finding new friends. Affectiveness is an emotional reaction to pages. An affective presentation captures viewer attention by being interesting and by having the emotion evoked match the message. Affect is difficult to achieve because we are not always consciously aware of the emotions we want or how to design them. Affect frequently takes several iterations to define the real users and a design that appeals to them. Nevertheless, the design tenets of contrast, repetition, proximity, and alignment all can be used to add (or detract) from page affect. A successful set of web pages must satisfy both affective and effective criteria. Pages must be complete and accurate to meet the intended goal. They must also be visually appealing to so the audience will continue browsing the pages.

ASSIGNMENT: Revise your web page to insert the commands and a disclaimer as discussed in this Step. As appropriate, use bold face, italics, underlining, and so on to provide repetition of design elements. Review your pages and try to ensure completeness and accuracy and desired emotional tone.

Exercises

  REVIEW QUESTIONS

1. Define *output*.

2. Explain the difference between soft copy and hard copy, and give an example of each.

3. List the various types of display screens and the benefits of each.

4. Explain the importance of pixels and bit-mapping.

5. Explain the main difference between impact and nonimpact printers.

6. Contrast the printing methods used by ink-jet and laser printers.

7. Define *spooling* and describe how it can be useful in printing.

8. Define *buffer* and describe how it can be useful.

9. Identify two kinds of plotters and explain the differences between them.

10. Describe *voice output* and give examples of how voice output is used.

11. Give two examples of output devices used with presentations.

12. Define *computer output microfilm (COM)* and describe its main purpose.

FILL IN THE BLANKS

1. _____ is processed data, such as text, graphics, or sound, that can be used immediately or stored for later use.

2. Permanent printed output is called _____.

3. A _____ creates temporary visual output on monitors.

4. A tiny dot on a monitor screen that can be lit with different colors is a _____.

5. An _____ printer prints by striking an inked ribbon against paper.

6. A _____ printer prints characters in a manner similar to the way numbers appear on a football scoreboard.

7. A complete set of characters in a consistent and unique typeface, such as Helvetica, is called a _____.

8. The printers that use heat, electricity, or laser technology to print output are called _____ printers.

9. A printer that sprays tiny drops of ink onto paper to create letters, numbers, and symbols is a _____ printer.

10. A _____ is used with a computer and overhead projector to project screen images during a business or educational presentation.

MATCHING

Match each term with its description.

a. laser
b. font
c. dot-matrix
d. spooling program
e. soft copy
f. plotter
g. monochrome
h. hard copy

i. COM
j. impact
k. buffer
l. nonimpact
m. music synthesis
n. liquid crystal display
o. output
p. VGA

____ 1. Output from a computer monitor.

____ 2. Computer-generated text, graphics, or sound.

____ 3. Printers that produce output by physically striking a ribbon to deposit ink on a page.

____ 4. Fastest growing segment of the printer market.

____ 5. Output medium that is used most often on laptop computers.

____ 6. Output printed on paper.

____ 7. Printers that use heat, electricity, and laser technology.

____ 8. Complete set of unique characters.

____ 9. Output monitor that displays text and graphics in black and white.

____ 10. Printer that produces output similar to numbers on a scoreboard.

____ 11. Technology for permanently storing large amounts of information, such as magazines.

____ 12. Output device for printing graphics, used primarily in mapping and design work.

____ 13. Conversion of data into sounds.

____ 14. Memory for temporary storage inside a printer.

____ 15. Allows information to be stored on a magnetic medium until a printer is ready to print.

____ 16. Current standard for color monitor resolution.

 **ACTIVITIES**

1. Check the "Computers for Sale" classified ads in your local newspaper. Make a list of all the used output devices available for sale. Record the prices and features of each device. From this list pick the one output device that you think is the best buy. Explain your choice.

2. Visit your school's computer lab. Make a list of the available output devices and how they are used in the lab.

3. Visit your school's library and talk with the librarian. Find out if your school uses computer output microfilm (COM). If your school does use this technology, ask the librarian to demonstrate its use with microfilm or microfiche readers.

4. Obtain an advertisement for each of the following kinds of output devices and write a few paragraphs describing the characteristics, including price, of each: (a) ink-jet printer, (b) dot-matrix printer, (c) laser printer, and (d) plotter.

Skills for Living

RESEARCHING RELIGIONS

In 400 BC, in China, subjects viewed emperors as godlike spokespersons for their real God. An emperor would literally spend his entire life planning and preparing for his death. At the time of passing, his tomb was filled with articles and relics needed during his journey to heaven. If the journey was successful, the past emperor would look favorably on those left behind and spread wealth and good fortune among them.

Discovered in 1974, the tomb of the First Emperor of Qin, Qinshihuang, considered by many to be one of the most powerful people who ever lived, contained over 8,000 life-size statues of soldiers, horses, and chariots to guard the emperor from evil spirits on his journey to heaven. The funeral park was 22 miles square. Over 2,000,000 people worked 40 years on the tomb. When opened, 21 other coffins were found. They contained the remains of the emperor's wife and handmaidens, all strangled at his death in order to accompany him and serve him in the next life.

As seen above, religion affects our behavior, our politics, and our relations with each other. What do you believe? What about others—what do they believe? The ancient Romans thought that gods and goddesses controlled lightning, the sea, and even the winner of the ancient Olympic Games! Native Americans believe in Mother Earth and Father Sun, and that all of the Father's creations—trees, water, air, animals, and humans— were meant to live in balance and harmony. At the core of Hinduism is a belief in Brahman, the One that is the All, the absolute and ultimate principle which is the core of all living things. Still many other religions believe in various prophets who lived solely to spread the true word—depending on the religion, the prophet might be Joseph Smith, Mohammed, Jesus, Moses, or another.

How have all these different perceptions of a deity evolved? Perhaps the Internet can give us the answer.

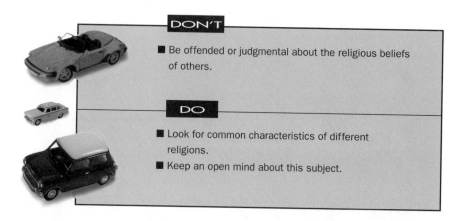

DON'T

■ Be offended or judgmental about the religious beliefs of others.

DO

■ Look for common characteristics of different religions.
■ Keep an open mind about this subject.

Student Activities

1. Assume you are taking a comparative religion class in college. One of the religions your professor lectured on in class caught your interest, so you have decided to do your term project on that religion. Locate one or two web sites on the religion to do research for this project. Some items to investigate include:

    a. When was the religion started and by whom?
    b. What are the basic beliefs and doctrines of this religion?
    c. How large a following does this religion have and in what countries?
    d. What do you find most unique about the religion and its beliefs?

2. Share your research process, findings, and Internet experience with others in the class. Was the Internet and the Web a good place to do your research? Why or why not?

CHAPTER 6

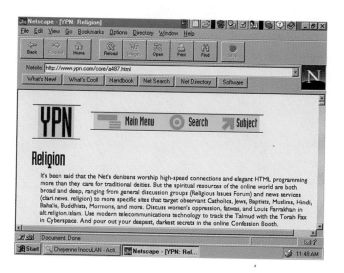

SECONDARY STORAGE

OBJECTIVES

AFTER STUDYING THIS CHAPTER, YOU SHOULD BE ABLE TO:
1. Understand and explain the need for secondary storage.
2. Explain the hierarchy of data and list its components.
3. Understand the differences among varying methods of file organization.
4. List the differences among hard disks, hard cards, and diskettes.
5. Explain how data are represented, read from, and written to magnetic tape.
6. List and describe different forms of magnetic tape.
7. State the advantages and disadvantages of using magnetic disks and magnetic tape.
8. Describe how a mass storage system operates.
9. List and describe the various types of optical disks and give examples of their uses.

CHAPTER OUTLINE

WHY USE SECONDARY STORAGE?

HIERARCHY OF DATA
Bits, Bytes, and Characters
Fields
Records
Files
Databases

DATA STORAGE AND RETRIEVAL
Sequential File Organization
Random File Organization
Indexed File Organization

MAGNETIC DISK STORAGE
Hard Disks for Large Systems
RAID
Hard Disks for Microcomputers
Hard Cards
Diskettes

MAGNETIC TAPE STORAGE
Representing Data
Reading and Writing Data
Blocking Records
System Backup

MASS STORAGE

OPTICAL DISK STORAGE
Laser Disks
CD-ROM
Jukeboxes
WORM
Erasable Optical Disks

SPECIAL-PURPOSE STORAGE DEVICES
Combined-Function Storage Device
Optical Memory Cards
Smart Cards

As you will see in this chapter, secondary storage technology has come a long way since the days of those huge magnetic tape drives you've seen in photographs of 1960s mainframes. Today's storage devices and media reflect the trend toward shrinking size and increasing power reflected in other computing components. The average diskette you use on your microcomputer can store around 1,440KB of data, and CD-ROMs, which resemble music CDs, can hold hundreds of times that amount, with much faster access times. These revolutionary changes in storage capacities and portability have helped fuel the boom in information storage and retrieval.

Consider the way consumers purchase products today. Some manufacturers and distributors are abandoning old-fashioned approaches to marketing goods, such as paper-based, direct-mail ads and catalogs, in favor of the use of electronic storage and retrieval media that allow potential customers to interact with images stored on that medium. Instead of passively turning pages in a paper catalog of goods—such as a brochure on the newest models of Chrysler's Jeep Eagle vehicles—today's consumers who own PCs can pop the car company's latest marketing disk into their home micro-computers and call up information as they want it. A typical marketing disk takes PC users on a "tour" of the product, complete with interior and exterior photographs, option packages, and pricing information. Jeep even offers a PC video game called PhotoQuest that puts potential buyers behind the wheel of Jeep Grand Cherokees to participate in a wildlife photo safari; the potential buyers "try out" the Jeep's features as they traverse the off-road terrain to win the game. Exciting marketing tools like this are just one example of secondary storage technology you'll read about in this chapter.

WHY USE SECONDARY STORAGE?

Recall that main memory provides only temporary storage of data. This memory holds data and instructions for current use by the processor and continually feeds these back and forth during processing. Also, main memory is both limited and volatile, which means that programs and data stored in main memory will disappear when the computer is turned off. Main memory is often called primary storage. When you want to permanently store programs, data, or information obtained from processing, you must use secondary storage. **Secondary storage** holds data and programs for future use in permanent nonvolatile storage areas. Processed data (information) can also be held in secondary storage. Other names for secondary storage are *external storage* and *auxiliary storage*. Secondary storage allows you to store unlimited programs and data, making it one of a computer user's most valuable assets. Try to imagine the thousands of filing cabinets needed to store all the military records held by the Department of Defense or to store all the employee records kept by Ford Motor Company. Secondary storage units make these types of paper-based filing systems obsolete. Five major advantages of secondary storage include:

- ■ **Convenience** Secondary storage allows you to locate and retrieve stored data, programs, and information easily and quickly.
- ■ **Economy** Storing data, programs, and information on a secondary storage medium is relatively inexpensive.
- ■ **Reliability** Data, programs, and information stored on a secondary storage medium are safe and protected.
- ■ **Capacity** When one secondary storage medium is filled with data, another can always be added, forming libraries of data and information with considerably less bulk than traditional systems of data and information storage.
- ■ **Portability** Secondary storage mediums may be transported to other sites for future processing.

There are a number of types of secondary storage from which users can choose, including magnetic disks, magnetic tape, and optical storage devices. After learning about the various secondary storage devices and media in this chapter, you will be more qualified to make your own secondary storage choices.

HIERARCHY OF DATA

The principles, operation, advantages, and disadvantages of secondary storage devices are discussed in terms of how data are organized within each particular device. Earlier you learned that data are raw, unprocessed facts and figures that are entered into a computer for processing. Data can represent small entities—so small that individual items have no meaning on their own. Consider the following data: brown eyes, red paint, 11/30/76, 15 steps, 1.5 miles, Maria Garcia, or safety belt. All of these are facts used to describe or represent reality. These representations of reality are called **data items,** or *data elements*.

By themselves, data items are meaningless. Usually, you must select, organize, or manipulate (process) data items in some way to give them meaning. How data items are related or organized so as to have meaning is called the **logical data structure**. How data items are stored and located by the computer for processing is called the **physical data structure**.

A common way to view data is from the smallest logical unit, called a *field*, to the largest logical unit, called a *database*. However, this is not the way data are stored by computers. Computers store data physically, rather than logically. The concept of data structures is depicted graphically in the data hierarchy shown in Figure 6.1 on page 182. Each level in the hierarchy is formed by combining elements of the preceding level.

Figure 6.1

In the hierarchy of data, each
level builds on the elements
of the preceding level.

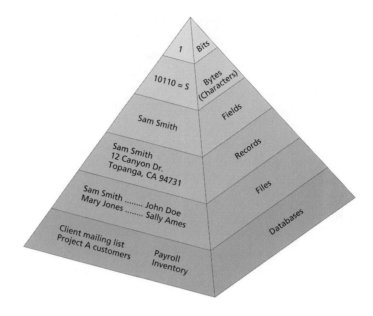

BITS, BYTES, AND CHARACTERS

You've already learned that a *bit* (0 or 1), shown at the top of the hierarchy, is the small-est unit of data a computer can store. You've also learned that a unique combination or sequence of bits, called a *byte*, represents a character, which is a letter of the alphabet, a number, or a symbol.

FIELDS

A **field** is a group of related characters (bytes). A field can consist of a combination of letters of the alphabet, the digits 0 to 9, and symbols such as *, @, $, +, or &. A field is the smallest amount of data that is meaningful to a computer user. For example, the letter *J* will probably not mean anything to you on its own. But when combined with other charac-ters to form the name John or the month January, it forms a logical unit. Some examples of fields are a name, a street address, a telephone number, or a catalog part number.

Each field must be of a certain **data type**, meaning that only certain kinds of data can be entered into them. For example, a field that contains a combination of alpha-betic characters and numbers is referred to as an **alphanumeric field**. A field that con-tains only numbers is a **numeric field**. The specific material in the field is called a **data item**. For instance, a street address is a field, but 1605 Elm Street is the data item. Fields are often given names, such as "Street," that identify the kind of data they include. Fields are given a fixed number of character positions, called **field length**. ZIP codes, for example, could have a field length of five or nine (or ten, if the hyphen is included). Fields that can vary drastically in the number of characters they contain, such as names, are given a field length to accommodate the longest data item.

RECORDS

A **record** is a group of related fields. A checking account record, for example, might include fields for the person's name, address, telephone number, account number, social security number, and checking account balance. A record is usually the smallest logical unit of data that you can retrieve from a file. For instance, if you wished to check your checking account balance, the bank teller would have to access your record from the bank's checking account file located in secondary storage to retrieve that field of information.

FILES

A **file** is a group of related records. A checking account file would contain a complete set of records including all customers that have an account with the financial institution. An address book is another example of a file, in which there is one record for each person. Your professor's class roster of students is another example. (The term "file" also refers to named areas on disk that contain programs, text, or graphics.)

DATABASES

A collection of related files is called a **database**. A retail firm might have a database that includes customer, employee, supplier, payroll, accounts payable, accounts receivable, and scheduling files. All of these data files comprise the firm's database.

Databases reduce the repetition of data. Data in a database system are often, but not always, stored in one location and shared by several individuals needing access to the data. For example, a retail firm's inventory balances can be stored in one location and used by employees in inventory control, accounting, purchasing, and sales-order entry. Any updating done to information in a file is immediately available to all who use the shared database.

DATA STORAGE AND RETRIEVAL

The relationship between logical and physical data structures is highly complex. For example, a physical record may consist of only a small portion of the logical record. In addition, many logical structures might be developed from a single physical structure. While the complexity of the relationship between logical and physical data structures is beyond the scope of this book, it is nevertheless important to recognize that while they are related, logical and physical data structures are different. *Logical data structures* are the way data items are related or organized to provide meaning. *Physical data structures* are the way data are stored and then accessed from storage.

Secondary storage devices employ various methods of accessing data. Magnetic tape can only access data in the order in which they are stored. This method is called **sequential access**. Consider music stored on cassette tapes. To hear the third song on the first side, you must first pass through the first two songs. Magnetic disks have sequential access capabilities. They also have the added benefit of random access capabilities. **Random access** means you can retrieve data in any order. Think of an audio CD. If you want to hear that third song, the CD player will skip over the first two songs and go directly to the third. But if you want to listen to the music in the order presented, the CD player will play the songs in sequence. Sequential and random access are tied to the following file organizations.

SEQUENTIAL FILE ORGANIZATION

In **sequential file organization**, also called *single-file organization*, each record is recorded and stored in ascending or descending order. Records are then accessed one after another (see Figure 6.2 on page 184). You can't jump from middle to beginning to end in this type of system. Sequential organization is ideal when you need to process all of the records in a file. For instance, it is a convenient system for processing payroll. It's also useful to banks and credit card companies that send out monthly statements to all of their accounts, even if the account balance is zero. Sequential organization is appropriate for any organization that updates large, ordered files on a regular basis.

Figure 6.2

In sequential file organization, you must pass through all records previous to the record you wish to access. This type of file organization is most efficient when processing all records in a file.

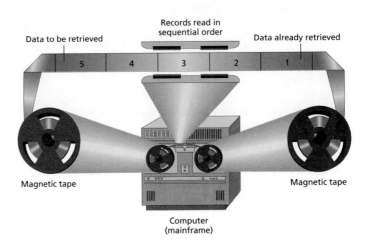

RANDOM FILE ORGANIZATION

Like the main memory in your computer system, **random file organization** relies on a system of addresses. Each file is recorded and stored to an address that can then be retrieved in any order (see Figure 6.3). This type of file organization is also referred to as *direct* or *relative*. It is best suited to organizations that need to access only a few records in no fixed pattern or sequence. For instance, car rental agencies place thousands of reservations each day. If they used a sequential file organization, they would not be able to respond very quickly to customers who wished to change their reservations. With direct file organization, they can quickly access individual records using the customer's last name. A **key field** is used to identify the record and determine where the record is stored on disk. In order to determine where to place a record on disk, the computer performs **hashing**, which is a mathematical operation, on the record's key field. Hashing uses a formula that almost always produces a unique number for the key field, which, in the case of car rental agencies, becomes the customer's confirmation number. Having a unique number is important in instances when you have key fields

Figure 6.3

Random file organization allows you to go directly to the record you wish to access.

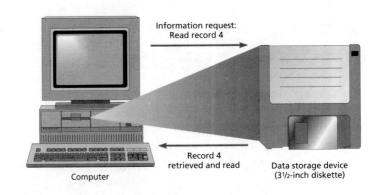

that contain identical information. For instance, if you have two customers named Harrison, you wouldn't want the second Harrison to override the first's record. Direct file organization is appropriate for organizations that update only a small portion of their records on an irregular basis.

INDEXED FILE ORGANIZATION

With **indexed file organization**, each file contains an index of the records stored within it (see Figure 6.4). This organization allows both sequential and random retrieval of files. Indexed file organizations are used most frequently with microcomputer storage systems. The method is very flexible. You can create more than one index for each file and access the file using different key fields. For instance, while it might prove beneficial for employee records to be stored sequentially for processing payroll, it becomes less efficient when you need to update information on a single employee. To get to that employee's record in sequential organization, you would first have to pass through all employee records preceding the one you desired. With indexed files, you could create two indexes. One, using the employee number, could be used for sequential processing of paychecks. The second, using social security numbers, could be used for random individual updates.

The drawback is that indexed file organizations are slower than direct access methods. They use up more storage space than the other file organizations, and their hardware and software requirements are expensive. They are also unavailable on tape systems. Indexed file organization is appropriate for organizations that process large batches of files on a regular basis but also need access to random files on occasion.

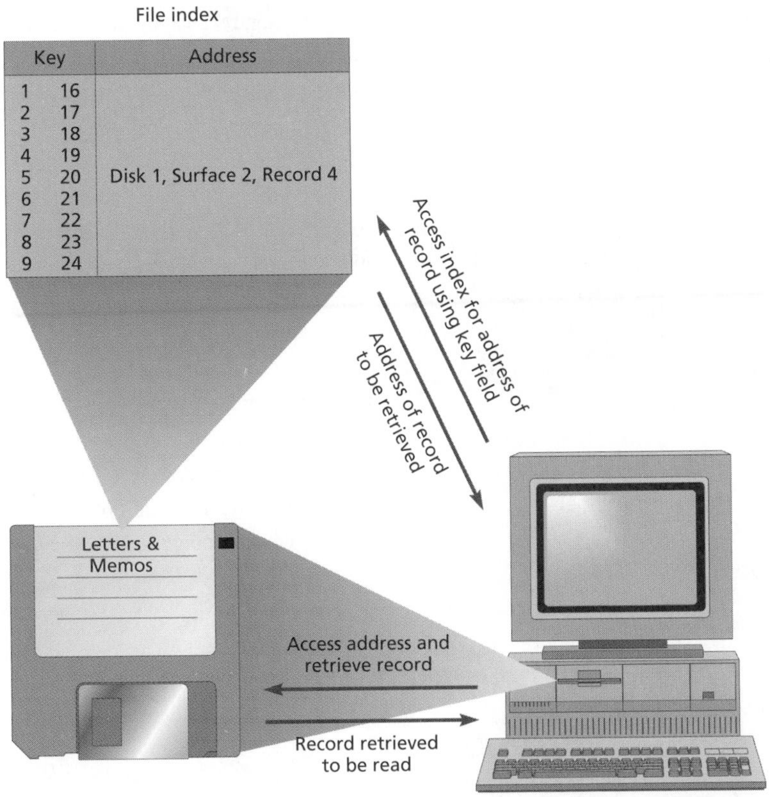

File index

Key	Address
1 16	
2 17	
3 18	
4 19	
5 20	Disk 1, Surface 2, Record 4
6 21	
7 22	
8 23	
9 24	

Access index for address of record using key field

Address of record to be retrieved

Letters & Memos

Access address and retrieve record

Record retrieved to be read

Figure 6.4

Indexed file organization is most often used with microcomputer systems. It allows both random (direct) and sequential access to records in a file.

MAGNETIC DISK STORAGE

Magnetic disks are the most common type of secondary storage technology for computer systems. Magnetic disks, which consist of platters made of rigid metal or flexible plastic coated with an easily magnetized substance, allow much faster storage and retrieval of data than magnetic tapes, discussed later in this chapter. Magnetic disks provide direct, pinpoint access to data. Recall that direct access means that a computer system can go directly to the location on a disk where data are stored and retrieve the data almost instantly. Because of this capability, magnetic disks are also called **direct access storage devices (DASDs)**. There are two main types of magnetic disks: hard disks and diskettes.

Hard disks are aluminum platters that are either *fixed*, meaning they are permanently installed in your computer system, or they are *interchangeable*, meaning they are loaded into your computer system as needed and stored off-line. Hard disks have large storage capacities, and they access data very quickly. There are many types of hard disks in use today in all kinds of computer systems.

Diskettes, also called *floppy disks* or simply *disks*, are an interchangeable storage medium made of a tough, flexible plastic called *mylar* and housed in a protective jacket. Their storage capacities are much lower than those of hard disks. They also store and retrieve data at comparatively slower rates. They are, however, convenient for the distribution and backup of small amounts of data, programs, and information.

HARD DISKS FOR LARGE SYSTEMS

Hard disks are aluminum platters. On super, mainframe, and minicomputer systems, the platters are typically 14 inches in diameter. They are mounted on a vertical shaft and housed in a container called a **disk pack**, as shown in Figure 6.5. A disk pack may contain from 2 to 22 or more platters that rotate on the shaft. A plastic covering protects the disks from dust and other contaminants. Disk packs come in both removable and nonremovable designs.

Removable disk packs are loaded into your computer system as needed and stored off-line. They are mounted on **disk units**, which are peripheral devices connected to the computer system. Since the top and bottom platters of interchangeable disk packs are somewhat exposed to dust particles, these layers are not used to store data. Though once very popular, interchangeable disk packs are now often replaced with nonremovable disk packs.

Nonremovable disk packs are permanently installed and sealed, making them much less vulnerable to contamination. All of their disk surfaces are available for the storage of data. And because they are permanently installed, data are always available to people who may be accessing the system from a remote location and are physically unable to exchange removable disk packs.

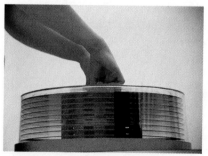

Figure 6.5

Hard disks in large computer systems are housed in disk packs to protect them from dust and other contaminants.

Courtesy of IBM Corporation.

Locating Data Each of the two sides of a hard disk contains tracks and sectors. **Tracks**, shown in Figure 6.6, are concentric circles around the circumference of the disk on which small magnetic fields are recorded. A **sector** is a pie-shaped section of a disk and is the smallest unit in which data can be stored. Each track on a disk has the same number of sectors.

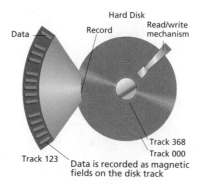

Hard Disk

Data — Record — Read/write mechanism

Track 368
Track 000
Track 123
Data is recorded as magnetic fields on the disk track

The number of tracks varies among disk manufacturers, but is typically several hundred. All tracks on a disk will have the same storage capacity even though tracks on the outer edge are much wider than those near the center. Making the capacity independent of the track or its position on the disk allows for a constant rate of data transfer.

Identifying Records In order to make it possible to directly place or find a specific record, a unique address is assigned to each record on a disk. There are several methods of creating record addresses on a disk. One method, called **cylinder addressing**, uses the same numbered tracks and sectors for recording and for finding data. A *cylinder*, shown in Figure 6.7, is a vertically aligned set of tracks on a disk pack. For example, an imaginary vertical line extending through the outermost track on all disk surfaces would comprise cylinder 1, the next track would comprise cylinder 2, and so on. In Figure 6.7,

Cylinder 146, Disk surface number 1 Record 5

Hard disk

Figure 6.7

With cylinder addressing, a combination of three locations is used to locate data.

cylinder 146 would include track number 146 on all disks in a disk pack. The cylinder address is a combination of three locations: the cylinder number, disk surface number, and record count. The three are somewhat like your address—city, street, and house number. For example, one record in a customer file might have the address 14615. This would mean the record is positioned at cylinder 146, disk surface 1, record count 5 (as shown in Figure 6.7).

The *surface number* identifies the surface within the cylinder where the record is located. Viewing a nonremovable disk pack from top to bottom, surface 1 would be the topmost recording surface in the pack; surface 2, the next recording surface; and so on. In our example, the particular customer record is located on recording surface 1. A combination of *cylinder number* and *surface number* identifies a particular track in a disk pack. The *record count* identifies the exact location of the record on the already-defined track in the disk pack. A record count of 1 would identify the first record on the track, as in our example. A record count of 5 would identify the fifth record on the track.

Another method, called **sector addressing**, divides each disk's recording surface into eight or more sectors, much like pieces cut in a pie, as shown in Figure 6.8. A disk

Figure 6.8

Sector addressing divides the disk surface into eight or more sectors. The point where the sector intersects the track marks data locations.

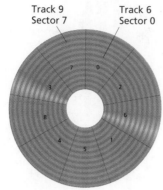

Track 9
Sector 7

Track 6
Sector 0

Figure 6.9

The access mechanism (shown close up on the right and as it is positioned within the system unit above) holds all of the read/write heads of a hard disk system. Although only one head can actively read or write data at a time, all heads move to the same track location.

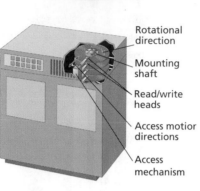

Rotational direction

Mounting shaft

Read/write heads

Access motion directions

Access mechanism

pack with 10 recording surfaces and 200 tracks with 8 sectors per track would have a total of 16,000 (10 X 200 X 8) sectors. Data locations are referenced at the point at which a sector intersects a track. The track number determines the location of the data.

Reading and Writing Data   Once attached to a computer system that's turned on, hard disks spin constantly at very high speeds. Although the actual speed can vary, it is commonly about 3,600 revolutions per minute. Data are written and read by a read/write head that "floats" on a cushion of air very close to each disk surface (within a few millionths of an inch). Each head is assigned to a specific disk surface, as shown in Figure 6.9. Read/write heads are attached to a device called an *access mechanism*. The access mechanism moves the heads together, in and out between the disks, at the same time and speed. Even when reading and writing data, the heads never touch the surface of the disk. The tiniest particles, for instance a smoke particle, a fingerprint, or a human hair, cannot fit between the read/write mechanism and the disk (see Figure 6.10). If present, they can cause damage to the surface of the disk. Such damage is called a **head crash** and usually means that some or all of the data on the disk will be lost.

Figure 6.10

The read/write head is so close to the surface of the disk that if it comes in contact with the smallest of particles, you can expect disk damage.

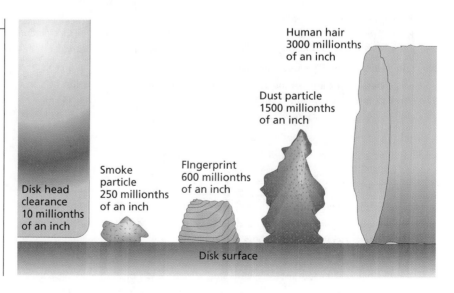

Human hair 3000 millionths of an inch

Dust particle 1500 millionths of an inch

Smoke particle 250 millionths of an inch

FIngerprint 600 millionths of an inch

Disk head clearance 10 millionths of an inch

Disk surface

Disk Access Time The time it takes between entering a request for data and receiving the data is called the **disk access time**. The time is dependent on three factors: seek time, rotational delay time, and transmission time. The procedure for reading data is as follows:

1. The read/write head moves to the desired track or cylinder. The time this takes is the *seek time*. This movement takes up the most of the total disk access time. Some hard disk drives contain mechanical access arms for both the inside and outside tracks. This reduces the average seek time significantly.

2. The mounting shafts, which are in constant movement, rotate the disks so that the heads are aligned over the position on the track where the data are stored. The time it takes to complete the alignment is the *rotational delay time*. On average, it takes 8 milliseconds for a hard disk spinning at average speed and 75 milliseconds for a diskette.

3. The data are read from disk and transferred to the computer. This is the *transmission time*. The transmission time is negligible compared to the total disk access time.

RAID

Large companies whose employees need to access millions of records are turning to **redundant arrays of inexpensive disks (RAIDs)** to manage their files. RAIDs replace the traditional 14-inch disk packs with multiple 5¼-inch hard disks that work together as a unit. The systems take up less space and cost less than disk packs. The smaller disks spin more quickly and steadily, speeding up access times. Access time is also greatly improved when the disks are configured to work in parallel, reading or writing data simultaneously. RAID systems may be used by organizations that require fast access to data and the ability to store updated data quickly. For example, an insurance company maintains millions of insurance records within its computer storage system. Using a RAID system for storage, records can be quickly retrieved, updated, and stored again.

HARD DISKS FOR MICROCOMPUTERS

In recent years, fixed hard disks have become very popular among microcomputer users. Hard disks for microcomputers are less commonly known as **Winchester disks**. The Winchester name comes from the old 30-30 Winchester rifle that had two barrels tiered so that one barrel was housed above the other. Similarly, early hard disks had two 30MB platters. Winchester disks are usually permanently installed in the system unit as fixed disks. There are, however, interchangeable Winchester disks that are inserted and removed in a manner similar to that of putting a cassette tape into a VCR.

HARD CARDS

Some microcomputer users find there's never enough room to store all of their data permanently. These users often prefer to store every program they acquire on a hard disk instead of on diskettes. In such cases, even a 1024MB hard disk can be filled rather quickly. Another option is a hard card.

Hard cards are add-in circuit boards that fit in a slot inside your computer. They work the same way as other hard disks. When adding a hard card to a microcomputer system, users are essentially adding a second hard disk without removing or replacing the hard disk already there. Hard cards are expensive, but they are ideal for people with limited space left in their system unit.

COMPUTER CURRENTS

When Paperless Is More

For over a decade now, researchers have talked confidently about the advent of a "paperless" office—one in which all records would be created and stored not in a filing cabinet but in a computer. Yet look around any office, and you'll see piles of paper. While some of this "paper trail" is the result of user fears about not having "hard copy," storage space on computers is also an issue, especially given the vast storage requirements of some software and virtually all graphics files.

New technologies now becoming available offer the prospect of far greater secondary storage in the future.

■ **Flash memory cards** Looking much like the traditional computer memory chip they are based on, these chips offer as much storage as some hard disk drives (currently 20 megabytes, with higher capacity "flash cards" due soon). But because they include no working parts, they are far less subject to damage than are hard disk drives. In addition, they consume 95 percent less power than hard disk drives and can read data far faster.

■ **Floptical disks** These disks pack more information onto a conventional-

sized disk by placing the disk "tracks" (concentric rings in which information is stored) closer together. Using special super-floppy drives, these devices can store 20.9 megabytes on a 3½-inch diskette, as opposed to the 1.44 megabytes stored on a standard 3½-inch diskette.

Courtesy of 3M Data Storage Division.

■ **Glass disks** While the idea of using glass instead of the typical aluminum platter has been around for some time, the fragility of glass kept such disks off the market until recently. However, Japanese engineers have now developed a chemical-hardening technique to overcome fears that a glass-based system might "crash" all too literally. Because of its extreme smoothness, computer read/write heads can "fly" closer to the surface of glass disks and cram more data into the same space—at least three times more than conventional disks in the case of the first glass units, and some analysts expect glass disks with 200MB capacity to arrive on the market shortly.

■ **Glass-ceramic disks** Another approach to strengthening glass disks, these devices have a core of MemCor, a substance developed by Corning that blends glass with ceramic implants, which is then coated with three layers: a base coat, a magnetic film, and a protective coating. In addition to providing greater strength than glass alone, MemCor allows for production of disks only 25mm thick (vs. 40mm for conventional aluminum disks), a serious consideration in producing disks for smaller and smaller computers. And because MemCor doesn't have to be textured or chemically strengthened as glass disks do, its cost is the same or only slightly higher than for conventional disks.

■ **"Wet" hard drives** These drives use liquid instead of air to cushion the drive head from the hard disk. Because a thin layer of liquid provides the same protection as a thicker layer of air, a "wet" drive head can get closer to a hard disk than can a "dry" one, which reduces the amount of space needed to read, write, and store the same amount of material. In addition, wet insulation makes such drives particularly resistant to damage. But whether wet or dry, floptical or glass, one thing's certain—they all hold a lot more in less space than that file cabinet.

DISKETTES

Most microcomputers now contain one internal hard disk and either one or two interchangeable disk drives. A **disk drive** is the device that contains the read/write head that stores and retrieves data from hard disks and diskettes. Diskettes are available in two popular sizes, measured in diameters: 3½ inches and 5¼ inches. Figure 6.11

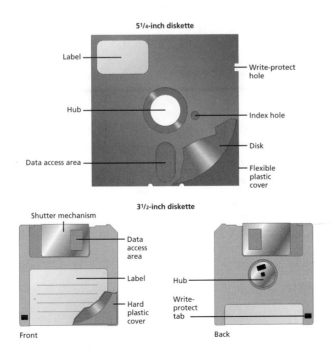

5¼-inch diskette

Label
Write-protect hole
Hub
Index hole
Data access area
Disk
Flexible plastic cover

3½-inch diskette

Shutter mechanism
Data access area
Label
Hard plastic cover
Front

Hub
Write-protect tab
Back

Figure 6.11

The data access area on 3½-inch diskettes is better protected from particles and dust than the constantly exposed area on 5¼-inch diskettes.

shows all the individual parts of the two diskettes. Because of their rigidity and greater capacity, 3½-inch diskettes are now most common. Inside the 3½-inch diskette case is a thin, circular mylar wafer, sandwiched between two sheets of cleaning tissue. This wafer spins and exposes its recording surfaces to the disk drive's read/write mechanisms. Diskettes are quite sensitive and should be treated carefully to avoid damaging the disk. Damaging a disk can alter or destroy the data it contains. Some "do and do nots" are identified in Figure 6.12.

Figure 6.12

Though 5¼-inch diskettes are more vulnerable, you should use extreme care when handling 3½-inch diskettes as well.

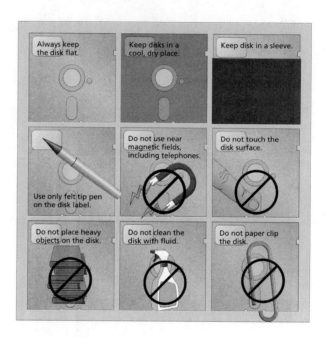

Preparing the Diskette for Use Before data can be stored on a diskette, the diskette must be prepared for use. Diskettes are *soft-sectored*, which means the size and number of sectors on the disk are determined by the microcomputer and software you are using; the number of sectors on the disk is not predetermined. The procedure for preparing a diskette for use and determining the number of sectors it will contain is called **formatting** the diskette. When a diskette is formatted on your microcomputer, a mapping pattern is inscribed on its surface that divides it into sectors, similar to the sectoring of hard disks as illustrated in Figure 6.8. As programs or data are stored on a diskette, the computer automatically maintains a file directory on the diskette to keep track of the contents of each sector. This directory shows the name of each file stored on the diskette, its size, and the sector in which the file begins.

Storage Capacity Although early diskettes contained only one side specially treated to store data, most in use today have two usable sides, as do hard disks. And like hard disks, the two sides contain tracks on which data are stored as a combination of tiny magnetic fields, or *bits,* which are either magnetized to represent a 1 or not magnetized to represent a 0. The amount of data that can be stored on a diskette depends on the number of tracks it has. For instance, most 3½-inch diskettes have 80 tracks, a few older types have only 40. The number of tracks is measured in *tracks per inch*. The storage capacity of a single diskette track is measured in *bits per inch*. Different types of diskettes vary in the number of bits they store per inch. Though high-density and double-density diskettes have the same number of tracks per inch, the capacity of the high-density diskette is twice that of the double-density diskette.

Density refers to how close together bits of data are packed on the diskette. Storage capacities that are common to 5¼-inch diskettes are 360KB (double density) and 1.2MB (high density). For 3½-inch diskettes, common capacities are 720KB (double density) and 1.44MB (high density). In recent years, manufacturers have introduced new diskettes with a storage capacity of 2.88MB. A 360KB diskette can store approximately 100 single-spaced typewritten pages of text. A 2.88MB diskette can store approximately 800 pages of typewritten text. Research to develop diskettes with even higher capacities is under way.

Reading and Writing Data A diskette is placed in the system-unit disk drive, which contains the read/write mechanisms necessary to store and retrieve data from a diskette (see Figure 6.13). When the user issues a command for data to be written to or read from the diskette, the diskette rotates as small electromagnetic read/write heads inside the drive perform the read/write task as instructed. Hard disks rotate constantly. With diskettes, the surface only rotates when data are read or written. This makes their performance much slower than that of hard drives. Another difference is that the read/write heads contained in hard disks never touch the disk surface while the read/write heads of disk drives do physically touch diskettes.

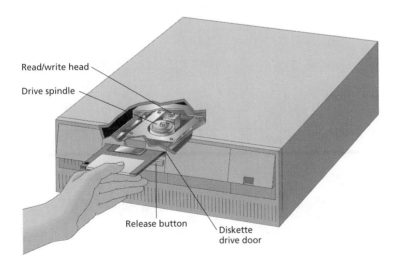

Read/write head

Drive spindle

Release button

Diskette drive door

Figure 6.13

Diskettes are placed in the system unit disk drive which contains the read/write mechanisms for storing and retrieving data.

A user can prevent writing to a diskette accidentally. The protective jacket of a 5¼-inch diskette contains a small notch on one side. By placing a small gummed label over the notch, data contained on the diskette cannot be altered. Newer 3½-inch diskettes contain a small shutter near one corner. Opening the shutter so that an opening appears through the diskette prevents the accidental alteration of the stored data. Closing the shutter allows data to be written to the diskette.

A special type of floppy disk drive from Iomega Corporation is the **Bernoulli disk drive**, also called **Bernoulli Box**. The Bernoulli Box, named after the Swedish scientist who discovered the principle of aerodynamic lift, is faster and has greater storage capacity than traditional floppy drives. As with the disk platters in hard disks, Bernoulli disks float between the read/write heads, so there is no actual contact between the disk and the heads. Like a floppy disk, a Bernoulli disk is flexible and removable. Because the disk is flexible, it is less susceptible than a hard disk to head crashes. Bernoulli disk drives, however, are not as fast as hard disk drives.

MAGNETIC TAPE STORAGE

Magnetic tape was developed to replace the earlier, bulky, expensive method of storing data on punched cards. It comes in either detachable reels or cartridges and is made of mylar coated with a magnetizable substance such as iron oxide. Magnetic tape made the task of sequential processing faster and more convenient. Though still used for this function in all types of computer systems, magnetic tape has been replaced in many instances with the more flexible direct access technology of magnetic disks. Today, magnetic tape is often used as a backup for magnetic disk files. A **backup** is a copy of data made and stored in a safe location to ensure that data are preserved in case the original data are damaged or destroyed.

   Detachable reel tapes, which look similar to the tape used on reel-to-reel audio tape systems, as shown in Figure 6.14, are typically ½-inch wide with lengths ranging

Figure 6.14

Magnetic tape is fed through the tape drive and wound onto the take-up reel.

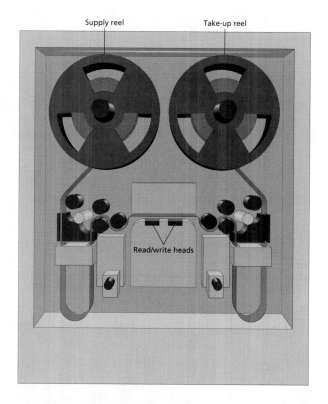

Supply reel   Take-up reel

Read/write heads

from 200 to 3,600 feet. The most common length is 2,400 feet with a reel diameter of 10½ inches and a weight of about 4 pounds. Detachable reel tapes use two reels: the *supply reel* and the *take-up reel*.

Magnetic tapes can hold up to 200 megabytes of data. Detachable tape reels are used with large computer systems, such as those found on many college and university campuses, and those used by many large businesses. A reel of tape may contain an organization's payroll file consisting of payroll data for all employees. After the tape reel has been installed onto a tape drive, the file is loaded from the tape drive into the computer along with the payroll program. Under control of the payroll program, all employee records are updated and checks are printed.

Cartridge tapes are smaller versions of the reels and are stored in plastic cases. Cartridge tapes are typically ¼-inch wide and 600 feet long, and they can hold several hundred megabytes of data along 24 to 32 tracks, depending on the tape drive (see Figure 6.15). The self-contained, ¼-inch cartridge tapes are often used for backup on microcomputer systems.

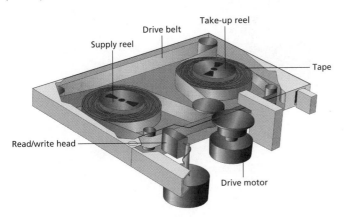

Special ½-inch cartridge tapes are made for backing up mainframe computers. These contain 18 tracks, twice as many tracks as detachable reels. They can store 200MB of data on 600 feet of tape. Their shell contains only the supply reel. As shown in Figure 6.16, the take-up reel and an automatic threading mechanism are built into the tape drive.

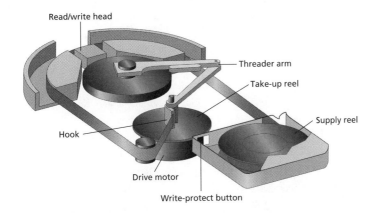

Figure 6.16

A jointed arm attaches to the hook at the beginning of ½-inch cartridge tape and loads the tape onto the take-up reel inside the drive.

REPRESENTING DATA

As shown in Figure 6.17, magnetic tape consists of tracks that extend along the length of the tape. The common coding method used for supercomputers and mainframe computers is EBCDIC. Microcomputers use ASCII. There are two types of tape formats. In *nine-track* formats, 1 byte (character) of data is recorded vertically across the tape (1 bit on each track) plus the error-detecting parity bit. In *serpentine* formats, the bits are recorded horizontally along anywhere from 18 to 32 tracks. Serpentine formats are used for backing up data. In Figure 6.17, only the magnetized bits are visible. However, a nonmagnetized bit is present in each of the seemingly vacant positions.

Figure 6.17

Bits are encoded either vertically across the track or in a serpentine manner along the track.

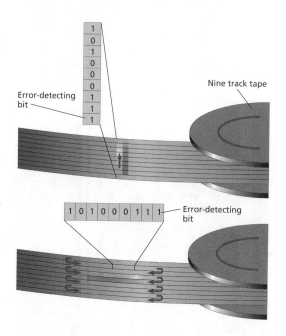

READING AND WRITING DATA

Read/write mechanisms inside tape drives, such as those shown in Figures 6.15, 6.16, and 6.17, are used for recording data on or retrieving data from magnetic tape. Read/write mechanisms include electromagnetic read/write heads that read the magnetic fields on the tape and convert them into electronic impulses. Read/write heads also write data on the tape by creating patterns of magnetic fields. The tapes contain beginning-of-tape markers, identification labels, and start-of-data markers. When tapes are loaded, they are first identified by the computer. If the identification number of the tape does not match that indicated by the data entry personnel, no new data will be stored on the tape. Another precaution taken to protect detachable reel tapes from accidental erasure is the inclusion of a plastic ring that must be inserted onto the reel. Tapes cannot be written to if the ring is missing.

BLOCKING RECORDS

If you've ever been driving along and had to slam on your brakes quickly, you know the car slides a few feet before stopping. The same is true for magnetic tape; it does not stop instantly. It is necessary to leave some space between records in order to stop the tape at the proper place. A blank space, as small as ⅕-inch, separates two records, and is called an **interrecord gap (IRG)**. You probably would not want to separate all records by IRGs because doing so would waste space on the tape and take extra processing time. Instead, you can group similar records together using a process called **blocking**. Blocking means placing logical records into one physical record, or block, which is separated from other blocks by an **interblock gap (IBG)**.

A *logical record* contains complete information about one person or thing, such as a customer or product. For example, a customer file containing information on 200 customers would have 200 individual, yet similar records. This block of 200 logical records would comprise one *physical record*. One IBG would be placed before and another following this physical record to separate it from another physical record. A block of 200 logical records is extremely large. It is often more useful to block records in smaller groups, such as three, four, or five. The number of blocked records is called the **blocking factor**. The blocking factor often depends on the amount of internal memory available and the size of the logical records. IRGs and IBGs are illustrated in Figure 6.18.

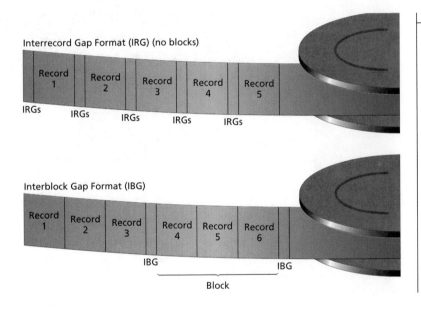

Figure 6.18

Interrecord gaps and interblock gaps are the blank spaces left on tapes to compensate for the time it takes to slow down and speed up when reading and writing data.

SYSTEM BACKUP

Experts agree that many businesses cannot survive for more than seven days if their computer systems fail. How long would a bank survive if account holders could not deposit or withdraw their funds? Yet, every individual and organization is exposed to the trauma and danger of system failure due to fires, earthquakes, floods, sabotage, human error, or equipment failure. How do individuals and organizations ensure that they can survive these calamities and recover in time? How well-prepared would you be if your computer were destroyed in a fire, your hard disk crashed, or important diskettes were stolen?

Magnetic tape backup is often the key to successful recovery. Whether the system is a mainframe or a microcomputer, backup tape systems are used to copy critical programs and databases, and store them in more than one location. After a system failure, they can then be reloaded on new equipment. Think of these systems as insurance against lost programs and data. Few people really appreciate the importance of this process until they experience such a disaster firsthand.

Copying the entire contents of a 1 gigabyte hard drive would require approximately 700 backup diskettes. Imagine the time and effort (and possibility of error) required for this task. Fortunately there is a better way. Special magnetic tape backup systems are available for all types of computers. These systems are fast, relatively inexpensive, and the high density storage tapes are compact. Figure 6.19 shows a typical tape backup system used with personal computers. Once the initial backup is completed, subsequent backup procedures copy only

Pete Saloutos/Tony Stone Images.

Courtesy of Living Books.

For generations of children, bedtime stories have represented not just one more way to stay up "a few minutes more," but a chance to enter a magical world where all things are possible. Before computers, the traditional bedtime story took place at parents' or grandparents' knees as the older generations read aloud from classics such as *The Tale of Peter Rabbit, Alice's Adventures in Wonderland,* or one of Dr. Seuss's lyrical books. Drawings in these volumes were an important component of the story, so children often curled up in the reader's lap to get a good look at the pictures as the story was read.

Today, CD-ROM disks display interactive "books." Not only can the computer read and patiently reread certain passages, they even allow children to point to parts of the screen and "ask" what the pictures mean. For example, in *Just Grandma and Me,* the CD-ROM "reads" the story in English, Spanish, or Japanese, with appropriate words on screen and contains a "Let Me Play" option. Choose it, use the mouse to click on some part of the picture, and hidden surprises appear. Though they can't replace the love and physical presence of caring adults, CD-ROM storybooks can introduce even preschoolers to the joy of reading, while providing hours of entertainment.

programs and data files modified since the last backup. These tapes are often stored in different locations to guard against loss or destruction. Should a disaster occur, the new computer is simply loaded with the contents of these backup tapes and processing can continue.

Courtesy of Iomega Corporation.

MASS STORAGE

Some very large organizations, such as federal agencies and insurance companies, store vast amounts of data. In response to this need, some manufacturers build special-purpose secondary storage systems capable of storing huge quantities of data. A **mass storage system (MSS)** is capable of storing up to 500 billion characters. This storage system is 500 times larger than a typical 1,000MB hard drive on a personal computer.

MSSs combine the low cost of magnetic tape with the direct-access capabilities of magnetic disks. The MSS consists of a set of magnetic high-density tape cartridges, each of which can be retrieved by a mechanical arm in a few seconds. Each cartridge is slightly less than four inches wide and two inches in diameter. Inside each cartridge is a reel of tape almost 800 feet long and 3.87 inches wide. Approximately 50 million characters can be stored on each reel of tape.

When data need to be stored or retrieved, a computer-controlled device retrieves the cartridge and brings it to a reading/recording device where the tape is loaded. After the tape is loaded, the data are copied onto a magnetic disk, providing the computer with direct access to the data.

OPTICAL DISK STORAGE

One of the newest forms of high-density storage is **optical disk storage**, of which there are several different types, including laser disks and CD-ROM. Optical disk storage takes advantage of laser technology that allows the etching and reading of marks on platters. The technology offers several advantages over magnetic tape and magnetic disks, including:

- Greater data density
- Less expense, bit for bit
- Extreme durability
- No "head crashing"

LASER DISKS

First developed by RCA for showing home movies, **laser disks** (also called *video disks*) have since evolved into an effective means of storing data for computer use. They vary in size from 5 to 14 inches in diameter and have a huge storage capacity—the larger ones can store over 7 gigabytes (7 billion bytes). Hundreds of these disks can be stored in automated disk libraries for mass storage capabilities. They are durable, lasting for decades, compared to the few years of use you can get out of magnetic media before they begin to wear out. Laser disks are also easy to handle.

Data are written to and read from laser disks as follows. A shiny coating of aluminum protects the light-sensitive surface beneath. To write to the photosensitive substance, a laser emits a narrow beam of light, one millionth of a meter in diameter (a *micrometer*). The light creates a long, narrow spiral of depressions called **pits,** which are separated by flat intervals called **lands** (see Figure 6.20). The pits and lands are microscopic, and they wind around the platter in a trail about 20 miles long. To read the stored data, a less intensive laser scans the platter. When the beam hits a pit, the scattered light that reaches the reflective lens in the disk drive passes through a *photodetector,* which produces an electrical signal that is converted into a color video signal. Laser disks are an analog medium.

Figure 6.20

A microscopic view of the surface of laser disks reveals regularly spaced parallel ridges. The pits are so small that you would have to line up 3,000 of them to equal a centimeter.

Disk surface

Laser disk

CD-ROM

Compact disk read-only memory (CD-ROM) is a digital medium. CD-ROMs use laser technology to read and write digital information. Text, images, and video are converted into their digital equivalents (strings of bits) and encoded on disks that are similar to audio CD disks. The pits on CD-ROMs equal 1, and the lands equal 0. With capacities of 550MB, CD-ROMs are capable of holding hundreds of times more information than magnetic diskettes. To give you an idea of optical disk capacity, one CD-ROM can store the entire *Encyclopaedia Britannica* (approximately 460 million characters) with room to spare.

CD-ROMs are used for entertainment applications like Microsoft's Golf game.

Courtesy of Microsoft Corporation.

Early versions of CD-ROMs used a variety of methods for indexing and retrieving information. This limited the medium's potential use. A standard, known as the *High Sierra format*, was developed to provide a uniform method of encoding CD-ROMs and to broaden the medium's applications. Now, CD-ROMs are effective teaching tools and are finding applications in multimedia.

JUKEBOXES

CD-ROMs are similar to audio CDs in another way. You are probably familiar with multidisk player/changers that can accommodate several audio CD-ROMS and allow a user to switch back and forth among several CD-ROM disks. Multidisk player/changers are now used with computers for storing and retrieving vast amounts of data. Large bodies of work that require the storage capacity of multiple CD-ROM disks are now stored on these multidisk player/recorders, sometimes called **jukeboxes**. A desired CD-ROM disk is loaded to the CD-ROM disk drive under a control program. Information is accessed to a monitor by pushing the appropriate buttons. For instance, the Library of Congress, which holds over 88 million items in print, has turned to jukebox storage for a number of its works. Works which are known for the nontext images on their pages are scanned, and the bitmapped information is encoded on disk. When possible, however, text is entered rather than scanned, saving space. Both methods work to preserve delicate materials and to give readers easy access to the information they seek.

FOCUS

Jukebox, Play Me Some Data

ODS Health Plans, Inc. (ODS) is a provider of medical and dental health insurance. The company currently has over 4,000 physicians in its network of providers. In 1995, the company processed well over one million claims, and annual revenues exceeded $200 million. The insurance industry, much like banking, the stock market, and real estate, is a paper-intensive industry. In the insurance industry, 4 percent of the clients incur 50 percent of the health care costs. Cost management and case management are critical for these special cases. Insurance claims typically produce a paper file containing from 1 to 100 pages of support forms and exhibits. In addition, by law, the industry is required to maintain past claim records for seven years. Imagine the space it would take to store these files. Optical disk storage comes to the rescue!

Courtesy of IBM Corporation.

Reprinted with permission from Eastman Kodak Company.

ODS is a national leader in the insurance industry in the application of optical storage technology to claims processing and is often a test site for new IBM storage systems. Currently paper claims are created by the insurance adjuster or the medical provider (doctor, dentist, hospital, etc.). The paperwork is then sent to ODS headquarters. ODS immediately scans these documents at 1,000 pages per hour, using a high-speed Kodak 900 scanner. The scanned forms are now computer processible. The computer can read individual fields of data on the claim form, such as the client's name, claim number, social security number, dollar amounts, etc. Each claim is then electronically transferred to a personal ODS claim representative who oversees the claim to its completion.

Once the claim is settled, the contents of the claim file are routed to a mass storage device called a *jukebox* for permanent storage on optical disks. This IBM 3995 jukebox has five direct-access optical-disk cartridge drives and an additional 144 on-line cartridges available for user access and storage. Each cartridge stores approximately 2GB of data on a permanently-enclosed 5-inch-diameter platter. The entire system can store 288GB—the equivalent of two million image pages. As older claims fill a jukebox cartridge, the cartridge is copied and removed. Using a dual backup system, one copy is stored on site for easy access, and a second copy is stored at an off-site location. Should information from a five-year-old claim be needed, the appropriate cartridge is simply retrieved from local storage, mounted in the jukebox, read, and processed. Photo copied images from an optical storage device are considered legal copies and meet the industry requirement for the seven-year storage life.

The company is currently developing a paperless, personal computer-based hardware and software system installed in a doctor's, dentist's, or hospital administrator's office for electronically preparing claim forms. This process is called *electronic data interchange* or EDI. At the end of the day, these claims are electronically downloaded (over phone lines) to an ODS computer and then entered into the normal processing system. According to Raymond Lee, an ODS systems administrator, "This is a giant step forward in creating a paperless claims processing system for us."

WORM

One type of optical storage that allows data to be written on a disk once, but read as many times as the user wishes, is called a **write once, read many (WORM)** disk. WORM disks are made of plastic or glass covered by a thin layer of metal that a laser beam can mark. The laser burns a hole, changes the metal's color, or raises a bubble to the surface of the metal. This permanent alteration is then read by a beam with less power. Once written, data cannot be erased or changed. This is beneficial for companies that need a permanent record of all past transactions.

ERASABLE OPTICAL DISKS

Several optical disk manufacturers have announced a new type of optical disk, called **erasable optical disks**, which allow users to store and change data. These disks are covered with a material that, when heated to a certain temperature, will change from a crystalline state to a duller, amorphous state, allowing information to be stored. When later heated to a slightly lower temperature, the material returns to its original state.

SPECIAL-PURPOSE STORAGE DEVICES

Beyond the standard secondary storage mediums discussed so far in this chapter, there are some interesting new applications where specialized storage mediums have been developed. Some of these combine normal storage functions. Others focus on specialized security or identification applications.

COMBINED-FUNCTION STORAGE DEVICE

One good example of a **combined-function storage device** combines CD-ROM capabilities with those of erasable optical disks in a system using an optical cartridge. With 650MB of storage, it acts like a CD player, but also reads and writes like a hard drive. Because the CD-ROMs are removable, the system can also be used as a backup device for hard drive programs and data. The unit is installed in a standard CD-ROM bay in a personal computer.

OPTICAL MEMORY CARDS

Optical memory cards, about the size of a standard credit card, are used to store an individual's medical history, prescriptions,

Courtesy of Panasonic Computer Peripheral Company.

CD-ROMs can play music like a CD player and, because they are removable, can also be used as a backup device for hard drive programs and data.

Courtesy of Drexler Technology Corporation.

Optical memory cards are the size of a credit card. They are ideal for healthcare systems; medical imaging; document storage; ID cards; secure off-line banking; access systems; and other business, consumer, and government applications.

driving records, educational background, finger prints, and even credit history. These cards are impervious to magnetic or electrostatic fields. The card is non-volatile, updatable, and readable through a special device attached to a personal computer. During an emergency or when requested, this card is read for the appropriate information and the necessary actions are taken. Almost 2,000 (6.6MB) pages of text, numeric data, and images can be stored on a single card.

Smart cards are an access key and are sold as a subscription to the Global System for Mobile Communications, a European mobile phone network.

Courtesy of GEMPLUS Card International.

SMART CARDS

Smart cards are credit-card-sized plastic forms that actually contain an embedded microprocessor chip filled with specialized information about the owner and the owner's property. These cards can be used like a key to start a car or open a door to a home. They can be used as a bank debit card initialized with a certain amount of credit and used to purchase items. Employees can use the card as a timecard at work, to check in and out and record their hours worked, or to gain access to high security facilities. Store owners can track shoppers' purchases and buying habits and even send them personalized birthday or anniversary cards.

Key Terms

alphanumeric field	interrecord gap (IRG)
backup	jukeboxes
Bernoulli Box	key field
blocking	lands
blocking factor	laser disks
combined-function storage device	logical data structure
compact disk read-only memory (CD-ROM)	magnetic disks
cylinder addressing	magnetic tape
data item	magnetic tape backup
data type	mass storage system (MSS)
database	numeric field
density	optical disk storage
detachable reel tapes	optical memory card
direct access storage devices (DASDs)	physical data structure
disk access time	pits
disk drive	random access
diskettes	random file organization
disk pack	read/write mechanisms
disk units	record
erasable optical disks	redundant arrays of inexpensive disks (RAID)

field	secondary storage
field length	sector
file	sector addressing
formatting	sequential access
hard cards	sequential file organization
hard disks	smart card
hashing	tracks
head crash	Winchester disks
indexed file organization	write once, read many (WORM)
interblock gap (IBG)	

Summary

Primary storage holds data, programs, and information for current use. **Secondary storage**, also called *external storage* and *auxiliary storage,* refers to devices and media that are used to store programs, data, and information for future use.

In the hierarchy of data, each level builds upon the previous level. Bits are combined to form characters which make up **fields**. Fields are grouped into **records** which are organized together as **files**. Related files form a **database**.

Sequential file organization allows for the processing of records one after another. **Random access file organization** allows you to process records in any order. **Indexed file organization**, used mostly with microcomputer systems, allows for either sequential or random processing.

Magnetic disks, the most common type of secondary storage are **direct-access storage devices (DASDs)** that store data on their flat, easily magnetized surface. **Hard disks** are rigid platters that are either fixed or interchangeable. **Hard cards** are hard disks attached to add-in boards.

Diskettes are small magnetic disks housed in plastic jackets convenient for storing software and small amounts of data or information.

Magnetic tape is used for sequential processing. **Detachable reel tapes** are used with large computer systems.

Mass storage systems (MSS) store data on compact magnetic reels that are converted to magnetic disk when needed.

Optical disk storage provides greater data density, durability, and reliability than magnetic storage systems, at less cost. **Laser disks**, an analog medium, and **CD-ROMs**, a digital medium, have storage capacities in excess of 550MB. **Jukeboxes** store multiple sets of CD-ROMs for quick access. **WORM** disks allow you to write to the disk once and read the data multiple times. **Erasable optical disks** allow you both to read and write to the same disk multiple times.

Some **special-purpose secondary storage devices** combine normal storage functions, while others focus on specialized security or identification applications. One **combined-function storage device** combines CD-ROM capabilities with those of erasable optical disks. **Optical memory cards** store an individual's personal history. These cards are non-volatile, updatable, and readable. **Smart cards** are credit-card-sized plastic cards that contain an embedded microprocessor chip filled with specialized information about the owner and the owner's property.

14 Easy steps to being a webmaster

STEP 6   LOADING TO THE WEB

In this step, we discuss two design issues and then load the pages to the Web. The design issues are to analyze what is not there and to reassess page decisions and page linkages. The ability to define links to pages all over the world is a feature unique to the Web. The purpose of analyzing what is not there in your pages is to add such links. Adding links should enhance the effectiveness of your pages without you having to maintain the pages. This step requires "new media" thinking in that you cannot think about traditional, paper-bound references to define these links. The idea is to provide information about the topic that is of interest to page users. For instance, you might link to the home pages of every company you have worked for. If you have a hobby that relates to dog training, you might add a link to pages for dog trainers, the New York Dog Show, or other dog-related pages. Links to other pages should be limited to those that are interesting, helpful, and related to your page. Too many links are confusing; too few may deprive users of information they would otherwise want and limit the use of your pages.

Several ideas relate to links and navigation between pages. First, the links from each page to other pages should provide clear threads of continuity that mirror the information hierarchy constructed in Step 1. Second, there is an optimal number of return linkages for each page, usually between two and five, to provide backward jumps. Last, many pages try to leave the navigation between pages to the user, providing links to every page from every other page. This reduces the clarity of threads, and confuses rather then helps page users.

Next, do an overall assessment of your pages to review consistency of information and links on each page. First, analyze your pages to determine that all information on each page relates to a single topic. Redesign the pages as needed to ensure their singleness of purpose. Reassess your pages for the use of contrast, alignment, repetition, and proximity. Then, analyze your links. There should be a clear thread of links that ties all of the pages for each audience and message together. Threads may be in hot text buttons used to select jump addresses. Each thread should be able to be followed easily from top to bottom of your information hierarchy, and without any sidestepping to pages not directly related. If you find that you cannot clearly identify the linkages from one page to the next, or that some sidestepping is done, redefine the page links as needed to fix the problem. In addition to not having clear links, many pages have too many links and you should also check for this problem. Knowing the right number and right links relies on a clear definition of the user and intended page uses. Some authors suggest a road map for complex page applications so users know how they got where they are (see Figure 6.21).

Finally, you are ready to load a page to the Web. To perform this step, we use a program called *file transfer protocol*, or ftp. The ftp program can be purchased and goes by different names, such as Fetch. Most commercial on-line services provide ftp software. Since each program

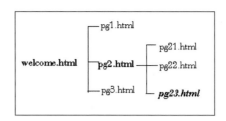

Figure 6.21

is a bit different, we discuss the steps to using ftp, but leave the details of your specific environment to your professor. The first step in using ftp requires the web site address at your location. For example, the web address for Netscape is www.netscape.com. You may also need access authorization from your school and a directory for your pages. Your professor will guide you in obtaining this information. Information objects on the Internet share a common addressing scheme (see Figure 6.22). The http stands for *hypertext transfer protocol*, and is the standard naming convention for all Internet services that expect all nodes to recognize the filenames. Files not using the standard http names are not recognized and not readily accessible via the Internet.

Figure 6.22

http//www.location.orgtype/x/y/z/page.html
An example is
http//www.cox.smu.edu/faculty/mis/conger.html

Where http//	identifies the item as a WWW object
	www.location.orgtype
or	
ftp.location.orgtype	identifies the web server address
	identifies the ftp site address
/x/y/z/	identifies one or more subdirectories for information storage on the web server
page.html	identifies the hypertext markup language (html) object page name

Make sure that you follow the conventions of your institution for moving pages up to the Web. Also, make sure that the names you expect your pages to have, that is, the names used in any links, are the names you give the pages moved up to the Web. All ftp programs require the following steps.

1. Identify the ftp address of the computer you want to enter.
2. Identify yourself to the computer.
3. Go to the directory you wish to access.
4. Transfer the desired file(s), giving them a name on the target computer.

This name must match any linkages referring to the page.

ASSIGNMENT: Reassess your pages adding links that enhance their effect. Upload your pages to the Web using ftp.

Exercises

REVIEW QUESTIONS

1. Explain the purpose of secondary storage.
2. List and explain the elements in the hierarchy of data.
3. What are the file organizations used by secondary storage devices.
4. Explain the differences among hard disks, hard cards, diskettes, and optical disks.
5. Explain how a diskette is prepared for use.
6. Explain how data are represented on magnetic tape.
7. What are the advantages and disadvantages of magnetic tape and magnetic disks?
8. How do mass storage systems operate?
9. What is a CD-ROM, and how might this technology be useful to an organization?

FILL IN THE BLANKS

1. A compact, self-contained roll of magnetic tape for microcomputers is called a _____.
2. A _____ is a removable disk made of mylar.
3. The hierarchy of data consists of the following levels of elements, each building upon the previous level: _____, _____, _____, _____, _____, _____.
4. Winchester disk systems are commonly referred to as _____ disks.
5. _____ means that a computer system can go directly to the location on a disk where data are stored and retrieve the data almost instantly.
6. The process of preparing a diskette for use is called _____.
7. An _____ system is a high-density storage system that uses laser technology to read data from and write data to a disk.
8. A file organization method in which records in a data file, such as an employee file or a customer file, are stored one after another is called a _____.
9. A _____ system uses multiple 5¼-inch hard disks in place of traditional 14-inch disk packs.
10. An _____ file organization is capable of retrieving files sequentially and randomly.

MATCHING

Match each term with its description.

a. jukebox
b. disk packs
c. density
d. IRG
e. field

f. magnetic disk
g. pits
h. DASD
i. platter
j. auxiliary

___ 1. Narrow spiral of depressions that store data on optical disks.

___ 2. Another name for secondary storage.

___ 3. Flat, rigid disk made from metal, such as aluminum substrate.

___ 4. How close together bits of data are packed on a diskette or other storage medium.

___ 5. Most common type of secondary storage in use today.

___ 6. Containers in which hard disks for large computer systems are stored.

___ 7. Device that stores volumes of data on multiple CD-ROMs.

___ 8.   Smallest logical unit in the hierarchy of data.

___ 9. Space between individual records on tape.

___ 10. Provides a user with direct access to stored records.

 ACTIVITIES

1. Write a report on manufacturers who are developing new and different secondary storage technologies.

2. Locate an article on secondary storage devices that can store data as microscopic living molecules. Write a report on how this technology works.

3. With a classmate, contrast laser disk and CD-ROM technologies. Find out what educational programs are available for each platform. Which technology is best suited for your studies?

Skills for Living

BUYING A TRUCK

Buying a home and buying an automobile will be perhaps the two biggest purchases you make during your lifetime. It is important that you spend some quality time investigating these two decisions. In this practice exercise, we focus on buying a truck. How can the Web help? This should be a fun exercise.

The Web is filled with auto-related resources. They include auto dealer home pages, accessory shops, new and used car (and truck) ads, auto rating services, opinions of current owners, and shopping manuals. When browsing the Internet for "new pickup purchase," we encountered literally thousands of sources related to this subject. A serious shopper should begin the data collection process on the Web. Then, armed with this background, move to the local newspaper ads, then to the dealer's showroom or fleet manager to negotiate the specifics of the deal.

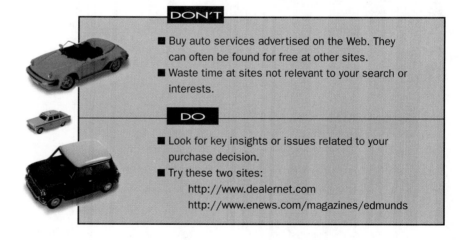

DON'T
- Buy auto services advertised on the Web. They can often be found for free at other sites.
- Waste time at sites not relevant to your search or interests.

DO
- Look for key insights or issues related to your purchase decision.
- Try these two sites:
  http://www.dealernet.com
  http://www.enews.com/magazines/edmunds

Student Activity

1. Assume you are considering buying a new small pickup. You have up to $19,500 to spend. You are considering a Chevrolet S-10, a Dodge Dakota, a Ford Ranger, and a Nissan XE. Use the Internet to help you do your analysis. Try to find information about price, consumer group ratings, safety features, insurance rates, resale value, gasoline mileage, standard features and accessories, and factory warranty for each model. Put your data in a table format and try to rate or rank each of your four alternatives. Which one would you pick and why?

CHAPTER 7

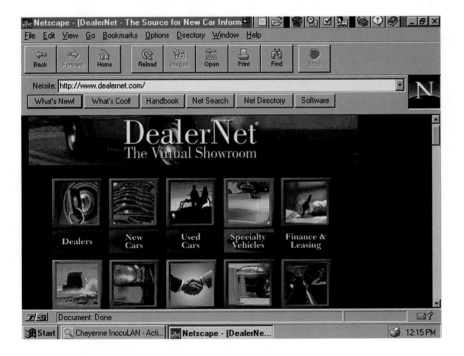

TELECOMMUNICATIONS AND THE INTERNET

OBJECTIVES

AFTER STUDYING THIS CHAPTER, YOU SHOULD BE ABLE TO:
1. Explain the concept of telecommunications.
2. List communications media and explain the differences among them.
3. Explain the differences between digital and analog transmission of data.
4. Explain modulation and demodulation.
5. Describe synchronous and asynchronous methods of transmission.
6. Contrast the differences among simplex, half-duplex, and full-duplex transmission.
7. List three grades of communications channels.
8. Define and give an example of a wide area network.
9. Define and give examples of local area networks.
10. List hardware and software tools designed to improve telecommunications links.
11. List several telecommunications applications.
12. Explain what the Internet is.
13. Gain access to the Internet.
14. Communicate with others using the Internet.

CHAPTER OUTLINE

TYPES OF MEDIA
Twisted Pair Cable
Coaxial Cable
Microwave Systems
Satellite Systems
Fiber Optic Cable

CHARACTERISTICS OF TRANSMISSION
Analog vs. Digital Transmission
Serial and Parallel Transmission
Asynchronous vs. Synchronous Transmission
Direction of Transmission
Speed of Transmission

NETWORKS
Wide Area Networks
Local Area Networks
Network Topologies
Gateways and Bridges

TELECOMMUNICATIONS PROTOCOLS

TELECOMMUNICATIONS IN USE
Voice Mail
Electronic Mail
Electronic Bulletin Boards
Teleconferencing
Fax Machines
Information Services
Telecommuting

THE INTERNET
What Is the Internet?
History of the Internet
Services Available on the Internet
Connecting to the Internet
The Internet Address
Searching and Browsing the Internet
The World Wide Web (WWW)
Surfing the Internet

magine coming home to a house with computers that control your physical comfort, the preparation of your food, and your evening's entertainment. Sound like a dream of the future? Yes and no. If you are like most Americans, your home already features several computers—even if you don't own a PC and have never touched a computer keyboard. The microwave oven in your kitchen and the VCR in your family room both rely on computer devices. Many thermostats and stereos also contain computerized controls.

If you're one of the millions of American households that owns a PC, the options available to you already read like the science fiction of 50 years ago. In addition to playing games and balancing the family checkbook with a PC, many households belong to one or more "on-line" interactive services that provide them with everything from advice to watchbands. America Online, the nation's largest on-line service and other large services such as CompuServe, and GEnie, let users:

- Make hotel, car, concert, and airline reservations
- Leave and read messages from others on electronic "bulletin boards" that address a variety of topics
- Place orders for goods from companies such as Sears and Spiegel
- Check on weather reports, stock market conditions, and sports scores
- Play games with other users

In addition, there are hundreds of specific bulletin boards and on-line services. For example, Dow Jones News/Retrieval Service is designed for those users who want to follow financial markets.

What lies ahead? Changes in virtually every aspect of daily life. Manufacturers of many home appliances, ranging from refrigerators to irons, from lamps to toasters, are working to improve their products with the help of tiny "computers on a chip." But the big news in home computing advances in the near future may well be the development of multimedia information and entertainment systems. Although these systems are still in development stages, major computer companies hold high hopes for these devices, not only in terms of their capabilities, but also in terms of projected sales.

Constructing such systems will be a complex task, however, in part because of the ambitious plans being proposed. If current developers are right, the home multimedia system of the future will be able to:

- Access over 500 television stations
- Enable viewers to select from tens of thousands of movies and past television episodes at any time
- Understand handwritten and verbal commands from users and reproduce human speech
- Offer interactive fiction in which the user can become part of the story and affect the outcome
- Allow game players, would-be athletes, and shoppers to enter into virtual realities. Users would not merely browse through on-screen catalogs or move icons around a screen, but would don garments and helmets that project images of a ball field, a game board, or a store, and allow users to hit that baseball, elude that dragon, or try on that jacket before they order

Achieving even a small portion of these lofty goals presents major obstacles of all kinds. Technological complications abound. At present, only the most sophisticated mainframes and supercomputers are capable of even rudimentary voice synthesis and recognition. Transmitting the flood of information these systems are to provide may mean that homes will need to be wired with cables capable of sending gigabytes every second. The software to run these systems will need to be so user friendly that users virtually won't be aware of it. (Given the number of adults in the United States who say they cannot program their VCRs, this task in itself is a major undertaking.) After years of fruitless argument over standards that would smooth out communications among types of existing computerized equipment in business, manufacturers will need to develop some standards for hooking together far more elaborate and numerous home devices.

Perhaps most important of all, the makers of these new systems will need to overcome consumers' resistance to change. Americans who currently own computers (and might otherwise be considered the most likely to desire exciting new technologies) have a lot of money and time invested in their existing machines. It will take a great deal to persuade them to jettison their hardware and software to make the hefty investment that multimedia systems will initially require.

In this chapter, you'll learn more about these and other developments in telecommunications.

Data communications is the process of transmitting data from one location to another, such as from one computer to another computer. A **data communications system** is a computer system that allows data to be transmitted and received over data communications media or communications channels, such as a telephone line. The combined use of computer systems and *communications channels* for sending and receiving data is called **telecommunications**.

TYPES OF MEDIA

A variety of communications media are now used to move data from one location to another. Telephone lines *(twisted pair cable)* and *coaxial cable* transmit data through electrical charges or pulses. *Microwaves* and *satellites* send data by way of electromagnetic waves. More recently, *fiber optic cable* and laser transmission allow data to travel as light pulses at the speed of light (approximately 186,000 miles per second). Your choice of communications media affects not only the speed of transmissions, but also the amount of noise (electrical interference) that will exist. For instance, data traveling across fiber optic cables does not have the electrical interference problems associated with media such as traditional telephone wire.

TWISTED PAIR CABLE

One of the older communications channels consists of insulated wires twisted together to form a cable called **twisted pair cable** (see Figure 7.1). These are often bundled in packs of thousands, placed underground, and branched to buildings and individual rooms where they await use in phone jacks. Besides telephone use, twisted pairs are often used to connect computers in networks and transmit data over relatively short distances. This technology is inexpensive, but susceptible to noise. To ensure intelligible transmissions, cable lines are refreshed (the signal is strengthened) every couple of miles at repeater stations.

Figure 7.1

Twisted pair cable.

Courtesy of AMP International.

Courtesy of National Wire and Cable Corporation.

COAXIAL CABLE

First introduced by the cable television industry to provide clear video transmission, coaxial cable gained popularity for other forms of data transmission due to its speed and lack of noise. **Coaxial cable** is a copper wire surrounded by a thick band of insulation, wire mesh, and rubber or plastic, as shown in Figure 7.2. It is more expensive than twisted pair cable, but it has a higher capacity: 100 million bits per second (bps), and can span longer distances than twisted pair cable before it needs refreshing. Telephone companies use coaxial cable for undersea phone lines as well as for replacing twisted pair cables underground. It is also popular for connecting computer systems located in the same office building.

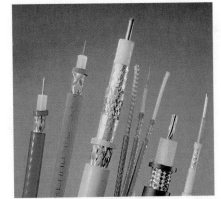

Figure 7.2

Coaxial cable.

Courtesy of Huber & Suhner, Inc.

MICROWAVE SYSTEMS

A **microwave system** transmits data through the atmosphere in the form of high-frequency signals similar to radio waves. Data is transmitted between microwave towers, as shown in Figure 7.3. Since signals do not bend, towers must be in line of sight of one another. (This means there must be no visible obstructions between the sending microwave station and the receiving microwave station.) The distance between the towers is dictated by the terrain in the surrounding areas, but is rarely more than 30 miles. At further distances, noise is picked up because of the moisture in the air and in the earth's surface. Microwave towers are often placed on top of mountains or tall buildings to ensure unobstructed transmission routes. Each microwave tower along the route picks up the signal, amplifies it, and relays the amplified signal to the next tower.

Figure 7.3

Because microwave signals do not bend, relay stations maintain line-of-sight links.

One limitation of microwave systems is the set number of frequencies through which data can be sent. Trying to send multiple communications over the same frequency causes scrambling. Since the data transferred over microwaves is limited to a range of frequencies, when this range becomes saturated, other mediums of transmission must be used.

SATELLITE SYSTEMS

Communications satellites are positioned 22,300 miles above the equator. They orbit the earth at exactly the same speed as the earth's rotation, making them seem to stay in the same place in the sky when viewed from the ground. This is called a *geosynchronous orbit*. A **satellite** is a solar-powered electronic device that contains a number of small, specialized radios called *transponders* that receive signals from transmission

FOCUS

The World at Your Fingertips

Nowhere in the world of networking have designers had higher hopes—or more troubles—than in constructing computer communications systems for our increasingly global economy. Rosy projections of networks linking everything from the world's financial markets to medical researchers are bumping up against some tough problems.

Many of the problems are technical. In particular, global networks suffer from the sheer physical difficulties of linking computers tens of thousands of miles apart. Paving what some have dubbed the *information superhighway* takes more than gravel and tar, or even elaborately engineered steel girders and cables. In part, this problem is the result of the vastly different types of "traffic" that attempt to navigate this superhighway: a mishmash of machines operating with different systems, at different speeds, and carrying different types of data.

The superhighway itself is really a series of vastly different "road" types. Within a single company location, communication between computers may be hard-wired, with physical cables literally linking each computer in a building. Radio waves may carry data from building to building within towns. Cellular technologies enable a driver in San Francisco to talk with a coworker in Atlanta with no more effort than placing a traditional telephone call. Conventional telephone lines and cable wires carry part of the ever-increasing volume of computer data within and between some nations. Fiber optic cables and broadband integrated services digital networks (ISDNs) offer the prospect of extremely rapid data transmission over long distances in the years to come. And, at least in theory, even the most remote regions of the world could be reached by satellite transmissions today.

Within a global network, the complexities of communication are, in part, those of any corporate network. Problems increase, however, because of differing standards and equipment common to various nations and the plethora of languages spoken by system users. While some systems offer at least basic translations, many industry observers believe the greater breakthrough may be the development of *e-forms*—simple forms that would be immediately recognizable by all computers in a network that need to do so. If, as projected, the answers to these forms are limited to a very narrow range, even a user's PC could be equipped to translate the form—and its responses—into various languages.

Finally, global networks must contend with differing political and economic constraints in the many nations of the world. Some observers worry that the rapid growth of information and communications technology may widen the gap between rich and poor nations. They

Courtesy of Samsung Electronics Company.

point out that the costs of constructing such networks are extremely high. (In 1990, U.S. investment in computer technology and the people to operate it were roughly equal to 10 percent of the gross national product: about $500 billion.) Yet without such investment in the so-called information infrastructure, a nation's economy is at a severe competitive disadvantage, unable to take advantage of the cost savings of better management, more efficient mechanized production, and tightly controlled inventories and inventory costs.

Nevertheless, some analysts believe that global networks will ultimately be the salvation of poorer nations. In eastern Europe, today's modest investment in telecommunications will lay the foundation for greater prosperity in these nations as they struggle to master capitalism in the years ahead. In desperately poor nations, the growing abilities of laptop computer users to access major databases and expert systems mean that, for example, global networks can supply poor farmers in remote regions of Africa with information on how best to farm in arid conditions. Such networks can also improve the distribu-

tion of food and medical supplies in poor nations. Highly educated citizens of third-world nations need not leave their native lands in order to earn respectable salaries, either by creating software for the global system or by using that system to better operate companies within their own lands. Either way, a poor country benefits, both in tax revenues on the individual's higher income and in terms of retaining well-educated citizens to serve as role models.

It may well be that critics of global networks are simply expecting too much too soon. Some observers have taken the analogy of an information superhighway and extended it to predict that just as every nation first developed its own roads—and its own unique approach to what kinds of roads to run and where—so nations will develop unique information roads that have uncommon advantages and disadvantages. Hooking these data routes together will be no easier than linking the world's physical roads. But in the end, we will all benefit from traveling over these different roads and gaining a variety of insights along our journey.

Figure 7.4

Satellites receive microwave signals, amplify the signals, and send them back to the earth's surface. Three satellites, properly positioned, can send signals over the entire earth's surface.

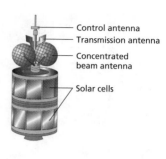

Control antenna
Transmission antenna
Concentrated beam antenna
Solar cells

stations on the ground called *earth stations*. The satellite amplifies the signals and transmits them to the appropriate locations (see Figure 7.4). One of the benefits of satellite systems is the small number of satellites and repeater stations needed to transmit data over long distances. In fact, three satellites properly positioned can provide access to the entire earth's surface.

Satellites transmit billions of bits per second, making them appropriate for transmitting large amounts of data. Because of the time it takes to send and receive data across such long distances, satellites are more appropriate for one-way communications (such as television and radio applications) than for interactive applications (such as telephone conversations or computer conferencing) where transmission delay times are quite noticeable. Some problems that are encountered with satellite technologies include:

- Noise interference due to weather conditions and solar activity
- Weakened signals due to the distance signals must travel
- Lack of privacy across open, easily accessed air waves

Satellites only last seven to ten years in orbit. The cost involved in building a satellite, sending it into orbit, maintaining it, and replacing it can be enormous. This has led to the formation of companies that supply the technology for a fee to those who wish to make use of it, but not incur the total cost. Such economies of scale make the technology affordable to a greater number of businesses. Several satellites are now orbiting the earth to handle domestic and international data, video, and voice communications. For instance, banks use satellites daily to transmit thousands of customer transactions to other banks. A bank in Los Angeles can transfer money from a customer's account at that bank to the customer's account at another bank in Rome, Italy, within a few seconds by using satellite transmission.

FIBER OPTIC CABLE

Fiber optic cable and lasers represent two emerging technologies that permit the transfer of data with the following benefits:

- High volume
- Speed
- Low error rate
- High security
- Long life

Courtesy of NYNEX.

Courtesy of Bellcore.

Figure 7.5

Splicing a .250 micrometer fiber is a precise and complex process. Any problems along the way can sabotage the movement of light through the fiber.

With fiber optic cable, data is converted to light pulses and transmitted by laser through tiny threads of insulated glass or plastic. Each thread, about 1/2,000 inch in diameter, is capable of carrying thousands of telephone conversations (see Figure 7.5). Billions of bits of data are transferred per second, as with satellites, but without the time delay. The speed of transmittal is about 10,000 times faster than with copper wire. There is no electrical noise interference, which allows data to reach its destination with far fewer errors. Fiber optic cable also offers a relatively high degree of safety: It is difficult to tap into a beam of light, and taps are more easily detected. Fiber optic cable may prove to be more cost-effective than other types of transmission media due to its very long life.

The communications channels or media described above are used throughout the world by individuals, businesses, and organizations. When data is to be sent over long distances, several different media are often used together, as shown in Figure 7.6. Large companies with branch offices throughout the United States, for example, often use combinations of channels to send data between locations. The same holds true for companies with offices in foreign countries.

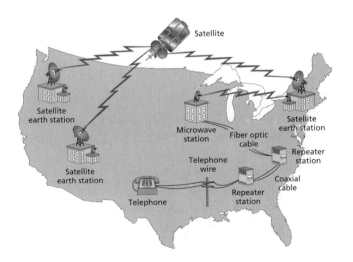

Figure 7.6

Several media channels work together to transmit data across long distances.

CHARACTERISTICS OF TRANSMISSION

Now that you are familiar with the types of media used for communications, it is time to examine how data is actually transmitted. Following are discussions of the characteristics that govern data transmission.

ANALOG VS. DIGITAL TRANSMISSION

There are two types of signals for transmitting data: analog and digital. With **analog transmission**, the signals form a continuous wave pattern, as demonstrated by human speech. The pattern stays within a frequency range and is repeated over time. Original communications media, such as telegraph and telephone lines, were designed to accommodate analog transmissions. Most computers, you'll recall, are digital machines. They process information by way of two distinct states represented by 0 and 1 bits. **Digital transmission** involves the sending of digital signals through the communications media.

Digital signals are distinctly different from analog signals, as illustrated in Figure 7.7. The emergence of computers in the communications arena brought with it the need to accommodate digital signals and the development of *modems.*

Figure 7.7

Digital signals represent two distinct states: "on" or "off." Analog signals form continuous waves.

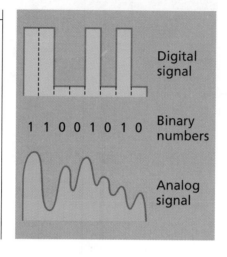

Parity Bits Occasionally, errors occur during transmission of digital signals. Interference on the line caused by electrical disturbances or mishandling of equipment, for example, might change a 0 to a 1 in one of the bytes. In order to detect such errors, a ninth bit, called a **parity bit**, is added to the end of every byte. Computer manufacturers design either odd-parity or even-parity systems. If your computer has an odd-parity system, the bit added to the end of a byte will cause the number of 1s in the byte to add up to an odd number. For instance, the letter *D* is converted to the binary string 01000100 in ASCII-8. If your computer has an odd-parity system, a 1 is added as the parity bit, making the total number of 1s equal to 3. If, when the byte is transferred, the CPU finds an even number of 1s, it will send you an error message. The CPU will not, however, be able to tell you the exact location of the error.

When errors are detected in the transmission of data, the receiving computer will request that the sending computer repeat the transmission of the byte that had the error. This happens in the background and at very high speeds, so users are usually not even aware that errors have been detected and corrected.

Modems Since a computer's digital signals are unable to travel across traditional analog telephone wires, the signals are converted to analog signals *(modulated),* sent

Figure 7.8

Modems convert digital signals into their analog equivalents for transmission across telephone lines, and then convert the analog signals back to their original digital format for processing.

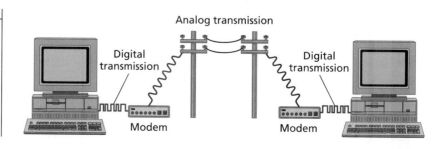

across telephone lines, and then reconverted to their original digital state
(demodulated). The device that performs
the necessary conversions is called a
modem *(modulate/demodulate)*. As shown
in Figure 7.8, both sending and receiving
computers must contain modems in
order to transmit data successfully.

The three main types of modems are
internal, external, and cellular, and all
types perform the same functions (see
Figure 7.9). An internal modem is contained on a circuit board which is inserted
into a slot inside a computer. An external
modem is a self-contained device, outside of the computer, that plugs into a
computer the same way you would plug in
a keyboard. Recently, cellular modems
which do not require wires are finding
popularity with laptop and notebook computer users. Cell stations resembling tall,
metal telephone poles pick up signals
from cellular modems in their vicinity and
pass along the communications through
regular telephone lines.

Figure 7.9

Internal modem.

Courtesy of Diamond Multimedia Systems, Inc.

External modem.

Courtesy of Diamond Multimedia Systems, Inc.

Cellular modem.

Gerard Yunker/Slight and TELUS Corporation.

Modem Transmission Speeds An
important factor to consider in choosing
a modem is the speed at which it can send data. This speed, called the **baud rate**,
refers to the number of times per second the signal being transmitted changes. With
each change, one or more bits can be transmitted. Each signal state can represent
multiple bits. Modems can transmit data at rates ranging from 300 to 38,400 bits
per second (bps). When a large amount of data is to be transmitted, a higher baud
rate may be preferred.

ISDN Although traditional communications channels are analog, digital channels
are also available that do not require a modem. Some telephone companies
now offer customers ISDN service. **Integrated services digital network (ISDN)** is a
technology that makes it possible for users to transmit information in digital form along
traditional copper-based telephone lines. ISDN is a set of international standards for
using software to control the transmission of data, voice, and video simultaneously
sent as digital signals over twisted-pair telephone lines. Twisted-pair lines traditionally
are used for analog transmissions. These networks carry several types of data including
voice messages, computer data, graphics, and video along the same channel. Sending
data along digital rather than analog lines greatly enhances the speed of communications. Most recently, large companies are looking to develop ISDNs that make use of
fiber optics for even faster, more secure communications.

SERIAL AND PARALLEL TRANSMISSION

In general, there are two methods by which digital signals and, hence, data and instructions can be transmitted to a computer: serial transmission and parallel transmission. These methods are also used to transmit digital signals within and between computer systems. In **serial transmission**, the bits that make up each byte are transmitted one after another over a single wire. In parallel transmission, each byte travels over a separate wire and arrives with the same byte. Figure 7.10 illustrates the movement of bits in both serial and parallel transmission.

Although faster than serial transmission, parallel transmission is usually a less attractive alternative over longer distances because the cost of running the additional wiring that is required is usually too expensive. Serial transmission is how most data is sent over telephone wires.

Figure 7.10

In serial transmission, bits are sent one at a time. In parallel transmission, all of the bits in a byte are moved together.

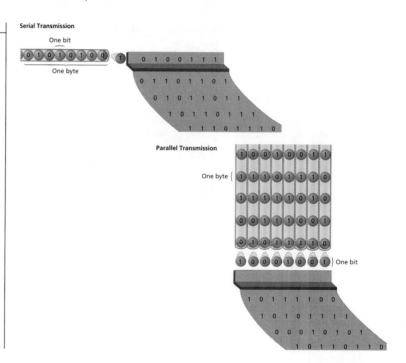

ASYNCHRONOUS VS. SYNCHRONOUS TRANSMISSION

Since the bits in serial transmission are sent out one at a time, transmission schemes have been developed to alert the receiving device as to where one character ends and the next begins. These schemes are called asynchronous and synchronous transmission. They are contrasted in Figure 7.11.

Figure 7.11

Asynchronous and synchronous transmissions.

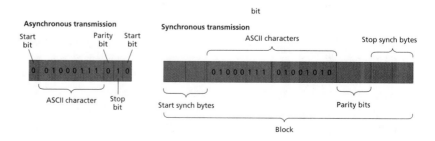

When **asynchronous transmission** is selected, each byte is surrounded by control bits. One extra bit is added at the front of the character and another one or two bits are added at the end. The front bit, called a *start bit,* indicates the beginning of a character. The bit at the end, called a *stop bit,* indicates the end of that character's signal. There is also the error checking or *parity bit.* Asynchronous transmission is slow. Out of ten or more bits, only eight bits are actual data, making the efficiency of the communications channel only 80 percent.

A faster and more efficient way of sending data is through **synchronous transmission**, in which blocks of bytes are wrapped in start and stop bytes called *synch bytes.* The data is sent more quickly and at a lower communications cost because more of the bytes are devoted to actual data. Synchronous transmission is most often used by large computer systems. However, PC users who wish to retrieve data from large computer systems can buy add-in boards that provide synchronous transmission.

Both the sending computer and receiving computer must use the same transmission method. If the sending computer sends data using the asynchronous method and the receiving computer is using the synchronous method, then the receiving computer will be unable to accept the data.

DIRECTION OF TRANSMISSION

The way a communications device is capable of sending and receiving data is called its *transmission mode.* Transmission modes are classified as simplex, half-duplex, and full-duplex, and are illustrated in Figure 7.12.

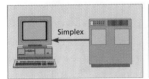

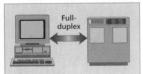

Simplex Transmission When the transmission of data can only occur in one direction, it is sent in **simplex transmission** mode. One analogy is a public announcement system at a basketball game. The announcer can make announcements to the audience but cannot receive messages back from the audience. Likewise, a computer that transmits data via a simplex channel can either send or receive data but cannot do both. Because it is often necessary to do both, simplex channels are seldom used for business communications applications.

Half-Duplex Transmission A two-way method of communicating is called the **half-duplex transmission** mode, with the limitation that data cannot be sent and received at the same time. A walkie-talkie system operates on the half-duplex system in that only one person can talk at a time. The person receiving cannot transmit, and the person transmitting cannot receive. When used as a mode of transmission over long distances, the half-duplex mode results in delays. It takes time for both computers to switch from sending and receiving modes as preliminary confirmation and okay signals are sent back and forth. The elapsed time between sending and receiving is called the *response time.* Half-duplex transmission is often used with a central computer system and the terminals connected to it. In these systems, the user usually needs to wait for a response from the main computer before continuing, making simultaneous transmission unnecessary.

Full-Duplex Transmission Simultaneous transmission in two directions is achieved through the **full-duplex transmission** mode. Full-duplex transmission eliminates delays due to response time, which can be an important advantage when large amounts of data are transmitted between minicomputers, mainframe computers, and supercomputers. Full-duplex mode is, however, more expensive than the other two modes.

SPEED OF TRANSMISSION

Communications channels vary in the speed, or bits per second, at which data is transmitted. Channels are usually classified into three grades, or bandwidths: narrowband, voice-grade, or broadband.

- **Narrowband channels** are the slowest category of communications channel, with a transmission speed ranging from about 45 to 150 bps. A narrowband channel is used in situations where very low-speed applications are performed. For example, a narrowband channel is often used for telegraph communications.
- **Voice-grade channels** have a wider bandwidth than narrowband channels and are of medium speed. Voice-grade channels average from 300 to 9,600 bps. Traditional twisted pair cable telephone lines are voice-grade channels that average about 2,400 bps. These channels are often selected because they are economical and already in place.
- **Broadband channels**, such as coaxial cables, microwaves, satellites, and fiber optics, are more suitable for applications requiring high-speed transmission of large volumes of data. They range from 19,200 to 500,000 bps. Large banks frequently use broadband channels for transmitting data representing thousands of financial transactions each day. For example, the Federal Reserve Branch Bank in Memphis, Tennessee, uses broadband channels (microwaves and satellites) to transmit over 100,000 transactions daily to the Federal Reserve District Bank in St. Louis, Missouri.

NETWORKS

Some computer systems use a single computer, whereas other systems use multiple computers that are connected by communications channels. When two or more CPUs are linked together in some way with communications media, the system becomes a **network**. A network is a collection of computers, terminals, and other equipment that uses communications channels to share data, information, hardware, and software. It allows individuals and employees convenient access to programs, data, and other information stored on another computer. It also allows employees to communicate with each other. A type of network in which data is sent over long distances among computers is known as a *wide area network*. On a smaller scale, local area networks send data among computers located in close proximity to each other, such as in the same building.

Many networks use the **client/server** method for sharing information. With this method, a user uses a personal computer or terminal (the client) to send information to another computer (the server), which then relays the information back to the client or to another computer (another client). For example, suppose you are a subscriber to the Microsoft Network and send an e-mail message to a friend who is also a Microsoft Network subscriber. The message is sent from your computer (client) to Microsoft's computer (server) which, in turn, relays the message to your friend's computer (client). In situations where users subscribe to different services, messages may be routed through more than one server.

WIDE AREA NETWORKS

Large geographic areas are spanned by **wide area networks (WANs)**. The oldest form of WAN is the long-distance telephone network. Though the long-distance monopoly was broken up years ago, many telephone companies in the United States are linked together electronically. They are also electronically linked with other international telephone companies. As communications media devices continue to improve in speed, capacity, and security, individuals and businesses are discovering more reasons and benefits in sending and receiving data long distances through communications channels. Today, the most prevalent WANs are public access networks and value added networks.

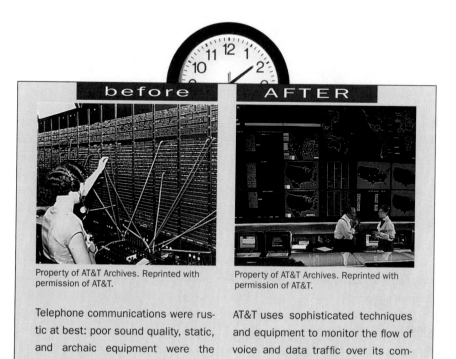

Property of AT&T Archives. Reprinted with permission of AT&T.

Property of AT&T Archives. Reprinted with permission of AT&T.

Telephone communications were rustic at best: poor sound quality, static, and archaic equipment were the norm, with service nonexistent in some areas.

AT&T uses sophisticated techniques and equipment to monitor the flow of voice and data traffic over its complex communications network.

Some networks are limited to a smaller geographical area, such as a city or town. In such a case, the network is often referred to as a **metropolitan area network**, or **MAN**.

Public Access Networks Networks maintained by telephone companies, called common carriers, such as Bell, MCI, US Sprint, and AT&T, are called **public access networks (PANs)** because they provide voice and data communications channels across long distances to anyone who can pay the fee. More recently, companies that own satellite transmission facilities have developed PANs also.

Value-Added Networks Companies that use the facilities of common carriers to offer the public additional communications services at a subscription fee are called **value-added networks (VANs)**. VANs create an economy of scale. Sharing communications lines among many users makes the cost of the service affordable. Services include access to network databases, electronic mail, and information processing. The value in VANs is that the company running them manages the network, provides conversions between differing systems, and ensures that subscribers receive the data they need with little effort and at less cost than if they pursued the same service through PANs.

Subscribers need only make a local modem call to access a VAN. Data is then routed between the subscriber's computer, the VAN's local terminal, and a long-distance host computer. One of the most popular services offered by VANs is information retrieval. Examples of VANs that provide this service include America Online, GEnie, MCI Mail, Prodigy, LEXIS, NEXIS, and CompuServe. The services offered by these and other VANs are discussed in the "Information Services" section later in this chapter.

LOCAL AREA NETWORKS

Local area networks (LANs) are private communications networks that serve the needs of companies located in the same building with two or more computers. LANs make it convenient to share not only databases, but also software and hardware, such as hard disks and printers. A LAN typically uses a dedicated microcomputer, called a **file server**, that allows other microcomputers to share its resources. With a file server and a high-capacity hard disk, called a **disk server**, users can access programs and data just as easily as if they were on their individual hard drives. Having these items on the disk server frees up space on the hard disks in their individual computer systems for their specific files. Similarly, a **print server** manages the flow of traffic on expensive printer devices. Sharing resources such as applications programs, expensive hard disk capacity, and high-quality printers over networks saves companies enormous amounts of money in software and equipment costs.

Local area networks are classified by their topologies (physical configurations): star, bus, ring, and token ring. The computers linked in networks are often called **workstations** or *nodes*.

NETWORK TOPOLOGIES

Network topology refers to the way computers and peripherals are configured to form networks. One way to think of a topology is to examine a map showing roads, rivers, highways, and other items such as cities and mountains. Looking down at the map, you can view the relationship of various physical locations. A diagram of a network topology is similarly viewed. This allows a viewer to locate each network component. In the following sections, we examine various types of networks, or topologies.

Star Networks In a **star network**, multiple computers and peripheral devices are linked to a central, or host, computer in a point-to-point configuration, as shown in Figure 7.13. A **host computer** is typically a more powerful minicomputer or mainframe computer. Any communications between the computers must be routed through the host computer. This topology is preferred by companies with multiple departments that need centralized access to databases and files. One downfall of the star topology is its dependence on the host computer. Since all communications go through the host, the network becomes inoperable if the host does not function properly.

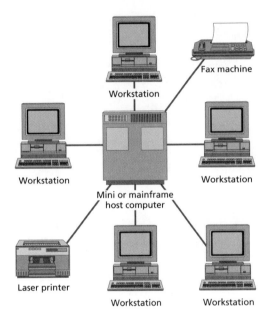

Workstation

Fax machine

Workstation

Workstation

Mini or mainframe host computer

Laser printer

Workstation

Workstation

Figure 7.13

In star topologies, computers and peripheral devices are connected to a host computer.

Bus Networks A **bus network** does not contain a host computer. Instead, all computers are linked by a single line of cable called a **bus** as shown in Figure 7.14. All communications travel the length of the bus. As they pass, each computer hooked to the network checks to see if it is the assigned destination point. Since there is no host computer, the malfunction of one computer does not affect communications among other computers. Bus topologies commonly use coaxial or fiber optic cables. The bus network is less expensive than the star network, but it is also less efficient.

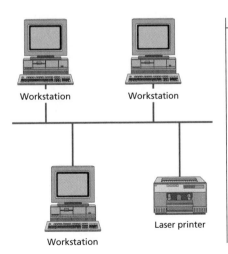

Workstation

Workstation

Laser printer

Workstation

Figure 7.14

In bus topologies, devices are connected to a central line; there is no host computer.

Ring Networks In a **ring network**, there is no host computer nor a central line of cable. Instead, each computer is connected to two other computers in the ring (see Figure 7.15). Communications are then passed in one direction from the source workstation to the destination. If one computer isn't working, the computer is bypassed. One difficulty with ring networks, however, is that if two computers are trying to send communications at the same time, one or both of the messages may become garbled. Ring networks are not used as often as the previous two configurations.

The devices in ring topologies are connected in a closed loop.

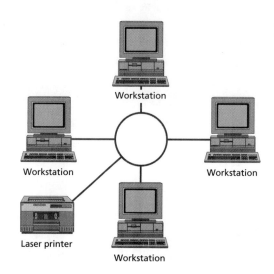

Token Ring Networks In order to eliminate errors due to two communications being sent at the same time, **token ring networks** were developed, in which a pattern of bits called a **token** is passed from one computer to another sequentially around the ring. Only when a computer has the token may the computer transmit a communication, as shown in Figure 7.16. The token ring network is more expensive than the others, but efficient.

Figure 7.16

In a token ring topology, only one computer can pass along a communication at a time by attaching the communication to a group of bits, called a token, that travels around the ring.

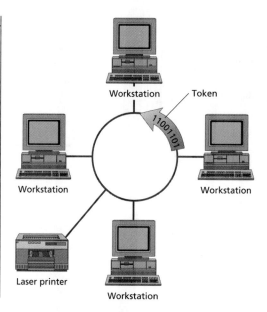

Multiplexers A special device that increases the efficiency of the network system by allowing 8, 16, 32, or more low-speed devices to share simultaneously a single high-speed communications channel is called a **multiplexer**. When used to connect devices with the host computer, the multiplexer accepts data from several devices, combines or *multiplexes* it, and sends it across a single high-speed channel to a second multiplexer that divides, or *demultiplexes*, the data and then transmits it to the host computer (see Figure 7.17).

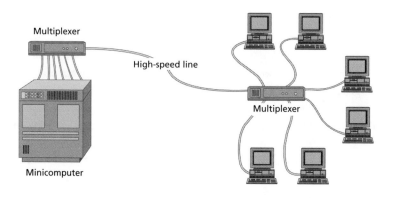

Multiplexer

High-speed line

Multiplexer

Minicomputer

Figure 7.17

A multiplexer combines the data of several low-speed devices and sends the results across high-speed lines to a second multiplexer, where it is divided into its original format for processing.

Some multiplexers contain a *protocol converter* that allows communications with systems using different standards.

Concentrators With a **concentrator**, data is transmitted from only one device at a time over the channel. The data is then multiplexed with other data and stored until there is enough data to make transferring it to another device worthwhile. Using a concentrator assumes that not all terminals will be ready to send or to receive data at the same time. Concentrators are usually minicomputers with memory functions that allow for the storage and forwarding of transmissions.

Front End Processors Usually a minicomputer located near the host computer is designated as the **front end processor**. It establishes the link between the source of the communication and the destination computer. Its main function is to relieve the host computer from the burden of controlling communications. It acts as a go-between for the main computer and the rest of the network, as shown in Figure 7.18.

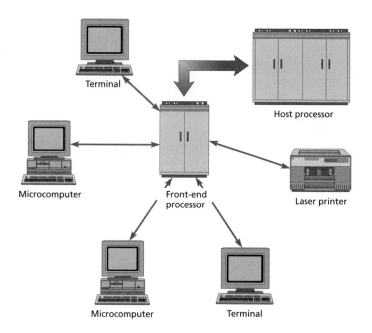

Terminal

Microcomputer

Front-end
processor

Host processor

Laser printer

Microcomputer

Terminal

Figure 7.18

The front end processor controls communications between devices, freeing the host computer for other tasks.

GATEWAYS AND BRIDGES

Sometimes it is necessary for networks to communicate. A LAN may need access to another LAN or to a WAN. For this communication to occur, networks must be equipped with resources called gateways and bridges. A **gateway** is the hardware and software that allows communication between dissimilar networks. For instance, if paralegals at a law office working on a LAN wished to use LEXIS (a law database on a WAN) to find information about supreme court rulings on sex discrimination cases, they would have to employ a gateway to make the connection.

A **bridge** is the hardware and software that allows two similar networks to communicate. If the paralegals' research turned up the name of a law firm from which they wished to gather more information, and that law firm maintained a LAN, the paralegals could connect with the firm's LAN through a bridge.

TELECOMMUNICATIONS PROTOCOLS

As is true for all microcomputer hardware, all communications channels need software to work. The software used with modems and networks is usually referred to as **communications software**. Because communications devices vary in their methods for transmitting data, communications software provides protocols for standardizing the process. **Communications protocols** are procedures for sending and receiving

transmissions. They are used to establish timing of the transmission, electronic connection of the devices, transmission mode, acknowledgment signal of the receiving device (called **handshaking**), and treatment of errors. Communications software packages permit a user to **download**, which means to transfer information from a larger computer system or network to a personal computer, and to **upload**, which means to transfer data files from a smaller computer system to a larger computer system or network.

TELECOMMUNICATIONS IN USE

Computer technology has revolutionized the way much work is done throughout the world. Let's examine a few applications made possible by this new technology.

VOICE MAIL

How many times have you missed an important telephone call or wasted your time trying to reach someone by telephone and failing? These frustrating experiences can be avoided with the use of **voice mail**, now popular for business use. Voice mail systems are the computer's version of a telephone answering machine. Instead of no one answering, or bouncing from one person's telephone to another when the original recipient is unavailable, voice mail allows you to leave a message in a voice mail box. The spoken message is digitized and stored in bit form. When the receiver retrieves the stored messages, they are reconverted into their analog form.

ELECTRONIC MAIL

Similar to voice mail is the application of **electronic mail (e-mail)**. E-mail is a fast and inexpensive way of sending, receiving, storing, and forwarding messages electronically. E-mail is effective for interoffice communications. When someone is on the phone or in a meeting, you can leave them messages, attach files if necessary, and get on with your business without the aggravation of trying to connect with the individual throughout the day. By using e-mail, you can send messages to those connected to the system whenever you want, and the recipients can read the messages at their convenience, as shown in Figure 7.19.

Everyone connected to the e-mail system is given a code that is an address. The address is not location specific; messages can be retrieved from remote locations. When logged into the system, a user is automatically notified when there is mail. This makes it convenient for a sales representative, for instance, who wishes to check for messages on a daily basis while on the road. A notebook computer can be connected to a main office through hotel telephone lines, giving the sales rep access to messages which can then be answered and forwarded as appropriate.

Figure 7.19

Electronic mail (e-mail) is a convenient and efficient means of sending and receiving messages.

ELECTRONIC BULLETIN BOARDS

You're already familiar with bulletin boards located in school hallways, dormitories, and student centers. An electronic bulletin board is merely a computerized extension of this bulletin board concept.

An **electronic bulletin board system (BBS)** is a computer system that maintains an electronic list of messages where anyone with access to the bulletin board can post messages, read existing messages, or delete messages. A bulletin board uses data communications systems to link personal computers with message systems. To use a bulletin board, you need a personal computer, a modem, and the number of a bulletin board service. Just dial the number to see a list of messages and follow the on-screen instructions to post a message or to read one. Bulletin boards represent a cost-effective means for communicating with groups of individuals who have information on topics they wish to share. The Internet is an example of a BBS used by universities and research institutions to facilitate the open exchange of information. The Internet connects hundreds of thousands of computers on networks throughout the world.

TELECONFERENCING

Teleconferencing allows an "electronic" (instead of face-to-face) meeting to be conducted between people at distant locations. The simplest system is a basic conferencing system, which is a single communications software package installed on a company's mainframe or minicomputer. Each conference participant must have a microcomputer with communications software already installed, plus a telephone and a modem. Once connected, all participants may send and receive messages via their computers. Messages can be directed to an individual, a group, or to all participants. The software notifies each participant of an incoming message.

By adding cameras to the teleconferencing system, you have a conferencing system known as **video conferencing**. A video conferencing system is shown in Figure 7.20.

Figure 7.20

A video-conferencing system.

Courtesy of PictureTel Corporation.

FAX MACHINES

A facsimile machine, commonly referred to as a **fax machine**, makes it possible to transmit documents and drawings over telephone lines from one location to another in a manner that is faster and often cheaper than sending the document overnight or through the mail. Virtually anything that can be written or drawn on paper can be sent to a receiving fax machine. However, fax machines are designed to handle paper that is a specific size, normally sheets of paper that measure $8\frac{1}{2}$ x 11 inches. Some machines use standard plain paper, while other machines require a chemically treated, thermal paper.

Each fax machine is given a standard telephone number, called its *fax number*. To send a document from one fax machine to another, the page(s) are inserted into the machine, and the receiver's fax number is dialed. The machine from which the fax is being sent notifies the receiving machine that the document is being transmitted. The digitized data is transmitted along a telephone line to the receiving machine, where the data is reconstructed into its original form and printed. The machine has a display which shows when the document has arrived at its destination. This process is shown in Figure 7.21. Fax machines are standard equipment in most modern offices.

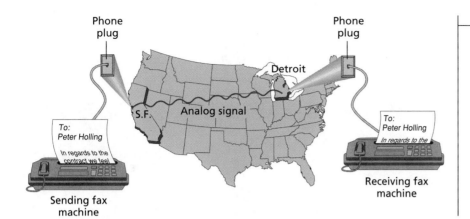

Figure 7.21

Sending documents across country via fax machines is quicker than sending them overnight, and often less expensive. Fax machines contain internal modems, which convert the fax machine's digital signals into analog form for transmission across telephone lines.

Microcomputers can be equipped with add-in boards that enable users to send and receive faxes using their computers.

INFORMATION SERVICES

An **information service** is a company or organization that uses its computer system to accumulate, store, and make available to subscribers information on subjects ranging from airline reservation services to stock market quotations. Subscribers are charged fees to obtain the information they want. The fees charged to subscribers may be periodic (for example, monthly) or based on the amount of time a subscriber uses the service or both.

The list of information services is growing, and the information you can gain access to is almost without limit. Some specialized services include LEXIS (which was discussed earlier as an example for the need of gateways and bridges), which provides access to court rulings, federal regulations, and articles in legal publications; NEXIS, which provides access to bibliographic information to magazine and newspaper articles; DIALOG, which is one of the largest suppliers of bibliographic material on topics ranging from agriculture to business to science and engineering; and Dow Jones News/Retrieval Services, which provides a statistical database covering stock market activity. Many other specialized services are available. Stockbrokers, lawyers, scientists, and engineers, among others, find that the databases save them incredible amounts of research time.

The emergence of PCs for home use has led to the creation of information services that provide a broad range of services, including America Online, GEnie, MCI Mail, CompuServe, and Prodigy. For instance, America Online is one of the largest commercial information services. It offers a variety of information services including travel arrangements, home shopping, electronic banking, up-to-date weather reports, and stock market quotes that can be downloaded into users' spreadsheet programs.

Prodigy is another example of a commercial information service. It provides many of the same offerings as America Online and CompuServe, including movie and book reviews, conferences on a variety of topics, games, and an on-line encyclopedia. Prodigy also provides financial information, but does not allow you to download the information onto your own spreadsheet package.

COMPUTER CURRENTS

Hurrying to Join the Internet

Would you like to read your morning newspaper or a back issue at your convenience? Soon you might be able to do just that if you have access to the Internet or the right information service.

Some of the nation's largest newspaper chains are forming a new company to help them create a national network of on-line newspaper services. The new company, called New Century Network, will consist of Cox Newspapers, Inc., Gannett Company, Inc., The Hearst Corporation, The Times Mirror Company, Knight-Ridder, Inc., and The Washington Post Company. Collectively, these companies own 185 newspapers with a combined Sunday circulation of more than 23 million readers. All but the smallest newspapers will be put on-line on the network within the next three years.

Some will be on-line within a few months.

The New Century Network will provide a wide range of services, such as helping members share news content and develop new content packages. Local services provided may include news items; features and sports information; ticket services; home shopping; and guides to community affairs, entertainment, and events.

Also offered will be Internet communications, including electronic mail and bulletin boards. The service will be accessible via the Internet and the World Wide Web.

The new company is expected to begin operations at a time when the demand for on-line time is increasing at a phenomenal pace. Existing on-line services such as The Microsoft Network, Prodigy, America Online,

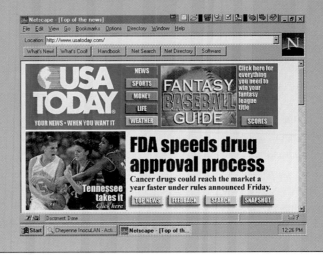

CompuServe, GEnie, and Delphi are already being challenged by the tremendous growth of the Internet.

Newspaper companies are not the only ones anxious to join the Internet mixture. Several banks are exploring the feasibility of providing banking services on the Internet. Some colleges and universities are examining the possibilities of allowing students to register via the Internet and providing information, including catalogs and schedules, to students the same way. Some colleges and universities already offer special courses on the Internet. Assignments are sent to students who are enrolled in a class. After completion of an assignment, the result is sent to the institution for evaluation.

It seems that the list of potential Internet applications is unlimited. What's next? The only logical response is that it's anyone's guess.

TELECOMMUTING

With rapid advancements in communications technologies, it was only a matter of time before individuals and organizations discovered that some people could perform work for their employers at home, on a part-time or full-time basis. Many employees who work from their homes are involved in data entry operations, such as accessing company files or updating company records. Their work can be accomplished at home using telecommunications systems that allow communication with their organizations' central computers. This is known as **telecommuting**. It is one of the fastest growing areas in computing today. Between 1987 and 1995, the number of Americans working at home, at least part of the time, was projected to increase from 23 million to 51 million.

Courtesy of AT&T.

Figure 7.22

Telecommuting is one of the fastest growing areas in computing today.

There are advantages and disadvantages associated with telecommuting. Benefits include:

- Higher productivity
- Increased job opportunities for persons who are physically impaired
- Savings on transportation costs

Disadvantages include:

- Lack of face-to-face interactions with fellow workers
- Inability to obtain technical help quickly if a problem occurs or if questions arise
- Lack of direct management supervision

So far, you have learned that information can be shared among computers connected by means of communications channels, and that information can even be shared among networks that comprise a wide area network. In the following sections, we will examine the Internet, which makes it possible for information to be shared virtually worldwide.

THE INTERNET

Nearly everyone has heard of the Internet and millions of computer users throughout the world have used it. For those who have not used it, the Internet remains somewhat of a mystery. It is the largest and best-known wide area network in existence.

WHAT IS THE INTERNET?

The **Internet** is a worldwide network of computer networks linked together via communications channels. Its actual size is unknown because of its rapid growth. In fact, the Internet is expanding so rapidly it is virtually impossible to keep track of the number of networks, information services, databases, hardware and software packages, and information being made available to users on an almost daily basis. At the 1995 International Telecom conference in Geneva, Switzerland, it was announced that the Internet included the following:

- 3,000 networks
- 35 million users worldwide
- 2.5 million computers connected to the Internet
- 21,500 organizations connected to the Internet
- 3 million computers connected
- Users located in over 110 countries

The Internet has been called a "virtual community," because users throughout the world can share useful information. For example, having the necessary computer equipment and software, a doctor at a small rural hospital in central Alaska can communicate with medical specialists at a large hospital in Anchorage. X-rays, EKGs, and other medical data can be sent to medical specialists in Anchorage for evaluation and the evaluation results sent to the doctor at the rural hospital.

HISTORY OF THE INTERNET

The Internet was started in 1969 for the purpose of linking researchers working on government projects at four universities. Soon other colleges, universities, and private sites were added. The Internet began expanding rapidly in the late 1980s when several public and private networks were linked together with the National Science Foundation network. Since 1989, the Internet has doubled in size every year. It is expected that in the year 2000 the Internet will serve 40 million users worldwide.

SERVICES AVAILABLE ON THE INTERNET

A variety of services are available on the Internet. Below are some of the more useful things you can do on the Internet.

Send and Receive Electronic Mail Electronic mail (e-mail) messages can be sent anywhere in the world by, and to, users with an e-mail address. An e-mail address is free and addresses are available from various sources, including company directories, newspaper advertisements, from individuals themselves, and from directories that can be purchased at bookstores.

Search Databases Most large universities and several large libraries have on-line databases that are available for users to review. Using the Internet, a user can specify a particular topic, such as "birds" and then view a list of books and magazines containing information on that topic (see Figure 7.23).

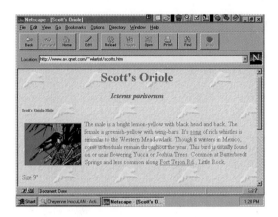

Figure 7.23

On-line databases exist on a variety of topics.

Transfer Files Millions of files are available for transfer. A person can use the Internet to obtain information on hundreds of subjects. Once a file has been retrieved, it can be edited, formatted, saved, and printed. For example, students can use the Internet to obtain information for term papers and projects and are no longer limited to the use of the university's library (see Figure 7.24).

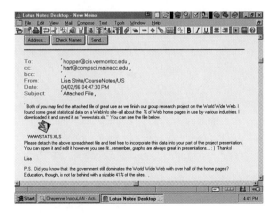

Figure 7.24

Users can use transfer files to obtain information for projects.

Participate with Discussion and News Groups A user can participate with other Internet users in a discussion of topics of mutual interest. Comments and opinions can be exchanged freely among users with common interests.

Play Games Single and multiple player games are available on the Internet. Users at remote sites can compete in a variety of games including chess, monopoly, and cribbage.

Order Products and Services A common practice by businesses now is to include an e-mail address with product advertisements that appear in newspapers, magazines, and on television. Products can be ordered by using the Internet to contact the company. Once contact has been established, a user need only answer questions appearing on the screen and have a credit card handy (see Figure 7.25). For example, a hungry Internet user can order a pizza via Pizza Hut's PizzaNet system. The order goes to the Company's Wichita, Kansas, computer where it is rerouted to a local Pizza Hut. The order is delivered to the customer in the usual manner.

Figure 7.25

Pizza Hut's PizzaNet system.

CONNECTING TO THE INTERNET

How can a potential user get on the Internet? There are the following four ways.

Connect via (Subscribe to) an Information Service An easy way to connect to the Internet is to subscribe to a commercial information service, such as the Microsoft Network (MSN), America Online (AOL), or Prodigy. For users wanting to link their home personal computer to the Internet, this is a popular choice. These services provide an electronic gateway to the Internet that allows subscribers to access many of the Internet's most popular features, including electronic mail. Communications over the Internet are possible because of the Transmission Control Protocol/Internet Protocol (TCP/IP). All Internet host computers must be able to communicate via TCP/IP. However, the protocol used by information services including Prodigy, America Online, and the other services is different than TPC/IP. The Internet gateways of these services enable communication between the information services communication protocols and TCP/IP.

Connect via an Internet Service Provider Many companies offer connections to the Internet for a fee. An example might be a telephone company, such as Bell-South. To sign up, some companies send the customer one or more diskettes and a packet of written information explaining the service, rate charges, and installation instructions. Once installed, the user dials into the provider's host computer as the user would into an information service. Once on-line, the user is on the Internet and has access to all of the Internet's features. The installed software provides a direct link via

TCP/IP. Connection is made through a Serial Line Internet Protocol (SLIP) service or Point-to-Point Protocol (PPP) service on the service provider's host computer.

Direct Connection to the Internet The fastest way to access the Internet is with a direct connection. To have a direct connection, a user's computer must be configured with TCP/IP software and must be connected to a local area network (LAN) that is linked to an Internet host computer. Many colleges, universities, and businesses are connected this way. At many colleges, all a student needs to do to access the Internet is to obtain an Internet address and password from the network administrator.

Connection via Long-distance Telephone Companies The federal government has eased regulations of the telecommunications industry. As a result, several companies are entering the competition of providing telecommunications services, and more technologies are emerging.

In 1996, AT&T began offering its 80 million residential long-distance customers access to the Internet at an initial cost to long-distance customers of $19.95 per month for unlimited access. Sprint and MCI have also announced plans to offer access to their customers and some smaller companies have plans to enter the competitive arena. Internet and World Wide Web service by long-distance telephone companies will make use of standard telephone lines and equipment already in place. Within a short time, almost any user having a telephone can have access to the Internet and World Wide Web.

THE INTERNET ADDRESS

Communication via the Internet is made possible through an Internet address. You might think of an Internet address as you would a mailing address. Let's break down the components of the following Internet address:

fuller@bobcat.lmc.edu

User ID At the left of the @ symbol, called the separator, is the user ID which is usually part or all of the user's name. In the address above, "fuller" is the last name of the user. Because there is only one user at this site whose last name is "fuller," this ID is acceptable. However, more than one "fuller" would require a distinguishing ID, such as "bob_fuller" or "sam_fuller." The underscore(_) is used to separate the two names.

@ Symbol The @ symbol indicates the user is at, or is connected to, a particular host computer or network.

Host/Network Identifier The part at the right of the @ symbol identifies the host or network. In our example, the user "fuller" is connected to the Lees-McRae College network, named "bobcat" after the school's mascot. The word "bobcat" is followed by a period (.) that separates the network's name from the college's initials, "lmc." Another period separates the college's initials from the letters "edu" that indicates that Lee-McRae College is an educational institution. Large universities, businesses, or organizations might have a network within a network. A user at one of these places might have an Internet address such as the one below, where the network in the CIS department is a part of the university's network.

john_williams@cis.statecollege.edu

Internet addresses, such as the one above, are determined by the person responsible for the network. For example, the network manager assigns "statecollege" as the name of the school's campus-wide network and "cis" as the name of the smaller network within the department of computer information systems. John Williams, a faculty member in the CIS department is assigned the name "john_williams." These three names within the address enable messages to be sent to the faculty member's computer.

SEARCHING AND BROWSING THE INTERNET

No person, group, or agency monitors the Internet or keeps track of information moving along it. As a result, there is no index for a user to determine what information is on the Internet or how the information is to be used. Because there are thousands of databases loaded onto servers that are connected to the Internet, millions of pieces of information are accessible to a user. An information server is an Internet host containing information that is made available over the Internet. To get the information, a user must look for it. The information can be obtained by searching, browsing, or asking for it.

Searching the Internet One way to search the Internet is by using Gopher, a system developed at the University of Minnesota, whose athletic teams are called the Golden Gophers. Gopher lets you "burrow" into a remote computer's files through on-screen menus.

Browsing the Internet Browsing can be interesting for a user seeking specific information, such as specific provisions contained in a specific piece of legislation passed by Congress, or a list of books offered by a certain publishing firm. A **browser** is software that allows a user to view the graphical "pages" on the World Wide Web. A number of browsers are available for purchase, including Mosaic and Netscape.

Most Internet users are willing to help other users in need. Someone needing help can post an inquiry on the Internet. Other users reading the inquiry might provide solutions. For example, a user wanting information about Levi's jeans can post an inquiry such as "How can I learn about Levi's jeans?" A typical reply might be "contact http://www.levi.com."

THE WORLD WIDE WEB (WWW)

The fastest-growing and perhaps most interesting part of the Internet is the **World Wide Web (WWW)**, simply called "the Web." It has multimedia capability, which means that users can obtain information from private companies, government agencies, and other sources that contain text, graphics, and sound. For example, some companies use the Web to provide information about their products and services. The Internet address for such a company begins with a Uniform Resource Locator (URL, pronounced *you-are-el*, not *earl*). The Internet address for all web URL sites begin with http:// prefixes. For example, you can view information about Microsoft's Windows 95 software at the following address:

http://www.windows.microsoft.com

The information might consist of several pages beginning with the home page. A home page is a main page, usually the first page, of information. Viewing a home page is similar to viewing a cover of a catalog. A home page might be followed by one or more additional pages (see Figure 7.26). Pages that follow the home page might contain detailed information about products or services.

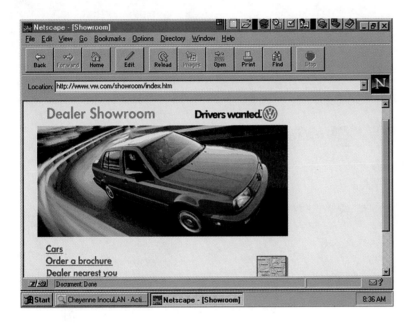

Figure 7.26

A home page, like this one from Volkswagen, might be followed by one or more additional pages.

Web pages are written and linked together by means of **hypertext markup language**, called **HTML**. HTML consists of hidden codes that allow a user to click on a highlighted word or phrase to automatically access a related site. The hypertext protocol (http) (explained earlier) is how information is sent over the World Wide Web.

The earlier development of applications for the Internet and World Wide Web was tedious and cumbersome. However, applications development became easier when Sun Microsystems introduced a new programming language, called **Java**, in May 1995. Written by a team of programmers headed by James Gosling, Java allows software developers to design software projects that can be distributed over the Internet using the World Wide Web, and will eventually allow all Java-based applications to run on any computer connected to the Internet. Java has become the most popular programming for developing Internet and World Wide Web applications.

SURFING THE INTERNET

The phrase "surfing" the Internet means exploring the World Wide Web. A user doesn't need a reason to explore. Surfing can be interesting, fun, and educational. Thousands of users surf every day. Enjoy your surfing and your travels through cyberspace.

In this part, several chapters were devoted to discussions of computer hardware. Computer software and data management are equally important. In Part Three, we will examine these topics.

Some World Wide Web Addresses

Topic	Address
Federal Government Information	http://www.febworld.gov
Careers in Education	http://www.chronicle.merit.edu
U.S. Small Business Administration	http://www.sbaonline.gov
Internet Shopping Network	http://www.internet.net/directories.html
Purchase Tickets On-line	http://www.ticketron.com
Chicago Field Museum of Natural History	http://www.bvis.uic.edu/museum
The White House	http://ww.whitehouse.gov

Key Terms

analog transmission

asynchronous transmission

baud rate

bits per second (bps)

bridge

broadband channels

browser

bus

bus network

client/server

coaxial cable

communications protocols

communications software

concentrator

data communications

data communications system

digital transmission

disk server

download

electronic bulletin board system (BBS)

electronic mail (e-mail)

fax machine

fiber optic cable

file server

front end processor

full-duplex transmission

gateway

half-duplex transmission

handshaking

host computer

hypertext markup language (HTML)

information service

integrated services digital network (ISDN)

Internet

Java

local area networks (LANs)

metropolitan area networks (MANs)

microwave system

modem

multiplexer

narrowband channels

network

network topology

parity bit

print server

public access networks (PANs)

ring network
satellite
serial transmission
simplex transmission
star network
synchronous transmission
telecommunications
telecommuting
teleconferencing
token

token ring network
twisted pair cable
upload
value-added networks (VANs)
video conferencing
voice mail
voice-grade channels
wide area networks (WANs)
workstations
World Wide Web (WWW)

Summary

Data communications is the process of transmitting data from one location to another. **Telecommunications** is the combined use of computer systems and communications channels such as cable, microwaves, and satellites.

Modems convert **digital** signals into their **analog** equivalent for transmission over communications channels and reconvert them to their original state for processing. The speed at which modems transfer data is called **baud rate**. Another measure of speed is **bits per second (bps)**.

A **network** is two or more computers connected by means of communications channels. A **wide area network (WAN)** connects computers over long distances, while a **local area network (LAN)** connects computers located in close proximity to each other. A **network topology** refers to the way computers and peripherals are configured to form networks.

Gateways allow communications between dissimilar networks. **Bridges** allow two similar networks to communicate. **Communications protocols** are procedures for sending and receiving transmissions.

Telecommunication applications and technologies include **voice mail systems, electronic mail, bulletin board systems (BBS), teleconferencing, fax machines, information services**, and **telecommuting**.

The **Internet** is a worldwide network of computer networks linked together via communications channels. The World Wide Web is the fastest-growing part of the Internet. Internet services include sending and receiving electronic mail, searching databases, transferring files, participating in discussion and news groups, and ordering products and services.

14 Easy steps to being a webmaster

STEP 7 | CRITIQUE PAGES

By now, you should have pages on the Web. In this step, we take an opposite perspective from the designer and shift to that of the user. You will give fellow students comments on their pages, applying the ideas presented in the first six steps. The ideas are presented in the table below. Each idea has questions to ask yourself about the web pages you are evaluating.

Step 1

Ideas	Review Questions
Audience	Who are the intended audiences of the pages you are reviewing? Is each audience clearly definable? List and define the audiences as you perceive them. Good audiences might be banks, all people from 18–26, entertainment software development companies.
Message Content	Define the message content you perceive as intended for each audience you identified above. Does the message content express whole ideas? Is the message content unique or valuable to its intended audience?
Clarity of Message	From your definitions of each audience and its messages, does the information on each page relate to the audience and its message? Do you understand the author's intentions from a short glance at the page?

Step 2

Ideas	Review Questions
Chunking	Do the information chunks make sense?
Proximity	Are all the chunks or identifiers for chunks that are related formatted together?
Clarity of Page	Is each page clearly written? Cleanly formatted? Concise?

Step 3

Ideas	Review Questions
Proximity	Are the chunk groupings designed to identify them as a group?
Alignment	Is alignment and indentation used to set apart information on the headers, details, chunk identifiers, and chunks?
7-second Rule	When you browsed through the pages, were you spending more than ten seconds per page trying to understand any one single idea?
White Space	Are there any pages that violate the 40–60 percent white space rule? Is the white space spread out over the whole page?

Step 4

Ideas	Review Questions
Contrast	When you glance at a page, is contrast evident?
Color	Is color use pleasing? Is color use consistent with page content and goals?
Font Size	Are font sizes varied to provide contrast?

Step 5

Ideas	Review Questions
Repetition	Is design element repetition obvious? Are all chunks of the same type designed the same? Do repeated elements help tie the design together?
Typeface Commands	Are typefaces varied? Does their use add to your understanding of the content? Is typeface command use consistent?
Disclaimer	Is a disclaimer present, or referenced, on every page? Is a last date of update on every page?
Contact Information	Are a contact person and contact information present on every page?
Effective Pages	Does all information appear to be complete (as you can best determine)? Does all information appear to be accurate?
Affective pages	Is the design emotionally pleasing to you? Does the design impart an emotional feel that is consistent with its purpose?

Step 6

Ideas	Review Questions
Missing Information	From your interpretation of the pages, is there any other related that you still want to know?
Links	Do links to other pages add value to the page contents?
Multi-page Decisions	Are page breaks logical? Do pages have clear threads that tie them together? (List as many as you can.)
Navigational Efficiency	Are links intuitive? Do links add to your understanding of threads to link pages? Are there too many or too few links for any single page?

ASSIGNMENT: Evaluate the pages of at least three other students in your class. Write a short summary of your critique, reviewing the above questions and giving reasons why you liked or disliked the pages, their composition, and their content. Be as specific in your comments as possible to provide the author of the pages enough information to improve his or her pages. Follow the procedure below.

1. Go through a whole set of pages for a single person quickly.
2. Review the questions from Steps 1–3 above based on your recall. Write any critique of the pages based on the quick review.
3. Review the pages more slowly, looking for the threads that tie them together. If you had problems with the 7-second rule see if you can identify why.
4. Review the questions from Steps 4–6 identifying particularly good and bad uses of the ideas. Take enough notes of the badly designed page elements to help the author correct the situation. Be critical and only identify the top/bottom 5 percent of the good and bad designs.

5. After you have reviewed all three sets of pages, grade them (with a single score for each set of pages) on a scale of one to ten, with one being the lowest score and ten being a highest score, in terms of their overall effectiveness, affectiveness, and efficiency of navigation. If you would like to participate in a nationwide study of web pages, go to http//www.cox.smu.edu/faculty/mis/conger/webpagesurvey/survey.html.

Survey results will be updated as they become available. This type of study can provide information on the criteria that people use to judge web pages. I would appreciate your participation; all answers will remain anonymous.

Exercises

REVIEW QUESTIONS

1. What is telecommunications? Cite examples of actual applications.
2. What communications channel would you use to connect the computers of a LAN? Explain your reasoning in terms of the appropriateness or inappropriateness of other communications channels.
3. What is the difference between digital and analog transmission?
4. Explain the meaning of the words *modulation* and *demodulation*.
5. How do synchronous and asynchronous data transmissions differ?
6. Explain the differences between simplex, half-duplex, and full-duplex transmission modes.
7. Name three grades of communications channels and give an example of each.
8. What is the difference between a wide area network and a local area network? Give examples of how they are used.
9. Distinguish between star, bus, ring, and token ring network topologies.
10. Explain the purposes of multiplexers, concentrators, and front end processors.
11. What is the purpose of communications protocols?
12. What is the difference between a gateway and a bridge?
13. List six current applications of telecommunications and explain the benefits of each.
14. Explain the meaning of the term *Internet*.
15. Identify three ways to connect to the Internet.
16. Name the three parts of an Internet address.

FILL IN THE BLANKS

1. _Data communications_ is the process of transmitting data from one location to another, such as from one computer to another.

2. A _____ is a communications channel that transmits data at the speed of light.

3. Communications satellites contain _transponder_ that receive signals, amplify them, and send them back to earth stations.

4. A modem is an electronic device that converts digital signals into analog signals, which is called _modulation_. When the signals reach their destination, another modem reverses the process, which is called _demodulation_

5. The number of times that a modem can change signal states per second is called its _Baud rate_

6. In _asynchronous_ transmission, a large group of bytes are surrounded by start and stop bytes and sent out via a serial transmission device.

7. _Full-Duplex transmission_ allows two-way, simultaneous transmission of data.

8. AT&T is an example of a _____ network. _public access_

9. LANs allow private groups to share resources such as a high-capacity hard disk called a _disk server_

10. A _star_ network consists of computers and peripheral devices linked to a host computer.

11. The computers linked in networks are often called _work stations_ or nodes.

12. _____ are procedures for sending and receiving telecommunications transmissions. _Communications protocols_

13. _Download_ is the process of transferring information from a minicomputer or mainframe computer or from a network to a personal computer.

14. The _Internet_ is a worldwide network of computer networks linked together via communications channels.

15. The fastest growing, and perhaps most interesting, part of the Internet is the _World Wide Web_

MATCHING

Match each term with its description.

a. handshaking
b. gateway
c. broadband channel
d. modem
e. multiplexer
f. refreshing
g. BBS
h. e-mail

i. microwave
j. fax
k. telecommunications
l. concentrator
m. ring network
n. half-duplex
o. baud rate
p. Internet

_o_ 1. Data communications speed.

_l_ 2. Combines data transmissions and sends them across high-speed channels.

_k_ 3. Process of transmitting data from one computer to another through communications channels.

_a_ 4. Acknowledgment signal from the receiving computer to the transmitting computer indicating that the system is ready for data transmittal.

_b_ 5. Hardware and software that allows communications between dissimilar networks.

_f_ 6. Process of strengthening a signal and sending it to the next station.

_d_ 7. Device that enables computers to communicate over ordinary telephone lines.

_g_ 8. Electronic list of public messages that can be accessed by any computer attached to a modem.

_c_ 9. Fiber optic cable is an example.

_m_ 10. Does not use a central computer.

_n_ 11. Method of transmission in which data can be transmitted in both directions, but not simultaneously.

_i_ 12. Data is transmitted as high-frequency radio signals.

_j_ 13. Makes it possible to transmit 8½ x 11-inch hard copies of documents electronically across telephone lines.

_h_ 14. Process of sending, receiving, storing, and forwarding messages electronically over communications channels.

_p_ 15. Worldwide network of computer networks linked via communications channels.

ACTIVITIES

1. Break into groups of three. Each student in the group should investigate one of the following VANs: America Online, Prodigy, and CompuServe. What are the membership fees? How are you charged for access time? What services are offered? Compare your lists. What are the advantages and disadvantages of each service?

2. Internet is a wide area network used by universities and research institutions to facilitate the open exchange of information. The network connects hundreds of thousands of computers on networks across the world. Find out if your school is connected to Internet. If it is not, as a class, prepare a letter to the computer lab requesting connection. Research the benefits provided by Internet and add these to the letter. Once the connection is made, explore Internet and write about what you find.

3. Assume you are the manager of a small office consisting of five PCs, a laser printer, and a minicomputer. You are assigned the task of joining the computers into a network. Before you make a decision, you are to research and write a report comparing the costs and benefits of two types of networks. After writing the report and choosing a network topology, research the costs of various communications channels such as twisted pair, coaxial, and fiber optic cables. Which kind(s) of communications channels will you use and why?

4. Using any available sources, such as magazines available at your school's library, find an Internet address for a product you would like to learn about; for example, a new car. Use a computer in the school's computer lab to retrieve information about the product you selected.

Skills for Living

TELECOMMUNICATIONS AND THE INTERNET
INTERNET EXERCISE: PLANNING YOUR VACATION TO MAUI, HAWAII

Background

It is said that the Hawaiian demigod, Maui, loved to fish. One day as he was fishing, he hooked a giant landmass under the sea. As he reeled it in, one part of the landmass broke free and floated to the surface to bask in the sun. The god then named this handsome island "Maui" in honor of himself.

Maui is the second largest of all the Hawaiian Islands. The island is approximately 55 miles long and 25 miles wide. Rainfall varies from under 4 inches per year on the southwest shore of the island to over 500 inches per year on the northeast coastal area (the second wettest spot on earth). Sugar, pineapple, flowers, potato chips, and cattle are the primary exports.

But dazzling sunsets, whale watching, snorkeling, sunbathing, tropical breezes, white sand beaches, breathtaking flowers, and luaus (parties featuring giant feasts and native dancing) are what really bring the tourists.

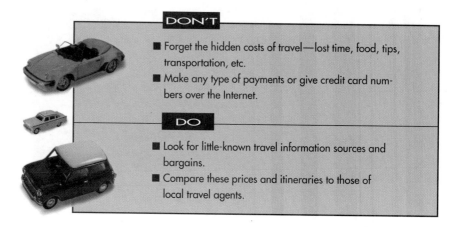

DON'T
- Forget the hidden costs of travel—lost time, food, tips, transportation, etc.
- Make any type of payments or give credit card numbers over the Internet.

DO
- Look for little-known travel information sources and bargains.
- Compare these prices and itineraries to those of local travel agents.

Student Activities

1. Imagine you are planning a trip to this island paradise. Money is no object, but you have only one week to stay (fly to Maui on a Sunday, return on the following Saturday).

Pick dates, then go about collecting information via the Internet. You might search the Internet for Maui, the American Automobile Association (AAA), airline carriers to Maui, Hawaii Visitors Information Center, etc. Be creative and have fun planning your trip.

■ Where will you stay? You might consider two beautiful, but expensive, resorts on the island: the Grand Wailea Resort Hotel and Spa on the southwest coast in Wailea (rooms range up to $10,000 per night!) and the Ritz-Carlton Kapalua at Kapalua on the northwest coast. Can you find a map of the island to see where these two hotels are located?

■ Where is the airport? Will you rent a car at the airport or somewhere else? How much will it cost and what types of vehicles are available? (Hint: You can rent Harley-Davidson motorcycles by the half-day, as well as sports cars such as Ferraris, Dodge Vipers, and Corvettes.)
■ What are you going to do there? You might consider a day-long, sailing-snorkel-ing-whale-watching catamaran trip to Lanai, a small neighboring island only a few miles away. One-hour helicopter rides into the Haleakala volcano crater (the world's largest dormant volcano) are a must! Also, no one should go to Maui without planning a one-day shopping trip to the city of Lahaina.

2. Organize and write about your search results for a class discussion. How does the itinerary and cost of your trip compare with those of your classmates? What terms did students use to search the Internet?

MAKING THE CONNECTION

Combining computer systems with communications channels such as cable, microwaves, and satellites enables us to communicate with virtually anyone in the world at any time. When two or more computers are connected by means of communications channels, a network is created. The largest and best-known worldwide network is the Internet, and the World Wide Web is the fastest growing part. Internet services include sending and receiving electronic mail, searching databases, transferring files, participating in discussion and newsgroups, and ordering products and services. With the list of potential Internet applications growing every day, our communications capabilities are becoming unlimited.

Courtesy of PictureTel Corporation.

Spotlights

Courtesy of Netscape Communications Corporation.

Courtesy of NYNEX.

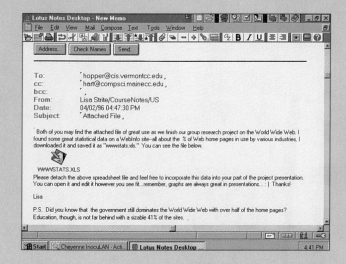

Courtesy of Samsung Electronics Company.

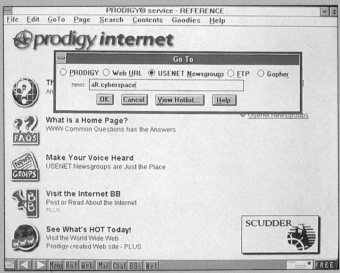

Courtesy of Prodigy Services Company.

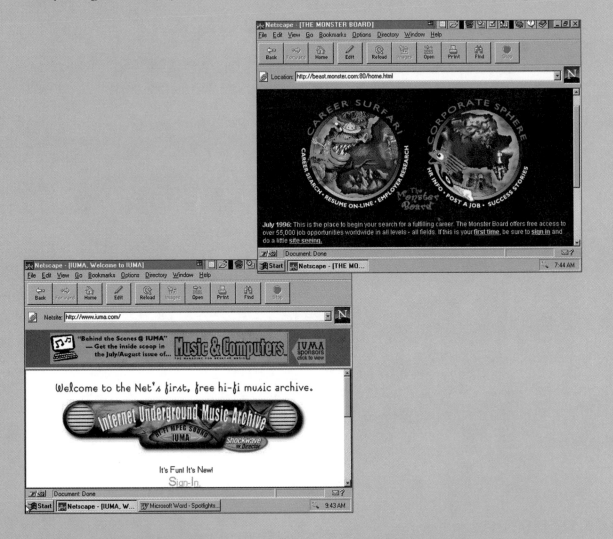

Property of AT&T Archives. Reprinted with permission of AT&T.

Courtesy of GEMPLUS Card International.

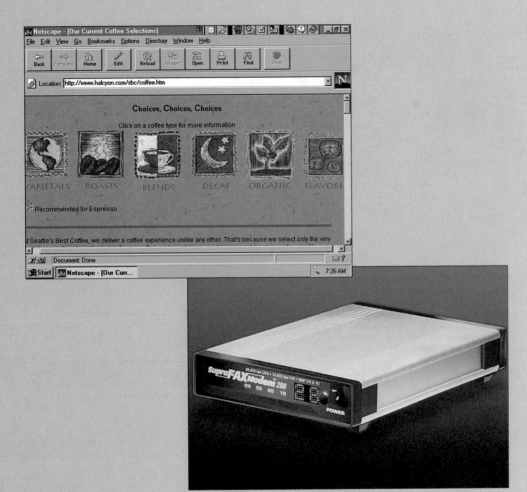

Courtesy of Diamond Multimedia Systems, Inc.

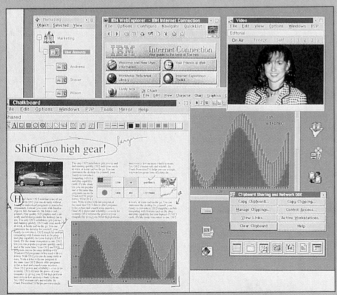

Courtesy of IBM Corporation.

Courtesy of Bellcore.

Courtesy of AMP International.

Gerard Yunker/Sight and TELUS Corporation.

PART THREE

SOFTWARE AND DATA MANAGEMENT

The operating system is a set of programs that runs or controls the computer hardware and interfaces with application software. A useful application software package is database software, which is indispensable for today's businesses.

OBJECTIVES

AFTER STUDYING THIS CHAPTER, YOU SHOULD BE ABLE TO:
1. Define system software and identify its role in a computer system.
2. Identify system software components.
3. Define the term *operating system* and state why an operating system is essential to a computer system.
4. Distinguish between internal command instructions and external command instructions.
5. List four operating system functions.
6. Define *operating system environment*.
7. Explain the meaning of serial processing, multitasking, time sharing, virtual memory, and multiprocessing.
8. List the features and capabilities of five microcomputer operating systems.
9. Explain the purpose of utility programs.
10. Contrast the properties of language translators.

CHAPTER OUTLINE

WHAT IS SYSTEM SOFTWARE?

OPERATING SYSTEMS
Common Computer System Tasks
Hardware Independence
Internal Command Instructions
External Command Instructions
Command Language Translators
Generic vs. Proprietary Operating Systems

OPERATING SYSTEM FUNCTIONS
Managing Memory
Coordinating Processing Tasks
Managing Peripheral Devices
Managing Resources

OTHER SYSTEM CAPABILITIES
Multitasking
Time Sharing
Virtual Memory
Multiprocessing

MICROCOMPUTER OPERATING SYSTEMS
PC-DOS/MS-DOS
Macintosh DOS
DOS with Windows
Windows NT
Windows 95
OS/2
UNIX

UTILITY PROGRAMS
Disk Toolkits
Data Compression Programs
Backup Utilities
Text Editors
Antivirus Utilities

LANGUAGE TRANSLATORS
Compilers
Interpreters

magine that you have decided to write a textbook. It might be a textbook on history, mathematics, or even computer science or information systems. Like most modern authors, you don't want to type and retype draft after draft of your book. Fortunately, both you and your co-author (who teaches at a university on the other coast) have computers with the same popular word processing program.

Two months of hard labor later, you confidently ship your collaborator a disk containing the first draft of Chapter 1. But instead of the congratulatory telephone call you had hoped for, you receive an alarming message from your fellow writer: "Help! My computer says it can't read your disk!"

Alas, you have fallen victim to a problem almost as old as the first computer: incompatible operating systems. The IBM computer on which you work uses PC-DOS (short for Personal Computer Disk Operating System), while the Apple Macintosh used by your co-author uses Apple's System 7. Without compatible operating systems, you might as well be speaking Greek to someone who understands only Swahili.

Operating system problems got their start when the first computer companies developed proprietary systems to which they had exclusive legal rights. Proprietary systems made it hard for customers to use machines from other companies. They also allowed computer companies to regulate the software developed for use on their systems.

The Apple II, the machine that started the microcomputer revolution when it was introduced in 1977, had a proprietary operating system (as have subsequent Apple offerings). Among Apple's earliest competitors, some developed their own proprietary systems, while a number used what they hoped would become the industry standard, a system called CP/M. Then, in 1981, IBM weighed in with the original IBM-PC. Forced to play "catch up" because of its late entry into the market, IBM departed from its usual practices and built the PC using nonproprietary software and hardware. IBM contracted with Microsoft Corporation to develop the PC-DOS operating system for the PC. IBM's enormous initial success (and the subsequent successes of those who "cloned" its machines) made the PC's operating system, DOS (called MS-DOS on IBM-compatible machines because it was developed by Microsoft), the standard for which the industry had been looking.

In the years since, Apple and IBM have continued their competition, while software developers have labored to devise versions of popular software for both standards and other software to translate between the two operating systems. For the home user, however, incompatibilities remain frustrating.

WHAT IS SYSTEM SOFTWARE?

System software is a collection of programs that starts the computer and coordinates all activities of the computer system. System software also manages peripheral devices. For instance, the operating system monitors the keyboard to determine when a key is pressed. It controls the flow of information from printers, monitors, and other devices back and forth from main memory.

The number and complexity of programs that make up system software depend upon the computer system being used. For example, system software for PCs may consist of 50 to 200 programs, whereas system software for mainframe computers may include many hundreds of programs. System software allows the end user and **application software** to communicate with the computer hardware. Without system software, your computer would be useless. System software programs are grouped into three main categories:

- Operating systems
- Utilities
- Language translators

OPERATING SYSTEMS

If you spend much time around engineering labs, you're bound to run into the term *black box*. In engineering jargon, a black box is a machine that somehow gets a job done without the user knowing *how*. The user only knows how to operate the black box to produce the desired results. Figure 8.1 shows a schematic diagram of a generic black box. Notice that the black box is defined by what you can do to it (input) and what the black box does in response (output). You are not concerned with how the black box does what it does—only that it does what is asked.

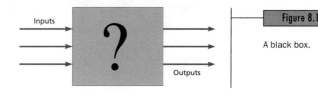

Figure 8.1

A black box.

There are many examples of black boxes in people's daily lives. To most, a television is a black box. People can manipulate the picture and sound with various dials and switches, yet they don't necessarily know how the television works. Figure 8.2 shows an example of the television as a black box.

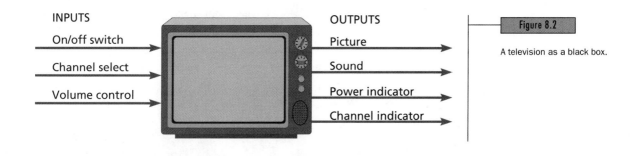

Figure 8.2

A television as a black box.

In a like manner, a computer can be thought of as a single black box, or collection of black boxes. In Figure 8.3, you can see a computer system separated into two black boxes: hardware and software. *Hardware* refers to the physical materials and circuits that constitute the computer. *Software* refers to the instructions that run the computer and tell it what to do.

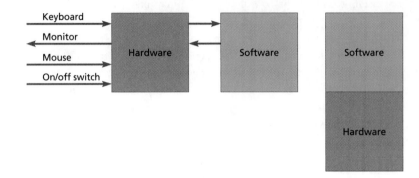

Figure 8.3

A computer as two black boxes (left) and a two-layer computer model (right).

The difference between hardware and software is relatively easy to recognize. When you switch from a word processing program to a spreadsheet program, the computer does not physically change, at least not significantly. What does change is the software, or the set of instructions that tells the hardware how to respond to your input from the keyboard.

Figure 8.3 shows the two black boxes, stacked one atop the other like layers in a cake. This "cake" model is referred to as a two-layer model of a computer system.

Figure 8.4 shows the computer system "cake" model broken into three layers. Notice that the hardware layer is the same as that of Figure 8.3, but the software layer has been further split into two layers: the application software layer and the operating system layer.

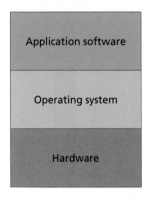

Figure 8.4

Three-layer computer model.

The application software layer is the layer with which you are familiar. Examples of application software are word processing (e.g., WordPerfect) and spreadsheets (e.g., Lotus 1-2-3). Although you are probably familiar with the look and feel of one or more application software products, the operation of the operating system layer is more subtle.

The operating system layer, designed to be invisible to the user, lies between the application software and the hardware. Looking at Figure 8.4, you can see that there is no direct path between the application software and the hardware. When the application layer needs something from the hardware layer, it first sends the request to the operating system layer. The operating system forwards the request to the hardware. The hardware performs the desired action and may return some information to the operating system, which in turn passes the information to the application.

An **operating system (OS)** is a set of programs that runs or controls the computer hardware and acts as an interface with application software programs. The operating system serves two purposes: to provide a common set of computer functions and to provide hardware independence.

COMMON COMPUTER SYSTEM TASKS

There are certain tasks that virtually all application programs must perform. These include

- Getting input from the keyboard
- Reading from and writing to disk drives
- Writing information to the computer screen

Each of these tasks is basic as far as the application software is concerned. However, the hardware layer may require many different instructions in order to complete one of these basic functions. It is the operating system that translates a simple, basic instruction into the set of instructions that the hardware requires. For example, suppose an application needs to read part of a data file. It may command the operating system:

Retrieve the eighty-seventh piece of information on disk drive F:

The operating system might translate this simple command to the hardware as follows:

Check disk drive F:
If it does not exist, tell this to the application program
Otherwise,
Start disk drive F:
Find the eighty-seventh piece of data
Read this piece of information
Send this information to the application program
Stop disk drive F:

In this case, the operating system simplifies the basic task of reading a piece of data from a disk drive. The application program need issue only one basic instruction rather than the eight or more that would be necessary without an operating system.

The typical operating system contains several hundred functions, each of which is translated to one or more instructions on the hardware side of the layer.

HARDWARE INDEPENDENCE

Looking back to Figure 8.4, notice that as far as the application program is concerned, the only other thing that exists in this world is the operating system. That is, the application program can only communicate through the operating system. Because of this, the operating system functions as a buffer, or interface, between the application and the hardware.

Suppose new hardware is designed that can operate much faster than before. Further suppose that this new hardware functions differently than the old hardware, requiring different instructions to perform certain tasks.

If operating systems did not exist, programmers would have to rewrite application software to take advantage of the new, faster hardware. Fortunately, because many applications usually share a single operating system, they need only redesign the operating system layer so that it translates the exact same set of commands on the applications side to the new groups of commands needed on the hardware side. Having an operating system layer allows programmers to design many thousands of applications for a single operating system and allows end users to use these applications on different types of hardware by simply adapting the operating system.

INTERNAL COMMAND INSTRUCTIONS

The operating system performs dual requirements of providing hardware independence and support for common computer functions through a combination of internal and external command instructions and command language translators.

Internal command instructions, also called *resident commands*, direct and coordinate application software and computer hardware. These are the most frequently used commands. They are so important to the functioning of your computer that they must be readily accessible to the CPU at all times. For this reason, they are loaded into main memory when you turn on your computer (called **booting** in microcomputer systems and **initial program loading (IPL)** in the minicomputers and mainframes). Internal command instructions remain in main memory until you turn off your computer.

The **control program** or *supervisor* is the internal command instruction that manages all other programs in the computer. It summons operating system commands as they are needed.

Internal command instructions take up much more room in main memory on minicomputers and mainframes than on PCs. This is simply because the larger and more complex the computer system is, the larger and more complex the operating system must be in order to manage the system. Although some high-end PCs now run more than one program at once, their capabilities are extremely limited when compared to the dozens of programs run by minicomputers and the hundreds of programs run by mainframes.

EXTERNAL COMMAND INSTRUCTIONS

General-purpose commands that are stored in secondary storage devices (usually on disk) and summoned by the supervisor program as necessary are called **external command instructions**, or *transient programs*. They are not as crucial as their internal cousins; they are not needed to run application software. Because transient programs are used infrequently, it is not efficient for them to remain in residence in the limited confines of main memory. A system program that allows a user to format a blank disk, for instance, might be used only once a week or less.

COMMAND LANGUAGE TRANSLATORS

The **command language translator** converts instructions into the specific machine language used by the CPU. The instructions, often written in *command language*, allow the user to specify orders (commands) directly to the operating system. For instance, you may wish to have the operating system save, delete, or rename a file; format a diskette; or copy a file from one storage location to another.

The way users initiate commands varies with operating systems. Both IBM and Microsoft versions of DOS (Disk Operating System) provide a **text interface**, where commands must be typed in. This type of interface is also referred to as *command driven*. In order to issue commands to these operating systems, you must know the commands for various operations. For instance, the command for deleting a file in DOS is DEL, a space, followed by the filename. The command is initiated by pressing the ENTER key. An example of a text interface as it appears on your monitor is shown in Figure 8.5.

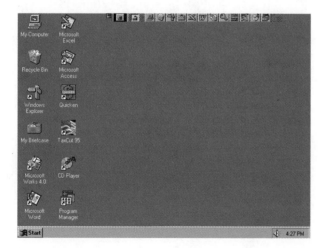

Figure 8.5

In order to issue commands in operating systems employing a text interface, you must know the command language syntax and type in commands.

The Apple and Macintosh operating systems, in contrast, use a **graphical user interface (GUI)**. Rather than remembering a command and its syntax, users are given visual representations, or icons, of commands to select. For instance, to delete a file, the user would use the mouse to point to a file folder icon, press and hold the mouse button, drag the file folder to a trash can icon, and release the mouse button. An example of a graphical interface is shown in Figure 8.6. Some people find the visual representations easier to use than text-based commands, while others find text-based commands faster once they are learned.

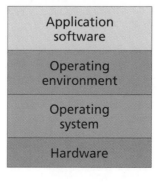

Figure 8.6

Some people enjoy the visual representations offered in graphical interface operating systems.

Recently, developers have come up with a way to offer a graphical interface to DOS users. Originally, this was accomplished through a program called an **operating environment**, which fit on top of the operating system as the next layer of software, as illustrated in Figure 8.7. Examples of programs that fit over DOS operating systems include Microsoft Windows and Hewlett-Packard's New Wave.

| Application software |
| Operating environment |
| Operating system |
| Hardware |

Figure 8.7

The operating environment acts as a layer between the operating system and application software, providing the user with a graphical interface.

Even more recently, Microsoft developed an operating system for IBM and compatible PCs that in itself makes use of a graphical interface. The operating system is known as Windows NT (New Technology) and is discussed, along with other microcomputer operating systems, in greater detail later in this chapter.

GENERIC VS. PROPRIETARY OPERATING SYSTEMS

Operating systems for PCs are often generic. This means that they are designed for compatibility with a number of computer brands. For instance, MS-DOS and Windows NT are operating systems designed for use with all IBM and compatible PCs. Most PCs are sold with operating systems preinstalled by retailers and included in the purchase price. When purchasing a PC, you should investigate what operating system is included with the system and whether this operating system fits your needs. Often there are trade-offs when selecting a particular operating system. Some that are easier to use are slower. Some that have many additional features are also more expensive.

Operating systems for Apple computers and for most mainframes are proprietary: they are designed to work on only one kind of computer system. In the case of mainframes, they are usually purchased separately from the computer system and are specially designed to fit the needs of the organization that will put them to use. The table below lists a selection of operating systems and the computers with which each can be used.

Proprietary and Generic Operating Systems		
Operating System	**Kind of Computer(s)**	**Type**
Apple DOS 3.3	Apple II and III Series	proprietary
Apple ProDOS	Apple II Series	proprietary
CP/M	Older (early 1980s) microcomputer brands	generic
GCOS	Honeywell mainframe computers	proprietary
MS-DOS	IBM-PCs and compatibles	generic
OS/2	IBM PS/2 and compatibles (Multichannel architecture)	generic
OSNS	IBM mainframe computers	proprietary
TRS-DOS	Tandy TRS-80 Series	proprietary
UNIX	Powerful PCs and some minicomputers mainframes	generic
VAXNMS	DEC's VAX series of minicomputers	proprietary
VM	IBM mainframe computers	proprietary
VMS	IBM mainframe computers	proprietary
Windows NT	Powerful PCs, minicomputers, and IBM mainframe computers	generic
Windows 95	Powerful PCs containing the latest microprocessors	generic

OPERATING SYSTEM FUNCTIONS

Now that you are familiar with the pieces that make up an operating system, the ways in which the operating system manages and controls a computer system's hardware and software applications can be examined in more detail. Keep in mind that the operating system you are using may not include every function examined. As previously mentioned, operating systems for large mainframe computers must be able to manage more resources and accommodate more users than an operating system for a PC. In order to meet the dual requirements of providing support for common computer system tasks and hardware independence, operating systems perform these four important functions:

- Managing the allocation of main memory
- Coordinating processing tasks
- Scheduling the use of peripheral devices such as secondary storage devices and printers
- Monitoring the use of all equipment

MANAGING MEMORY

One of the functions of the operating system is memory management. Memory management includes protecting programs in memory from accidental erasure and accommodating programs that exceed the physical limitations of main memory.

An operating system keeps track of its own location and how much main memory it occupies. It prohibits other programs and data from being stored in its space. An operating system also protects all programs and data by assigning them memory space. Once memory is assigned to a particular program, it cannot be used for other programs or data.

Some operating systems contain memory management programs that automatically separate main memory into equal, fixed-size blocks called **partitions**. The operating system is stored in one partition, application programs in another, and data in another. Operating system memory management programs are equipped to expand or reduce the size of a partition to accommodate the data or program if it is too large to fit into a single partition. Using this technique, the main memory is allocated on the basis of need; that is, longer programs and data are allocated more main memory space. Figure 8.8 illustrates this situation.

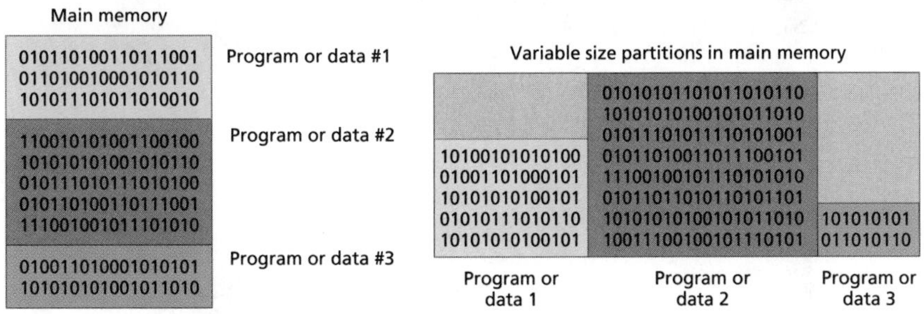

Figure 8.8

The operating system contains memory management programs that automatically adjust the size of partitions to accommodate program length.

COORDINATING PROCESSING TASKS

Each separate program run by a computer system is called a **job**. Each job requires special instructions or commands for assigning input, output, and secondary storage devices. For maximum efficiency, some operating systems have **job control programs** that allow opera-tors to line up (queue) several jobs so that the computer can start executing the next job as soon as the current job is completed. At the beginning of each job in the queue, a group of instructions is inserted in a special language, called **job control language (JCL)**. These instructions provide the operating system with information such as the name of the user; the specific programs to use; and the input, output, and secondary storage devices to be used. After finishing the first job, the job control program reads and follows the next set of JCL instructions and sets up the next job.

Some operating systems also contain a **scheduling program**, which examines the jobs in the queue and schedules each job according to the criteria specified by the com-puter staff. Normally, a scheduling program determines a job's priority and estimates the amount of time required to complete the job. Many organizations use some method for prioritizing computer jobs, especially when several users share the same computer.

MANAGING PERIPHERAL DEVICES

An operating system is also responsible for coordinating the operation of the processor with its peripheral devices. One of the operating system's main tasks is to identify the various peripheral devices attached to the processor, as shown in Figure 8.9. For example, disk drives on most personal computers are identified by the letters A, B, C, and so forth.

Figure 8.9

One of the tasks of the oper-ating system is to identify the peripheral devices attached to the system and coordinate their use.

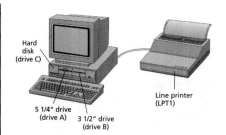

Hard disk (drive C)

5 1/4" drive (drive A)   3 1/2" drive (drive B)

Line printer (LPT1)

In large computer systems, a unique **device address** is assigned to each peripheral device to identify it and its location, as illustrated in Figure 8.10. For example, architects in a large firm might use monitors, keyboards, and digitizing tablets to enter designs into their workstations. The designs are sent over coaxial cable lines to a large central com-puter for processing. After processing, each architect designates one of several output devices in the office to receive the results. For example, the command "Queue=LPT3" would instruct the operating system to send the output to the plotter designated as LPT3.

Figure 8.10

In large computer systems, the operating system assigns unique device addresses to each peripheral device.

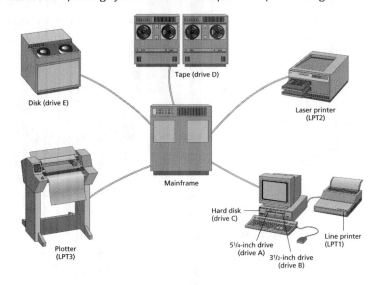

Disk (drive E)

Tape (drive D)

Laser printer (LPT2)

Mainframe

Plotter (LPT3)

Hard disk (drive C)

5¼-inch drive (drive A)   3½-inch drive (drive B)

Line printer (LPT1)

MANAGING RESOURCES

Operating systems manage computer system resources. Computer system resource management includes

- Keeping track of computer access and usage
- Keeping track of peripheral device usage
- Providing up-to-date reports of system utilization costs

Access to and usage of a computer system can be monitored for security and control so that unauthorized use of a computer system and user files can be prevented. Nearly everyone has heard of or has read horror stories about unauthorized users gaining access to computer files and changing, damaging, or destroying valuable information. An operating system can keep track of each time the computer is used and which programs and files were accessed by each user. Each time a user accesses the computer system, the operating system electronically stores information about the access in a **run log**, as illustrated in Figure 8.11. In the log, entries include the ID number and name of the user, the programs executed, all files accessed, the date, and the time the user logged on and off the system. A run log provides an audit trail for monitoring computer access that can be used to improve user service and establish security and accountability procedures in the computer system.

User	Name	Program	File	Date	Time in	Time out
3231	Roberts	GENLDGR	INVENT	03–OCT–1993	0923	1040
1287	Blimlic	GENLDGR	PAYROLL	03–OCT–1993	0945	0949
1108	Crimmins	GENLDGR	PERSONNEL	03–OCT–1993	1028	1035
0893	Sanders	GENLDGR	ENGINEER	03–OCT–1993	1145	1710
2543	Mitchell	GENLDGR	WAREHOUSE	03–OCT–1993	1151	1155
7634	DeLoache	FORECAST	SALES	03–OCT–1993	1208	1220
1186	Tribble	FORECAST	SALES	03–OCT–1993	1342	1350
4301	Simmons	GENLDGR	SURVEY1	03–OCT–1993	1455	1725
5569	Tanner	MARKET	CUSTOMER	03–OCT–1993	1532	1535
3337	Yadkin	GENLDGR	PERSONNEL	03–OCT–1993	1557	1601
1217	Ruffins	MARKET	DISTRIBUT	03–OCT–1993	1611	1622
5588	Perry	MAINT2.5	DPPROG	03–OCT–1993	1646	1820
0057	Mason	FORECAST	SALES	03–OCT–1993	1721	1729
9783	Benjamin	GENLDGR	ACCOUNTING	03–OCT–1993	1733	1901
9102	Wilkes	MARKET	R&DEVEL	03–OCT–1993	1758	1814

Figure 8.11

Run logs provide a means for monitoring computer use.

Some organizations want to keep track of how often and how much computer peripheral devices are used. Having this information on hand can help in making resource allocation decisions. If an organization learns that a particular terminal or printer is rarely used, it might decide to move the device to another area where the need is greater. Some operating systems also keep track of this information in the run log.

Some organizations allocate the costs of operating a computer system among users or departments. This is done by first preparing a fee schedule that identifies cost items such as processor time, disk storage space, printer time, and the number of pages printed. The operating system retrieves this information from the run log and produces an accounting report. Accounts and accumulated charges are billed according to individual user passwords or account codes.

A company can also use these reports for budget preparation and for predicting future computer usage. The main advantages are:

- They allow administrators to monitor usage.
- They make it possible to estimate future computer resource needs.

An example of a utilization report is shown in Figure 8.12.

Figure 8.12

Utilization reports allow administrators to monitor computer usage and make charges to departments' budgets accordingly.

Employee name	CPU usage	Disk usage	Paper usage
Adams, Jason	8.01 sec	4 pages	131 sheets
Blalock, Agnes	4.23 sec	5 pages	97 sheets
Blalock, Bill	5.67 sec	12 pages	101 sheets
Fuller, Michael	6.54 sec	10 pages	116 sheets
Fuller, Edith	7.31 sec	11 pages	99 sheets
Marsh, Cathy	3.94 sec	6 pages	77 sheets
Marsh, Gerald	4.45 sec	8 pages	63 sheets
Marsh, Doris	5.21 sec	7 pages	54 sheets
Sanders, Kay	7.46 sec	5 pages	71 sheets
Taylor, Rich	9.03 sec	11 pages	88 sheets
Winbon, Cindy	6.08 sec	9 pages	109 sheets
Winbon, Doug	4.47 sec	5 pages	66 sheets
Wyse, Brian	5.54 sec	8 pages	73 sheets

Total department charges. $91.26

OTHER SYSTEM CAPABILITIES

Operating systems and computers are constantly improving. As personal computers become more powerful, they are able to perform many of the functions that were previously done only on larger computers. For instance, the earliest type of operating system, called a **serial processing** operating system, allowed only a single user to run a single program at one time. If there were a number of jobs to be processed, these were done in a series. This type was used on the first computers in the late 1940s and early 1950s. Many PCs still use this type of system. Later, more advanced operating systems, called **multiprogramming** operating systems, were developed for minicomputers and mainframes that allowed several users to run their programs at one time. Now, tasks such as running more than one program at a time or supporting more than one user at a time can also be accomplished on PCs. The following sections examine methods that allow the scheduling and assignment of multiple jobs at the same time.

MULTITASKING

Most early computers were serial processing computers, which meant that programs were processed one after another, in a series. Because processing occurs at much higher speeds than any other phase of the computer cycle (such as input and output), most processors were idle much of the time. **Multitasking** operating systems allow single users to run more than one program at a time, whether they are using PC systems or larger systems. With multitasking, single users can work with a spreadsheet application, for example, and a database application concurrently. Multiple applications are in process at a time, but because the computer is so fast, the user does not realize that multiple tasks are occurring.

Multitasking is possible through partitioning, discussed earlier in this chapter. The CPU can process only one instruction at a time, but the instruction can come from any partition. After the processor performs operations per the instructions in the first program, the operating system directs the processor to retrieve instructions and accompanying data from another partition, such as the second program, then the third, and so on. This procedure is repeated until all instructions in all the programs, along with the data, are processed, as shown in Figure 8.13.

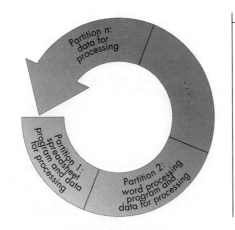

Figure 8.13

Multitasking processes jobs concurrently. The operating system directs the CPU to perform small sections of a program at a time, cycling through partitions until all processing is complete.

TIME SHARING

Time sharing (also called *time slicing)* is similar to multitasking in that both allot short periods of time for the processing of multiple programs on one CPU on a rotating basis. They differ, however, in how they allot time for processing. In multitasking, the CPU processes a program until it comes to a logical stopping point and then moves on to the next program. With time sharing, the CPU spends a fixed amount of time with each program and moves on, no matter whether its stopping point is logical or not. For example, if five programs run simultaneously, a CPU set up for time sharing will spend perhaps 1 second with a program (the actual time slice can be much smaller than this) and then move on to the next program, cycling through until all programs are completely executed.

The benefit of time sharing is that users executing small programs are not held up while waiting for the CPU to come to a logical stopping point in processing a large, complicated program, as might be the case with a multitasking computer system. With time sharing, no single program dominates the CPU's time.

VIRTUAL MEMORY

With most computers, main memory is a limited and, therefore, valuable resource. The more users there are, the less main memory is available for each user. Moreover, when programs and data are partitioned, it takes more main memory because of the necessary system recordkeeping and the small, unfilled storage areas in the partitions. Both of these factors can cause a shortage of main memory that can be overcome by using virtual memory.

Virtual memory uses a technique for managing the limited amount of main memory and a larger amount of low-speed secondary storage, such as hard disk storage, in such a way that the difference in speeds between the two types is not perceived by the computer user. The technique entails swapping segments of the program and data from the low-speed secondary storage (such as a hard disk) into high-speed internal storage (main memory). The high-speed internal storage is called *real storage*. The low-speed secondary storage is called *virtual storage*.

The segment of the program or the amount of data swapped back and forth is referred to as a *page*. Thus, the virtual memory process is called **paging**. This technique divides programs and data into equal-size sections, or pages. Each page consists of a block of a few thousand bytes or characters. From one to a few pages are kept in main memory with the remaining pages kept in secondary storage. The operating system keeps a list containing the number of pages in the program and their locations in memory. When another page is needed during processing, the operating system scans the list to find the page and its location and retrieves the page. After the computer finishes with the first page, the page is moved to secondary storage, and the next page is brought into main memory from secondary storage. This procedure is called **swapping**—an old page is swapped for a new page. This way, only a portion of a program needs to be in main memory at one time, freeing main memory space for other program pages (see Figure 8.14).

Figure 8.14

A virtual memory technique called paging separates programs and data into segments and stores them in secondary storage. The pages are swapped into main memory as they are needed for processing.

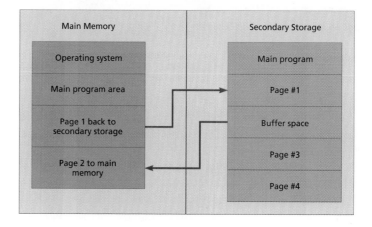

Virtual memory can be implemented in both multitasking and serial processing environments. However, its use is more prominent in multitasking environments because of the greater demand for main memory when multiple programs are being executed.

MULTIPROCESSING

When a multiuser computer has an exceptionally heavy workload, it tends to slow to the point that it is unable to perform its data processing tasks as quickly and as efficiently as users would like. To increase processing speed, some computers combine more than one CPU in order to share the workload, as illustrated in Figure 8.15. Computers having more than one CPU are called **multiprocessing** systems, and they can have a variety of different configurations. With multiprocessing systems, processing is accomplished simultaneously on two or more CPUs, rather than concurrently on a single CPU as discussed with the other processing methods. Scheduling applications on multiple CPUs is complex and requires a large, sophisticated operating system.

An organization using a multiple-CPU system must decide how to divide the work among the CPUs. In some systems, the operating system divides the work almost equally. In other systems, a single application may be split between two or more CPUs. Still other systems may be designed to allocate special tasks to each CPU, such as controlling user input and output. Recall from Chapter 4 that systems employing many microprocessors (up to tens of thousands) are called *massively parallel processing systems.*

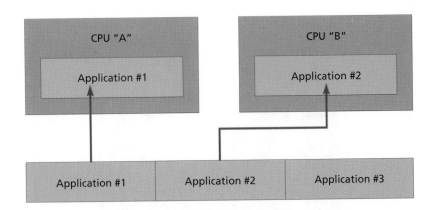

Figure 8.15

With multiprocessing, two or more CPUs share processing chores. The processing is accomplished simultaneously.

MICROCOMPUTER OPERATING SYSTEMS

You are likely to encounter and be expected to become familiar with a number of PC operating systems. In the past, DOS was the overwhelmingly predominant system, but the development of increasingly powerful processors and sophisticated software, coupled with some built-in limitations of DOS, have given rise to several competing types of PC operating systems. The following sections take a look at the most popular operating systems on the market today and explain the main differences among them.

PC-DOS/MS-DOS

In 1981, IBM announced its entry into the PC market. Before that, IBM had always developed and supplied its own operating system software for its hardware. However, with the introduction of the PC, IBM contracted with Microsoft Corporation, which was then a small company near Seattle, Washington. Microsoft developed PC-DOS for the IBM PC and MS-DOS, its generic equivalent, for IBM-compatible PCs.

Microsoft licenses the source code of MS-DOS to hardware manufacturers who make slight changes or additions and change the name to refer to their systems. For instance, variations of DOS include COMPAQ-DOS, NEC-DOS, and Zenith DOS. The changes are so slight that applications written for one DOS operating system will also work on any of the others. All of these operating systems are commonly referred to simply as DOS. DOS is a serial processing system, meaning that it is a single-user, single-task operating system.

IBM became interested in the PC market in 1979 because of the development of the new 8088 microprocessor chip from Intel Corporation. This chip contained more main memory capabilities and greater processing speeds than its predecessors. DOS was designed to take advantage of these capabilities. Since then, PCs have evolved through six generations of Intel microprocessor chips (the 8088, 8086, 80286, 80386, 80486, and 80586—the Pentium). Each chip supplied the user with new capabilities and features. In order to maintain its crucial role of offering hardware independence, as each generation of Intel chip has evolved, so too has DOS.

Yet even with all of the upgrades, DOS by itself remains primarily a command-driven operating system for single users performing single tasks at a time. In addition, DOS is incapable of fully exploiting the 32-bit wordsize offered with the new Pentium chip.

MS-DOS 7 (see Figure 8.16) is the current industry standard for IBM-compatible personal computers. Various versions of MS-DOS operating systems appear on about 65 percent (60 million) of all PCs in the United States. This is largely due to the number of applications written to work with this operating system.

Figure 8.16

Users of Windows 95 can access MS-DOS 7 to execute DOS commands.

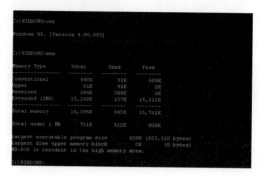

COMPUTER CURRENTS

Beyond the Speed of Light

Over the last two decades, computer processing speed has doubled about every 2 years. This has been great news for scholars, scientists, and engineers who rely on computers to analyze enormous quantities of data. After all, the faster a computer can complete a single calculation, the faster it can work its way through the thousands, millions, or even billions of calculations necessary to send a man to the moon . . . or design the new best-selling car.

Such speed has not come cheaply, of course. The mighty supercomputers that have most often been used in such undertakings have usually come with price tags as breathtaking as their accomplishments. Now many experts are questioning whether the ultimate answer may not only be faster but less expensive: *massively parallel processing*.

For years, super-computers have been the "work harder and smarter" solution to solving large problems. But computer speeds are increasingly nearing what may be the physical limit—the speed of sound. Thus many experts in the field are suggesting that it's time to "hire more help": to let "many hands make light work" by putting many computers (microprocessors) to work on a complex problem simultaneously. When the "many" is thousands, or even tens of thousands, of microprocessors, the result is massively parallel processing (MPP).

The difficulty of making MPP work is in coordinating the labors of the various computers involved. Using MPP means first deciding how the task will be divided between computers, then allocating the efforts of those computers.

There are two basic ways of dividing a task in MPP: single instruction multiple data (SIMD) and multiple instruction multiple data (MIMD). As their names imply, in SIMD, all the computers perform the same calculations, but on different sets of data, while in MIMD, each computer manipulates the data differently. While it is more difficult to divide up the task to achieve MIMD, such systems may offer the greatest potential for coping with the computing challenges of the future.

These challenges are coming from all directions. Leading the pack (in part because of its "deep pockets") is the U.S. government. For example, at NASA, scientists are using MPP to analyze the enormous volume of data being generated as part of a study of the earth's climate. Other U.S. government researchers hope that a giant MPP system will help them understand what happens in the core of a nuclear reactor so that they can create safer reactors —perhaps even eventually making nuclear fusion a viable energy supply. In addition, medical researchers are now using MPP to study the effects of toxins on the human body.

Private industry is also leaping on the MPP bandwagon. The oil companies have begun using MPP instead of supercomputers to analyze seismic data and locate potential new oil fields. Firms that need to access very

Courtesy of IBM Corporation.

large databases may be best suited to MPP. For example, airlines, insurance companies, banks, and credit card companies have shown keen interest in MPP. So have retailers. Indeed, Wal-Mart stores currently use MPP to analyze 8.8 *trillion* bytes of data on inventory levels and sales. Neodata Corporation, a multinational direct-marketing company that handles more than 13 million transactions and 3 million telephone calls each month, uses MPP to analyze its huge database.

The reasons for MPP users' enthusiasm are obvious when you consider what MPP can do . . . and what it *doesn't* cost. The fastest supercomputers today operate at speeds of a "mere" 1.3 billion calculations per second. Experts say that MPP could more easily achieve "teraflops"—1 trillion calculations per second—with some saying that even 2 trillion calculations per second could be achieved in the near future, using MPP. And best of all, this great speed can be made available at far more modest cost than that of supercomputers.

MACINTOSH DOS

Apple's first microcomputer, the Apple II, was introduced in 1979 and came with an operating system that made use of an icon-oriented graphical user interface. Apple computers employ Motorola processors, which have a completely different architecture than the Intel processors for IBM PCs and compatibles. The two systems are unable to share data without special equipment and software. The original Apple operating system was called Apple DOS. It was designed for single users performing single tasks at a time.

With the Macintosh line of computers came the more powerful operating system called Macintosh DOS. This operating system supports multitasking and virtual memory. System 7 is a recent version of Macintosh DOS. A sample screen is shown in Figure 8.17. Apple's icon-oriented operating system set a standard in ease of use that many other operating systems are trying to emulate.

Figure 8.17

Macintosh System 7.5 provides an easy to use graphical interface that other operating systems are striving to emulate.

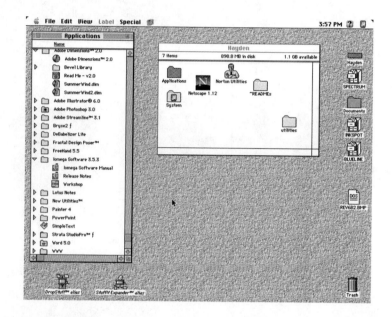

DOS WITH WINDOWS

In the mid-80s, Microsoft Corporation introduced Windows, a program designed to give DOS a graphical interface similar to the icon-driven operating systems of the Apple Macintosh and make it easier to use and more powerful. Windows is not an operating system itself, but rather a shell for the DOS operating system. It is often referred to as an operating environment. The feature that makes Windows so easy to use is an intuitive graphical user interface in which users work with on-screen icons and pull-down menus rather than with commands typed in from the keyboard.

A main feature of Windows is the use of a concept called a *window*. A **window** is a portion of the display screen dedicated to some specific purpose. The computer screen can be divided into multiple windows, as illustrated in Figure 8.18, that can be moved around on the screen and made larger or smaller.

The Windows program allows the user to treat the computer screen like a desktop where several programs can remain open simultaneously, moving back and forth among them without having to close one and open another, as is necessary in DOS.

For example, the user can be working with one program while printing output from another. Or, the user can transfer information or visuals from one window (application) to another. In these ways, the Windows shell program offers the user a multitasking environment.

Windows software has some disadvantages. Because the program is so large, current versions require a minimum of 8 megabytes (8 million characters with 16 million recommended) of memory. It cannot be used with all microcomputers, particularly older ones (since it requires an 80386 or newer processor, such as Intel's Pentium processor). Also, only those application programs designed for use with Windows function well within that environment. However, many popular DOS programs have been rewritten to work with Windows. In fact, most newer versions of popular application software are being written for Windows and are thus being influenced by its popularity.

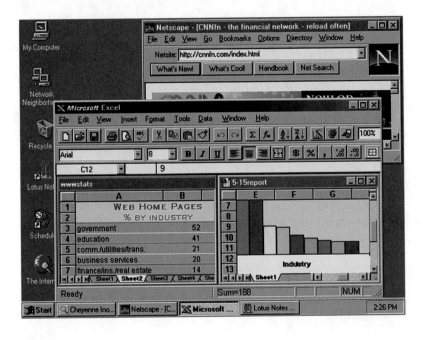

Figure 8.18

Windows provides a graphical interface and a multitasking environment.

WINDOWS NT

Microsoft took the shell concept and made it into a new category of operating system for the PC. Windows NT (for New Technology) was targeted as the successor to both DOS and DOS with Windows. It was designed to take advantage of the newer 32-bit processors and features multitasking and network capabilities. These features are also a part of OS/2, IBM's entry into the competition for a successor to DOS.

WINDOWS 95

The newest version of Windows for IBM compatibles is Microsoft's Windows 95. Unlike earlier versions, Windows 95 includes the newest version of DOS. The features contained in earlier versions of Windows have been improved in this latest version. In addition, several new features have been added. Following is a list of some of these new features.

A New Interface Windows 95 features a new Start button and task bar (see Figure 8.19). By clicking on the Start button, the user can open documents quickly, find documents, and use system tools, such as the text tool and drawing tool. The task bar allows the user to switch between programs and files in a manner similar to changing channels on a television.

Figure 8.19

Windows 95 features a new Start button and task bar that allow the user to open documents quickly and switch between programs and files.

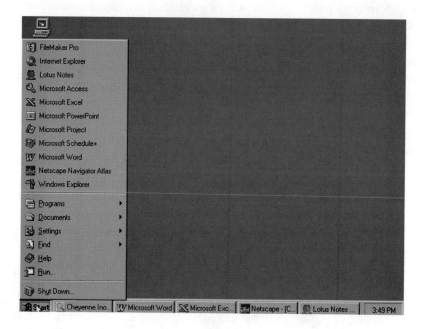

Windows Explorer This feature allows the user to browse through and manage files, drives, and network connections. By using Windows Explorer, the user can locate programs and files quickly and easily (see Figure 8.20).

Figure 8.20

The Windows Explorer feature allows the user to browse through and manage files, drives, and network connections.

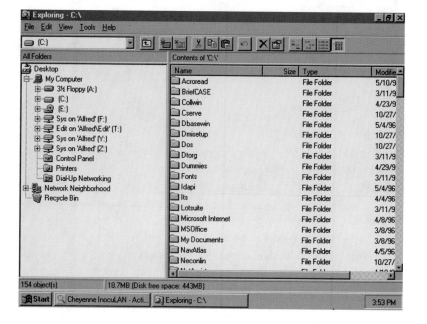

Long Filenames Windows 95 allows for longer filenames than do earlier versions. Earlier versions limited a filename to eight characters. Windows 95 has removed this limitation.

Improved Game and Media Support Windows 95 provides faster video capability for games, enhanced support for MS-DOS-based games, and improved performance for playing video and sound files.

Plug and Play Hardware Compatibility This feature makes the installation of additional peripheral devices easier. With Windows 95, the user simply inserts the card for the device. When the computer is turned on, Windows recognizes and automatically sets up the newly installed hardware.

32-bit Preemptive Multitasking Windows 95 allows the user to use several programs at once. The user can switch back and forth between applications quickly and easily.

Microsoft Exchange Microsoft Exchange allows the user to view and work with all types of electronic communications, including e-mail and faxes.

Microsoft Network This is Microsoft's new information service, similar to America Online and Prodigy (see Figure 8.21). The user needs only to answer a few on-screen questions to gain access. Once on-line, the user can communicate with people worldwide, use e-mail and bulletin boards, and have access to the Internet. There is a subscription fee for access to the Microsoft Network, which can be paid monthly or annually.

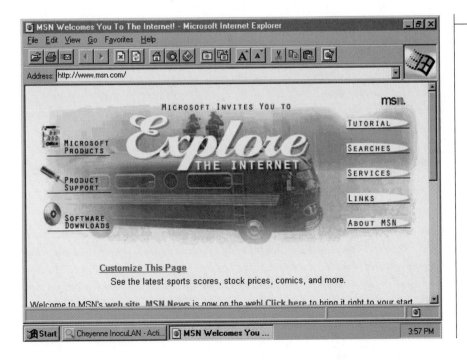

Figure 8.21

Microsoft Network, a new information service, allows users to use e-mail, bulletin boards, and have access to the Internet.

OS/2

IBM supplies OS/2 (Operating System/2) for its high-end PS/2 family of personal computers. It can also be used with other current more sophisticated PCs. It is designed for a single user working on multiple applications at once (see Figure 8.22). OS/2 is packaged with a shell program called Presentation Manager, which provides a graphical user interface similar to that of Microsoft Windows. OS/2 can run multiple applications simultaneously, whether they are programs designed for Windows, OS/2, or DOS. OS/2 takes advantage of 32-bit wordsize processing and multitasking capabilities. OS/2 comes in a standard edition and an extended edition, which offers built-in networking and database features.

Figure 8.22

OS/2 has a graphical user interface that makes it convenient for users wishing to work on multiple applications at once.

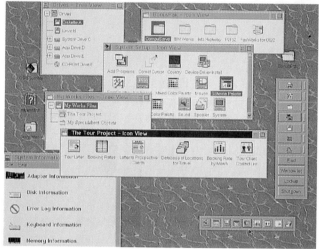

Courtesy of IBM Corporation.

OS/2 was originally developed as a joint venture of IBM and Microsoft and was designed to replace MS-DOS. At the same time, Microsoft was developing Microsoft Windows independently, as an interim graphical user interface shell for DOS. Because of the immense popularity of Windows and early poor sales of OS/2 (it required more expensive hardware and had far fewer application software programs available), Microsoft and IBM went separate ways. Microsoft focused on new versions of Windows and IBM concentrated on developing OS/2.

A more recent version of OS/2 is called OS/2 Warp, version 3 (for warp speed). While the newer version retains most of the features of earlier ones, it does run faster, particularly on newer computer models.

UNIX

UNIX, from AT&T, is another very powerful operating system that was first developed to run on minicomputers as a multiuser, multitasking operating system. UNIX also offers virtual storage and time sharing capabilities. The operating system was rewritten in 1973 to allow its use on a larger range of computers, from mainframes to high-end microcomputers. UNIX is known as a *portable* system because it is "portable to" a very wide range of hardware. A portable operating system is extremely flexible. Because it is the same for various sizes of computers, it is easy to move programs and data among computers or to connect

FOCUS

IBM Developing Products for Windows

In the PC operating systems arena, IBM and Microsoft have been fierce competitors for many years. Today, IBM's OS/2 and Microsoft's Windows NT and Windows 95 are the dominant players in the operating system market. Both companies have spent millions of marketing dollars touting the virtues of their respective OS products. Windows NT and Windows 95 have emerged as the dominant network and PC operating systems.

An agreement between the companies enables IBM to develop new versions of some of its popular applications software for use with Windows NT and Windows 95. In December 1995, IBM released its popular database, DB2 Version 2, for Windows NT. Earlier DOS-based versions of DB2 have been profitable to IBM. Databases represent a substantial portion of the network software market and this new product gives the company a competitive presence in this market.

The agreement also enables IBM to develop other products in its software portfolio for Windows NT and Windows 95. The company's goal is to give customers the broadest set of options for implementing or enhancing enterprise (an organization's) net-

works. "There's a lot of interest among customers wanting to retain freedom of choice—where they can pick the platform they want and implement the best tools," said Tim Negris, vice president of sales and marketing for IBM's Software Solutions Division, in

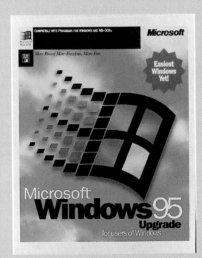

Courtesy of Microsoft Corporation.

Somers, New York. "We'll be extremely aggressive moving to Windows NT and Windows 95—not just porting, but being exemplary on those platforms," he said. Negris emphasized that these efforts are not a capitulation to rival Microsoft Corporation, but an attempt to give customers a strong alternative to Microsoft products.

Source: This FOCUS article is paraphrased (except for the quotes) from two articles obtained from *PCWeek* via the Internet. The two articles are:
1. Taschek, John. "IBM's DB2 for Windows NT Looks Powerful, Not Pretty." December 4, 1995.
2. O'Regan, Rob. "Big Blue Readies 3-pronged Software Strategy for '96." February 8, 1996.

mainframes and PCs together to share resources. UNIX can also run programs designed for different operating systems, even in a network where individual computers are using different operating systems. A sample UNIX screen is shown in Figure 8.23.

UNIX, however, is relatively slow compared to operating systems built specifically for certain families of computers. With continuing improvements being made to it, UNIX is becoming a more versatile and popular operating system. UNIX is often used in government, scientific research institutes, universities, and large companies where a cost-effective networked environment that can support a variety of computer systems is needed for day-to-day operations.

Figure 8.23

UNIX runs on a large range of computers from micros to mainframes.

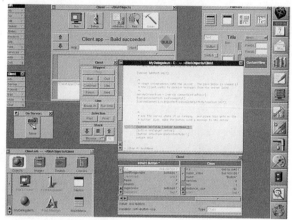

Courtesy of Sun Microsystems.

UTILITY PROGRAMS

Another important type of system software program is the **utility program**, which provides commonly needed services. A utility program assists the user in maintaining and improving the efficiency of a computer system. Typical utility programs provide such services as transferring data from one storage medium to another (for instance, disk to tape); sorting, merging, copying, deleting, or renaming files; and transferring files from one location inside a computer to another or from the CPU to a printer. Utilities usually reside in secondary storage and are summoned by the user or the operating system supervisor program as needed. Utility programs are packaged in a variety of ways. Some are built directly into the operating system, while others are packaged as independent programs that can be acquired from third-party vendors.

Large operating systems supply a set of utility programs. These utilities are designed to aid the operation of the computer for a number of different applications. Examples of specific utilities are programs that print the contents of memory, identify errors in user programs, and store files more efficiently. The table on the next page shows a partial list of utilities included with Microsoft's MS-DOS 6 operating system. However, utilities are available from vendors that include additional programs, such as disk toolkits, data compression programs, backup utilities, and text editors. The range and variety of available utilities programs is enormous. The following sections examine a few of the more common ones.

MS-DOS 6 Operating System Utilities

Utility	Function
COMP	Compares the contents of two files to see if they are identical.
COPY	Copies a file from one disk to another disk.
DEL	Deletes a file from a disk.
DIR	Lists all files stored on a disk.
DISKCOMP	Compares the information on one disk to another disk.
DISKCOPY	Makes a copy of an entire disk onto another disk.
FORMAT	Prepares a new diskette for use, checks the diskette for unusable segments, and creates a directory of files.
RENAME	Allows you to change the name of a file.
TYPE	Displays the contents of a file on the screen.

DISK TOOLKITS

A popular and useful utility package for PCs, called Norton Utilities, allows you to recover accidentally erased data, repair damaged files, and recover from a crashed disk. Norton Utilities contains a program that analyzes a disk to identify potential problems and offers solutions for correcting problems. For example, the program can determine if a disk is damaged and, if it is, suggest corrective action by the user. This software is easy to use. It allows you to choose options from a main menu (see Figure 8.24). When you choose the option "Diagnose Disk," for example, a disk is analyzed and any problems with the disk are displayed on the screen. Then, the utility program suggests the corrective action for you to take. Although the check-disk utility supplied with DOS can perform similar activities, many users feel Norton Utilities is more thorough and easier to use.

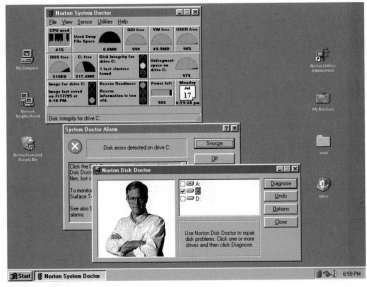

Courtesy of Symantec.

Figure 8.24

Norton Utilities is an example of a disk toolkit utility that allows you to recover or repair lost or damaged files.

The bit-mapped schemes of some graphic files are too large to fit on a diskette without first being condensed by a data compression utility.

Courtesy of Sun Microsystems.

DATA COMPRESSION PROGRAMS

Some graphics files are so large that they cannot fit on a single diskette without the use of a data compression program. A data compression program, such as PKZip, contains a scheme for organizing data in such a way that extremely large files are compressed to a fraction of their original size. This helps not only in fitting unwieldy graphics files onto diskettes, but also in saving time and cost in sending large files over communications channels. The data are unreadable in their compressed format, but the same software that compresses data contains a decompression program that restores data to their original form.

BACKUP UTILITIES

Backup utilities allow you to back up your hard disk in a fraction of the time it would take to do so using operating system commands. They also allow you to decrease the number of disks you use when you perform a complete system backup by compressing the data.

TEXT EDITORS

Text editors allow you to manipulate lists and records easily and quickly. They are particularly helpful for manipulating lines of computer code and columns of data. They allow you to make global changes, such as correcting errors in the ordering of fields, with one easy command. Programmers and those who work with databases find text editors extremely useful.

ANTIVIRUS UTILITIES

Other very popular and practical utilities are known as antivirus utilities. A **virus** is a small, destructive program that finds its way into a computer system and attacks and destroys data files, programs, or even the operating system itself. Your computer can become contaminated with a virus by executing a program containing that virus. Frequent backup of hard disk files reduces the loss potential, but the best answer is to use antivirus utilities to combat these intruders.

When virus-protection utilities are first loaded (called *inoculation*), they immediately search for known viruses on floppy disks, hard disks, and computer memory. If detected, the virus is identified, the user is alerted, and the virus is removed.

Symantec is a leading supplier of antivirus utilities. When installed, its antivirus utility scans each new diskette or file entering the system for virus contamination. The company keeps the utility current through periodic upgrades to fight new virus strains. Viruses are discussed in more detail in Chapter 13.

Numerous antivirus software packages are available. Many are designed specifically for use with Windows 3.1 and others for Windows 95. Some are capable of detecting and eliminating viruses transmitted over the Internet. For example, Symantec Corporation's Norton AntiVirus for the Windows 95 utility program can detect and eliminate more than 7,300 different viruses, including those transmitted via the Internet.

Courtesy of U.S. Postal Service.

Courtesy of Brother International Corporation.

Individuals and businesses depended on the delivery schedule of the U.S. Postal Service. Often, it took five business days for a letter to travel from coast to coast. In the days before overnight delivery services, the only alternatives were UPS and other parcel delivery companies, which did not at that time guarantee overnight or even two-day delivery.

Not much has changed in the manner in which typed or handwritten letters are sent and delivered today by the Postal Service. One thing that has changed is the cost. The cost of producing a single one-ounce, first-class letter is approximately $1.24. This includes labor, stationary, postage, and time and travel cost for delivering the letter to the post office.

With the right computer equipment and software, messages can be sent and received within a few seconds and, in some cases, are free of cost. Immediate electronic communications are made possible by computers and the Internet.

If you have a user account at your school, you can send e-mail messages to, and receive e-mail messages from, anyone having access to the Internet including family members and friends.

Another fast way to communicate is to send a letter or document in seconds to any location in the world using a facsimile (fax) machine. Fax machines digitize text and graphics, serially transmit the data over telephone lines, and re-create the images at the receiving end.

LANGUAGE TRANSLATORS

In Chapter 4, we explained that a computer can understand and execute only programs that are represented in machine language (0s and 1s). A machine language program consists of a long series (perhaps millions) of 0s and 1s. It is unreadable by most people. Although a programmer could write a program using machine language, the process is cumbersome, tedious, and very seldom done. For these reasons, programmers write application programs using higher level programming languages, which the computer then converts into machine language using a language translator. A language translator converts a user-written source program into its machine language equivalent so that the program can be executed by a computer.

Language translator programs are usually transient programs that are purchased separately from operating systems. One notable exception for microcomputers is the BASIC translator (QBASIC), which is included as a part of some disk operating systems. Language translators include compilers and interpreters.

Figure 8.25

Compilers convert high-level language programs (source code) into machine language (object code) that the computer can process.

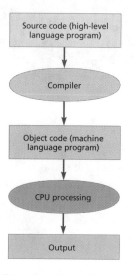

COMPILERS

A **compiler** is a language processor that translates an entire high-level language program into its machine language equivalent before the program is executed. Every high-level language requires its own compiler. A COBOL program, for instance, cannot be sent through a BASIC compiler. The high-level language program is called the **source code**. The machine language translation is called the **object code**. If the programmer has written the source code without any errors, it becomes operative after compilation, as illustrated in Figure 8.25. The object code can be saved and used again and again, saving translation time. Almost all commercial software is run through compilers and saved as object code before it is mass-produced and packaged.

Figure 8.26

Interpreters convert source code one line at a time, immediately display errors on the monitor screen, and send the translation to the CPU for processing without first creating an object code.

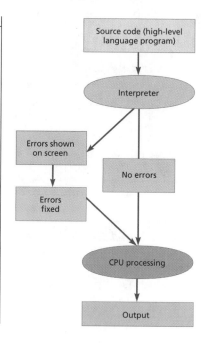

INTERPRETERS

An **interpreter** does not create an object code. Instead, it translates high-level language code one line at a time and will immediately display any errors it uncovers on the screen, as illustrated in Figure 8.26. The immediate feedback makes it ideal for teaching situations. Interpreters, however, are much slower than compilers. It takes them about five times as long to interpret source code. Since the translation is not saved to an object code, the program needs to be reinterpreted every time it is used.

Key Terms

application software

booting

command language translator

compiler

control program

device address

external command instructions

graphical user interface (GUI)

initial program loading (IPL)

internal command instructions

interpreter

job

job control language (JCL)

job control programs

language translator

multiprocessing

multiprogramming

multitasking

object code

operating environment

operating system (OS)

paging

partitions

Program Manager

run log

scheduling program

serial processing

source code

swapping

system software

text interface

time sharing

utility program

virtual memory

virus

window

Summary

System software is a collection of programs that starts the computer and coordinates all activities of the computer system. System software also controls **application software**, which is a collection of related programs designed to perform specific tasks. System software consists of operating systems, utility programs, and language translators.

An **operating system** is the core layer of software. It is a collection of programs that controls and manages a computer system.

Internal command instructions, also called *resident commands*, direct and coordinate other types of software and your computer's hardware. The **control program**, or supervisor, is the internal command instruction that manages all other programs in the computer. **External command instructions**, called *transient programs*, are general-purpose commands that are stored in secondary storage devices and summoned by the supervisor program as necessary.

The **command language translator** converts instructions into the specific machine language used by the CPU. Some provide **text interfaces** and are command-driven, while others provide **graphical user interfaces**. Shell programs work in conjunction with text-based operating systems to provide users with a graphical **operating environment**.

The operating system performs important memory management tasks, including protecting all programs in memory from accidental erasure and accommodating programs that exceed the physical limitations of main memory through a process called **partitioning**.

A **job** is a computerized application. Each job requires special instructions or commands for assigning input, output, and secondary storage devices. Many operating systems contain **job control programs** that permit this to be done. At the beginning of each job in the queue, a group of instructions is inserted in a special language, called **job control language (JCL)**. Some operating systems also include a **scheduling program** that examines and prioritizes the jobs in the queue and schedules each job according to the criteria specified by the computer staff.

An operating system is also responsible for coordinating the operation of the CPU with the peripheral devices connected to the CPU. In large computer systems, a unique **device address** is assigned to each peripheral device.

Operating system resource management tasks include keeping track of computer access, usage, and peripheral device usage with a **run log** and providing up-to-date reports of system utilization costs.

Most early computers were **serial processing computers**, which means that the computer was capable of processing only one application or job at a time. Most modern computers are **multitasking** machines capable of accommodating more than one user at a time by processing more than one job at a time. **Time sharing** systems work similarly to multitasking systems, except the allotment of time is divided equally among programs, not at logical breaking points as in multitasking systems.

Because main memory is limited, many multiuser computer systems use **virtual memory**, in which unused portions of programs are kept in secondary storage until needed. A common virtual memory technique, called **paging**, divides programs into equal-size sections called pages. Each page consists of a few thousand bytes. As new pages are needed, used pages are exchanged for unused pages, a processed known as **swapping**. **Multiprocessing** is possible when a computer system consists of two or more processors. Multiple processors share the workload of a computer system.

DOS is a single-user, single-task operating system for IBM and compatible PCs. Macintosh DOS System 7 is a single-user operating system that supports multitasking and virtual memory. Windows is an icon-based shell program for PCs that divides the screen into **windows** dedicated to specific purposes. Windows NT is a new 32-bit operating system with networking and multitasking capabilities. The newest version of Windows is Windows 95. OS/2 is a 32-bit operating system designed for a single user working on multiple applications at once on IBM's PS/2 family of personal computers and compatibles. UNIX is a multiuser, multitasking operating system that offers virtual storage and time sharing capabilities on everything from PCs to mainframes.

Utility programs provide services that make a user's job easier. These programs allow programs and data to be transferred from one storage device to another, data to be sorted and merged, and output to be sent to an output device. They usually reside in secondary storage and are summoned by the user or the operating system supervisor program as needed. Utility programs are packaged in a variety of ways. Some are built directly into the operating system. Others are packaged as independent programs that can be acquired from third-party vendors.

14 Easy steps to being a webmaster

STEP 8 | GRAPHICS AND OTHER ANCHORS

There are several different types of external files you might want to reference in your web pages: graphics, other pages that are yours, and pages that are someone else's. Recall from Step 3 that the general reference for another web page is called an *anchor*, and it can include *hot text* that a browser clicks to display the referenced page. In addition, different types of graphics and icons can be imbedded in an anchor or with other text to increase a page's visual interest. Graphics are variously referred to as icons, graphics, or images; in this step, we call them all graphics. The vocabulary you need for this step is:

.gif	A graphic stored in graphic image format
.xbm	A graphic stored in x bitmap format
.tiff	A graphic stored in TIFF format
href	A URL identifying a hypertext reference, for instance, another web page (ending in .html) or a movie (ending in .mov)
img src	A URL identifying an image source that may be one of .gif, .xbm, or .tiff

Creating .gif, .tiff, or .xbm graphical files can be performed in many graphics and photographic manipulation software packages, such as Photoshop™ or Corel™. The format for all the options in an anchor are:

```
<a href="URL">
<img src="imageURL" alt="Alternative text" align={middle | top | bottom}>
Text to select the URL</a>
```

The "Text to select the URL" is the *hot text* that shows as blue (unless otherwise stated) on the Netscape page or red if the link has been used. Embedding the graphic within an anchor makes it part of the *hot* area. The "imageURL" will show as a *button* before the hot text. It is aligned with the text by selecting one of the keywords from the list (middle, or top, or bottom). The alignment command positions the text relative to the graphic. The most common alignment is *middle*. Here is an example of an anchor with its Netscape version shown below it.

```
<a href="http:www.sample.com/sample.html">
<img src="http://www.sample.com/samphoto.jpg" align=middle>
Sample hot text</a>
```

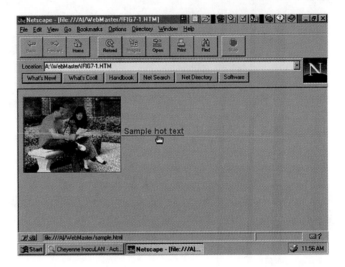

Anchor code can be imbedded in a paragraph, unnumbered list, or header to give many design alternatives. Because of the numerous alternatives, judicious use of graphics is important to developing an interesting, but uncluttered page. There are three design principles relating to the use of graphics: repetition, contrast, and color. As with text in the other steps, the *repetition* principle suggests the use of a single graphic to link related items.

For *contrast*, make multiple icons or graphics different enough so they don't get confused with each other. For instance, do not use red balls and pink balls because on an eight-color monitor, they will appear the same. Try to use primary colors, not shades of a single color.

Colors can be repeated both within and between pages to provide continuity and repetition. Selection of multiple colors leads to the *color principle* that the use of colors should be limited.

Some caveats on using graphics and links are important in designing your pages. Most important is that every graphic adds to the load time of your page. Keep graphics small, under 5K is best. Use no more than 256 colors in any image, and design all graphics to fit a 13" monitor, that is, under 480 pixels in width. Try to keep the sum of all loadable elements in a page under 100K.

ASSIGNMENT: Apply the principles of repetition, contrast and color to imbed photos, icons or other graphics in your current design, replacing bullets, or otherwise adding visual interest to your page. Replace your old page with the new version.

Exercises

REVIEW QUESTIONS

1. Define *system software*, list its components, and explain briefly its role in the operation of a computer system.

2. What is an operating system? Explain why a computer system cannot operate without an operating system.

3. Identify some operating system functions.

4. What is an operating environment?

5. Define and contrast *multitasking* and *time sharing*.

6. What is virtual memory, and how does it work?

7. Define *multiprocessing*. In what situations is multiprocessing beneficial?

8. Compare and contrast PC-DOS/MS-DOS, Macintosh DOS, and Windows NT.

9. What are some of the new features included in Windows 95?

10. What type of computer system was OS/2 designed for? What are the benefits and drawbacks of OS/2?

11. What are the main characteristics of UNIX? When is this operating system most beneficial?

12. What are utility programs? Identify two utility programs available for microcomputers.

13. What is a language translator? List two types of language translators and explain the differences between them.

FILL IN THE BLANKS

1. Three main categories of system software programs are _operating systems_, _utilities_, and _language translators_.

2. The _control program_ is the internal command instruction that manages all other programs in the computer.

3. The Apple operating system was the first to introduce a _operating system_ that makes use of icons.

4. A _window_ is a portion of a computer screen dedicated to some specific purpose.

5. _Serial processing_ operating systems allow only one user at a time and can process only one application at a time.

6. _Multitasking_ operating systems allow several applications to be executed concurrently.

7. A common virtual memory technique, called _paging_, divides programs and data into sections, called pages.

8. _____ allows users to provide the operating system with special instructions, such as the name of the user; the specific program to use; and the input, output, and secondary storage devices to use for an application.

9. Computer systems that have more than one processor are called _multiprocessing_ systems.

10. Windows 95 from Microsoft Corporation allows a user to sign up for Microsoft's information service called _Microsoft Network_

MATCHING

Match each term with its description.

a. operating systems

b. booting

c. partition

d. utility programs

e. language translator

f. multitasking

g. transient commands

h. source code

i. supervisor

j. run log

k. paging

l. resident commands

m. job

n. window

---

a   1. The core layer of software.

N   2. Portion of a computer screen.

L   3. The most often used commands that are immediately loaded into main memory when the computer is turned on.

E   4. A program that translates a high-level language into machine language.

G   5. General-purpose commands that are stored in secondary storage and summoned when they are needed.

B   6. The process of turning on a microcomputer system.

I   7. Program that controls the entire operating system.

D   8. Provide services such as disk management, data compression, or backup.

m   9. Each separate program run by a computer system.

H   10. The name for the high-level language code before it is translated into machine language.

K   11. A technique whereby segments of programs and data are swapped.

__C__ 12. A block of memory.

__J__ 13. The way in which an operating system keeps track of computer access time.

__F__ 14. Processing programs concurrently.

ACTIVITIES

1. With your classmates, form five panels of equal numbers. Each panel should choose a microcomputer operating system to investigate. Research the current uses of the operating system by looking through computer and business publications. Contact the manufacturer for more information on system requirements and retail prices. What types of businesses are using the operating system? Are they finding it easy to use? What do you think the future holds for the operating system? Prepare a presentation to share with your class.

2. Some computer experts believe that differences between microcomputer operating systems will disappear in the not-too-distant future. Research articles for and against this argument. Are you convinced that we will move to open architectures? How long do you think it will take for computer users to move in this direction once the technology is in place and why? Write a report that supports your theories.

3. Locate a department in your school that uses a mainframe computer. Find out what operating system the mainframe uses. Ask the system administrator how the operating system was decided upon and how the system was tailored for the department's use. Also ask the administrator to show you the manuals that accompanied the operating system and to explain their role in keeping the system running.

4. Using computer journals and magazines, find some articles that explain Windows 3.1 and Windows 95. What are some differences between the two?

Skills for Living

STUDY YOUR STATE

Our country is truly an integration of united states. Foreign visitors are constantly amazed by the size and diversity of our country and fascinated by how our state and national governments operate in relative harmony. These are characteristics we often take for granted.

How much do you know about your state? What is its population, size, flower, bird, song, and tree? How does it compare in size and age to other states? Can you tell a little about the history of your state? When was it settled? By whom? In what year did it become a state?

How is the state represented as an entity in the U.S. government? Name your two U.S. senators and your representatives to the U.S. House? Who represents your district in the House? How would you contact this person? Do your representatives have personal web pages? Who is your governor?

What about industry and commerce? Who are the biggest employers in your state? What are your primary industrial and agricultural products? How many colleges and universities are there in the state? Which is the biggest, smallest? What is your state's most significant claim to fame on a national level? Perhaps the Web can help you answer these questions.

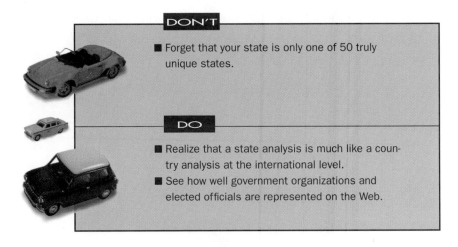

DON'T
- Forget that your state is only one of 50 truly unique states.

DO
- Realize that a state analysis is much like a country analysis at the international level.
- See how well government organizations and elected officials are represented on the Web.

Student Activities

1. Assume that you have volunteered to host a foreign student in your home as part of a college exchange program. As part of the program, the coordinator has asked you to prepare a short briefing on your state for this student. Use the Internet to help. Review topics such as political structure, demographics (population characteristics), city sizes, judicial system, major products and services, history, major companies and employers, tourist attractions, and colleges and universities. Find three extremely unique characteristics about your state.

2. Document your research and discuss in class. Perhaps you class could go on to develop a collective report and submit it to your local city government and to your state department of tourism and development. Be sure to mention the research was done via the Internet.

9

COMPUTER FILES AND DATABASES

OBJECTIVES

AFTER STUDYING THIS CHAPTER, YOU SHOULD BE ABLE TO:

1. Explain the importance of data management.
2. Describe file management systems.
3. Explain the purpose of a database.
4. Describe the function of database management systems (DBMSs).
5. Explain how records can be linked together to provide users with valuable information.
6. Distinguish between a hierarchical database, a network database, and a relational database.
7. Distinguish between batch processing and real-time processing.
8. List important system and procedure issue.

CHAPTER OUTLINE

DATA MANAGEMENT
Review of the Hierarchy of Data
Entities, Attributes, and Keys

FILES AND FILE MANAGEMENT

DATABASES
The Need for Databases
Database Management Systems

DATABASE MODELS
Hierarchical
Network
Relational
Multimedia

DATABASE PROCESSING METHODS
Batch Processing
Real-Time Processing

SYSTEMS AND PROCEDURES

DATABASE ADMINISTRATION AND DESIGN

lectronic databases and the data they contain are critical tools for running an efficient modern business. For example, consider a local video store. When you browse through the hundreds of videotapes available for rental, you probably don't think about the store's inventory database. The inventory database contains fields such as title, distributor, and rental fee. These and other fields describe the characteristics of every video in the inventory.

Once you have selected a video to check out, the clerk will probably use a scanning device to read the bar code data on the video's box, thus changing the data in the database to record your rental of that tape. In addition, the store maintains a database of customer information. On your initial visit, you probably provided the store with some key data about yourself, such as your name, address, and phone number. These data were added to the customer database. After you returned your first video rental, the transaction and whether you returned the video on time were also recorded in the database. Every subsequent exchange is then kept "on file" — that is, organized logically within the database.

Data are collected by our hypothetical video store and used by the store's owner to make decisions about inventory ("Should I continue to carry this video if it is rented only twice a year?"), marketing ("How can I convince customers to rent more videos at a time? Would a two-for-one offer encourage more rentals? Would it be cost-effective?"), and employee performance ("I'd like to reward Ida's excellent performance this month; she's really done a great job at customer service, and her cash register receipts are always on the money").

Small and large businesses alike are finding databases essential for speeding up processes and keeping on top of information.

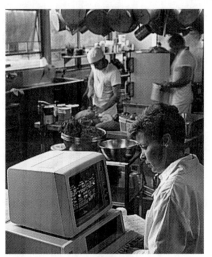

Gabe Palmer/The Stock Market.

Several multi-featured database software packages are available for large computers and microcomputers. Some popular databases for use with microcomputers are Access, FoxPro, Paradox, dBase V, and R:Base. These and other database packages are updated regularly. All allow the user to access and update the data, and to add new and delete old data quickly and efficiently.

In this chapter, you'll learn more about how data are organized into files and databases, and why databases are indispensible for today's businesses.

DATA MANAGEMENT

A company's ability to organize and process data is directly linked to how well that company will survive in today's business world. In order to stay competitive, organizations must have efficient data storage and retrieval processes. They must be quick to send out bills, order new inventory, credit accounts, access account information, pay vendors, and produce the information managers need for decision making. To help speed up these processes, companies make use of electronic files and databases.

REVIEW OF THE HIERARCHY OF DATA

In order to transform data effectively into useful information, companies must figure out how to organize it in a meaningful way. In Chapter 6, you learned about the hierarchy of data. Recall that these buildings blocks (see Figure 9.1) begin with the smallest piece of data that the computer can process (a bit) and progress through bytes (characters), fields, records, files, and databases. The most basic form of information is a *character*. Characters are joined together to form *fields*, a collection of related fields makes up a *record*, a collection of records makes up a *file*, and a collection of linked files makes up

Figure 9.1

The hierarchy of data represents the building blocks for turning data into information.

a *database*. The database is the highest level of the data hierarchy. It is used as the holding place for the data needed for all of the applications used by an organization. A **database** is a collection of data organized in a manner that allows users to retrieve and use those data. When thinking about database systems, organizations must consider

- What information the database will contain
- How much access should be given to various users
- How the database should be physically organized
- How to make the database structure seem logical to the user

ENTITIES, ATTRIBUTES, AND KEYS

Items in the hierarchy of data are sometimes given alternative names when referred to in terms of their functions in database systems, as illustrated in Figure 9.2. For instance:

- An **entity** is another name for a record. An entity is any person, place, or item for which data are collected, stored, and maintained. For example, an entity could be an employee, a department, or a grocery item.

SSN	Last name	First name	Hire date	Dept. number
005-10-6321	Johns	Francine	10-7-65	257
549-77-1001	Buckley	Bill	2-17-79	650
098-40-1370	Fiske	Steven	1-5-85	598

Entities (records)

Key field

Attributes (fields)

Figure 9.2

The records contained in a file represent entities. The attributes, or fields, represent characteristics of the entities. Key fields are unique attributes that can be used to distinguish one entity from another.

■ An **attribute** is another name for a field. For instance, for the entity "employee," attributes might include such things as name, address, and social security number. These attributes are used to identify the employee.

■ A **key** is an attribute used to uniquely identify an entity. For instance, machinery parts are assigned numbers that identify them as different from every other part. For some records, more than one key is needed to make a unique identification. For instance, personnel records would include keys not only of employee names, but also of their social security numbers. This ensures that organizations with identically named employees will be able to access records correctly.

FILES AND FILE MANAGEMENT

You have already encountered the word *file* in this and other chapters of this book. A file used to store data, often called a *data file*, is the computer counterpart to an ordinary paper file you might keep in a filing cabinet. In the traditional approach to data management, one or more data files are created for each application, as shown in Figure 9.3. The thing to remember about this type of approach is that each data file houses information on the attributes of a single application only.

A **flat file** is a single file consisting of records (rows) and fields (columns) of data. A spreadsheet program, for example, uses the flat file format for data storage, processing, and retrieval. When files are designed for a specific application and when an organization has many applications, the files will often contain **redundant data**, which means the same data are stored in more than one file. For example, an employee's name and address might be contained in both a personnel file and a payroll file. In addition to requiring more auxiliary storage space, redundant data present updating problems,

Figure 9.3

When a database is not used, files are linked to specific applications. There is no sharing of data among applications.

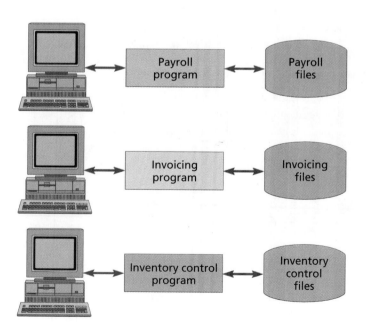

since data updated in one file will be reflected in another file. Data redundancy adversely affects **data integrity**, the ability to rely upon data as being accurate no matter which file is accessed. Smooth business operations require a high degree of data integrity.

In order to better organize and manage flat files, file management programs have been developed. A **file manager** is a software package used to organize data and to access data one file at a time. File managers enable you to search for records with specific characteristics, sort records, and produce summary information and detailed reports from selected records. They also allow you to add, delete, and modify data. File managers use on-screen **templates**, or standard forms, that have fields available for entering data into files. File managers usually give you the option of designing your own template. For instance, you may wish to design a template for your employee file that includes fields for employee name, street address, city, state, zip code, telephone number, and so on. The records in your employee file must then conform to the template that you've created.

You can use a file manager to create and store as many files as you want. But because you can work on only one file at a time, file managers can be difficult to use for interrelating data located in different files, and they don't solve the problem of data redundancy—the same data must sometimes be entered into separate files.

DATABASES

A flat file can be useful in keeping track of such things as customers, inventory items, and mailing lists. However, many applications require linking data contained in different files. For example, a mail order business would need to link several files, or lists, in order to fill customer orders. Ideally, data are accessible to any authorized person in an organization for whatever application and in whatever format desired. Flat files, however, do not allow this type of access. Flat files are designed to be used for just one application and by the set of programs associated with that application. They generally have little or no relation to other data used and required within an organization because they are initiated and developed independently. For applications where relationships between files are important, a database model makes more sense.

Databases were developed to overcome data redundancy, program dependency on data, and users having to dig through data unrelated to their needs. As noted earlier in this chapter, a database is a collection of data organized in a manner that allows users to retrieve and use data. A database is designed to allow a large number of users to draw information from it for many different purposes in many different formats.

THE NEED FOR DATABASES

When an organization grows in size and diversity, so do the problems of managing large and complex amounts of data. Suppose you are the owner of a business that has grown from 100 customers to 10,000 customers. It becomes much more difficult for your firm to keep track of the data, keep the data current, and give the right people access to the data they need. Databases reduce duplication in different files and keep data current in all critical files.

Databases manage and process information. A number of recent organizational trends are emerging that emphasize the importance and usefulness of databases. These are:

1. Businesses need up-to-date and accurate information. Information is one of an organization's most vital resources and is essential for its survival and growth.
2. Managers need up-to-date information in order to make timely and effective decisions.
3. More and more, customers are insisting on current information about the status of orders, invoices, and accounts.
4. Businesses use databases to maintain up-to-date inventories of products, materials, and supplies.
5. Database users want to develop their own personal applications in less time than that required by older and more traditional development methods.
6. A number of manufacturers have implemented the manufacturing strategy called *Just-In-Time (JIT)* manufacturing. Because manufacturers often order large quantities of raw materials used in producing finished products, and because storage of the materials is costly, JIT assures that materials purchased arrive just prior to when they are needed. This conserves warehouse storage space and reduces the cost of keeping large quantities of raw materials in inventory.

Databases span a broad range of computer systems and application areas. Some are used with personal computers and are adequate for small retail stores or other smaller organizations. Others use several interconnected mainframe computers that can support large-scale transaction processing. For example, suppose an automobile manufacturer needs to keep track of the quantity and location of more than 200,000 automobile and accessory parts. Without a reliable database, thousands of labor-hours could be wasted just looking for parts or inventory data.

DATABASE MANAGEMENT SYSTEMS

Managing a database is a complicated task. Fortunately, software packages called *database management systems* can do the work of manipulating databases for you. A **database management system (DBMS)** is a software package used to interact with a database. In some cases, users may interact directly with the DBMS. In others, users may

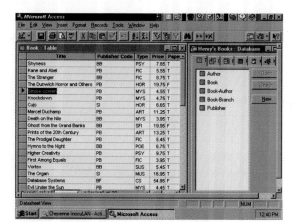

Database management systems like Microsoft Access allow you to build customized forms and reports by linking related tables in the database.

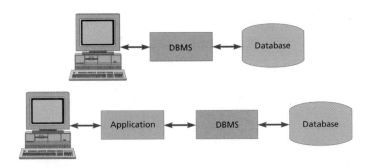

interact with programs that interact with the DBMS. For all systems it is only the DBMS that actually accesses the database, as illustrated in Figure 9.4.

For example, suppose a manager wants to check the account activity of a major buyer. The manager could request that the DBMS find the account, and the system would either locate this account and list the data or report that no such account exists in the database. All of the work involved in this task is performed by the DBMS. If the account is in the database, the manager could then query the system for the latest invoice sent to the account, and again the system would perform all of the work involved in locating the invoice. Likewise, when the manager wishes to add a product to the list of those that the account purchases regularly, the DBMS would perform all the tasks necessary to ensure that the request is added to the appropriate account. Other users accessing the same account from a different application would see the alteration made to that account. Instead of having a collection of separate files, all users in the organization would be able to share a common database managed by the DBMS, as illustrated in Figure 9.5.

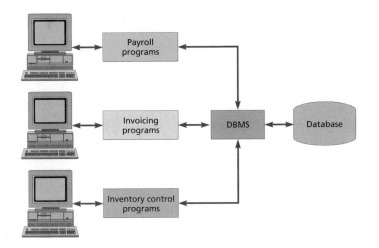

Many database packages contain special programs that facilitate using and managing the database. A typical database management system offers several useful features, including some or all of the following:

1. **Data dictionary** A data dictionary defines each field in the database files. Information typically found in a dictionary includes field name, field size, the type of data that can be entered into a field (numeric, text, or alphanumeric), and the default values.

2. **Query language** A valuable feature of a management information system is the query language, a specialized language for requesting information from a database. Query language allows the user to retrieve the desired information from the database in a specified format. For example, the query

SELECT ALL WHERE age > 35 AND name = "Wilson"

requests all records in which the name-field is "Wilson" and the age-field has a value greater than 35. The most widely used query language for accessing database information from mainframes and minicomputers is structured query language (SQL). SQL is now being used by PC database systems because it can be used for distributed databases (databases that are spread out over several computer systems).

3. **Utilities** DBMS utility programs permit easier maintenance of the database. These programs allow the user to add and delete files, monitor the database's performance, copy files, and update existing data.

4. **Data recovery** Some database management systems automatically keep a log of all records before and after changes are made. The log is used to restore the database in the event of a hardware or software malfunction.

5. **Database system security** More sophisticated database management systems permit the user to specify different levels of access privileges, such as adding and deleting files, retrieving files, and updating files. For example, senior managers might have the privilege of performing all of these tasks, whereas junior managers might only be allowed to retrieve files. These database management systems permit files or groups of files to be locked to prevent unauthorized access.

DATABASE MODELS

A DBMS must furnish a method for storing and manipulating information about a variety of entities, the attributes of the entities, and the relationships among the entities. DBMSs are often categorized by the method they use to manage data. Since a DBMS must both store and manipulate data, both of these facets must be addressed in a data model. Thus, a data model has two components, usually called structure and operations. The **structure** refers to the way in which the system constructs, or structures, the data. More properly, it refers to the way in which users perceive that the system structures data. The **operations** are the facilities given to the users of the DBMS for the purpose of manipulating data within the database.

When choosing a model for a database, it is important to describe the overall characteristics of the database. Basically, the model selected identifies the major parts (fields, records, and files) of the database and the way in which these parts are to work together. One of the underlying concepts for all database models is that there must be a way for records to be located and linked together. **Linking** is the ability to access all records in the database that contain one or more identical fields. For example, an insurance agent may need to link all customers whose policies need to be renewed within the next 30 days. The agent can use a computerized database system to find those customers. To link data elements (customer names and policy expiration dates) together, there must be relationships among the data elements. The relationships (the

FOCUS

Databases on the Move

Thanks to today's network computing tools, insurance adjusters are hitting the road. In particular, one suitcase-sized database-oriented system in place at The Travelers Corporation in Hartford, Connecticut, has increased production by 15 percent and boosted service by 50 percent. This graphical system from Automatic Data Processing, Inc. (ADP), the ADP Penpro, is estimated to save insurance providers about $100 per automobile repair estimate.

ADP describes the pen-based electronic clipboard as a "smart" estimating machine. When provided with detailed text about an automobile's repair, it accesses its database, calculates vehicle repair costs, and provides an estimate in moments. The database contains data on labor time and associated costs for overlapping functions, such as a similar task to be performed if the hood and fender are to be repaired. Static information, such as car design part numbers and prices, are refreshed each month on each user's mobile system.

The system has accomplished the impossible: it has helped to smooth relations between insurance adjusters and repair shops, who are traditionally at odds over accident adjustments. The insurance adjusters carry the portable version of the system, and the repair shops

Courtesy of ADP, Claims Solution Group.

have a similar desktop model, so that both sides have access to the same information. When both repair shop and adjuster are using the ADP system, the insurer will often waive on-site inspection of the vehicle because the insurance company trusts that both sides are working with the same data. The ADP Penpro has streamlined the process of getting the consumer's wheels back on the road.

The adjuster's version consists of a portable PC with a built-in modem that allows users to access mainframes in the corporate office that contain fluctuating data, such as the changing inventory of salvage yards. The PC also features a tiny printer that allows users to print an estimate on site.

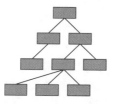

Hierarchical database

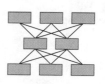

Network database

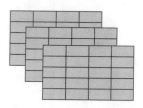

Relational database

data structures) represent the ways in which data elements can be linked logically, as determined by the user. The most common data structures and, therefore, database models, are hierarchical, network, and relational, as illustrated in Figure 9.6.

For the descriptions of the three types of databases on the next several pages, let's use the following hypothetical application. A company owns a computer store in Chicago and a computer store in Dallas. Each store has an inventory of parts and computer components which it sells. These parts and components are purchased from various vendors. Each part and component has a unique description. The stores receive orders for various parts and components. The set of data that could be used for this application is illustrated in Figure 9.7. The owners of the company want the data to be organized into a database so that they can answer questions such as "What are the outstanding orders for the Dallas store?" or "How many PT-1 devices does the store in Chicago have in stock?"

STORE

Store name	City
Store 1	Chicago
Store 2	Dallas

VENDOR

Vendor number	Vendor name
3428	Spinetics
4911	Electro Inc.
5726	Magno-tek

INVENTORY

Store name	Part number	Quantity
Store 1	PT-1	50
Store 1	PT-3	20
Store 2	PT-2	100
Store 2	PT-1	30

PART

Part number	Description
PT-1	Printer
PT-2	Diskette
PT-3	Disk drive
PT-4	CRT monitor

ORDERS

Store name	Part number	Vendor number	Order number	Quantity
Store 1	PT-3	3428	0052	10
Store 2	PT-2	3428	0098	7
Store 2	PT-3	3428	0098	15
Store 2	PT-4	5726	0099	1

HIERARCHICAL

The first conceptual model to be considered is the hierarchical database. A **hierarchical database**, shown in Figure 9.8, consists of elements that act in a **parent-child relationship**. In the computer store example, the parent element STORE is linked to, or points to, child elements INVENTORY and ORDERS. In order to obtain information from the ORDER element, the search must first go through the STORE parent element. For example, to answer the question, "What orders are outstanding in the Dallas store?", the DBMS that controls the database would first go to the STORE element (the parent element). The parent element then points to one or more child elements that contain the information requested.

There are several characteristics of hierarchical databases about which one should be aware. First, data stored on lower levels of the hierarchy can only be accessed through the parent element. Thus, to gain information about the inventory in a store, the INVENTORY element must be accessed through the STORE parent element. Second, the relationships within the hierarchical database are established when the database is created; that is, the person who designs the database must indicate that an inventory record is a child element of the STORE element when the database is created. Subsequently, all access to the database must be made through previously established links. Third, an element within a hierarchical database can have only one parent element. Therefore, in Figure 9.8, the INVENTORY element can have only one parent element, in this case the STORE element.

HIERARCHICAL DATABASE

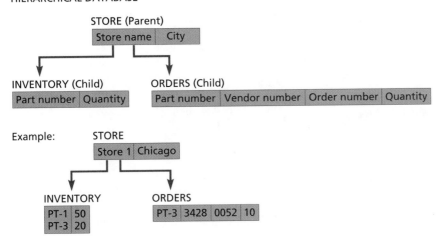

Figure 9.8

The hierarchical database shown here contains the parent element, STORE; and two child elements, INVENTORY and ORDERS. In order to retrieve data from either of the child elements, control must pass through the parent element. For example, to obtain the number of parts ordered on a given order such as order 0052, the inquiry must specify that the order was for Store 1.

The hierarchical database is the oldest type of conceptual database. Better designs are currently available.

NETWORK

A **network database** acts in much the same manner as a hierarchical database except that an element can have more than one parent. In network database nomenclature, a parent is called an **owner** and a child is called a **member**. A form of network database that has received wide usage is the *Conference on Data Systems Languages (CODASYL)* database. A CODASYL database consists of conceptual files and owner-coupled sets.

A **conceptual file** is the location of record keys and fields in the records of the file from the user's perspective. For example, a computer store may have five conceptual files: the STORE conceptual file, the VENDOR conceptual file, the INVENTORY conceptual file, the PART conceptual file, and the ORDERS conceptual file. In the STORE conceptual file, the store name is the key; in the VENDOR conceptual file, the vendor number is the key; and so on. It is important to understand that the conceptual files described here do not reflect the physical storage of the files on disk. A conceptual file presents the view of the data as the user or database administrator sees them.

An **owner-coupled set** in a CODASYL database (see Figure 9.9) is a set made up of owner and member records from the conceptual files. Each of these owner-coupled sets must be specified when the CODASYL database is created. For example, in Figure 9.9, three owner-coupled sets are defined—one with STORE as owner and INVENTORY as member; one with STORE as owner and ORDERS as member, and one with PART as owner and INVENTORY as member. To retrieve data, the user must specify the owner and the member to be retrieved. For example, to display the inventory of the Chicago store, the owner (STORE) and the member (INVENTORY) must be specified. Note that this arrangement is quite similar to a hierarchical database in that the data relationships must be defined at the time the database is created and that certain paths of data structure (i.e., owner-member) must be followed. The difference is that a member can have more than one owner (such as both STORE and PART being owners of INVENTORY).

Figure 9.9

This CODASYL network database has three owner-coupled sets. In each set, the owner-member relationship is called a 1:n relationship, meaning that for each owner there can be one or more members. For example, for each store there can be one or more orders; and for each part, there can be one or more stores with that part in inventory.

NETWORK DATABASE

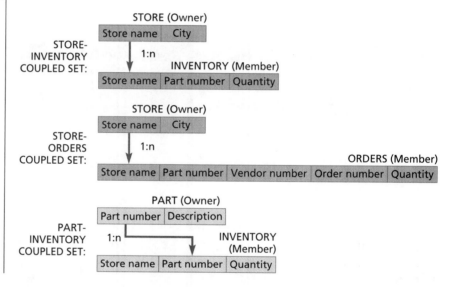

All of the owner-coupled sets and relationships established for a given network database are called the **database schema**. Since a database can contain hundreds of owner-coupled sets, it is often the case that not everyone using the database should have access to all of the sets. Therefore, user **subschemas** that specify those relationships available to given users can be defined. For example, if a user is writing a program to list the inventory in the stores, the program need not have access to the STORE-ORDER or PART-INVENTORY sets. Instead, a subschema would be defined allowing the program access to the STORE-INVENTORY owner-coupled set only.

While a network or CODASYL database is more flexible than a hierarchical database, it still has limitations: the database schema must be defined at the time the database is created, and retrieval of data is based solely on the schema. Network databases, however, have been successfully implemented and marketed by a number of software vendors.

before

AFTER

Culver Pictures.

Reprinted with permission from Lands' End, Inc.

Before computers, paper documents were often stored in endless rows of file cabinets, which were not always physically accessible to the workers who required the data stored on these documents. As a result, duplication of documents was common; the same data were often stored in several locations within an organization, and sometimes updates were not made in every location, resulting in inaccurate data.

Today, databases allow workers within an organization to share, update, and store data in a relatively small physical area. When one branch or department changes the data in its files, it can always be certain that the other branches or departments will be updated on those changes as well. The results are data that are always accurate and easy to access.

RELATIONAL

The most important advantage of a **relational database** over the other models is that the relationships among data sets can be determined at the time of use and changed at any time. In a relational database, data are organized in tables that are referred to as relations. A **relation** is a conceptual file in which each record is unique while having the same number and type of fields as all other records in that file. Files are also called **tables**. The tables are further divided into rows, or **tuples**, and fields, or **attributes**. The range of values that a field (attribute) can have is called the **domain**.

The data illustrated in Figure 9.7 are organized in relations. The five relations are the STORE relation, the PART relation, the VENDOR relation, the INVENTORY relation, and the ORDERS relation. Each record within the relation must be unique. When a request for information from the relational database is made, one or more of the three relational operations are performed: *selection*, *projection*, or *natural join*. Each of these operations creates a new relation (table) based upon the request for information.

A **selection** operation selects certain records from a given relation based on criteria specified by the user. For example, in Figure 9.10 on page 316, when the request is, "Find and list parts in inventory with a quantity greater than 40," the selection operation is applied to the INVENTORY relation to create a new relation containing those records with a quantity greater than 40. Once the new relation is created, the report or listing can be prepared from the data in the new relation.

REQUEST:
Find and list parts in inventory with a quantity greater than 40.

INVENTORY

Store name	Part number	Quantity
Store 1	PT-1	50
Store 1	PT-3	20
Store 2	PT-2	100
Store 2	PT-1	30

Selection operation

SELECTED RELATION

Store name	Part number	Quantity
Store 1	PT-1	50
Store 2	PT-2	100

A **projection** operation selects specified columns from a given relation, which will produce a new conceptual file. The projection operation then removes any duplicate records, creating a new relation (recall that in a relation, each conceptual record is unique). To illustrate the projection operation, suppose the request for information is, "Display the part number and vendor number for any part that has been ordered in a quantity greater than five on a single order." First, the projection operation finds all records in the ORDERS relation with a quantity greater than five. In the example of the two-step process shown in Figure 9.11, there are three records. Then the projection operation eliminates any duplicates. After the second step, a relation is created that includes only those part and vendor numbers for parts that have a quantity of more than five on order.

REQUEST:
Display the part number and vendor number for any part that has been ordered in a quantity greater than 5 on a single order.

ORDERS

Store name	Part number	Vendor number	Order number	Quantity
Store 1	PT-3	3428	0052	10
Store 2	PT-2	3428	0098	7
Store 2	PT-3	3428	0098	15
Store 2	PT-4	5726	0099	1

Projection operation Step 1

CONCEPTUAL FILE

Part number	Vendor number
PT-3	3428
PT-2	3428
PT-3	3428

Projection operation Step 2

PROJECTED RELATION

Part number	Vendor number
PT-3	3428
PT-2	3428

A **natural join** operation is used to join two different relations. The process is controlled through the use of common fields found in each of the relations. For example, the PART relation and the INVENTORY relation have a common field—the part number. Therefore, a natural join operation can be performed on the two relations based on the part number field. Suppose, for example, a request is made to "Display all parts in inventory and include the part description." The data in the INVENTORY relation must be joined with data from the PART relation to satisfy this request. This process is shown in Figure 9.12. Note that the essential process is to replace each occurrence of the part number in the INVENTORY relation with the PART record containing the same part number.

REQUEST:
Display all parts in inventory and include the part description.

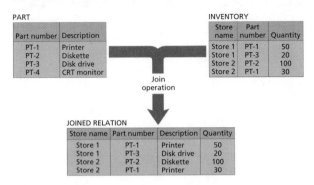

Figure 9.12

The natural join operation creates a joined relation from two separate relations. The joined relation is based upon the common field(s) found in each of the separate relations. The part number and part description from the PART relation have replaced the part number from the INVENTORY relation.

Requests for information from a relational database can be considerably more complex than those just illustrated. The same relational operations are performed on the data, however. The strength of relational databases is that the operations are performed at the time the request is made, without requiring the predetermined schemas of hierarchical and network databases. Thus, a relational database is much more user-oriented because the user can ask virtually any question and the relational database management system will perform the necessary relational operations to create the data relation requested. Virtually all modern database management systems support relational databases. They are presently the best and most versatile way to make data available to users.

MULTIMEDIA

Until now our attention has been focused on databases that involve text data. In Chapter 12 you will learn about multimedia, the integration of text, graphics, video, animation, and sound. Computer applications that use different types of data (text, pictures, sounds, and so on) need to be managed effectively.

Computer systems with multimedia capability are becoming much more popular. They are being used for a variety of applications, including education, entertainment, training, and marketing. In education, they are used for a variety of interesting learning activities. For example, a CD-ROM containing an encyclopedia can be used to retrieve information about dinosaurs, complete with text, pictures, sounds, and animation. For entertainment, a system containing a video disk player might allow the user to view a movie on the computer monitor just as the user would at a movie theater. Many companies use multimedia computer systems for training, such as training in the correct way to service customers in a fast-food restaurant. In marketing, multimedia systems are used to exhibit products for potential customers. For example, a salesperson in a furniture store can use a system to demonstrate how various pieces of furniture appear when placed together in a room.

A multimedia database is a special type of database capable of managing files that contain a combination of text, graphics, sound, and animation. Files transmitted over the Internet are often multimedia files in that they include text, graphics, sound and animation. Specially designed multimedia databases are capable of handling these complex files.

As the volume of multimedia data increases in all these areas, the data need to be managed effectively and efficiently. Although some multimedia data management systems are now available, managing these types of data will be a greater challenge for multimedia developers in the future.

DATABASE PROCESSING METHODS

When we use the term "database processing," we mean that the data to be processed are stored in a database and that the data in the database are being manipulated by a DBMS. Depending on an organization's needs, data can be processed in one of two ways: batch or real-time.

BATCH PROCESSING

Batch processing is a technique used to collect data transactions, sort them into groups or batches, and then process the transactions all at once. Batch processing was used almost exclusively when computers were first implemented in business environments. In many cases, source documents containing the data to be processed were brought to a central location where the data were punched in on cards or into the computer for processing. Thus, many of the early applications implemented on computers, such as payroll or billing operations, were best processed in a batch environment. Today, batch processing is still the best way to implement some applications, even though real-time processing, discussed next, has become more prominent.

Suppose you are going to update your employee file each month. The existing employee master file contains a list of all employees in the organization, with relevant data about each employee. The transaction file contains a list of the persons hired since the master file was last updated, persons no longer employed by the organization, and any other personnel changes associated with existing employees (pay raises, transfers, new dependents, and so on). These changes need to be added to the current master file. The processing results in a new, up-to-date employee master file. This activity is illustrated in Figure 9.13.

Figure 9.13

Using batch processing to update an employee master file, data are keyed from source documents and stored on diskette. The old master file is entered into the computer and updated by an application program that will create a new master file.

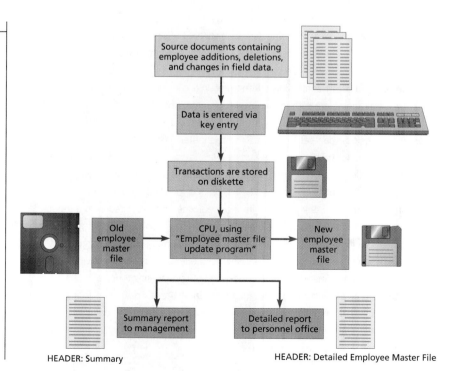

Before batch processing occurs, a transaction file must be sorted so that the order of the records in the transaction file matches the order of those in the master file. A computer program written specifically to sort records in a specific order is used. Records are normally sorted into sequential order using a record key, such as an employee number. A record key is like the information written on folder tabs. It distinguishes the record from all other records in the file. Once records in the two files are in the same order, they can be easily matched and the master file updated.

During processing, a new master file is created. This file includes all unchanged data from the original master file, plus the current changes from the transaction file. Most updating programs also generate error reports that indicate any problems. Requests for employee additions and deletions that have already been made or requests for changes in a record that does not exist in the master file are typical examples of transactions that might be included in the error report.

Batch processing is more efficient than other types of processing for some applications. Usually, it is also less expensive. If master files need to be changed only periodically, such as payroll files or files of student grades in each quarter or semester, batch processing is excellent. Also, if a high percentage of the records in the file are to be processed, batch processing is a good approach. One disadvantage of batch processing is that the master file is updated only periodically. Between update runs, data in the master file may become outdated or inaccurate. For example, creditors and suppliers must wait until the end of the processing cycle (which may be daily, weekly, or monthly) for payment checks. If you mail a deposit to the bank, the bank will likely record your deposit by means of batch processing sometime during the evening on the day the bank receives your deposit. Deposit batches are run before withdrawals in order to assure that these deposits are credited and accounts not mistakenly overdrawn.

REAL-TIME PROCESSING

Real-time processing, also called *on-line transaction processing*, is a processing technique in which master file records are updated as soon as individual transactions are entered into the computer system. An individual transaction is processed fast enough for the results to be used almost immediately. For example, a customer enters a bank, fills out a deposit slip, and hands it along with $50 to a teller. The teller enters the depositor's account number contained on the deposit slip into a terminal. The record is retrieved from the master file and displayed on the teller's screen. The teller verifies that the master record is the correct one by checking the name and other fields if necessary. The teller enters the transaction data. The master file is updated with the transaction record. The new master file record is written back to the master file in the correct location. This process is illustrated in Figure 9.14 on page 320.

With real-time processing, the intermediate step of temporarily storing data in a transaction file is not necessary. Instead, transactions are immediately recorded on a direct-access storage medium, such as magnetic disk. The record is retrieved from magnetic disk and displayed on a computer screen, the changes are then made by keying new data in specific data fields, and a new, updated record is created.

Real-time processing is particularly important in situations where up-to-date information is essential. Airlines use real-time processing systems in order to provide passengers with correct data about flights. Law enforcement agencies also need real-time systems in order to retrieve criminal records and other key information.

Figure 9.14

In this example of real-time processing, the following takes place: (1) The teller enters the transaction data. (2) The program retrieves the corresponding record from disk and places it in main memory. (3) The calculations take place. (4) The customer's receipt is printed. (5) The disk record is rewritten with the new account balance.

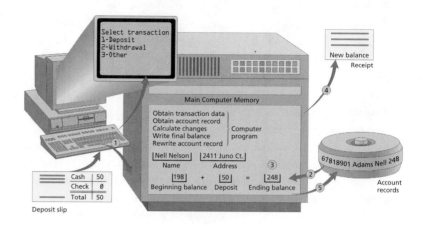

COMPUTER CURRENTS

Protecting the Corporate Database

The 1991 U.S. Supreme Court decision of Feist v. Rural Telephone removed a large portion of the protection corporate databases had previously been given. The Court ruled that data compilations are not copyrightable, likening them to "white pages" telephone directories, the contents of which may be copied "at will."

The Feist decision was a crucial one in that it rejected the long-held notion that in compiling facts, publishers deserved copyright protection because of their "sweat of the brow" efforts to pull together data. However, the opinion, written by Justice Sandra Day O'Connor, stated that facts can be copied, even directly from a competing compilation.

Initially, many information providers concluded their businesses would be ruined by the decision. Their costly efforts to gather data and put them into logical, marketable form could indeed be free for others to take. They probably were not comforted by the Court's explanation that the "primary objective of copyright is not to reward the labor of authors" but, according to the Constitution, to "promote the Progress of Science and useful Arts."

Taken in that light, supporters of the Court's decision point out that data compilers, especially information systems (IS) professionals concerned with protecting corporate databases, have some alternatives. Proprietary data (a firm's internal data, usually considered confidential within the firm) can be protected utilizing trade-secrets law. Trade-secrets protection can cover data that are substantial, secret, and valuable, such as computer programs, product ideas, and database compilations. Protection is put in place when the data are designated as secret and measures are taken to keep them protected. Firms considering depending

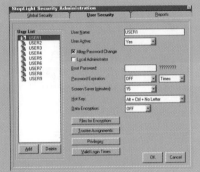

Stoplight® picture courtesy of Safetynet, Inc.

on trade-secrets law need to be aware that the law does not routinely protect data shared on-line, and it also is limited because it only allows firms to collect damages if they can convince the courts that the data were designated as confidential, that measures were taken to protect them, and that they were obtained and used illegally.

Deciding whether corporate databases are protected or not is a tricky call. The Court's decision was based

somewhat on the arrangement of facts in the database—for example, the alphabetical listing of names in a telephone book is not copyrightable because it does not possess the minimal creative spark required by the Copyright Act and the Constitution. Similarly, many corporate databases have no copyrightable "arrangement" of the data they contain. In fact, the software sorts the data into a form requested by the user. Because raw data are not protected by copyright, directory publishers and database providers may want to consider taking a different approach: presenting their compilations in subjective terms, which is probably copyrightable. For instance, a compilation of the hotels in a resort area by itself is not copyrightable; however, if a publisher presents a compilation of the 50 best hotels, ranked subjectively, the compilation would be protectable. Another sticky point arises, however, if a second publisher reprinted information on the hotels listed in the "50 best" compilation; the protection concerns only the selection criteria, not the basic data themselves.

Real-time processing offers significant advantages for users. One advantage, as discussed, is that a more current master file can be maintained because the master file is immediately updated whenever transactions occur. Another advantage is that input errors can be quickly detected. For example, the computer program can immediately alert the user of an error if the user attempts to enter the number of hours worked for an employee whose record is not currently in the employee master file.

Real-time systems also have some weaknesses. Most real-time systems are more expensive to implement and maintain than batch processing systems. They require more expensive direct-access devices (recall from Chapter 6), such as magnetic disk; whereas batch processing systems typically use less expensive magnetic tape storage. To guard against unauthorized access to data and as protection against costly human errors that can damage or destroy important on-line information, elaborate and sophisticated control and backup procedures are often needed. Also, real-time systems must run continuously to stay current. Auditing a real-time processing transaction is more difficult and time-consuming than auditing batch processing transactions. Because hundreds of users might have access to information stored on a direct-access system, the chances of human error are greatly increased.

Most organizations use a combination of both batch and real-time processing systems, such as the banking applications in the previous examples. Checks and loan payments, for example, can be batch processed, while in-person account balance inquiries must be done in a real-time processing environment.

SYSTEMS AND PROCEDURES

Data cannot be organized, loaded, and stored on auxiliary storage using either files or a database for use by personnel within an organization without an extensive set of systems and procedures. Among other things, the systems and procedures must address the following issues:

- Who has access to what data?
- What are the backup procedures, including what data are backed up and how often are they backed up?
- What controls must be placed on the data so that only authorized personnel have access to them?
- When and how are data to be updated?
- If data are downloaded to personal computers, what controls will be placed on the data?
- In a distributed database environment where data are placed on multiple computers in different geographic locations and the computers are linked by data communications, how are access and updating of these data to be controlled?

Addressing these issues is vital if data are to be successfully organized, processed, and used within an organization.

DATABASE ADMINISTRATION AND DESIGN

In small organizations, the responsibility of selecting, implementing, and managing a database system may rest with anyone management selects. In large organizations, this is usually the responsibility of a computer professional, called a **database administrator (DBA)**, who possesses extensive knowledge of database systems. The database administrator typically has the following responsibilities:

- **Database design** The DBA is responsible for the design of the database. This individual determines how, when, and where records are to be added, modified, and deleted.

■ **User training and coordination** The DBA oversees the training of database users and makes certain users are informed of what data are available and how they can retrieve them. Users also have responsibilities, including being familiar with the system, and updating, adding, and deleting data.

■ **Backup and recovery** Data that are centralized are particularly vulnerable in the event of a computer failure. The DBA is responsible for making sure that data are backed up frequently, that risks are minimized, and that a plan is in effect to restore the system to full operation quickly if an emergency occurs.

■ **Monitoring system performance** Most large database systems allow the DBA to monitor the efficiency of the system, such as user response time. Utility programs allow the DBA to make adjustments for a more efficient use of the database.

■ **Database system security** A main responsibility of the database administrator is to prevent unauthorized use of the organization's data. It is generally agreed that an organization's data are among its most valuable assets. Some organizations have lost millions of dollars as the result of unauthorized users gaining access to stored information.

We have learned that the responsibility for designing a database for a large organization rests with the database administrator. For individual personal computers, the responsibility rests with the user. Commonly accepted rules for designing a database (regardless of the type) include the following guidelines:

■ **Decide how the data will be used**. Records should contain data useful to the organization or individual. Fields should not be included for unnecessary data. For example, a field for "graduate student" would be unnecessary for a college that does not have a graduate program.

■ **Design the file on paper**. Create a list of every field you want to include on the database form and organize the fields into groups.

■ **Always include a unique key field**. Examples of unique key fields include social security numbers and student ID numbers. Only one record should contain these data because a person's social security number is unique. Records are often accessed by entering the record's unique key.

■ **A distinct item should have its own field**. An example of a distinct item is a person's last name or date of birth.

■ **Do not include separate fields when information can be derived from other fields**. For example, there may not be a need to include a field for sex and another field for gender.

■ **Allow ample space for each field.** If only eight spaces are allocated for a person's last name and someone's last name consists of more than eight characters, the person's name will not fit into the space allocated.

■ **Set defaults for frequently entered data**. Some database programs allow for a specific kind of data to be entered into a particular field. For example, the user can specify that only numeric data can be entered into "Amount Owed." If a user enters data other than numbers into this field, the database will not accept the data and display an error message. This minimizes the potential for entering incorrect data or entering data into the wrong field.

Databases provide users with opportunities to manage data effectively and efficiently. The potential uses for databases are virtually unlimited. Imagine the enormous task of the Social Security Administration in managing the records of millions of U.S. citizens. For users of personal computers, applications range from maintaining records of friends' and relatives' birthdays to keeping track of household assets for insurance purposes. Whatever the application, a knowledge of databases can be a valuable tool for any computer user.

Key Terms

attribute	network database
batch processing	operations
conceptual file	owner
data integrity	owner-coupled set
database	parent-child relationship
database administrator (DBA)	projection
database management system (DBMS)	real-time processing
database schema	redundant data
domain	relation
entity	relational database
file manager	selection
flat file	structure
hierarchical database	subschemas
key	tables
linking	templates
member	tuple
natural join	

Summary

A company's ability to organize and process data is directly linked to how well that company will survive in today's business world. The hierarchy of data starts with bits and progresses through bytes, fields, records, files, and databases. A **database** is a collection of data organized in a manner that allows users to retrieve and use those data.

An **entity** is another name for a record. An **attribute** is another name for a field. A **key** is an attribute used to uniquely identify a record.

In the traditional approach to data management, one or more data files are created for each application. The crucial aspect of this type of approach is that each data file houses information on the attributes of a single application. These files are often called

flat files. These files will often contain **redundant data** which conflict with **data integrity**, the ability to rely upon data as being accurate, no matter which file is accessed.

A **file manager** is a software package used to organize and access data a single file at a time. File managers use **templates**, which are standard on-screen forms with fields available for entering data into files.

Databases were developed to overcome data redundancy, program dependency on data, and users having to wade through data unrelated to their needs. Managing a database is a complicated task. Software packages called **database management systems (DBMSs)** are used to interact with a database. DBMSs furnish a method for storing and manipulating information about a variety of entities, the attributes of the entities, and the relationships between the entities.

The way the DBMS stores and manipulates data is addressed in a data model which has two parts: structure and operations. The **structure** refers to the way in which users perceive that the system structures data. The **operations** are the facilities given to the users of the DBMS for the purpose of manipulating data within the database. **Linking** is the ability to access all records in the database that contain one or more identical fields.

A **hierarchical database** consists of elements that act in a **parent-child relationship**. Data stored on lower levels of the hierarchy can only be accessed through the parent element. The relationships within the hierarchical database are established when the database is created. An element within a hierarchical database can have only one parent element.

A **network database** acts in much the same manner as a hierarchical database except that an element can have more than one parent. In network database nomenclature, a parent is called an **owner** and the child is called a **member**. One type of network database, the CODASYL database, consists of **conceptual files** and **owner-coupled sets**.

In a **relational database**, the relationships between data can be determined at the time of use. When a request for information from the relational database is made, one or more of the three relational operations is performed: **selection**, **projection**, or **natural join**.

A **multimedia database** is designed to manage files consisting of text, graphics, sound, and animation. As the popularity of multimedia systems increases and the volume of applications grows, specialized databases are required to manage multimedia applications.

Batch processing is a technique used to collect data transactions, sort them into groups or batches, and then process the transactions all at once. **Real-time processing** is a processing technique in which master file records are updated as soon as individual transactions are entered into the computer system.

Data cannot be organized, loaded, and stored on auxiliary storage using either files or a database for use by personnel within an organization without an extensive set of systems and procedures.

In large organizations, the responsibility for designing and maintaining the database falls to the **database administrator (DBA)**. The DBA has several specific responsibilities and duties.

14 Easy steps to being a webmaster

STEP 9 | TABLES

A home page that is an index to other pages can be made beautiful only in a limited way using icons and text. A list of links probably contains more items than can fit on a single 4-x-6-inch screen (the default Netscape window). Tables provide the ability to convert simple lists, using icons or text, all to tabular, columnar form. Many web pages use tables, combining icons with graphics to provide a visually interesting page.

Figure 9.15

Html code for a basic table.

html Commands(s)	Text Function
<table> </table>	Identifies the beginning and end of a table.
<tr> </tr>	Identifies a table row.
<td> </td>	Identifies table data or the contents of a row and column combination (a cell).
<th> </th>	Identifies a table header with a boldface and centered default.
<caption> </caption>	A table caption is a table header that is outside of the table border.
border=value	Borders allow emphasizing of table outlines. The value is a number from zero (no border) to a maximum of 9.
cellspacing=value	Cell spacing is the amount of space inserted between individual cells in a table. The default is one, a maximum is 9.
cellpadding=value	Cell padding is the amount of space between a table border and its cell contents. The default is one, a maximum is 9.
width=value-or-"percent"	The width describes the width of the table. The value is used to express an absolute width in pixels (picture elements, $1/7''$ each). A percentage is used to describe a width relative to a Netscape window.
rowspan=value	A cell attribute that allows a single cell to span multiple rows.
colspan=value	A cell attribute that allows a single cell to span multiple columns.

align=left/center/right	A cell or caption attribute that allows alignment relative to the horizontal borders as left, right or center.
valign=top/center/bottom	A cell attribute that allows alignment relative to the vertical borders as top, bottom, or center.

Figure 9.15 shows the code for a basic table, using a default border without headers, that displays at 50 percent screen width. Table attributes are separated by a space within the table command. Cell contents are left-justified in the center of the cell.

Note that the percentage is enclosed in double quote marks, indicating non-numeric characters. Always code the cell (a <td> command) on a single line to ensure proper spacing within the cell, for example, <td>cell contents</td>. To get an empty cell with borders, code a blank line, either <td> </td> or <td>
</td>. Figure 9.16 shows the Netscape table that results from the table definition in Figure 9.15. For a detailed explanation of table html, print the Table Primer from Netscape at http//www.netscape.com.

Tables can provide design element repetition with icons or by using the same table for several pages (e.g., for all return buttons). Background, color, and other graphical techniques can enhance table effect.

Tables should always be followed by a bulleted list or other low-tech presentation of the same information. Many users turn off graphics to speed page transmission. To ensure that these users can access your information, always provide both a high-tech and a low-tech version of each page's content.

ASSIGNMENT: Reevaluate your pages. If a table might more effectively format some portion of one or more of your pages, revise the pages and replace the current code with a table. If you have no information that is amenable to tables in your pages, define a table to look like a set of calculator keys.

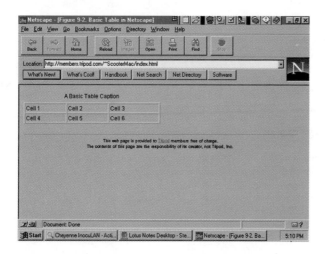

Figure 9.16

A Netscape table.

Exercises

REVIEW QUESTIONS

1. Explain why computerized data is more useful when the data are well organized and structured.
2. Relate entities, attributes, and keys to the hierarchy of data.
3. Define *flat file*.
4. Describe the functions of file management systems.
5. Explain the importance of databases.
6. Define a database management system (DBMS) and identify its main features.
7. Describe how data are linked in a hierarchical database.
8. Explain the differences between hierarchical and network databases.
9. Describe the operations of a relational database.
10. Contrast real-time processing with batch processing.
11. Explain the role of the database administrator (DBA).
12. Identify specific guidelines for designing a database.

FILL IN THE BLANKS

1   A *database* is a collection of related data or files.
2. A *entity* is any person, place, or item for which data are collected, stored, and maintained.
3. A *key* is an attribute used to uniquely identify a record.
4. A *flat file* houses information on a single application and the attributes of that application only.
5. Two ways data are normally processed are in batch and in *real time*.
6. When the same data are stored in more than one file, the data are referred to as *redundant data*.
7. File managers use *templates*, which are standard forms that appear on screen with fields available for entering data into files.
8. Software packages called *DBMS* do the work of manipulating databases.
9. *Linking* is the ability to access all records in the database that contain one or more identical fields.

10. A ~~relational~~ database model uses one or more tables or files and establishes relationships among them on the basis of a common field in each table or file.

11. A ~~multimedia~~ database model manages application files that contain a combination of text, graphics, sound, and animation.

12. In a large organization, the ~~database administrator~~ is responsible for designing and maintaining the organization's database system.

MATCHING

Match each term with its description.

a. projection
b. operations
c. schema
d. subschema
e. member
f. database
g. real-time processing
h. network database

i. natural join
j. templates
k. parent-child relationship
l. master file
m. file manager
n. batch processing
o. structure

F 1. Collection of related data or files.

J 2. Standard forms that appear on-screen with fields available for entering data into files.

L 3. File that contains data that are used as a source of reference and is updated periodically.

O 4. Way in which a DBMS constructs data.

D 5. Specify only those coupled-set relationships available to a given user.

N 6. Data is collected over time, sorted, and processed all at once.

E 7. In network database nomenclature, the name of the CHILD.

C 8. All of the owner-coupled sets and relationships established for a given network database.

B 9. Facilities given to users of a DBMS for the purpose of manipulating data.

I 10. Used to join two different relations in a relational database.

a 11. Selects specified columns from a given relation in a relational database which will produce a new conceptual file.

H 12. Database model using owner-coupled sets.

K 13. Basis of the hierarchal database model.

G 14. Master files are updated as soon as individual transactions are entered.

M 15. Used to locate information in other files.

 **ACTIVITIES**

1. Think of ways you might use a database. Make a list of elements you think should go into the database. Talk with your instructor or friends about the kinds of data you want to be able to store and retrieve, and get their opinion on the most appropriate kind of database for your needs. Report your findings to the class.

2. Write an essay describing the problems a large firm might encounter if it could not use a computerized database.

3. Forecast what database applications will be like ten years from now.

Skills for Living

STUDY YOUR FAVORITE SPORT

What is your favorite sport? How much do you know about it? How can you go about learning more? The Internet, of course.

A personal friend began collecting antique golf clubs, balls, postcards, and books when he was a child. Today his collection is worth over $2 million. He has gone on to write several books and produce four golf videocassettes. He has made his sport his business.

Sports captivate the world. The 1996 Summer Centennial Olympic Games were held in Atlanta in July. Over 16,000 athletes and officials from 195 countries and 2 million visitors attended. The world television audience was estimated at 3.5 billion.

Imagine the technology needed to support this effort. IBM supplied three of its largest computers to the Olympic Games. They also supplied 80 AS/400 advanced server systems and 7,000 IBM desk and laptop PCs. Sports and technology make a good team. The Internet is the newest example.

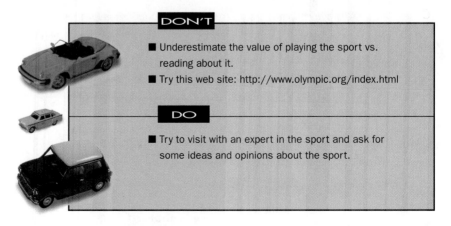

DON'T
- Underestimate the value of playing the sport vs. reading about it.
- Try this web site: http://www.olympic.org/index.html

DO
- Try to visit with an expert in the sport and ask for some ideas and opinions about the sport.

Student Activities

1. Do a thorough analysis of one sport. Review its history, players, status, future, critical skills necessary, tournaments, organizational issues, and financial matters. Then, from your research, make a list of ideas of how you could become more proficient in this sport. How useful was the Internet in improving your understanding of this sport? Share your ideas with your professor and class.

2. Find out more about the Olympic Games. When and where were the first games held? How many times have they had the Olympic Games? Have the Games ever been canceled? If so, for what reason? What events are included in the Summer Games? The Winter Games? Which would you rather attend? When and where will the next Games be held? And, what events would you attend? Create an itinerary for your dream trip to the Olympic Games (Winter or Summer), including a brief history of the Olympics, dates you will travel, and events you hope to attend.

NOT SO LONG AGO

Not so long ago, society experienced a revolution—the computer revolution—sparked by the invention and proliferation of computers. It was just 50 years ago that computer engineers at the University of Pennsylvania turned off the lights in their lab and turned on the first general-purpose computer—the Electronic Numerical Integrator and Computer (ENIAC). Today, scientists are on the verge of building computers that can run 100 billion times faster than the ENIAC. As the uses and capabilities of computers continue to increase, so too will the ways in which computers influence every aspect of our lives.

Courtesy of IBM Corporation.

Spotlights

Courtesy of IBM Corporation.

Courtesy of IBM Corporation.

Courtesy of IBM Corporation.

Courtesy of IBM Corporation.

Ron Sherman/Tony Stone Worldwide.

Courtesy of Apple Computer, Inc.

Courtesy of Apple Computer, Inc.

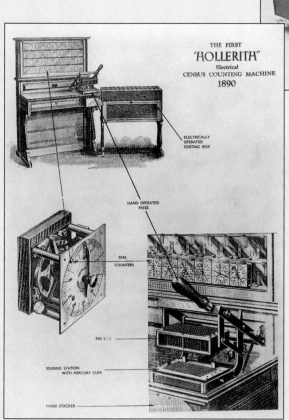

Courtesy of IBM Corporation.

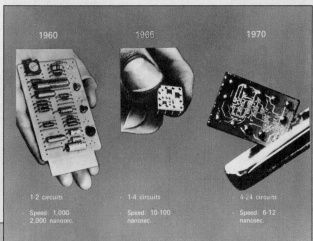

Courtesy of IBM Corporation.

Superstock.

Superstock.

Reprinted by permission of Texas Instruments.

Courtesy of IBM Corporation.

Reprinted by permission of Texas Instruments.

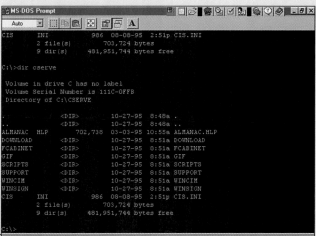

Courtesy of IBM Corporation.

Chris Collins/The Stock Market.

Property of AT&T Archives. Reprinted with permission of AT&T.

Courtesy of IBM Corporation.

J. Barry O'Rourke/the Stock Market.

Clayton Price/The Stock Market.

PART FOUR

SYSTEMS AND DEVELOPMENT

Computers are often used as problem-solving tools. To solve problems effectively, it's important to understand the methods involved in designing problem solutions and the programming languages used to solve those problems. With today's emphasis on problem solving, visual systems convey the meaning and implications of data and improve communication.

CHAPTER 10

Computer-Based Problem Solving

CHAPTER 11

Software Development and Programming

CHAPTER 12

Visual Systems

COMPUTER-BASED PROBLEM SOLVING

OBJECTIVES

AFTER STUDYING THIS CHAPTER, YOU SHOULD BE ABLE TO:

1. Explain and give examples of good and bad problems.
2. Explain the management hierarchy.
3. Define six levels of information systems and applications of each.
4. Explain the role of the systems analyst.
5. Identify five phases in the system life cycle.
6. Name four methods that can be used for system conversion.
7. Explain prototyping and its importance in system development.
8. Define *CASE* and the changes it may make in problem solving for computer-based information systems.
9. Understand key trends in systems development.
10. Explain how microcomputer use has evolved in the information systems of both large and small organizations.
11. Define *end-user computing*.

CHAPTER OUTLINE

WHAT IS A PROBLEM?
Sources and Causes of Problems

THE MANAGEMENT HIERARCHY

LEVELS OF INFORMATION SYSTEMS
Transaction Processing Systems
Management Information Systems
Decision Support Systems
Expert Systems
Executive Information Systems
Interorganizational Information Systems

SYSTEMS ANALYSIS AND DESIGN
The Role of the Systems Analyst

THE SYSTEM LIFE CYCLE
Phase 1: Preliminary Investigation
Phase 2: Systems Analysis
Phase 3: Systems Design
Phase 4: System Acquisition and Implementation
Phase 5: System Maintenance

PROTOTYPING

CASE TOOLS

THE FUTURE OF SYSTEMS DEVELOPMENT

MICROCOMPUTERS AND END-USER COMPUTING
Microcomputers in Small Organizations
Microcomputers in Large Organizations
End-User Computing

sk Debbi Fields, founder and CEO of Mrs. Fields Cookies, whether cookies are just a passing craze, and she'll argue that as long as cookies are "fresh, warm, and wonderful and make you feel good, are you going to stop buying cookies?"

Making people feel good is a passion with Mrs. Fields, a passion that is built into—and largely responsible for—a remarkable computer software system used by the more than 700 Mrs. Fields stores in the United States and around the world. The system, known as *Retail Operations Intelligence*, is the brainchild of Fields's husband, Randy. Enough companies expressed interest in the software for Randy to form his own software company, Park City Group, to market the system. Burger King is among the largest of Park City Group's clients. Although Retail Operations Intelligence is a complex system, Randy's reasons for creating it were simple: to "leverage" Debbi Fields's skills and standards so that they—and she—were accessible to all the firm's store, district, and regional managers. At the same time, the system, running on an IBM AS400, was designed to allow employees to do those things that only people can do, such as managing other people and interacting with customers.

Randy Fields's version of electronic mail, called FormMail, lets store managers contact not only their immediate superiors, but also home-office personnel—including Debbi Fields herself—with a guaranteed reply within 48 hours. The system also incorporates a sophisticated database with a series of some 20 "modules," application programs designed to help managers in specific aspects of their jobs.

For example, at the start of each day, the Day Planner module asks each store manager to identify the day of the week and other relevant information, such as whether it is a holiday or a sale day. Using these data with data bank records of past cookie sales on similar days, the computer sets hour-by-hour, product-by-product performance goals and suggests a mixing and baking schedule for each product in order to maximize sales and minimize losses. (Company policy states that any cookies over two hours old are to be removed and donated to local charities.) Throughout the day, information from the store's computerized cash registers enters the system. The system analyzes performance and offers suggestions if sales are slow (send a worker into the mall to give out free samples) or volume is down (remind workers to step up suggestive selling). The system even recognizes that some days are just bad days for cookie sales, regardless of past experience, and will downgrade projected sales and recommended baking schedules.

In addition to Day Planner, other major modules include a series of training modules and an interviewing module that asks applicants key questions and advises managers as to which applicants offer the best prospects. A personnel management module keeps track of all records on an employee and suggests when further training is indicated. There's even a maintenance module that helps managers cope with broken equipment by first asking a series of questions ("Is it plugged in?"). If the manager can't fix the machine, the computer notifies the home office of the problem, along with the age and previous service history of that machine and the name of the local repair service. When the repairs are made, the store manager tells the computer, which pays the bill automatically.

How successful is Retail Operations Intelligence? Mrs. Fields's managers love the fact that it has cut their administrative paperwork time by 60 to 70 percent. Shop workers seem to like its training modules. In the future, Mrs. Fields may find silicon chips bring success as sweet as any chocolate chip.

WHAT IS A PROBLEM?

In business, a **problem** is any event or situation, good or bad, that offers the opportunity to improve the organization in some way. When people hear the word *problem*, they tend to think of something bad. In the business world, a poorly trained sales staff, a decline in sales, and equipment failures are all examples of bad problems. However, many problems can be good. A company experiencing higher-than-expected sales has the problem of maintaining a high sales volume. A company with a large surplus of funds may have a problem investing the surplus. Solving a problem requires action. **Problem solving** is responding successfully to both good and bad problems. As you have seen in earlier chapters, computers are often used as problem-solving tools.

SOURCES AND CAUSES OF PROBLEMS

Problems originate from many different sources. An *internal problem* is one that arises from within a firm. For example, the firm may experience a shortage of resources, such as too few employees to complete a task in a timely manner. An *external problem* is one that results from factors outside the firm. A local government's decision to increase business taxes can pose an external problem for a business firm.

In almost all cases, there is more than one solution to a problem. The trick is to find a good solution in an acceptable amount of time. Because each problem is unique in some way, problem solving can be an interesting challenge. Even so, problem solvers usually follow the same processes in finding solutions. Figure 10.1 on page 346 shows a five-step problem-solving process.

Figure 10.1

FIVE STEP PROBLEM-SOLVING PROCESS

1. Problem Recognition/Identification

2. Generation of Alternatives

3. Evaluation of Alternatives

4. Implementation

5. Follow-up/Control

THE MANAGEMENT HIERARCHY

Today's business landscape is dotted with large, complex corporations whose appetite for information is insatiable. These organizations are working alongside small, vibrant, growing businesses with the same informational needs. Information has become the lifeblood of modern business enterprises. Without essential information at their fingertips, many businesses could not survive.

Decision makers need good information to assess situations, identify problem areas, plan changes, communicate those changes, and evaluate and control organizational programs and projects. Information technology supports these important managerial activities.

Effective information management requires managers to have solid personal computing skills. The ability to examine and implement information systems is critical and is one of the keys to success. Managers working at different levels within organizations need different kinds of information from a wide variety of sources. Their information needs are based on the nature of their organizations and the kinds of decisions they make.

Organizational structures are rapidly changing and evolving, as illustrated in Figure 10.2. During the 1970s, organizations formed **hierarchical structures** based on a chain-of-command similar to the military's. There were generals, (presidents), colonels (vice presidents), majors (assistant vice-presidents), and so on. The lines of authority and communication were well defined.

Old: Hierarchical Structure

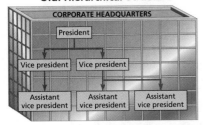

Newer: Matrix Structure

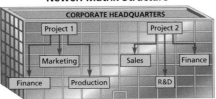

Newest: Nodal/Networked Structure

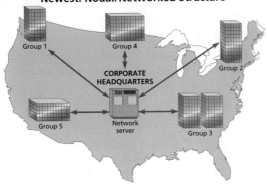

Figure 10.2

Organizational structures are changing from the traditional hierarchical structure to newer matrix and nodal/networked structures.

In the 1980s, due to competitive pressures and to new technologies, organizations began to adopt **matrix structures** or *cross-functional* organizational structures. Management teams or groups were formed by members from different functional areas (finance, accounting, marketing, and so on) to work on special projects. Communication lines and levels of authority began to blur. Many people reported to more than one manager or supervisor. A systems analyst might report to both a vice president in charge of information systems (who might be the function manager) and a product or division vice president. The function manager would set standards and procedures for systems development, and the product manager would decide on which projects and which project teams the employee would work on.

The problem that many employees in matrix organizations faced was in setting priorities. Specifically, if both managers assigned projects due on the same day, they had to decide which manager outranked the other. Many organizations dealt with this conflict by giving the product managers more authority than the function managers to ensure that the project teams completed work on schedule. Other organizations dealt with this situation by returning to the hierarchical structure.

Today, computer technologies, competitive pressures, and total quality management principles have fostered a new organizational structure—the **nodal/networked structure**. Through computer networks, geographically dispersed groups are formed to solve critical organizational problems. Once its work is done, the team disbands, and its members are reassigned to new groups working on new projects. Organizational communications flow freely in all directions, at any time, and at any distance, inside or outside the organization through these computer networks. All employees are linked together in a real-time, decision-making environment.

Even though organizational structures are changing, the hierarchical structure is still prevalent in business organizations. For this reason, the following sections on the role of information systems in business focus on the hierarchical view.

The hierarchical structure can be thought of as a management pyramid (see Figure 10.3) that includes the following levels:

- **Non-management Employees** The non-management employee level is where day-to-day business activities occur. Procedures are established that enable the firm to provide goods and services to the organization's customers. At this level, one would expect to find applications such as sales order entry, accounts payable, accounts receivable, billing, production control, and inventory processing.

- **Operations Management** At this next level, managers devote their attention to planning and controlling activities that occur at the level below. Operations managers plan and control the functional areas of accounting, manufacturing, marketing, and so on. Operations managers are mainly concerned with the day-to-day activities of the organization.

- **Tactical Management** At the middle management level, employees are involved in the tactical planning and controlling of operations. Here, budgets are prepared and rules and procedures are established. Tactical managers are usually responsible for making sure that all established rules and procedures are carried out. Tactical managers are involved in short-range planning—up to one year in the future.

- **Strategic Management** At the top level, managers are responsible for making overall corporate policy decisions. Their decisions are considered strategic because they affect the general welfare and future stability of the entire organization. Strategic managers formulate long-range goals and objectives for the entire organization and establish plans to meet them.

Figure 10.3

As you travel up the management hierarchy, decision making becomes a less structured process.

The evolution in information system technologies is changing the shape of the management pyramid. The lower and middle management sections of the pyramid are collapsing (see Figure 10.4). Historically, middle management has been the communication link between top management and the lower levels of managers and employees in the organization. Now, electronic communication performs this function. In the last ten years, there has been a 35-percent reduction in the ranks of middle management in U.S. organizations, and the trend is expected to continue.

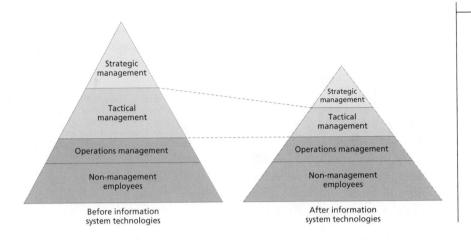

Figure 10.4

Information system technologies have increased the speed of decision making and decreased the need for large numbers.

LEVELS OF INFORMATION SYSTEMS

An organization's information needs, and the information systems that serve them, closely parallel the management activities at each level of the hierarchy. Figure 10.5 shows some of the information systems that have emerged to assist organizations. These systems are continuously evolving.

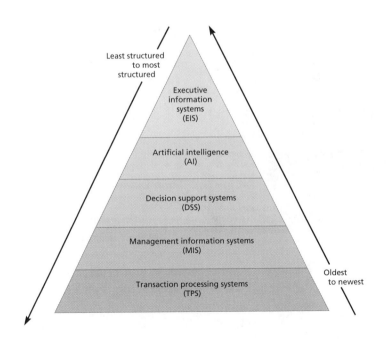

Figure 10.5

Information systems are continuously evolving to meet the growing needs of organizations. The oldest systems tend to be the most structured.

TRANSACTION PROCESSING SYSTEMS

Many people are familiar with transaction processing systems because they come into contact with them in their work or when they purchase goods and services. A **transaction**

processing system (TPS) is an information system that uses standard procedures to collect and process the day-to-day data that routinely flow through an organization. Because the processing cycle is routine and sequential with little variation it is classified as a *structured* information system.

Computerized information systems used for transaction processing have the following characteristics:

- They process routine business transactions quickly and efficiently.
- They are used mostly by non-management employees (the majority of the employees that work in organizations).
- The people using these systems are required to make few, if any, decisions.
- They are designed to process large amounts of detailed data generated by the daily activities of the business.

TPSs evolved from manual systems that became too labor intensive. TPSs were the first computer applications implemented by many organizations. Early in their history, TPSs were used primarily for *batch processing* applications. For example, in many organizations employee time cards were collected at the end of designated time periods, and all employee paychecks were processed at once (in a "batch"). TPSs also automated the processing of accounts payable. Invoices would be collected over a certain period of time, and then the data from all invoices would be entered into the computer and processed for payment.

Thousands of TPSs are currently in operation in a wide variety of organizations. One example is an airline reservation system. A reservation or travel agent follows a standard set of procedures when requesting information from or entering information into a

Figure 10.6

Transaction Processing Systems (TPSs) require few or no decisions on the part of those who use the system. They provide for quick input of data into the system, such as an order at a fast-food restaurant.

Courtesy of PAR Technology Corporation.

flight database. For instance, the agent will query the database as to whether there is a seat available on a specific flight and then enter appropriate information when a reservation is made. As in Figure 10.6, an agent must enter the purchaser's name, the time and date of departure and arrival and where the ticket is to be picked up. (Some airlines are now using ticketless travel systems—you simply prepay with a credit card and enter directly from the gate.)

Another example is an order-entry system. When an order is received, a trained order-entry clerk follows standard procedures to enter the order into the system. After an order has been entered, the computer system follows a set of standard procedures to process the order.

TPSs are used in many other industry processes as well, including banking systems, commercial loan processing, stock and bond management, transportation, health care, legal practices, manufacturing, retail operations, and utilities. TPSs are used for accounts receivable, accounts payable, inventory control, invoicing, order processing, payroll, purchasing, shipping and receiving, and general ledger applications. Essentially, most common business functions use TPSs.

Besides providing many organizations with the ability to process routine day-to-day business transactions quickly and efficiently, TPSs can also be set up to collect historical information on sales, customer buying habits, financial information, and so on. These historical databases are valuable sources of input data for the organization's other information systems.

MANAGEMENT INFORMATION SYSTEMS

Although TPSs can provide an organization with detailed data and data summaries, they are not designed to provide managers with the kinds of information needed to make major business decisions. For example, because TPSs often process data only at specific time intervals, a manager needing a report must wait until the complete payroll, inventory, or billing cycle is finished to obtain needed information. But managers need quick and easy access to information. The inability of TPSs to provide managers with this quick, easy access limits their contribution to decision making. A response to this shortcoming came in the late 1960s and early 1970s with the development of management information systems. A **management information system (MIS)** is any type of computerized information system that focuses on the production of decision-oriented information needed by decision makers.

Information is useful to a manager only when it is accurate, timely, complete, concise, and relevant. The first three characteristics (accuracy, timeliness, and completeness) can often be facilitated by using a computer. The fourth and fifth characteristics (conciseness and relevancy) can be achieved only with a carefully designed MIS. Well-written software and a well-trained computer staff are essential to an effective MIS. In organizations with MISs, managers should be knowledgeable about computers and their processing capabilities and should have a clear understanding of their own information needs.

A well-designed and implemented MIS generates useful information in a concise format that is easily read and understood. The information is often generated in the form of one or more reports. A **report** is a grouping of related information useful to the manager for decision-making purposes. Reports can be printed or displayed on a computer screen. Below are examples of some typical management reports generated by an MIS.

- A **custom report** is one that is specifically tailored to a manager's needs. A personnel manager, for example, might need a list of employees who speak both Spanish and German.
- A **demand report** is one that is prepared when requested by a manager. Manufacturing managers often request reports showing their labor costs by shift and by product.
- An **exception report** is one that shows differences or exceptions to predetermined norms or standards. For example, an exception report might identify only those employees who were absent from work three or more days during the previous month.
- A **summary report** contains summary information, such as averages or totals, instead of detailed data. A summary report might contain only sales totals for each salesperson, but not information about individual sales to customers.

Reports such as these are sometimes collectively called **capsule reports** because each contains only the information requested by the manager. Detailed data are sacrificed in favor of information overviews.

Many MISs are capable of accessing on-line files so that managers can find needed data and information quickly. Most of the better-designed MISs support query programs for database reporting or other types of report generators. A **database query program** or **report generator** is a program that allows users to produce reports containing data organized in a format selected by the users. In addition, many MISs provide for the integration of data from multiple files. All of these features make it possible for MISs to satisfy users' information needs for printed demand and custom reports and for immediate access to on-line data.

The primary objective of MISs is to provide the right information to the right manager at the right time. MISs give managers the tools needed to improve the quality of the managers' decisions and to reduce the time needed to make those decisions. An effective MIS can give the entire organization a competitive advantage by improving the effectiveness of management within the organization. Achieving this objective requires careful planning, design, and development. Development must include active participation of current and future users of the systems who can inform designers of the types of

Lawrence Migdale/Tony Stone Worldwide.

before

Mail-order companies mailed each customer a personally typed letter encouraging the customer to buy a new product.

AFTER

Today, these companies use computers, mailing lists, and sophisticated programs to sell and distribute large quantities of merchandise. With the advent of e-mail, FAX, home shopping channels and the Internet, many more shopping technologies will soon be available.

managerial information that will be needed. Systems designers need good technical skills, but they also must have good communication and business skills to develop effective MISs for their organizations.

DECISION SUPPORT SYSTEMS

As one moves up the hierarchical pyramid from the operational level to the management planning and control level, the decision-making process becomes more complex. At this higher level, problems tend to be less structured. Therefore, typical problems usually cannot be solved with clearly defined step-by-step procedures. The main obstacle to error-free planning is uncertainty about the future. Planning for quarterly or semi-annual budgets requires input from all departments within the organization. Stronger-than-expected competition may force a firm to quickly alter its advertising budget or its pricing policies, making earlier budget projections in those areas invalid.

You've learned that MISs are designed to provide managers with the kinds of information needed for making routine decisions on a day-to-day basis. Decision support systems go a step beyond MISs. A **decision support system (DSS)** is designed to provide managers with information they can use to make their decisions in unique, semistructured, and unstructured situations. Decision support systems help managers analyze and interpret the information they receive from MISs.

Suppose a company finds itself with a larger-than-expected cash reserve that is not needed immediately. Management decides to invest these extra funds for a 90-day period. Based upon company policies and objectives, the company has several investment options. The company could invest the funds in safe, short-term government securities, such as bonds or treasury bills, each with its own interest rate. Or, the company could earn higher interest rates with riskier kinds of investments, such as private corporate bonds. DSSs help managers weigh these options and make decisions based on their analysis of key information.

A DSS helps managers choose among alternatives. A typical DSS includes a set of quantitative, modeling, and simulation programs. These programs allow the DSS user to manipulate data in a variety of ways. When designed properly, a DSS has the capability to rank or to rate alternatives based on the decision maker's criteria. Also, many DSSs can access and use existing company data, generated by TPSs and MISs, to help assess these alternatives. Many DSSs provide managers with the flexibility to look into the future to determine the best answers to "what if" questions. Electronic spreadsheets, for example, allow decision makers to analyze the impact of "what if" financial, marketing, or production alternatives.

There are two major enabling conditions necessary for DSS development within an organization: (1) users must have a need to solve unstructured or semistructured problems (problems without known answers and without clear procedures for finding easy solutions), and (2) there must be existing corporate databases and user-developed databases that can be analyzed.

EXPERT SYSTEMS

A computer application that captures much of the expertise, experience, decision rules, and logic patterns used in the thought processes of an expert in a specific field is called an **expert system**. Medical diagnosis, investment counseling, legal defenses, engine repair, credit card authorizations for customers, and petroleum exploration are just a few examples of fields currently using expert system applications.

Since the mid-1970s when they were first introduced, many expert system programs have been developed and made available. In fact, the development of expert systems software is currently one of the fastest-growing segments of the computing industry. A well-designed and implemented expert system provides a user with answers to questions and solutions to problem situations similar to those that a human expert would provide.

Expert systems are valuable to a business when specific expertise is not evenly distributed throughout the organization. For example, consider a large bank whose senior loan officer (the in-house loan expert) is located at the main office in a large city, and its junior loan officers are located at each of the bank's branches in smaller, neighboring towns. If the senior loan officer's expertise has been captured and included in an expert system, junior loan officers may be able to make the same decisions as the senior officer by using the system. As a junior loan officer interviews a loan applicant, the data is entered into an expert system and processed. The expert system then recommends whether or not the loan should be granted. Although the output is only a recommendation, a junior loan officer may have more confidence about making the correct decision.

Expert systems contain a warehouse of knowledge. They provide users with queries that lead the user to informed conclusions.

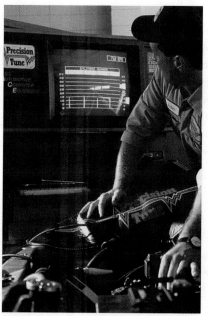

Courtesy of Precision Tune, Inc.

Consider another example. A young physician at a remote site discovers a number of unusual symptoms while examining a patient. The physician has never before treated a patient with these symptoms. Using a microcomputer, the patient's medical data is entered into an expert system and processed. The output from the expert system first suggests a list of additional lab tests. Then, when these test results are input, the expert system diagnoses a rare illness and recommends treatment. Based upon information provided by the expert system, the physician prescribes treatment and then closely observes the recovery process.

Expert systems are similar to DSSs in that they both require interactive dialog with users (see Figure 10.7). They differ in that expert systems deal with relatively structured problems, whereas DSSs are better suited to addressing unstructured problems. In addition, expert systems require clearly defined input—some are unable to deal with "what if" conditions. The real value of expert systems is their ability to store vast amounts of expert knowledge.

Courtesy of Promised Land Technologies.

Many large-scale expert systems are very expensive because they can run only on large computers. Implementing and maintaining large, complex systems is expensive for the following reasons:

- It is difficult to assemble expert systems and build the original set of information and rules for the system.
- New information must be entered often to keep the system current.
- The accuracy of the expert system's problem-solving capabilities must be checked frequently.

For these reasons, some complex expert systems are not cost-effective. However, in recent years, a wave of more cost-effective expert system software for microcomputers has been developed. This development has made expert systems more popular among small- and medium-sized businesses.

EXECUTIVE INFORMATION SYSTEMS

An **executive information system (EIS)** is a computer application used by senior managers to plot the course of the organization. An EIS is a DSS that provides top management with a window into the information and performance indicators stored in the company's computer systems. Executive information systems allow top managers to look quickly at summarized business information to spot trends and variances, allowing for timely reactions to changing market and organizational conditions.

EISs need good TPSs and MISs as foundations to collect and store quality information. EISs must provide a long-range view of the market, perhaps up to five to ten years down the road. **Drill-down systems design** allows for interrogation of divisional performance and the aggregation of those performance indicators into forecasted performances. Human, financial, and environmental issues are often combined and analyzed in these systems. Visual displays (graphs, charts, trend lines, variation charts) show variations between current and expected performance by department, by geographic area, or by product line. Spreadsheets carry performance data from different parts of the organization (finance, human relations, marketing, production, and so on).

EISs are often built over the top of these spreadsheet files, allowing the senior executive to query through these layers of spreadsheets and interrogate the database for performance indicators, critical variations, and emerging trends.

For EISs to be effective, senior executives must thoroughly understand the problems to be solved and how to apply the necessary computer problem-solving technologies. Executives must ask the right questions and use the right technologies to make the best-informed decisions.

Many senior executives lack technical computer skills. Therefore, EISs must be easy to use and the results easy to understand. The goal of an EIS is to complement the imagination and intelligence of senior management, not replace them.

INTERORGANIZATIONAL INFORMATION SYSTEMS

Communications and data-sharing among organizations is the newest information system application and is of great interest to researchers and practitioners alike. Consider a case where four organizations are electronically linked together: a local business school, a city government, a local bank, and an international athletic apparel company. The apparel company is considering a large expansion and wants help analyzing the project. Where should the expanded manufacturing facilities be located within the city? What would be the financial impact to the company and the community? Who else has recently completed a similar expansion? How long will the project take? Who within the four organizations would be available to help and how? A cooperative information and communication system linking these four participants would be an excellent first step to answering these questions and to the ultimate success of the project.

An **interorganizational information system (IOIS)** describes any social or technological system used to support the work of an organization by facilitating the collection, flow, and analysis of information between organizations. New tools needed to manage this type of system are still in the development stage. Possible benefits include lower costs, improved productivity, and better production and marketing strategies. Some companies are using electronic data interchange to share information as a first step in developing interorganizational information systems. **Electronic data interchange (EDI)** is a procedure that allows for exchange of data from the computer of one organization to the computer system of another organization. As communication and computer technologies improve, more developments will arise in this area.

SYSTEMS ANALYSIS AND DESIGN

A typical large business organization utilizes a number of computer-based information systems, such as a transaction processing system, a management information system, a decision support system, and an expert system. To be effective, all systems require careful planning and coordination. The process of analyzing, planning, designing, implementing, and maintaining any kind of system is referred to as systems analysis and *design* or *system development*. The process consists of analyzing an existing system, making changes to an existing system or designing a new system, acquiring the hardware and software needed for the new system, implementing the system, training users, and making certain that the new system works as it should.

FOCUS

International Computing

Texas Instruments (TI), a company respected for its hand-held calculators, is a major worldwide manufacturer of computer chips. TI shrank the time required to develop a calculator by 20 percent when it implemented its around-the-clock, around-the-world development system; since then, the development time has shrunk another 17 percent. Today, the sun literally never sets on TI's chip design and manufacturing efforts.

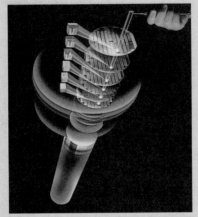

Reprinted by permission of Texas Instruments.

Like most global companies, TI used to lose days of precious time when designers and engineers in various parts of the world worked together to develop a new product. Drawings might take weeks to travel from one office to another. Even faxing didn't solve that problem, because blurry fax copies of blueprints were inadequate for employees' needs.

Today, far-flung sites work together electronically on various parts of a new design. The process engineering might begin in TI's Bangalore, India, office. Engineers working in the Dallas, Texas, and Miho, Japan, branches would then feed needed components to the Bangalore employees. When a design is complete, Bangalore sends it to Dallas for manufacturing; it's then sent back to Bangalore for testing and debugging. The projects that formerly took three years, now take one year.

Time gets compressed in another way. Now TI engineers work on projects 24 hours a day, thanks to time zone differences and the electronic workplace. A typical Monday begins in Dallas, where design engineers work eight hours on a project. When quitting time rolls around, the

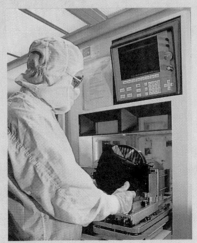

Courtesy of IBM Corporation.

Dallas engineers send their design drawings and progress reports electronically to their counterparts in Tokyo, Japan, who have just arrived at work. Eight hours later, when the Tokyo engineers' day ends, they ship their work electronically to TI designers in Nice, France. Finally, at the end of their work day, the Nice workers send their work to Dallas, where engineers are just reporting for work on Tuesday morning. Projects thus get a 24-hour effort from a worldwide workforce.

The process can be illustrated with an example. Suppose your firm buys items from a local supplier that goes out of business. You may be able to use your computer database to locate other suppliers in your area and in surrounding areas. If you can, the computer and database contain a possible solution to your problem: another good supplier.

Your next step is to obtain information from each potential supplier, including prices, procedures for ordering, purchasing terms and conditions, delivery schedules, and so on. These characteristics are the evaluation criteria on which you will make your decision. The acquired information can be stored in a database and, thereby, made available when needed. This information will allow you to evaluate each alternative supplier on the defined criteria so that you can make the best decision.

Finally, after making a decision and implementing the solution, you follow up to make certain it is effective. Does the supplier satisfy your requirements? Does the supplier offer fair and competitive prices, meet delivery schedules, and so on? Follow-up on a problem solution is an ongoing process. If the supplier you selected fails to meet your needs, the problem will need to be re-examined.

The process of systems analysis and design will vary among organizations and among applications. No two firms will develop the same payroll system, nor are they likely to have any identical systems. A system implemented by an automobile manufacturer, for instance, is likely to be quite different from one implemented by a large national retailing company.

THE ROLE OF THE SYSTEMS ANALYST

In a large organization, the overall responsibilities for systems analysis and design rest with trained computer professionals called systems analysts. A **systems analyst** is a skilled and experienced problem solver who can determine user information requirements and design systems that satisfy those requirements. The systems analyst does this by talking to the user and the user's work group to determine their information needs. This requires talking to all users, from clerks to managers. With this knowledge, the systems analyst can then design and plan for the development of an appropriate computerized system. A systems analyst must have technical skills plus well-developed social skills. The systems analyst will work closely with computer users, programmers, outside vendors, and managers. His or her job is to look at the problem, keeping all perspectives in mind, and to make decisions that will best serve them all.

THE SYSTEM LIFE CYCLE

Computer professionals generally agree on a phased approach to describe the **system life cycle**, the process of considering a new system from its inception through its development, implementation, and maintenance, until the system is either replaced or no longer useful to the user or organization (see Figure 10.8). However, there is some disagreement over exactly what the phases are, how they should be described, and how they are applied. Though the process can be broken down into anywhere from five to eleven steps, the flow of the process always remains the same. The most popular premise shows the system life cycle consisting of five phases:

Phase 1: Preliminary Investigation
Phase 2: Systems Analysis
Phase 3: Systems Design
Phase 4: System Acquisition and Implementation
Phase 5: System Maintenance

In the following sections, we will examine each of the phases in more detail.

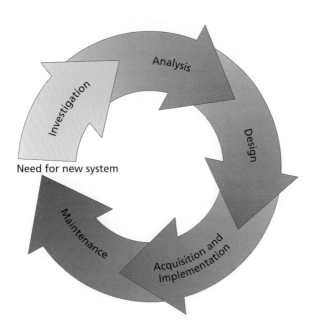

Figure 10.8

Because the needs of organizations are constantly changing, the system life cycle is a process that is often repeated.

PHASE 1: PRELIMINARY INVESTIGATION

The first step in system development is for the systems analyst to conduct a **preliminary investigation** of the problem so that it can be clearly and thoroughly defined. This investigation is launched at the request of the user or client. After identifying the specific problem, the analyst determines the extent and effects of the problem, suggests some possible solutions, and determines the approximate costs and benefits of alternative solutions.

The analyst also must determine the seriousness and magnitude of the problem. Many people have problems they would like solved, but some user's problems will prove more critical than others. The analyst needs to prioritize and solve the more serious problems first.

Identifying the Problem In trying to identify the problem, the analyst must distinguish between problems and symptoms. While a **symptom** is an indication that something may be wrong, analyzing a symptom without researching the cause can lead to an erroneous conclusion. For example, suppose an analyst learns from personnel in the computer center that the organization's mainframe computer is operating near full capacity, and that staff members are recommending a larger computer be purchased and installed.

After further investigation, the analyst finds that several noncritical applications were set up to run interactively on the mainframe computer. By taking these applications "off-line" and by processing them during the slower night shift, the computer's operating capacity can be improved. In addition, after talking to a number of computer-user teams, the analyst finds that time-consuming software development activities running on the mainframe could be transferred to the company's powerful PC workstation computer. Making these two system improvements may make the purchase of a larger computer unnecessary. In this case, the fact that the mainframe is operating near capacity is a symptom of the larger problem of managing system resources and applications.

Determining the Scope of the Project During the preliminary investigation, the analyst has to determine the scope of the problem. **Scope** refers to the extent of the problem, employee and management attitudes toward the problem and alternative solutions, and the amount management is willing to spend to resolve the problem. Installing a new computer system might cost several million dollars, but management might be willing to spend only a few thousand dollars.

A systems analyst soon learns to function within certain limitations or constraints. Developing a completely new system is not always the best solution. Sometimes, the analyst finds it best to modify an existing system. Modification may not be the ideal solution from a systems perspective, but budget constraints usually prevail.

Determining Costs and Benefits An important part of the preliminary phase of systems analysis and design is to determine a project's cost and potential benefits. The central question is whether the time and money spent on a new system are worthwhile. Unless the potential benefits exceed the expected costs, management is likely to veto the project.

Determining costs and benefits is not as easy as it might seem. For example, employee anger and frustration at having to learn new procedures might offset any gains from a new system. It can also be difficult to assign dollar values to potential benefits, such as more efficient information access for decision making.

Reporting to Management Upon completion of the preliminary investigation, the analyst prepares a written report for management that includes a description of the problem and recommendations. A summary of information gathered during the preliminary investigation, including costs and benefits, is also included. After reading the report and discussing it with those affected, management can decide on a course of action. Management can decide to abandon the project, implement a recommended solution, or continue on to the next phase of the system development process—systems analysis.

PHASE 2: SYSTEMS ANALYSIS

Assuming that management decides to go ahead with system development, the analyst begins the **systems analysis** phase of the system development cycle. Here, the analyst determines what the system is to do. During this phase, the analyst will gather pertinent facts, thoroughly analyze the existing system, and prepare and submit another report to management.

Gathering the Facts During systems analysis, the analyst obtains facts from available sources and determines what the current system does and what information the users and managers need. To obtain needed information, the analyst reviews technical data contained in the system's documentation, talks to users, and assembles useful data that will aid in making decisions about the project. Facts are gathered from written documents, questionnaires, interviews, and by personal observation. The analyst compiles useful data from these sources.

Analyzing the Existing System After the analyst has finished gathering information, he or she analyzes it using analytical tools such as diagrams and checklists. Prior to submitting a report to management, the analyst condenses and simplifies the information so that it can be easily understood by users. Diagrams, such as data flow diagrams and system flowcharts, can be particularly useful to a systems analyst.

A **data flow diagram** illustrates the logical flow of data and information through the system of users. It illustrates what is happening, not how the task is being performed. Thus, systems modeled with data flow diagrams could operate either manually or through the use of computers. Data flow diagrams are particularly helpful during meetings with users and managers because they are designed to be understood by nontechnical people. Data flow diagrams use four primary symbols, illustrated in Figure 10.9.

- ■ **Data flow lines** indicate the direction data move through the system.
- ■ **Process symbols** reveal activities that are performed.
- ■ **Entity symbols** show either the source or destination of the information flow.
- ■ **Data storage symbols** indicate the storage location for the data.

Data Flow
Symbols

Process Symbol

Entity Symbol

Data Storage
Symbol

Figure 10.9

The four primary symbols used in data flow diagrams.

Figure 10.10 illustrates a typical data flow diagram for an order processing application.

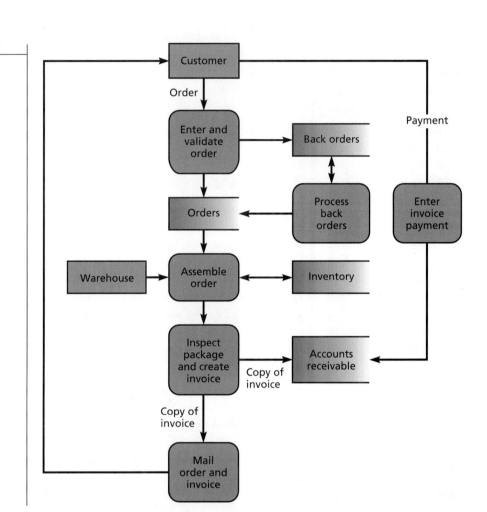

Figure 10.10

Data flow diagrams help analysts, end users, and managers visualize the flow of information as it travels through a system.

A **system flowchart** is a map that depicts the overall physical structure and flow in the system, including manual procedures, computer processing, and data files. It is more technically oriented than the data flow diagram and is used by the systems analyst to lay out the fine details of the system under development. The flowchart makes use of symbols standardized by the American National Standards Institute (ANSI). A full list of the symbols is illustrated in Figure 10.11. Using a system flowchart, the analyst views an entire system along with all of the individual system components. Figure 10.12 shows a sample system flowchart for the same order processing application diagrammed in Figure 10.10.

Using a system flowchart, the analyst can describe the structure of the current system and the relationship of its individual parts. There is no standard procedure for constructing system flowcharts, and they can vary greatly in size and complexity. The flowchart for a small system can be simple, while one for a large system can be very complex. Flowcharts are also discussed in Chapter 11 on Software Development and Programming.

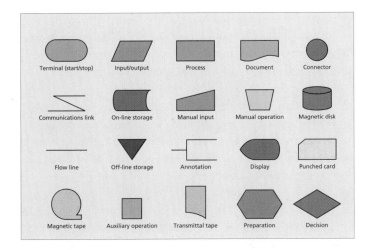

Figure 10.11

ANSI standardized symbols are used in system flowcharts.

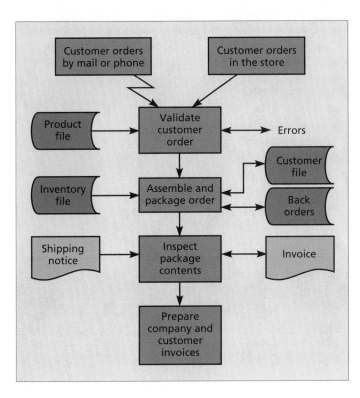

Figure 10.12

System flowcharts are used to document system designs.

Reporting to Management Upon completing the analysis phase, the analyst prepares a more comprehensive and detailed summary report to management. The main objective of this report is to help management decide whether or not it should continue on to the next phase.

PHASE 3: SYSTEMS DESIGN

During the **systems design** phase, analysts determine how the new system will operate. The design phase involves thoroughly reviewing the results of the previous systems analysis; developing a model of the new system; designing the outputs, inputs, processing steps, and storage systems for this new system; analyzing its costs and benefits; establishing a time schedule for implementation; and preparing the systems design report for management. This written document is often supplemented by oral presentations to those user teams involved in the processing change.

Reviewing the Project At the end of the previous phase, management decided to continue with the project, based on information contained in the analysis report. As a first step in the design phase, the analyst should review that report for the scope and goals of the project as approved by the management team. All of these materials will provide direction, constraints, and expectations for the project.

Developing a Model of the New System During systems design, the analyst prepares diagrams of the new system. This task is made easier by using data flow diagrams, system flowcharts, and other materials prepared during earlier phases. Collectively, such diagrams and flowcharts reveal how physical components of the system (including computer hardware) fit together to make up the complete system.

Some analysts begin by drawing an overall diagram of the system, which includes the components shown in Figure 10.13. These components are:

- Output requirements
- Input requirements
- Processing requirements
- Storage requirements
- Controls
- Personnel and procedural requirements

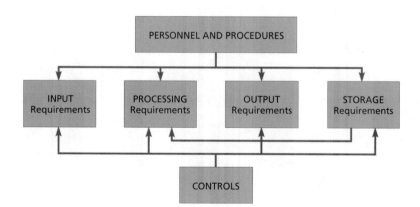

Figure 10.13

During the systems design phase, analysts start by drawing an overview model of the new system. The diagram shows what procedures must be determined and implemented for each phase of the information processing cycle.

The systems analyst first examines the system's output requirements by asking a number of questions. "What information do users need?" "When is the information needed?" "Where is it needed?" "In what form is the information needed?"

After output requirements are determined, data input requirements are defined. When reviewing input requirements, questions will arise. "What types of data contain the information required by the outputs?" "Where will the needed data be obtained?" "How should they be collected (manually or electronically)?" "How much data will the system process and store?" Storage might require multiple, on-line storage devices and media for fast access to information, as well as off-line storage for permanent storage and occasional processing needs.

Next, the analyst studies processing requirements. "What kinds of hardware and software are needed to convert the inputs into the desired outputs for team decision making?" "Does this process require a mainframe or a smaller computer?" "How much power and speed are required?" "Are there existing systems that might be purchased and adapted to solve this problem or must the company develop its own?"

Personnel requirements are of great importance to virtually any system. Typically, questions such as these are asked by the analyst: "What personnel are needed to operate the system?" "Can the organization afford additional personnel?" "Can users operate the system?" "What type of training is required?"

Finally, as with most systems, adequate controls and safeguards must be developed and implemented. Measures must be taken to ensure the security of the system, safeguard against unauthorized access to data files, and protect the privacy of individuals. Without adequate controls in place, the system can prove to be more harmful than helpful to the organization.

Analyzing the Costs and Benefits In information-intensive, "paper-based" industries such as insurance, banking, and investments, it is common for information system costs to exceed 30 percent of the company's total operating budget. Measuring the cost-effectiveness of these systems and their contribution to the performance of the company is done through cost/benefit analysis.

An attempt to identify and then to weigh or to compare the benefits of each alternative against its cost is the goal of **cost/benefit analysis**. Even if a project's benefits exceed its costs, there may be other alternatives that generate even greater benefits for less cost. Figure 10.14 portrays the concept of weighing costs against benefits.

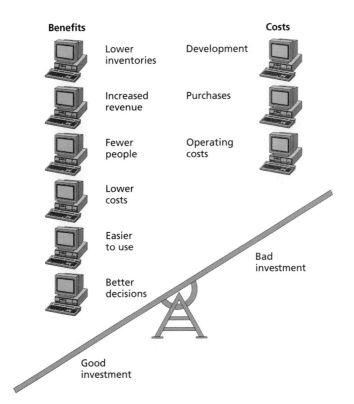

Benefits

Lower inventories

Increased revenue

Fewer people

Lower costs

Easier to use

Better decisions

Costs

Development

Purchases

Operating costs

Bad investment

Good investment

Figure 10.14

By weighing the costs and benefits of implementing a new system, managers can see clearly whether the system is a good or bad investment.

Most organizations have many more investment alternatives than they have resources to invest. Information system development competes with other organizational alternatives for the firm's limited time and money. Firms look at the costs and benefits of a new, computer-based inventory control system and compare the return on this project with, for instance, that of an investment in a new advertising campaign or with hiring five new salespeople. New systems must generate a positive return on invested resources. Organizations hope that the benefits resulting from the choices they make will exceed the benefits of the alternatives they discard. In information systems, the key commodity is information, and the business requirement for those systems is to deliver that information when and where it is needed.

The ideal investment is a low-risk option leading to a quick payoff and high cash flow. There are costs involved in generating information necessary for good decision making. The total of all these costs might be called the "cost of thinking." This is always a significant cost for the organization. Information systems increase the thinking power of the organization.

The table below lists the major types of costs and benefits in an information systems project. Costs are classified as either developmental costs, one-time fixed costs, or as ongoing variable costs. Intangible costs occur as a result of another, measurable cost. When a firm loses a key employee, the loss is difficult to measure. Similar problems occur when estimating benefits. Benefit categories relate to either lowering costs, increasing revenues, or returns from improvements in intangible categories. Benefits, such as labor saved by a new system can be estimated with relative ease. However, other intangible benefits, such as a happier work force, are more difficult to quantify. Perhaps the economic value of a happier work force might be measured by estimating employee turnover rates before and after a system is installed. Then, by multiplying employee training costs per year by the new, lower turnover rate, an estimate of the intangible benefit could be made.

Cost and Benefit Considerations in System Selection

Costs	Benefits
INITIAL DEVELOPMENT COSTS (FRONT END) Personnel (in-house staff and consultants) Equipment (computers and other resources)	**LOWER COSTS** Lower processing costs Reduced inventories Fewer personnel
FIXED COSTS (ONE-TIME) Computer equipment purchases Software purchases Building and facilities preparation Education and retraining Conversion process	**INCREASED INCOME** New customers New products and services Larger profit margins from more efficient operations

OPERATING COSTS (ONGOING)
Equipment lease fees
Programming and operations personnel
Maintenance
Security
Utilities
Insurance
Computer supplies
	NONMONETARY BENEFITS
	More satisfied existing customers
	Easier, user friendly system
	More professional industry and
	    community image
	Attraction of better, new personnel
	Lower turnover of existing personnel
	More efficient and timely
	    decision making

As you can see from the above table, cost/benefit analysis considers both numerical data and qualitative information. Cost elements include equipment, maintenance, facilities, software, communications, personnel, and conversion. *Conversion* is an estimate of the cost of getting out of the existing system. Retraining staff members and end users is an often-ignored expense. It is estimated the cost of conversion and retraining is usually twice that of the actual hardware and software required by the new system. A long-range perspective on cost/benefit analysis considers both acquisition and disposal issues related to the new system. Any analysis should show how a new system makes the organization leaner and more responsive.

Cost/benefit analysis should also consider the timing of when the organization will receive the benefits or have to pay the costs. The value of smaller benefits realized earlier may be greater than larger benefits occurring later in the life of a project due to the time value of money.

Finally, in today's total quality-management, customer-oriented marketplace, cost/benefit analysis must also include assessment of customer impact. The analysis should address what management has defined as the customer objectives for the system and what effect the new system will have on product and process quality, deliveries, service, customer attitude, and market competitiveness.

Deciding to Make or Buy Software When a new information system need arises, a key part of the design phase is determining whether software should be written internally or purchased from an outside vendor. This is the **make-or-buy decision**. Purchased software is usually general-purpose and may not perfectly match the needs of the company. Yet, developing software internally is slow and expensive, and extensive testing of commercial software can help determine its appropriateness. Make-or-buy decisions are often not clear-cut.

The focus of software assessment should be on the outputs needed, the inputs required, and the conversion process. Also, purchased software must blend seamlessly with other software applications currently running in the system. Integrating purchased software may make it difficult to achieve software consistency. Also, for ease of use, the user interface in purchased software must be relatively consistent with that used in current applications. Deploying purchased software requires the same planning and execution that in-house software requires.

Purchased software may reduce the design time for the system's life cycle, but the other phases of the cycle (preliminary investigation, analysis, implementation, and maintenance) are very similar to those used with in-house software. Considerations for the make-or-buy decision include:

- Access to future software upgrades by the vendor
- Capabilities of in-house programmers
- Current systems development backlog
- Delivery times
- Education and training supplied by the vendor
- Financial strength of vendor
- Financing
- Hardware requirements
- Industry reputation

- List of current customers
- Ownership or license
- Payment schedule
- Priority of this application
- Purchase price
- Quality of sales and systems maintenance people
- Ability to modify software
- Software return policy
- Testing and performance indicators
- User-friendliness
- Software and performance warranties

Today, with the large number of quality software vendors and relatively low software prices, many operating systems and application programs are being purchased. Industry associations and publications, competitors, customers, and vendor creditors are excellent sources of information. Note that many of the same considerations in the preceding list are relevant when it's time to purchase software for your own personal computer.

Systems Design Report for Management After the systems analyst has completed the design phase of the project, a report is again submitted to management. The systems design report includes all facts gathered during previous phases of the study, plus all the hardware, software, procedures, and contracts that will be required. The report identifies specific software to be purchased and specifies the software that will be written by the organization's own programmers.

After a summary of primary recommendations and other important information, the report contains detailed information on the system design, along with costs and benefits. Management's decision whether or not to proceed with the acquisitions phase of the project will be based largely on information contained in the report, on recommendations of the systems analyst, and on the response of the proposed system's users.

PHASE 4: SYSTEM ACQUISITION AND IMPLEMENTATION

Following a lengthy review of the systems design report, management will decide whether or not to acquire and implement the new system. Assuming that management decides to move forward with the new system, the analyst must decide which vendors or manufacturers will supply the necessary hardware and software components. This is the first major task of the **system acquisition and implementation** phase of the cycle.

Gathering Bids Most large organizations, including government agencies and schools, follow a practice of allowing vendors to offer bids on expensive projects, a practice called the **bid system**. The goal of the bid system is to obtain the best price by allowing rival firms to compete for sales of their equipment and other products. The systems analyst, in cooperation with the purchasing department, prepares a document called a **request for proposal (RFP)**, which contains a list of the technical specifications for hardware and software needed for the new system. The RFP can vary in length, from one page to several hundred pages, depending on the size and complexity of the project. Once it is completed, the document is sent to all vendors who might wish to submit bids. Vendors are notified of the date and time when all bids will be opened for review.

Most organizations have their own methods for evaluating bids. Figure 10.15 shows an evaluation form and bid scoring process that a company might use.

Evaluation criterion	Maximum score	Vendor 1	Vendor 2	Vendor 3
Quality	100	83	77	71
Cost	100	75	85	64
Warranty	100	61	88	63
Support	100	57	79	71
Documentation	100	66	69	65
Ease of use	100	82	88	73
TOTAL POINTS:		424	486	407

Vendor 2 has highest score

Figure 10.15

Many organizations use a form to evaluate vendors that submit bids. In this example, each vendor is evaluated on the criteria of quality, cost, warranty, support, documentation, and ease of use. Each of the criteria is assigned a maximum number of points that can be earned. The vendor earning the highest number of points is given primary consideration.

Implementing the System After bids have been evaluated and decisions have been made concerning the acquisition of system components, the system is ordered and installed. Depending on the size and complexity of the system, the time required for implementation can range from a few days to several months.

Rarely are all components delivered at the same time. Therefore, the analyst must prepare a timetable for implementing the new system. Systems analysts use a number of project management software tools, such as Gantt charts, to assure that implementation will proceed smoothly and with a minimum of difficulty. A **Gantt chart** is a bar chart commonly used to depict a series of activities, schedule deadlines, and milestones. Figure 10.16 shows a simplified Gantt chart for implementing a new computer system.

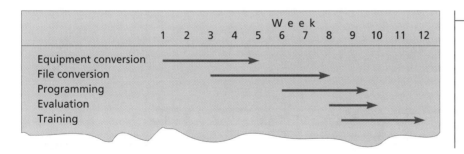

	Week											
	1	2	3	4	5	6	7	8	9	10	11	12
Equipment conversion												
File conversion												
Programming												
Evaluation												
Training												

Figure 10.16

Gantt charts depict a series of activities. They are used to schedule deadlines and milestones in system implementation.

Changing over from an old system to a new one is called **system conversion**. Such conversions can be frustrating. Also, system conversion means discontinuing use of the old, familiar system, which temporarily makes work difficult for users. There are four suggested ways to handle this conversion (see Figure 10.17 on page 370).

Direct conversion means that the user simply stops using the old system and begins using the new one. This is risky, because the new system might not function as planned, and the old system is no longer available to fall back on. Direct conversion would likely be done only if the old system were no longer usable or if there were insufficient resources to use both systems.

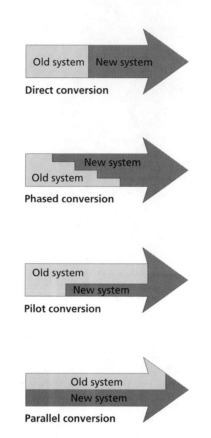

Figure 10.17

System conversions.

A *phased conversion* is one in which the organization eases into the new system one step at a time. Eventually, users will entirely abandon the old system and use the new system for all applications.

A *pilot conversion* is one in which the new system is used by some users, while other users continue with the old system. After a period of time all users will use the new system. This approach is used more frequently in companies having separate divisions or large geographical areas with separate computing facilities in each region.

In a *parallel conversion*, the most prolonged and expensive conversion method, both the old and the new systems operate simultaneously for a period of time. Once users are satisfied that the new system performs to their standards, the old system is abandoned.

System conversion is stressful and confusing for analyst and users alike. Conversions often require additional education and training for operators and users of the new system. Poor preparation of personnel is a leading cause of new system failures. Training, supplied by vendors or in-house personnel, should be done well in advance of the actual installation.

COMPUTER CURRENTS

PC: The Physician's Colleague?

It doesn't have a medical degree, and it certainly doesn't have much of a bedside manner. If you're ill, however, the personal computer could be one of the best "doctors" you'll ever see. Thanks to a new series of computerized medical information systems, computers today are helping physicians improve both the diagnosis and treatment of a host of diseases.

Medical information systems fall into two categories: communications systems and advice systems. Physicians can access both network systems using PCs with modems. While communications systems simply allow doctors to collect and store data for later retrieval, advice systems analyze data and apply it to a specific patient's situation.

Bruce Ayres/Tony Stone Worldwide.

To understand how these systems work, suppose you are the victim of an accident in New York City and are taken, unconscious, to the hospital. The emergency room doctors find your driver's license, which indicates that you are from a small town 300 miles away in Pennsylvania. By tapping into a national computer network of hospitals, the doctors in New York can see that you underwent treatment for a broken leg in Pennsylvania four years ago. They can also discover the name of your physician and learn the vital information that you are allergic to penicillin.

During your hospital stay nurses on your floor access the hospital's mainframe system to record your condition and treatment. This same system has a built-in "advice" component that flashes an alert if an ordered test duplicates one already run, or if a new medication reacts adversely with one you are currently receiving.

You return home after being released from the hospital, but begin to suffer from persistent headaches. Your family physician isn't sure whether these are a result of the accident or the beginning of a pattern of migraines like those experienced by other members of your family. By accessing Roundsman, an experimental advice system, your doctor can get summaries of the most recent studies on headaches and their causes. Your doctor can also enter your specific medical history and condition and receive the Roundsman's "expert" opinion—a synthesis of expert opinions on recent studies related to patients with similar medical conditions.

Valuable as they are, modern medical information systems are just the beginning of a computer revolution in medicine. Hospitals, insurance companies, and government agencies are all looking eagerly to computerized systems to reduce the skyrocketing cost of health care. For example, IBM and Blue Cross/Blue Shield have teamed up to develop a system that electronically links providers, patients, and payers in order to streamline the claim-filing process.

As the ability to transmit computer images improves, so do the prospects for expanded use of the computer in diagnostic settings. Residents of rural areas are one group likely to benefit, as their physicians will be able to consult with experts in state-of-the-art facilities across the country.

PHASE 5: SYSTEM MAINTENANCE

After acquisition and implementation have been completed, the new system must be maintained. Maintaining a computer system is an ongoing activity lasting the lifetime of the system. **System maintenance** is keeping the entire system operating and up-to-date. Additional internal memory might need to be installed, or software (such as a payroll program) might need to be rewritten and stored on the system. Also, all system components are continually monitored to ensure all parts of the system perform according to acceptable standards. It is estimated that 60 to 80 percent of an organization's system development effort is spent on system maintenance. It's no wonder that organizations are constantly looking for tools and methods to lower this enormous expense.

PROTOTYPING

Sometimes it is not practical, or possible, to follow the system development phases in precise order. Computer systems are very expensive and do not always perform as expected. Large systems development projects may take several years to complete. In the meantime, users' needs may change. Organizations and their activities must constantly adapt to changes in their internal and external environments.

To avoid the disaster of developing an expensive system that, in the end, does not meet user needs, some analysts develop a small working model of the system, called a **prototype**. For many years manufacturers have used prototypes to develop new products. Perhaps you've seen automobile prototypes in television commercials. An automobile manufacturer is not likely to commit to the expense of setting up a production line to manufacture a solar-powered car without first building and testing a prototype. Prototypes are built in many different organizations to test products and processes before time and money are invested in systems that might later prove unsuitable.

CASE TOOLS

Due to rising costs and increasing backlogs, applications development productivity is becoming an increasingly important issue in information systems development. **Computer-aided software engineering (CASE)** is a rapidly emerging technology that facilitates design, development, and maintenance of information systems. CASE tools automate almost everything a human does in the system development process—designing, coding, graphing, structuring data, generating output reports, and controlling the project timeline.

CASE tools include automated screen or report format design, software code generation (they can generate machine-readable instruction codes directly from design diagrams and specifications), program documentation, data flow diagrams, and structure charts. Once applications are developed using CASE tools, they can be quickly modified to meet changing hardware, software, or data requirements.

CASE tools include analysis and design workbenches that graphically show the application's structure and design; repositories or data dictionaries that provide common data definitions; application generators to produce program code; and project management tools to track and display system development progress. CASE tools improve productivity in the system life cycle, improve the quality of the software generated, and improve business performance due to better support systems. CASE tools also support joint or team-based application development in which programmers, systems analysts, and end users jointly interact to design new systems.

One very popular CASE tools software program is Excelerator. Using a structured, top-down approach, an analyst designs the major components of the system and then refines each segment of the system. Eventually, individual data record formats can be designed. When the analyst is done, the software creates graphic representations of the entire system using different levels of data flow diagrams.

In the future, CASE tools will be able to automate information systems projects from design to implementation to maintenance to disposal, and be able to show users every interaction and interface. These systems will even have the ability, using expert system technologies, to identity flaws in proposed designs and make recommendations. Finally, CASE tools will assess and improve design consistency among analysts. If one analyst uses techniques that are not be understood by other team members, the CASE program will notify the developer and recommend changes.

THE FUTURE OF SYSTEMS DEVELOPMENT

Systems development tool suppliers plan to bundle multiple software tools into a single, object-oriented, application development package. Programmers will apply these new development tools, called **software factories**, to applications requiring rapid development and assembly in a client/server environment. Developers will become system component builders. **Software warehouses** will store inventories of coded solutions for reuse in similar applications.

The software factory/warehouse combination will drastically shorten development times, increase the quantity of error-free programs, and allow application sharing among network users. Suppliers will also provide installation teams to train on-site staff. Object-oriented graphic user interfaces shrink learning curves and allow developers to easily transfer from one application to another. The annual worldwide market for development tools is expected to exceed $18 billion by 1997.

Historically, organizations have been data rich and information poor. Many organizations remain structurally incapable of providing useful business intelligence to management. Data warehousing facilitates the creation of internal intelligence systems that support decision-making systems.

Data warehousing is the process of acquiring data from multiple internal and external sources and integrating those data in a single database. Then, with flexible reporting and analysis tools, users can access specific information for more detailed analysis and decision making. Many organizations are expected to pursue new data warehousing applications.

MICROCOMPUTERS AND END-USER COMPUTING

Historically, most people have viewed the microcomputer as a tool for personal applications. In recent years, microcomputers have become important information-producing tools in many businesses due to technological improvements in microcomputer hardware and software. The expanding role of microcomputers for MISs has gained recognition and acceptance. However, the role of the microcomputer has evolved somewhat differently for small and large businesses.

MICROCOMPUTERS IN SMALL ORGANIZATIONS

Before microcomputers were introduced, many small business firms could not afford to purchase their own computer system. Many that could afford a computer system did not have computer-literate employees. Hence, data were processed manually or by a data processing service. Today, the low cost of microcomputer systems make them affordable and practical for most, if not all, small businesses. Microcomputer systems and employee training now represent a practical and necessary investment for small businesses.

Usually the first applications for which businesses use microcomputers are word processing and basic transaction processing systems, such as record-keeping, payroll, accounting, and customer billing. Over time, the volume of data stored on a microcomputer system increases. Management uses the data for marketing and inventory analysis, and to prepare budgets. In effect, the microcomputer system is being used as an MIS.

As managers gain experience, more complex applications are done on the microcomputer system. Integrated databases are developed, and sophisticated reporting and decision support systems are purchased or developed. Microcomputers are linked by communications software and communications channels. Business data and other resources, such as software programs and business files, can be shared by managers at various work sites. Also, managers can communicate electronically with other businesses and services, including suppliers, banks, and information services.

The role of microcomputers in small business has expanded dramatically in recent years. Today, the presence of a microcomputer system in a small business organization is about as common as the presence of a desk or a telephone. In fact, many businesses have microcomputers on every employee's desk. Most of these employees use word processing, spreadsheets, databases, graphics, electronic mail, the Internet, and other software applications as part of daily business.

MICROCOMPUTERS IN LARGE ORGANIZATIONS

Large business firms used mainframe computer systems long before microcomputers were introduced to the market. However, managers in these firms were often not experienced computer users. In many cases, only a few managers in departments outside of the computer department were involved in developing information systems.

Many large businesses have already installed microcomputers throughout their organizations. Because microcomputers are so easy to use, managers are motivated to become more involved in designing new MIS systems using the power and versatility of state-of-the-art microcomputer systems.

Because many of the organization's basic applications (accounting, transaction processing systems, payroll, and so on) are already being done on large, centralized mainframes or on minicomputers; microcomputers are often used by managers who are aware of the advantages of personal computing. Early applications often include DSSs that use electronic spreadsheet, graphics, and database programs. Other early applications include MISs that use file managers for reporting, and programs for personnel and project management.

With the assistance of computer personnel, microcomputer networks are installed, and microcomputers are linked to the firm's large computer and to various peripheral devices. This system allows managers to have access to the firm's large database files. Files can be downloaded from the mainframe to microcomputers or uploaded from microcomputers to the mainframe. Certain MIS and DSS applications can be moved from the large computer to microcomputers. EISs link microcomputers to databases inside the organization as well as to external databases in order to get the most up-to-date information for the strategic planning process.

Microcomputers are already serving important roles in small and large business organizations. As improvements continue in microcomputer hardware and software technologies, microcomputer systems will play an even more prominent role in the business world and in society.

END-USER COMPUTING

End-user computing is the process whereby the programming and operation of a computer are done by the person who uses the results for decision making and problem solving. With the advent of low-cost, user-friendly hardware and software, the demand for individual control of information and processing has increased over the past 15 years. End-use computing developed as an alternative to the year-long backlogs and perceived unresponsiveness of centralized computing departments.

Quicker response time, fewer communication errors, decreased dependence on others for information, and experimentation and innovation at all levels of the organization are just a few of the advantages of end-user computing. Drawbacks include a hefty financial commitment to computer training for all employees, possible user over-analysis, an antagonistic attitude toward the centralized computing department and their resources, poor documentation, and hardware and software incompatibility.

Most end-user training currently focuses on software and does not adequately prepare employees to solve business problems. Training should cover systems development, why computer projects fail, good documentation procedures, and database design principles. Users need training in systems analysis and design in order to understand the relationship between end users and centralized computing groups. Users also need to know how small, user-developed applications complement organization-wide computing efforts.

Key Terms

bid system

capsule reports

computer-aided software engineering
(CASE)

cost/benefit analysis

custom report

data flow diagram

data warehousing

database query program

decision support system (DSS)

demand report

drill-down systems design

electronic data interchange (EDI)

end-user computing

exception report

executive information system (EIS)

expert system

Gantt chart

hierarchical structures

interorganizational information system
(IOIS)

make-or-buy decision

management information system (MIS)

matrix structures

nodal/networked structure

preliminary investigation

problem

problem solving

prototype

report

report generator

request for proposal (RFP)

scope

software factories

software warehouses

summary report

symptom

system acquisition and implementation

system conversion

system flowchart

system life cycle

system maintenance

systems analysis

systems analyst

systems design

transaction processing system (TPS)

Summary

The word **problem** refers to any event or situation, good or bad, that offers an opportunity to improve an organization in some way. **Problem solving** is responding successfully to both bad and good problems.

Organizational structures are constantly evolving. The traditional business structure is **hierarchical**, while newer **matrix** and **networked** structures are being tried in some organizations in response to changes in the business world and in computer technology.

The management hierarchy pyramid includes four levels of information systems users: non-management employees, operations managers, tactical managers, and strategic managers. Moving up the pyramid, decision making becomes a less structured process.

An organization's information needs, and the information systems that serve them, closely parallel the management activities at each level on the management hierarchy.

Transaction process systems (TPSs) use computers to process detailed data such as payroll, accounts receivable, and inventory data.

Management information systems (MISs) evolved in the mid-1960s to aid middle managers in making intermediate-range decisions. These systems are computerized and capable of generating brief reports, such as **summary reports**, **exception reports**, **demand reports**, and **custom reports** for solving structured problems.

Decision support systems (DSSs), first introduced in the mid-1970s, aid all levels of management who deal with unstructured problem situations. **Expert systems (ESs)** capture the knowledge of experts in specific fields. **Executive information systems (EISs)** present high-level, summarized, graphical information to an organization's top decision makers for use in long-range planning decisions.

Interorganizational information systems (IOISs) electronically link organizations with **electronic data interchange (EDI)** to facilitate cooperative decision making.

The process of planning, designing, and implementing a new system is called *systems analysis* and *design* and varies from one organization to another. The responsibility for system development belongs to the **systems analyst**.

The **system life cycle** involves five major phases: (1) preliminary investigation, (2) systems analysis, (3) systems design, (4) system acquisition and implementation, and (5) system maintenance. Each phase includes several activities or tasks that must be completed before entering the next phase of the system development process.

During the **preliminary investigation**, systems analysts identify problems, determine the scope of the project and the costs and benefits, and report to management.

In **systems analysis**, analysts gather facts, analyze the existing system, and develop data flow diagrams and system flowcharts. **Data flow diagrams** are used to show the logical sequence of relationships and activities, not physical processes. **System flowcharts** are more technically oriented maps of the physical process components of systems.

During the **systems design** phase, systems analysts use **cost/benefit analysis** to identify and compare the benefits of each alternative against its costs. Even if a computer project's benefits exceed its costs, there may be other alternatives in the company that generate even greater benefits for less cost.

When a new information system need arises, a key part of the **systems design phase** is to determine whether software should be written internally or purchased from an outside vendor. This is called the **make-or-buy decision**.

Systems analysts then move to the **system acquisition and implementation** phase. The analyst prepares a **request for proposal (RFP)** document that lists the hardware and software required. The company puts outside vendors through a **bid system** to determine who can supply items needed for the system at the lowest price.

Depending on the complexity of the new system, system implementation can take anywhere from a few days to many months. A **Gantt chart** is used to plot the time frame of the conversion. The approaches to **systems conversion** include direct, phased, pilot, and parallel.

System maintenance is the last phase and consists of keeping the system operating and up-to-date.

Prototyping is developing and testing a smaller working model of a new system prior to developing the actual system.

Computer-aided software engineering (CASE) facilitates the design, development, and maintenance of information systems. Think of CASE tools as the automation of anything that a human can do in the systems development process.

Systems development tool suppliers plan to bundle multiple software tools into a single, object-oriented, application development package. Programmers will apply these new development tools, called **software factories**, to applications requiring rapid development and assembly in a client/server environment. **Software warehouses** will store inventories of coded solutions for reuse in similar applications in the future.

Historically, organizations have been data rich and information poor. Data warehousing facilitates the creation of internal intelligence systems that support decision-making systems. **Data warehousing** is the process of acquiring data from multiple internal and external sources and integrating those data in a single database.

End-user computing is the process whereby the programming and operation of a computer are done by the person who uses the results for decision making and problem solving.

14 Easy steps to being a webmaster

STEP 10   PHOTOGRAPHS

Photographs add visual interest to any web page because we relate to other people better than to text. Photos are good for showing people who give testimonials about a company, for demonstrating steps in a process (such as how to bake a cake), or for giving a viewer a sense of location (such as photos of a campus).

There are two ways to get photos into a web presentation. Paper-printed photos or slides can be scanned and digitized, or photos can be taken with a digital camera. Digital cameras take from 15 to 100 photos, in color or gray-scale, and with low or high resolution. A low resolution photo takes about 30K of disk storage while a high resolution photo takes about ten times that. Usually, you take photos in high resolution and save them in low resolution for web presentation. To use such a digital camera,

■ Take the photos desired

■ Attach the camera to a computer

■ Download the photos using special software from the vendor

■ Look at each photo and correct its lighting, size, composition, and so on, using features of the software

■ Save each photo as a .jpg file for linkage in an anchor to a web page

■ Test the file using a browser such as Netscape

■ Ftp the photo to the web site using a name and .jpg extension.

Photos liven a web presentation, adding an effective element that is not conveyed by words. For instance, organizations can appear to be serious or fun, people-oriented or not, and interesting or boring, all depending on the content of photos. Pictures of buildings with no people convey a serious, prosperous, non-people oriented look. Pictures of people smiling at a camera are better, but may appear posed and unnatural. Pictures of people going about their business are best, showing action, interest, and fun-people orientation. This does not mean that photos are not posed, only that the finished product should not look posed. It also does not mean that head shots and buildings are never used, only that they should be used for a conscious purpose. Finally, distorted photos that are stretched, reverse-video, or otherwise doctored, can be effective in conveying a sense of humor and fun.

In addition to animation; contrast, proximity, and alignment are all important elements for photo composition. Request that models' clothing colors be simple. Make sure backgrounds are not the same color and not too busy. Try to take outdoor photos on clear, sunny days with the subjects facing the sun. Do not have people wear blue clothes outside in a shot that has mostly blue sky background. Arrange the main characters or photo elements so that the eye will find them easily. If you already have a web page composition in mind, arrange the photo to fit with the rest of the web page. For instance, a photo to be in the bottom right of a page should be composed with the main elements also bottom right of the photo (see Figure 10.18 on page 380). This causes the viewers' eye to return to the page rather than "falling off the bottom."

Frames and other photographic tricks are created with software, such as Photoshop, and saved as .jpg files. Photos add to the time needed to load a page. Therefore, try to keep the combined size of all photos and graphics to under 100K per page.

Design of photo page placement requires several decisions. The design issues are photo angle, background, caption, and alignment with text and borders. Photos can be slanted or parallel to the sides of the web page (see Figure 10.19 on page 380). Slanted positioning is more artistic and less formal than parallel positioning. Similarly, a background to the photo can be square-edged or ragged. A square-edged frame gives the look of a real-life photo frame and is more formal (see Figure 10.18). A ragged-edge frame is casual, giving a scrapbook look (see Figure 10.19). Ragged-edge backgrounds are effective especially with slanted photos.

Figure 10.18

A photo showing proper alignment of elements.

Figure 10.19

A slanted photo with a ragged edge border.

The color, size, and placement of the background are also important to integrating a photo in a page. A background might be extended on one side of a photo with overlapping text that integrates it with the other content. Or, text color might match the photo background color, leading the users' eyes to pull them together.

The photo caption is another design element. All photos, unless used for strictly artistic purposes, should have a caption describing their contents or purpose. There is nothing more irritating than to view a "tour of the . . ." with 20 or 30 photos, none of which has a caption. Captions should explain the content, purpose, and importance of photos.

ASSIGNMENT: If your school or you have access to a digital camera, compose, take, and store one or two photos, and include them in your web pages. If you have old photos, scan, store, and include them in your web pages. Upload the new pages to the Web. If you do not have access to the necessary technology, evaluate two web sites that use photos. Write a paragraph on each, comparing their use of contrast, alignment, and proximity in both the photo composition and the arrangement of the photos on the page.

Exercises

REVIEW QUESTIONS

1. How has the management hierarchy changed over time?

2. How do management information systems (MISs) differ from TPSs?

3. What is a decision support system (DSS)? At which management level are DSSs most likely to be used?

4. How did executive information systems (EISs) evolve? Who uses them and how are they used?

5. Define *expert system*. Give examples of how an expert system is used.

6. What is the role of the systems analyst?

7. How are system flowcharts used?

8. What are the components that need to be considered when developing a new system?

9. Explain *cost/benefit analysis*.

10. What are some of the factors in the make-or-buy decision?

11. What are the four methods for system conversion identified in the chapter?

12. What is a prototype? What advantage does prototyping offer an organization?

13. What is a data warehouse?

FILL IN THE BLANKS

1. Responding successfully to both good and bad problems is called _problem solving_

2. During the _identifying the problem / preliminary investigation_ phase, the systems analyst distinguishes between problems and _symptoms_

3. A _data flow diagram_ illustrates the logical flow of data and information through the system.

4. One very popular _case_ tool software program is Excelerator.

5. A diagram that depicts the overall structure of a system, including manual procedures, computer processing, and data files is called a _system flowchart_

6. _Transaction processing_ systems are computerized information systems designed to process routine operational data.

7. _Expert_ systems capture the experience, decision rules, and thought processes of key people in specific fields.

8. _Electronic data interchange_ is a procedure that allows the exchange of data from the computer system of one organization to the computer system of another organization.

9. _Database query_ software is used to process data arranged in rows and columns.

MATCHING

Match each term with its description.

a. expert system
b. decision support system
c. transaction processing
d. strategic planning
e. EDI
f. end-user computing
g. system flowchart

h. Gantt chart
i. systems analyst
j. phased conversion
k. CASE tools
l. prototype
m. parallel
n. system maintenance

_K_ 1. Automated software program that includes workbenches, data dictionaries, application generators, and project management tools.

_L_ 2. Working model of a system designed to find flaws before a complete system is implemented.

_G_ 3. Depicts the overall structure of a system.

_H_ 4. Bar chart that depicts deadlines and milestones.

_I_ 5. Person responsible for systems analysis and design.

_J_ 6. Organization eases into new system one step at a time.

_M_ 7. Most prolonged and expensive conversion method.

_N_ 8. Keeping the entire system operating and up-to-date.

_D_ 9. Important, long-range planning process.

_B_ 10. Perform "what if" analysis on problem solutions.

_A_ 11. System that might be used to diagnose a rare illness or disease.

_C_ 12. System used to process large volumes of data in a short period of time.

_E_ 13. Process of linking data from one computer system to another in a communications network.

_F_ 14. Process whereby the programming and operation of a computer system are done by the person who uses the results for decision making and problem solving.

 **ACTIVITIES**

1. Select a business in your community that uses computers for transaction processing applications. Ask the manager to explain how the system operates and what data are collected. Take notes during your visit. Following your visit, write an essay that answers the following questions:

   a. What kinds of equipment does the business use? Does it use a specific brand name?

   b. What information does the business use?

   c. How do managers use the collected data?

   d. What are the advantages and disadvantages of the system now in use?

2. Suppose you plan to start a business selling music CDs and audiotapes. What kind of information system would you install to enable you to efficiently serve your customers?

3. Try to imagine what a familiar organization (perhaps your college) will look like ten years from now. Then, based on the information systems discussed in this chapter, analyze how the utilization of each type of system might affect the organization. What changes will result? How might people in the organization react to these changes? What will be the benefits and drawbacks of these changes? What will happen if this organization does not change in the next ten years? Prepare a short written report and oral presentation of your analysis.

4. How good are you at solving problems? Select a recent problem you encountered. Make a list of steps you took to solve the problem. How successful were you? What would you do differently if you had to solve the problem again?

Skills for Living

DOING MEDICAL AND HEALTH RESEARCH

Have you ever heard the saying, "May you grow up to be healthy, wealthy, and wise."? Notice that *healthy* is listed first. Without good health, the value of wealth and wisdom is greatly diminished. But how do we stay healthy? Doctors tell us that each person faces controllable and uncontrollable health factors. Controllable factors might include diet, exercise, drinking, smoking, hygiene, and stress. Uncontrollable factors are age, gender, family heredity, and blood type. At any point in time, the overall condition of our health is the current balance point between all of these controllable and uncontrollable factors. To improve our health, we must work on improving the positive impact of the controllable factors—better diet, more exercise, less drinking and smoking, less stress, etc. With any sickness or illness, information and understanding are the first steps toward a successful cure. The Internet is a wonderful source of information for managing our health.

How's your health? How do you know? How much do you know about health and about how you can learn more? How can you improve your ability to avert a sickness? No one should be more interested in your personal health than yourself!

What illnesses or diseases are in your family history—coronary disease, high blood pressure, hypertension, diabetes? What do you know about their causes and cures? Do you have a relative or friend who is stricken with a life-threatening disease? Maybe you can help.

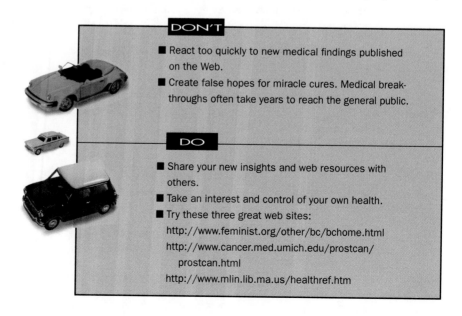

DON'T
- React too quickly to new medical findings published on the Web.
- Create false hopes for miracle cures. Medical breakthroughs often take years to reach the general public.

DO
- Share your new insights and web resources with others.
- Take an interest and control of your own health.
- Try these three great web sites:
  http://www.feminist.org/other/bc/bchome.html
  http://www.cancer.med.umich.edu/prostcan/prostcan.html
  http://www.mlin.lib.ma.us/healthref.htm

The Internet is an excellent source for the most current understanding about health and medical issues. Hospitals, societies, support groups, and even diseases have their own home pages on the Web. Because of the speed of publishing and distribution, new research findings often appear on the Web before they appear in the medical journals.

Try using this resource to improve your quality of life and that of those around you. What information is available about preventative medicine, herbal medicines, meditation?

Student Activities

1. Using the Internet, do some research and reading about an illness or disease of interest to you. What resources did you find? Did you find support groups or associations related to the malady? Are you now more familiar and aware of issues related to this topic? Can you identify other health issues where the Web could be a valuable resource?

   Do your research, write up findings, and discuss them with your classmates. Also, share your findings with other members of your family and friends. Share your insights with those you feel might be most susceptible or prone to encounter this type of illness or disease. Urge them to do their own health research on the Web.

2. Assess your own controllable and uncontrollable health factors. List five ways you could improve your health. How can the Internet help you improve your health?

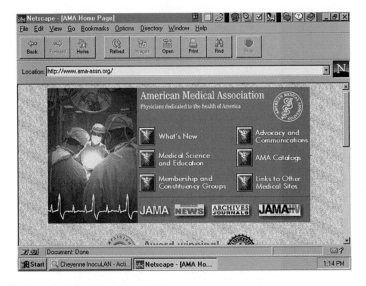

CHAPTER 11

SOFTWARE DEVELOPMENT AND PROGRAMMING

OBJECTIVES

AFTER STUDYING THIS CHAPTER, YOU SHOULD BE ABLE TO:

1. Explain what programming languages and computer programs are.
2. Identify the main steps in the software development cycle and briefly explain what each step involves.
3. Identify the main programming tools available.
4. Identify five generations of programming languages.
5. Distinguish between general-purpose and special-purpose programming languages.
6. Compare and contrast machine language and assembly language.
7. Identify several third-generation languages and explain "procedural" languages.
8. Explain what fourth-generation languages are.
9. Discuss natural languages and object-oriented programming.
10. Know which questions should be asked when selecting a particular programming language.

CHAPTER OUTLINE

APPLICATION SOFTWARE
    Commercial Software
    User-Written Software

COMPUTER PROGRAMMING
    Programming
    Programming Languages

THE SOFTWARE DEVELOPMENT CYCLE
    Defining the Problem
    Planning the Solution
    Coding the Program
    Testing the Program
    Documenting the Program
    Maintaining the Program

THE DEVELOPER'S TOOLKIT
    Structured Programming
    HIPO Charts
    Flowcharts
    Pseudocode
    Decision Tables

FIFTH-GENERATION LANGUAGES
    Language Classifications
    Machine Language (First Generation)
    Assembly Language (Second Generation)
    High-Level Programming Languages (Third Generation)
    4GLs (Fourth Generation)
    Natural Languages (Fifth Generation)
    Object-Oriented Programming

SELECTING A LANGUAGE
    Considerations

"I am sorry," sighs a distraught software user on the phone with a customer service representative at the maker's hotline. "I just can't seem to get my new SuperWonderWorks to run."

Each year, millions of Americans make similar calls to software makers across the country. Why should the users be apologizing? If people can't use a system, shouldn't it be the maker who apologizes?

For decades, computer software was designed "by computer geeks for computer geeks." As computers move out of research laboratories and into homes and offices, users increasingly call for "friendly" software. Yet whether it's the software that enables users to "program" their VCRs or top-selling spreadsheet, database, and word processing packages, incomprehensibility remains a problem. Indeed, an entire "how-to-use-your-software" publishing subindustry has arisen, thanks to some "user-friendly" systems that aren't and their accompanying reference manuals that may as well be printed in hieroglyphics.

Faced with the need to make products stand out in a crowded market, the nation's software makers are realizing the importance of user-friendly software in accessing a new generation of customers with limited computer literacy. Consider the following situation. Until 1990, WordPerfect, maker of the world's best-selling word processing software, did no special usability testing of its product. After attending the Conference on Human Factors in Computing Systems, WordPerfect's director of testing confronted the developers of the company's low-end word processor, LetterPerfect, about the difficulty of installing the program. Initially, the developers of the system insisted that the installation instructions were fine. But after witnessing the installation problems encountered by six inexperienced PC users *and* by WordPerfect's lead developer, LetterPerfect's developers rewrote their installation program. Today, WordPerfect is building its third usability testing lab.

Nor is WordPerfect alone in jumping on the usability bandwagon. While some companies, such as IBM, have conducted usability studies as a matter of routine for years, nearly every major software company has recently set up at least a small usability lab. It seems that, at long last, computer companies have figured out what other industries have long known: in the words of Black and Decker's CEO, "Customers don't want quarter-inch drills; they want quarter-inch holes."

APPLICATION SOFTWARE

A common saying among programmers and other computer professionals is that "software drives hardware." In Part Two, we discussed various hardware components of a computer system. All of these components, no matter how sophisticated or expensive, are useless without software. To be effective tools, computers need software that can produce the kind of information and output users desire.

As you learned in Chapter 8, system software handles the very basic details of managing a computer's hardware and software resources, making it possible for users to accomplish their tasks. The user is often not aware of the work of the systems software. Users are more aware of **application software** because this software determines the kinds of tasks the computer can accomplish, such as word processing, spreadsheets, databases, and graphics.

In this chapter we examine the process of developing application software, the methods involved in designing problem solutions, and the programming languages used to solve those problems. Programming tools for writing efficient and effective application programs are discussed, as are considerations for choosing programming languages for particular types of applications.

Application software is generally divided into two categories: *commercial software* and *user-written software*. Many commercial software application packages are available and more are being introduced daily. The number and variety of available application packages make it possible for a user to purchase a program for solving almost any kind of problem. Still, many users, including some large businesses, prefer to produce their own application programs. Some cannot afford to purchase commercial programs for all their needs. There are also situations in which commercial application programs are unavailable or are not exactly what is needed. Moreover, for some applications, writing one's own application program is more practical.

Courtesy of Lotus Development Corporation.

Courtesy of Microsoft Corporation.

The number and variety of software packages available make it possible for users to fill most of their application needs.

COMMERCIAL SOFTWARE

Every experienced computer user has used commercial software. **Commercial software** is a package that can be purchased from a software vendor. Sources include computer stores, mail-order companies, industry associations, and software development companies. They are typically referred to as *packages* because they include more than simply a computer program. Also included in most microcomputer packages are a user's manual, a registration card, and other documentation. A user's manual contains instructions for using the program. A registration card is used to record information about you and the product with the manufacturer so that the manufacturer can warranty the product. When you register software by sending in the registration card, the manufacturer will notify you of software upgrades or of releases of important new products.

before	AFTER

Courtesy of IBM Archives.

Courtesy of ADP, Inc. ADP is a registered trademark of Automatic Data Processing, Inc.

Before computers were introduced, performing complex mathematical operations or a lengthy series of mathematical operations was extremely difficult. For example, a payroll clerk might find it necessary to spend many hours using an adding machine to calculate the net pay for hundreds of employees. Errors were frequent. Try to imagine how frustrating it would be to calculate the gross pay, deductions, and net pay for every employee in a large organization. Accounting departments often employed several full-time payroll clerks.

Computer hardware and software have made the payroll process much more accurate and efficient. Today almost all organizations use computers to process their payrolls. An organization can have its programmers prepare a personalized payroll program, or it can purchase a commercial payroll program and modify that commercial program to fit the organization's needs. Once the program is stored in the computer, payroll clerks need only input specific data for each employee. The computer system can then process the payroll by performing the necessary calculations, printing the checks and stubs, and producing payroll reports.

The number of commercial software manufacturers, as well as the number of different software packages, has increased rapidly over the past two decades. In fact, growth in the software industry has been phenomenal, largely due to the dramatic increase in the availability and use of personal computers. Today, there are more than 3,000 commercial software producers making over 20,000 products.

A more recent trend, however, is toward acquisitions and consolidations in the software industry. Several large software companies acquired smaller companies. Some companies acquired products originally produced by other companies. While some companies downsized by selling popular products to other companies, other companies expanded their product lines by purchasing product rights from other companies. These transactions resulted in some software companies disappearing completely from the software industry.

USER-WRITTEN SOFTWARE

Problems vary among individuals and among organizations. In some situations, software programs for doing certain tasks are unavailable, and, therefore need to be created. Such programs are called **user-written software**. They are typically written using a high-level programming language (such as BASIC, C++, COBOL, or another currently popular language) by individuals who have the appropriate programming knowledge and skills. These languages will be described in more detail later in the chapter.

Although individuals can be proficient computer users without knowing how to write programs, the ability to write application programs enables users to take greater advantage of a computer's capabilities. People who know how to program are not restricted to using application software prepared by someone else.

COMPUTER PROGRAMMING

Programs instruct the computer about what to do. The process of writing those instructions is called programming. Programs are written in one of a number of specific programming languages, and the person who creates the program must be able to think and write instructions in the terms and rules (syntax) of that language.

PROGRAMMING

The process of expressing a problem's solution in a set of instructions that a computer can understand is **programming**. The computer language instructions are expressed in combinations of letters, numbers, and symbols according to a well-defined set of rules. The "character set" (letters, numbers, and symbols) together with the "grammatical rules" of the language, form the **syntax** or structure of the language. Every programming language has a unique syntax which must be learned before that language can be used.

Application programs are written by applications programmers. A **programmer** is someone who designs, writes, enters, and tests the computer programs that instruct a computer to perform particular tasks. Figuring out an organization's payroll is an example of a task a program might perform. Figure 11.1 shows a simple program.

In the program in Figure 11.1, lines 10 and 20 document what the program does. The program computes the average score for one student's tests. Line 30 instructs the computer to find the sum of the seven test scores contained in the instruction. In line 40 the computer finds the student's AVERAGE by dividing the TOTAL by 7. Line 50 tells the computer to display the message "THE STUDENT'S AVERAGE IS" on the screen, followed by the value of the student's AVERAGE. Line 60 ENDs the program. The RUN command starts the execution of the program. The processing results are shown on the printout next to the program.

Figure 11.1

A simple program for computing a student's total points in a course reveals some of the basic concepts necessary to understand programming.

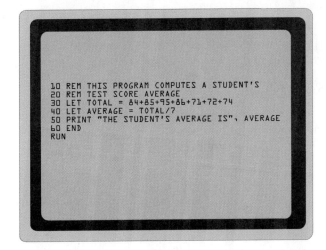

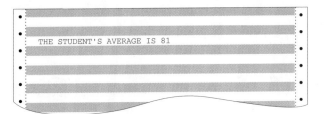

The computer does exactly what the programmer tells it to do, which, unfortunately, is not always what the programmer wants it to do. It is the programmer's responsibility to carefully prepare instructions. If a programmer tells a computer to add 10 and 4, the computer will always output 14 as the result. If the programmer actually intended for the computer to add 10 and 40, but keyed in 4 instead of 40, the program will still get 14. Faulty instructions or data will consistently produce a wrong answer. Programmers routinely refer to this as *GIGO* (garbage in, garbage out).

PROGRAMMING LANGUAGES

Programmers use **programming languages** to prepare step-by-step sets of instructions that are input into computers in order to solve problems of varying complexity. Each programming language has specific capabilities and limitations. If you choose a career as a professional programmer, remember that the company you work for will often choose the programming language to be used. It pays to know a number of programming languages.

Courtesy of Microsoft Corporation.

Courtesy of NeXt Software, Inc.

Each programming language has a specific set of characteristics.

Before writing a program, the programmer considers which language to use. To make this selection, the programmer considers some key factors. First, the programmer must use a language he or she knows. Second, *language translation software* (a type of system software) must be available for the language selected. Third, the programmer must choose a language that can be used with the computer system on which he or she is working. Finally, the programmer should select a language, such as a business or a scientific language, that was designed for the application.

Before describing how to choose the right programming language, we'll look at the general software development cycle and at the specialized tools programmers use in developing software.

THE SOFTWARE DEVELOPMENT CYCLE

Programming is a problem-solving process involving a set of sequential steps known as the **software development cycle**. The steps in the process are as follows:

1. Define the problem.
2. Plan the solution.
3. Code the program.
4. Test the program.
5. Document the program.
6. Maintain the program.

With the exception of documentation, the steps progress logically and should be followed in sequence. Documentation should begin at the start of the development cycle and continue throughout.

DEFINING THE PROBLEM

As you go through life, you undoubtedly encounter many problems that need to be solved. However, you may find that there are times when you cannot solve a problem because you cannot define it. Suppose your automobile will not start. After raising the hood and looking at the parts, you still cannot locate the problem because you do not know enough about cars. Therefore, you bring your car to an automobile mechanic. The mechanic performs a series of tests to determine the problem, perhaps with the aid of a computerized engine analyzer. After the problem has been identified (defined), the mechanic makes the necessary repairs to your car.

Programmers follow a similar process. The programmer first analyzes the problem in order to define it or works together with a systems analyst (discussed in Chapter 10) who has already determined the need for new software. The problem needs to be defined before proceeding further in order to determine whether the problem should be solved using a computer. Would you go to the trouble of writing a program that would add five three-digit numbers? Probably not. Instead, you might use a small calculator or perform the calculations with a pencil and paper. The benefits of using the computer must exceed the "costs" (time and effort) of applying it.

Defining the problem is simply determining what needs to be done. How a problem is defined is often dictated by the training and experience of the person solving the problem. For example, suppose the problem is to calculate the average price of ten grocery items. If you are a mathematician, your problem definition might be:

Average = Sum of the prices of ten grocery items/10

If you are not a mathematician, the above definition might not be useful to you. Instead, you might define the problem using the following steps:

1. Add the ten grocery item prices.
2. Divide the sum by 10.

The result, in either case, will be an arithmetic average (or *mean*). In both cases, you defined an algorithm. An **algorithm** is a set of rules that, when followed precisely and in sequence, will lead to a solution or indicate when the problem can't be solved.

PLANNING THE SOLUTION

After the problem has been clearly defined, start planning the solution. Complex problems demand complex solutions.

You've learned that a problem can be defined in terms of an algorithm. Now re-examine the grocery list problem. Suppose you want to solve this problem using a pocket calculator. Your algorithm would require the following steps:

1. Clear the calculator display.
2. Enter the price of one grocery item.
3. Press the add (+) button.
4. Repeat Steps 2 and 3 until the prices for all items are entered.
5. Press the divide (÷) button followed by the number 10.
6. Press the equal (=) button to obtain the average price of all items.

Program this process into a computer and you can use it any time you wish to compute an average.

Consider another problem. Suppose your family decides to build a larger house. First, have an architect draw up a set of blueprints that includes the features you want in your new house. Revise the blueprints until you and your family are satisfied. Build the house according to the blueprint specifications. Building a house without blueprints could be disastrous.

A clearly written solution prevents potentially serious mistakes. In this sense, programmers are like building contractors. Both need logically expressed plans to do their jobs and avoid mistakes.

During the planning stage, programmers use many of the tools discussed in later sections, such as flowcharts, pseudocode, and decision tables. A word of caution: as you begin to learn more about programming, you may be tempted to skip planning and preparation and begin immediately to write program instructions. Do not make this mistake! As your programming skills improve, you may find yourself attempting increasingly difficult problems, but the need for careful planning never diminishes.

CODING THE PROGRAM

The third step in the software development cycle is coding of the program. **Coding** expresses the solution in a programming language. During coding, the plan for the program is translated from written step-by-step instructions, flowcharts, or pseudocode into a programming language.

TESTING THE PROGRAM

Before a program processes data, it should be thoroughly tested to determine whether it is accurate. Program results are accurate only if the program is correctly written.

Syntax Errors A program must be free of syntax errors in order to run on a computer. A **syntax error** is a program instruction written in an invalid format. Your English teacher may not fail you for incorrect punctuation in a term paper, but a computer is unforgiving. When a computer runs a program containing syntax errors, you will get an error message like the following:

ERROR IN 30

Run-Time Errors A **run-time error** occurs when the programmer tells the computer to do something it cannot do. If the programmer tells the computer to add the six student test grades contained in line 90 of the program but inputs only five grades, a run-time error will occur when the computer can't find the sixth test grade. The following is a run-time error message:

OUT OF DATA IN 90

Logic Errors A programming mistake that causes the wrong processing to take place even though the syntax is correct is a **logic error**. Logic errors do not produce error messages, but their output is incorrect. For this reason, logic errors are serious and often difficult to find. Suppose you write a payroll application program using the BASIC language and enter an instruction telling the computer to calculate NET_PAY. Yet, in computing deductions, you failed to subtract the employee's monthly contribution to his or her credit union's saving plan. Since NET_PAY must reflect this deduction, you have incorrectly instructed the computer. The program will compute NET_PAY, but the amount will be wrong. Therefore, you have committed a logic error.

One method of reducing errors in program development is by **desk checking** the program. When desk checking, also called *desk debugging*, the programmer pretends to be the computer by reading each instruction and mentally "picturing" how the computer will process the data and the instruction. Most programmers will also check the output of each calculation. The few minutes spent desk checking can save a programmer hours of searching for and correcting logic errors.

Another way to test for logic errors is to run the program several times using data designed to test all possible input, branch, and output options. These data should be similar to the real data that are to be used later. The reason for doing this is to determine whether there is any way to run the program and not get the correct results; that is, the purpose is to test the validity and reliability of the program. A *valid* program does exactly what it is supposed to do. A *reliable* program is consistent.

DOCUMENTING THE PROGRAM

Documentation is the manuals and tutorials that accompany a commercial applications software package. The user's manual (see Figure 11.2) explains how to use the software. Today programmers often build help text into the program itself. *Help text* is on-line, on-screen documentation called up by the user.

Figure 11.2

Commercial software comes with both a user's manual and on-line tutorials outlining instructions on how to use the program. Programmers provide detailed instructions for user-written software as well.

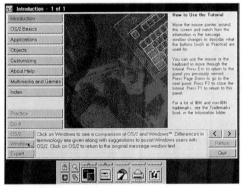

Courtesy of IBM Corporation.

Documenting a user-written program requires keeping records throughout the program's development. Included in the documentation are the program's author and purpose; the amount, kinds, and sources of input data needed to run the program; program flowcharts and pseudocode; an accurate instruction-by-instruction listing of the program; and sample inputs and their corresponding outputs. Changes in the software are much easier to make when well-prepared documentation is available. As changes are made to the software, these changes should also be reflected in the documentation.

Creating a well-written program is time-consuming. Some programs are intended for daily use. Operation of these programs becomes routine for users. Other programs are used only occasionally. Users may forget how to run them. Therefore, programs should be well-documented. Some computer professionals believe that documenting the program is the most important phase in software development.

MAINTAINING THE PROGRAM

The final phase in the software development cycle is program maintenance. After a program has been used for some time, it often is necessary for a programmer to modify the program to reflect a process change or to incorporate the solution to a new problem. Modifying a program is much easier when the documentation is accurate, complete, and up-to-date.

THE DEVELOPER'S TOOLKIT

All builders or developers need specialized tools in their work. Carpenters use tools such as hammers, levels, and tape measures. Automobile mechanics use wrenches, pliers, and screwdrivers. The software developer's toolkit includes structured programming, HIPO charts, flowcharts, pseudocode, and decision tables.

STRUCTURED PROGRAMMING

Before a program can be written to solve a problem, there must be a plan explaining how the program will work—there must be a problem solution. In order to develop these solutions, programmers use the structured approach, or top-down approach, to design program solutions.

Structured programming is an approach that emphasizes the disciplined use of professionally accepted programming standards and logic. Structured programming is promoted by the computer industry as the most productive way to prepare computer programs. Many companies require their programmers to follow structured programming standards because it makes their programs cost-effective. Cost-effective programs are:

1. Easy to write
2. Easy to understand
3. Easy to check and debug
4. Easy to maintain

Structured programming divides a problem into identifiable tasks. Then a program module is written for each task. The computer begins by executing the first instruction in the first module and then each of the following instructions sequentially. Structured programs use a common standard for instruction processing: sequence, iteration, and branching. Unless instructed otherwise, the default order of instruction execution is **sequential**, or "one after another." **Iteration**, or *looping*, means the program is instructed to repeat a sequence of instructions, usually using new data. For example, a payroll program iterates its payroll computations module for each employee. **Branching** allows the program to test for certain conditions ("Is this the last employee?") and then transfer to different locations in the program, depending on the results of that test. Branching statements can temporarily override the normal, sequential statement execution order.

Figure 11.3 on page 398 shows a simple example of a structured program. Line 10 (REM statement) identifies or states what the program does. REM statements are reminders or comments that help document or explain the program's operations. Lines 20, 30, and 40 display column headings when the program is run. Line 50 tells the computer that five sets of data (for five employees) will be entered (READ) and processed. Line 60 reads into COUNT the first DATA item (Line 110), indicating that the gross pay for five employees will be computed. Line 70 instructs the computer to READ the Name, Hours, and Rate for the first employee (Jim). In line 80 the computer calculates Jim's gross pay by multiplying his hours worked by his pay rate. Line 90 tells the computer to PRINT (display) Jim's name, hours worked, rate of pay, and gross pay. Then line 100 instructs the computer to branch back to the beginning and reiterate the procedure for the next employee (David). Notice the program is executed from the first instruction to the last, or from top to bottom.

Figure 11.3

This payroll program is written in an interpretive programming language called BASIC. When the user executes the program by typing RUN, the computer produces the output shown on the printout.

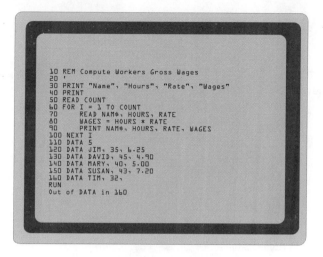

```
10 REM Compute Workers Gross Wages
20 '
30 PRINT "Name", "Hours", "Rate", "Wages"
40 PRINT
50 READ COUNT
60 FOR I = 1 TO COUNT
70     READ NAM$, HOURS, RATE
80     WAGES = HOURS * RATE
90     PRINT NAM$, HOURS, RATE, WAGES
100 NEXT I
110 DATA 5
120 DATA JIM, 35, 6.25
130 DATA DAVID, 45, 4.90
140 DATA MARY, 40, 5.00
150 DATA SUSAN, 43, 7.20
160 DATA TIM, 32, 5.50
RUN
Out of DATA in 160
```

Name	Hours	Rate	Wages
JIM	35	6.25	218.75
DAVID	45	4.90	220.50
MARY	40	5.00	200.00
SUSAN	43	7.20	309.60
TIM	32	5.50	176.00

HIPO CHARTS

A **hierarchy plus input-processing-output (HIPO) chart** is a tool that identifies which program segments are to be included in the program, thereby providing programmers with an overview of the entire program. The advantage of HIPO charts is that they encourage programmers to systematically arrange program segments into logical modules; that is, from the general to the specific, as illustrated in in Figure 11.4. This process results in a computer program that should be easier to maintain.

Figure 11.4

HIPO charts allow programmers to move from the general to the specific, breaking problems down to their logical units.

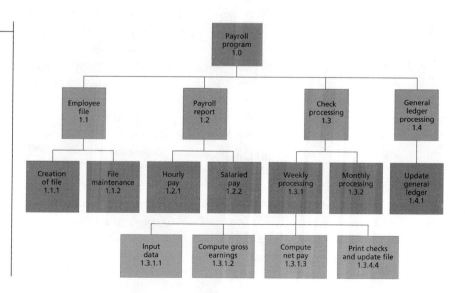

FLOWCHARTS

A **flowchart** is a symbolic diagram that represents the activities and flow of logic in a program. Arrows show the directional "flow" of control within the program. Arrows connect boxes and other symbols to represent the sequence of specific actions.

As discussed in Chapter 8, the American National Standards Institute (ANSI) developed special symbols to represent tasks performed by programs. Each symbol has a special meaning. Programmers often use a *flowcharting template* to draw their flowcharts. The plastic or metal template contains cut-out figures of the most commonly used flowchart symbols. The template's purpose is to allow programmers to trace the shapes of symbols onto paper. Flowcharting software, such as ObjectVision, is also available to make the programmer's job easier.

The flowchart in Figure 11.5 shows a logical solution for calculating a total grocery bill. Notice that the solution flows from the start, or from the top of the flowchart, to the end. The top symbol on a flowchart indicates the first step in the process, the next symbol indicates the second step, and so on. The programmer uses the sequence of steps in a flowchart as a model for writing a program with the same step-sequence. Flowcharting is a major part of the documentation process.

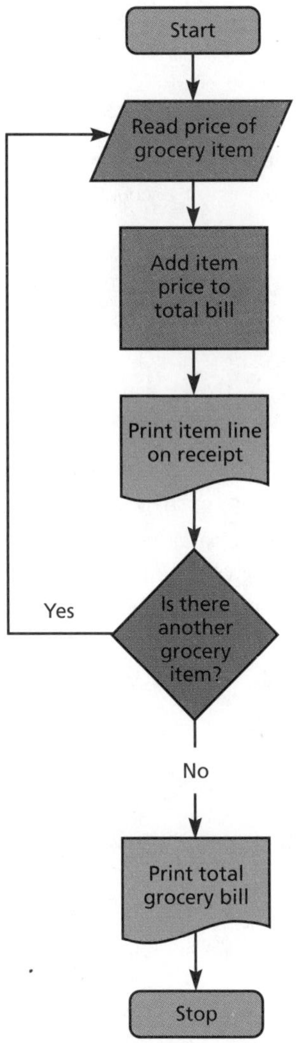

Figure 11.5

Flowcharts present logical solutions to programming tasks. Using standardized symbols, they visually present the flow of a program from beginning to end.

Notice that after reading the price of an item and adding it to the total bill, the cashier must determine whether the price of another item needs to be read and added. If so, control is passed back to that part of the process. This procedure is an example of looping or iteration, and it is often performed in both manual and computer tasks.

PSEUDOCODE

Pseudocode is a set of sentences or phrases listed in the same order as the actual program instructions, and describing in ordinary language what the program will do. The prefix *pseudo* means "false." Pseudocode is false program code because pseudocode statements cannot be executed by the computer. Legitimate program instructions must be written in a programming language. Preparing pseudocode before writing a program is analogous to preparing an outline before writing an essay. Both help the writers organize their thoughts.

Pseudocode's real value is as a programming aid. Think of it as a list of logically ordered actions you want the computer to perform. Sometimes flowcharts and pseudocode are used together. However, the two are independent and one may be used without the other.

DECISION TABLES

A programming tool called a **decision table** outlines the set of conditions that a computer program might encounter and indicates what processing action should be performed for each condition. A decision table depicts what happens in a system or program if and when specific combinations of conditions occur. The table is divided into four quadrants or sections: (1) condition stub, (2) condition entries, (3) action stub, and (4) action entries. Figure 11.6 depicts a decision table.

Figure 11.6

A decision table follows a four-quadrant format.

Condition stub	Condition entries
Action stub	Action entries

A decision table is based on a programming concept called **conditional logic**, which makes use of "IF . . . THEN" scenarios. Meaning that IF this set of conditions is met, THEN this specified action will be taken. Suppose you are the purchasing agent for a supermarket. In deciding which suppliers to buy from, you use three main criteria: price, delivery time, and quality. You then develop a decision table to use as a convenient reference in selecting suppliers. The decision table might resemble the one shown in Figure 11.7.

Figure 11.7

This decision table shows the decision rules followed in selecting suppliers. Three conditions are the basis for accepting or rejecting a supplier. Decision rule 6 indicates that a supplier who does not offer a low price or high quality will be rejected.

	Decision Rules							
	1	2	3	4	5	6	7	8
Conditions								
Low price	Y	Y	Y	Y	N	N	N	N
Fast delivery time	Y	N	Y	N	Y	Y	N	N
High quality	Y	Y	N	N	Y	N	Y	N
Actions								
Buy	X							
Consider buying		X	X		X		X	
Do not buy				X		X		X

Condition stubs — Condition entries
Action stubs — Action entries

In the table, a "Y" indicates a condition that is satisfied, and an "N" indicates a condition that is not satisfied. An "X" indicates the action to be taken. After examining the table, you should be able to determine the logic. For example, the table reveals the conditions you will consider and the actions to be taken based on the conditions. In the table, if a supplier offers the lowest price, fastest delivery time, and high quality products, an "X" indicates you will buy from the supplier. If some of these conditions are met, you will consider buying. If required conditions are not met, you will not buy from the supplier. Information contained in a decision table can also be incorporated in a flowchart or in pseudocode.

FIFTH-GENERATION LANGUAGES

Because programming languages have developed over a period of time, their evolution is often described in generations. To date, there are five generations of programming languages. These are shown on the continuum in Figure 11.8.

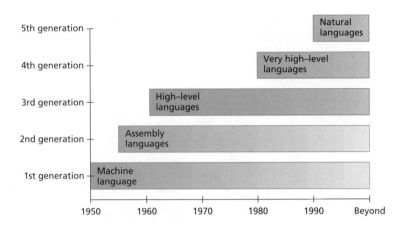

Figure 11.8

Five generations of programming languages have been developed over the past several decades. All five generations are still in use today.

Each new generation of programming languages has made developing applications a little easier. However, this does not mean that the fifth generation is the most commonly used. In fact, if a programming survey were to be taken today, you would likely find that third-generation languages remain the most popular languages for most applications.

LANGUAGE CLASSIFICATIONS

Rather than grouping languages in terms of their generations, you can classify them on the basis of their primary use or originally intended purpose (see Figure 11.9). A **general-purpose language** is used to write programs for a variety of applications, such as those found in business, science, and education, whereas a **special- purpose language** is used for specific applications. Some languages can be used for several programming applications. Most, however, were originally developed to satisfy the needs of aparticular application. In the following sections, some of the more important programming languages are classified in terms of their generation and their purpose.

Another way that languages are described in the following sections is by considering whether the language is pro-cedural or nonprocedural. A **procedural language**, such as COBOL, requires a programmer to write a series of step-by-step instructions for solving a problem. The program must include a detailed list of logical instructions for the computer to follow. For all procedural languages, structured programming is recommended.

Business languages

COBOL

C

RPG

Ada

Mathematical and scientific languages

FORTRAN

APL

Educational languages

BASIC

Logo

Flexible, multipurpose languages

Pascal

PL/1

Figure 11.9

It is sometimes helpful to classify languages in terms of their primary use.

More recently, new nonprocedural languages have emerged. **Nonprocedural languages**, such as RPG II, allow users to specify what they want to know or accomplish and query the system for this information, rather than actually writing a program to produce the needed information.

MACHINE LANGUAGE (FIRST GENERATION)

Early computers were programmed in **machine language**. Machine language programs are considered low-level because they can be executed without any translation. A machine language instruction is written as a string of binary numbers that can be processed directly by the computer. For this reason, writing a computer program in machine language is difficult and time-consuming. For example, the word "hello," which might be used as an introductory message in a program, is shown in its extended binary code or machine language equivalent:

1100100011000101110100111101001111010110

Imagine programming hundreds of words in machine language!

Machine language is *machine-dependent*, meaning it varies according to the specific hardware used. Although coding is difficult and time-consuming, machine language programs execute quickly. Some U.S. Defense Department programming is done in machine language to save critical seconds and to gain a competitive advantage in computerized national defense applications.

ASSEMBLY LANGUAGE (SECOND GENERATION)

Also considered low-level, **assembly languages** require little translation. These languages were developed in the late 1950s as an alternative to machine language. Assembly language uses convenient abbreviations, called *mnemonics*, to communicate with the computer. Mnemonics are key, abbreviated words (which are often abbreviations for complete English words) and character patterns used to denote the computer action requested. A programmer can write instructions using these abbreviated forms. For example, assembly languages use mnemonic codes like MUL for multiply, COM for compare, and DIV for divide. For most programmers, using these mnemonic codes is more convenient than machine language 0s and 1s, but it is less convenient than other, higher level languages.

HIGH-LEVEL PROGRAMMING LANGUAGES (THIRD GENERATION)

Each statement in a **high-level language** corresponds to several machine language or assembly language statements, making them easier to use. High-level languages resemble written speech more than their predecessors, as illutrated in the brief BASIC program shown in Figure 11.10. High-level languages are preferred for most programming applications.

BASIC One language that allows computer users to write programs in almost any discipline is called **Beginners All-purpose Symbolic Instruction Code (BASIC)**. It was introduced in 1965 to make it easier for students to write complex mathematical programs with little instruction. There are several versions of the BASIC programming language, including DOS BASIC, Visual BASIC, Microsoft's QuickBASIC, and True BASIC.

```
10 REM *** SIMPLIFIED PAYROLL PROGRAM ***
20 PRINT "ENTER HOURS WORKED";
30 INPUT H
40 PRINT "ENTER HOURLY PAY RATE";
50 INPUT R
60 REM *** COMPUTE WAGE ***
70 LET W = H * R
80 PRINT "WEEKLY WAGE IS $"=; W
90 END
```

Figure 11.10

High-level language programs, like this one written in BASIC, are closer to written language than their low-level counterparts. This makes programming errors easier to locate and correct.

Some versions of BASIC are *interpreted*, which means programmers are immediately aware of errors, while others like True BASIC are *compiled*, which means a listing of errors is generated when the program is executed. Some newer versions, such as Visual BASIC for Windows, are object-oriented versions. Object-oriented programming is explained later in the chapter.

Visual BASIC, like some other object-oriented languages, allows a user to build programs by pointing and clicking on icons and diagrams (called objects) displayed on the screen. Visual BASIC has become the computer industry's standard version for many programming applications. Some versions of BASIC even instruct the programmer what to do next. Figure 11.11 is a sample program written in BASIC that finds the square roots of the integer numbers (whole numbers) from 1 to 10.

```
10 CLS
20 FOR X = 1 TO 10
30 PRINT "THE SQUARE ROOT OF";X;"IS =";SQR(X)
40 NEXT X
RUN
```

```
THE SQUARE ROOT OF 1 IS = 1
THE SQUARE ROOT OF 2 IS = 1.414214
THE SQUARE ROOT OF 3 IS = 1.732051
THE SQUARE ROOT OF 4 IS = 2
THE SQUARE ROOT OF 5 IS = 2.236068
THE SQUARE ROOT OF 6 IS = 2.44949
THE SQUARE ROOT OF 7 IS = 2.645751
THE SQUARE ROOT OF 8 IS = 2.828427
THE SQUARE ROOT OF 9 IS = 3
THE SQUARE ROOT OF 10 IS = 3.162278
```

Figure 11.11

In BASIC, program instructions are executed in numerical order, from lowest to highest, unless a looping or branching statement instructs the program to act otherwise.

In BASIC, all instructions are numbered in the order in which they are to be executed. The computer executes the instructions from lowest to highest, unless a looping or branching statement is encountered. Statement 10 instructs the computer to erase everything presently showing on the screen. In Figure 11.11, statement 20 sets the parameters for the loop; that is, it tells the computer to perform some action or collection of statements a total of ten times. Statement 30 instructs the computer to display the message "THE SQUARE ROOT OF" on the screen, followed by the value of X (the numbers 1 through 10) and then the square root of the number represented by X. Statement 40 causes the cycle to be repeated. When the user types RUN, the program executes the command and the loop repeats a total of ten times, as you can see in the output.

Pascal A Swiss computer scientist named Nicklaus Wirth developed and introduced **Pascal** in 1971. The language was named after Blaise Pascal, the inventor of the first mechanical calculator. For several years after its introduction, Pascal was a popular programming language. However, in recent years, its popularity has decreased somewhat among personal computer programmers due to an increased interest in newer languages. Like BASIC, Pascal was developed as a vehicle for teaching programming concepts to students. Although its programming rules make Pascal more difficult to learn than BASIC, many programmers agree that Pascal is easier to learn than many other languages.

Figure 11.12 contains a sample Pascal program that calculates net pay. Note the similarities and differences between the Pascal program and the BASIC program shown in Figure 11.10. Unlike BASIC, Pascal statements are not numbered. Statements are executed in the order they are entered into the computer unless looping or branching is required. Instructions are included for calculating an employee's gross pay, deductions, and net pay. WRITELN, an abbreviation for WRITE LiNe, tells the computer what information to produce.

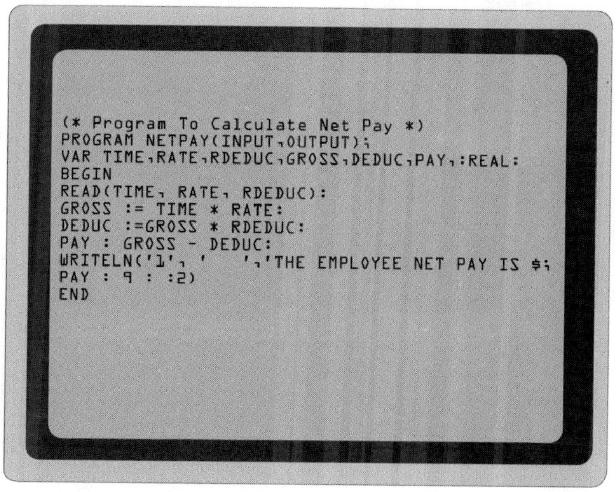

Figure 11.12

Pascal is similar to BASIC, yet it does not include program line numbers, which some believe make it more difficult to learn.

```
(* Program To Calculate Net Pay *)
PROGRAM NETPAY(INPUT,OUTPUT);
VAR TIME,RATE,RDEDUC,GROSS,DEDUC,PAY,:REAL:
BEGIN
READ(TIME, RATE, RDEDUC):
GROSS := TIME * RATE:
DEDUC :=GROSS * RDEDUC:
PAY : GROSS - DEDUC:
WRITELN('1', '    ','THE EMPLOYEE NET PAY IS $:
PAY : 9 : :2)
END
```

COBOL The first language developed especially for business applications is **COBOL** (an acronym for COmmon Business-Oriented Language). Currently, COBOL is one of the most widely used programming languages, especially with large computers. Its development resulted from a need for a machine-independent, business applications language.

Though COBOL has its disadvantages, for business applications COBOL's large file-processing capabilities are a definite plus. Compare the sample COBOL payroll program in Figure 11.13 with the previous payroll programs in BASIC and Pascal. Although all programs calculate employees' net pay, the COBOL program requires many more instructions. COBOL programs typically require up to seven times more instructions than similar programs written in other languages.

```
        IDENTIFICATION DIVISION.
        PROGRAM-ID. SAMPLE.
        *
        ENVIRONMENT DIVISION.
        INPUT-OUTPUT SECTION.
        FILE-CONTROL. SELECT EMPLOYEE-FILE ASSIGN TO TAPE-1.
                      SELECT PAYROLL-REPORT ASSIGN TO PRINTER.

        DATA DIVISION
        FILE SECTION.    FD  EMPLOYEE-FILE LABEL RECORDS ARE STANDARD.
        01  EMPLOYEE-RECORD.
            05  EMPLOYEE-NAME                PICTURE A(20).
            05  HOURS-WORKED                 PICTURE 9(2).
            05  HOURLY-RATE                  PICTURE 9V99.
        FD  PAYROLL-REPORT LABEL RECORDS ARE OMITTED.
        01  PAYROLL-RECORD.
            05  FILLER                               PICTURE X(5).
            05  NAME-OUT                       PICTURE A(20).
            05  FILLER                             PICTURE A(5).
            05  HOURS-OUT                      PICTURE 9(2).
            05  FILLER                               PICTURE (5).
            05  RATE-OUT                        PICTURE 9.99.
            05  FILLER                               PICTURE (5).
            05  NET-PAY                         PICTURE 999.99.
            05  FILLER                              PICTURE (81).
        WORKING-STORAGE SECTION.
        01  EOF                                      PICTURE 9
        VALUE 0
        *
        PROCEDURE DIVISION.
            OPEN INPUT EMPLOYEE-FILE
                 OUTPUT PAYROLL-REPORT.
            MOVE SPACES TO PAYROLL-RECORD.
            READ EMPLOYEE-FILE AT END MOVE 1 TO EOF.
            PERFORM WAGE-ROUTINE UNTIL EOF = 1.
            CLOSE EMPLOYEE-FILE
                  PAYROLL-REPORT.
            STOP RUN.
        WAGE-ROUTINE.
            MOVE EMPLOYEE-NAME TO NAME-OUT.
            MOVE HOURS-WORKED TO HOURS-OUT.
        MOVE HOURLY-RATE TO RATE-OUT. MULTIPLY HOURS-
                 WORKED BY HOURLY-RATE GIVING NET-PAY.
        WRITE PAYROLL-RECORD AFTER ADVANCING 2 LINES.
            READ EMPLOYEE-FILE AT END MOVE 1 TO EOF.
```

Figure 11.13

COBOL requires many more lines of instructions for an application than other similar programming languages. However, it is capable of processing a great quantity of files, making it useful for large business applications.

As MIS organizations expand their efforts to downsize and off-load applications from mainframe computers, personal computers are taking up the slack. Many software companies are now selling PC-versions of COBOL to run these new applications. COBOL appears to be regaining momentum as a viable programming language in the micro-computer systems development environment.

FORTRAN Developed and introduced by IBM in 1954, **FORTRAN** (an abbreviation for FORmula TRANslator) was one of the first high-level languages. The development of FORTRAN was an effort by IBM to meet programmers' scientific, engineering, and mathematical applications needs. FORTRAN is still widely used in the scientific community. FORTRAN's main value lies in its ability to execute the complex formulas typically used in engineering and mathematical analysis. It is known and appreciated for its brevity, a factor partly responsible for its popularity. However, because it lacks the large file-processing capabilities of COBOL, it is considerably less appealing for business programming.

Almost all computers, including mainframes and personal computers, can use FORTRAN. A sample FORTRAN program is shown in Figure 11.14.

Figure 11.14

FORTRAN programs are much shorter than others, but they lack large file-processing capabilities. FORTRAN's ability to execute complex formulas makes it popular with scientists and engineers.

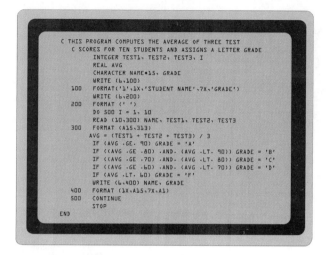

```
C THIS PROGRAM COMPUTES THE AVERAGE OF THREE TEST
C SCORES FOR TEN STUDENTS AND ASSIGNS A LETTER GRADE
        INTEGER TEST1, TEST2, TEST3, I
        REAL AVG
        CHARACTER NAME*15, GRADE
        WRITE (6,100)
100     FORMAT('1',1X,'STUDENT NAME',7X,'GRADE')
        WRITE (6,200)
200     FORMAT (' ')
        DO 500 I = 1, 10
        READ (10,300) NAME, TEST1, TEST2, TEST3
300     FORMAT (A15,3I3)
        AVG = (TEST1 + TEST2 + TEST3) / 3
        IF (AVG .GE. 90) GRADE = 'A'
        IF ((AVG .GE .80) .AND. (AVG .LT. 90)) GRADE = 'B'
        IF ((AVG .GE .70) .AND. (AVG .LT. 80)) GRADE = 'C'
        IF ((AVG .GE .60) .AND. (AVG .LT. 70)) GRADE = 'D'
        IF (AVG .LT. 60) GRADE = 'F'
        WRITE (6,400) NAME, GRADE
400     FORMAT (1X,A15,7X,A1)
500     CONTINUE
        STOP
END
```

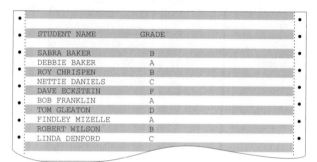

STUDENT NAME	GRADE
SABRA BAKER	B
DEBBIE BAKER	A
ROY CHRISPEN	B
NETTIE DANIELS	C
DAVE ECKSTEIN	F
BOB FRANKLIN	A
TOM GLEATON	D
FINDLEY MIZELLE	A
ROBERT WILSON	B
LINDA DENFORD	C

RPG One of the major processing tasks of large businesses is generating business reports, such as payroll reports, inventory reports, and sales reports. A language called **Report Program Generator (RPG)** was developed in the 1960s to simplify the production of business reports. RPG is an extremely popular language.

RPG is a problem-oriented, highly structured, and easy-to-learn language. Developed by IBM and introduced in 1964, RPG allows users to generate useful reports using existing or newly created files. Brief RPG programs can perform complex and sophisticated reporting tasks.

Because many instructions for preparing reports are included in the language, programmers using RPG II need only describe the file to be used, and specify the input, calculations, and output. In newer versions (RPG IV is the most recent), only the name of the file needs to be specified. The programmer uses specialized coding forms to write the specifications.

Ada One of the world's biggest users of computer software is the U.S. Department of Defense. In the early years of computing, the Department of Defense spent approximately $25 billion on a "hodgepodge" of computer software and languages. The department needed a powerful language capable of processing many kinds of applications.

FOCUS

Ada to the Rescue

The U.S. Department of Defense (DOD) developed the Ada language in the 1960s for use in military programming, but it was rarely used elsewhere in the programming world. 90 percent of Ada code in the United States today is written by contractors working for government customers, including the DOD, NASA, and the Federal Aviation Administration (FAA). In 1989, the DOD declared that Ada *must* be used—when cost-effective—in all DOD projects.

But Ada has not always been the language of choice, even for military program development. For example, several radar system programs developed by the U.S. Air Force in the 1970s and 1980s used FORTRAN or other languages for the original design and modification. However, the Air Force has recently announced that it will use Ada to modify the large phased array radar system, Cobra Dane, located in the Aleutian Islands and built before the DOD Ada mandate. The Air Force also has a plan to enter the computer-aided software engineering (CASE) field using Ada. For these reasons, Ada is gaining a new-found popularity.

Ada did not catch on in the non-military computing world for a number of reasons. Some features of Ada are not considered well-suited to real-time applications. However, with careful use of Ada, supporters say,

Crown copyright/Charles Babbage Institute.

most of these pitfalls can be avoided. In addition, Ada requires a large amount of software *overhead*—computer code needed for communications between software processes. Some experts do not consider Ada well-suited to performing several computations simultaneously and sharing data between many tasks, so when Ada is used in such situations, additional overhead is required.

To ensure Ada would prove sufficient as the Cobra Dane programming language, the developers spent $7 million to have both Raytheon and General Electric perform real-time demonstrations by programming a prototype radar scheduling module in Ada. This module is considered the most challenging aspect of the project's demanding real-time software requirements, with the transfer of up to 20,000 bytes of data within 10 microseconds. The scheduler plans how the radar will be used to collect the data required over the next cycle of time. Not only did the prototype force the developers to face real-time issues in advance—it is expected to make software development in the production phase easier.

In the case of the Air Force's entry into CASE, Ada brings some positive characteristics: it was designed for modular software development; it is almost objectlike—in other words, a programmer or designer can tie together several functions into a neat, reusable package; and it includes environment, such as a set of rules for maintaining system integrity by prohibiting programmers from taking undocumented shortcuts, thereby making it a "safe" computer language.

To meet its language requirements, the department adopted a language called **Ada**, named in honor of Lady Ada Augusta Von Byron for her work as the world's first programmer.

Introduced in 1980, Ada was originally intended to be a standard language for weapons systems. Ada has also been adopted by other government agencies and business firms and is endorsed by several large computer manufacturers. Ada is now also used on some microcomputers. Some users feel that Ada is too complex, while others say that it is easy to learn, can increase programming productivity, and is superior to established languages such as COBOL and FORTRAN. The Defense Department has obtained a trademark to exercise control over Ada's use.

C When AT&T decided to start manufacturing computers, engineers and programmers at its Bell Laboratories concluded that system programming (including that of the UNIX operating system, which AT&T was in the process of developing) was too time-consuming and difficult. The company began developing **C** (C is the full name and stands for its version designation). As a result, the UNIX operating system and C programming language were developed concurrently.

Because UNIX and C were designed to be used together, UNIX operating system application programs can be written more quickly with C than with most other languages. Now a variety of operating systems and application programs for computers of all sizes are capable of handling C. In fact, many vendor-written software packages are written in C. Even special computerized effects in several films (any *Star Trek* movie, for example) were developed using C.

C is a powerful programming language and has been used to develop a variety of software. Operating systems and applications packages, such as spreadsheets, word processing, and a variety of business applications, have been developed using C. C can also be used with personal computers. As more programmers become skilled in its use, an even larger number of software packages written in C language will become available. Figure 11.15 shows an example of C language.

C++ Developed at Bell Laboratories in the 1980s, **C++** (pronounced C plus plus) is an extension of C that makes effective use of object-oriented programming. C++ includes all of the original C language in addition to features for working with objects. C++ can be difficult to learn. However, once mastered, C++ is a good programming language for use in developing application software. C++ offers programmers flexibility. Although it is a procedural language, it also supports object-oriented programming. Many traditional COBOL programmers have switched to C++ because of its extensive programming features and capabilities.

A sample C program that calculates and produces the average of 20 numbers

```
#include <stdio.h>

main ( )
{
     int i, num;
     float sum;
     printf(Enter numbers \n");
     sum = 0;
     for (i = 0; I < 20; i++)
     {
             scanf("%d",&num);
             sum = sum + num;
     }
     printf("Sum = %3.1f\n",sum);
     printf("Average = %3.1f\n",
     sum / 20.0);

}
```

Figure 11.15

C is a popular language for developing microcomputer applications. This language is also used for a variety of business applications.

Versions of C++ are available for large computer systems and personal computers. It has become the programming language of choice for many organizations for both internal programming applications and for commercial software development. A version of C++, called Visual C++, has become one of the most popular software development languages for Windows-based applications.

PL/1 In 1964, IBM introduced a new programming language called **Programming Language One (PL/1)**. Before PL/1 was introduced, there were no languages suitable for both scientific and business use. PL/1 was designed as a compromise and contained some of the better features of both COBOL and FORTRAN.

PL/1 offers considerable programming flexibility and is relatively easy to learn. Critics of this language argue that the language is so loaded with options and defaults that it loses its effectiveness as a powerful programming language.

PL/1 uses a modular structure. The modules can be used alone or combined into more complex PL/1 programs. For this reason, the language is useful for novice users who need to learn only the basic modules of the language for their simpler applications and for expert programmers who can use all of its features.

4GLS (FOURTH GENERATION)

During the past two decades, a new generation of programming languages, **very high-level languages (4GLs)**, has evolved. Fourth-generation languages are essentially abbreviated programming languages. Recall from earlier third-generation sample programs that a single task often requires many (in some cases hundreds of) lines of program statements. To perform the same operation in a 4GL, fewer (sometimes only five to ten) program statements are required. Thus, many 4GL users, formerly alienated from the systems development process, have been able to fulfill their information needs.

Unlike procedural third-generation languages, 4GLs are nonprocedural. Recall that with a procedural language, the programmer must tell the computer *how* tasks are to be done. With a nonprocedural language, the programmer need only tell the computer *what* is to be done. In short, the programmer does not have to explain to the computer how to do something. This obviously makes 4GLs easier to use and has the potential to increase programmer productivity, in some cases by as much as 25 times. Most computer experts believe that 4GLs deliver the largest cost and time savings of any software tool because of their rapid application development capabilities.

Figure 11.16

Fourth-generation languages such as Focus require the programmer to code what is to be done, not how to do it. This saves the programmer time and increases productivity.

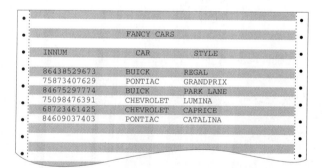

Examples of popular fourth-generation languages are Clarion, Focus, and DataFlex. Figure 11.16 shows a sample program written in a fourth-generation language called Focus. Notice how few statements are needed to produce a report showing the cars in inventory.

NATURAL LANGUAGES (FIFTH GENERATION)

If 4GLs seem easy to use, try one of the several **natural languages**. These languages permit a user to obtain information stored in a computer by using "natural," or ordinary, words.

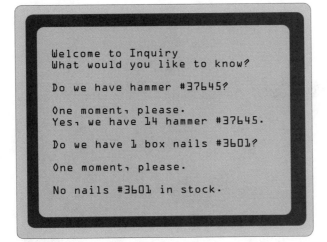

Figure 11.17

Natural languages permit users to enter ordinary words into the computer in order to retrieve information. The natural language Inquiry might produce a screen similar to the one here.

Here's how one natural language called Inquiry works. The language serves as a messenger between a user and a database. After starting the computer and typing the word "Inquiry," the user is asked what he or she would like. If the user wants to know whether a particular item is in stock, he or she inputs a question containing the item. Inquiry responds by displaying a message telling the user whether or not the item is in stock. Figure 11.17 shows an example of the Inquiry system.

Fifth-generation languages are making computer systems much more user-friendly. However, natural languages suffer from ambiguity in the ways that key words are used. These languages will require strict syntax and vocabulary limitations to reduce this ambiguity. At present, fifth-generation languages are used mostly for information retrieval, but the possibilities for future applications are limited only by people's imaginations.

OBJECT-ORIENTED PROGRAMMING

A significant departure from conventional programming languages are **object-oriented programming (OOP) languages**. These work with objects and messages rather than with a set of instructions and a separate set of data. Object-oriented programming was pioneered by Alan Kay at the University of Utah in the late 1960s in his programming language, Smalltalk.

As he developed Smalltalk, Kay envisioned a small computer with a flat screen. The user simply points to graphical icons or buttons on the screen. Each icon and button represents an object that includes both programs and data. The object might be a picture of a trash can. By moving a mouse to point to the trash can and then clicking the mouse button, a file displayed on the screen is deleted.

Other object-oriented programming languages have been developed in recent years. These include Visual BASIC, C++, and Object COBOL. Some people believe that object-oriented programming languages will eventually replace conventional programming languages. This user-friendly family of programming languages may prove to be an important factor in simplifying the development of complex programs in the future.

COMPUTER CURRENTS

Toward Environmentally Correct Software

Order any major brand of application software, and chances are you'll receive a box bigger than what your portable computer arrived in. In addition to the software you'll receive a reference manual, warranty information, and probably a host of other "support" materials, ranging from a guide to using the tutorial disk to a plastic template to lay across your keyboard—all neatly boxed in a cloth-covered case, which, in turn, is packed in what looks like more plastic "popcorn" and cardboard than Tiffany's uses to ship fine crystal. No sooner do you unload all this material and begin to grasp it, however, than the maker of that software is sure to come up with a new version of the program—yours for a nominal fee.

Like an increasing number of Americans, you may be left wondering what you can do with the old software and documentation. Short of dumping it in the trash and contributing to the growing landfill problem, you have several alternatives. If you plan to discontinue using a software program altogether, you might want to place an ad in the local newspaper and sell it. Many schools and charitable organizations are desperate for software (and hardware,

too) and are more than happy to get "outdated" copies. (However, don't try to sell an old copy of software and keep the new, or you can be arrested for software "piracy.")

Or you might want to consider sending the old version off to the GreenDisk Company. GreenDisk will break down the package into its paper and plastic components and arrange to recycle them. It will erase and reformat the disks and resell them with the GreenDisk label.

GreenDisk is the only such business at work now, but more such companies are probably coming, given increasing recycling requirements in the United States and abroad. In fact, in Germany, a new law will require

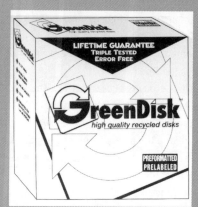

Courtesy of GreenDisk, Inc.

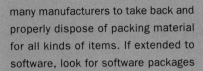

many manufacturers to take back and properly dispose of packing material for all kinds of items. If extended to software, look for software packages consisting of only program disks and a CD-ROM disk with everything else you need on it—what you might call "software lite."

SELECTING A LANGUAGE

So far, you've learned about some of the languages that allow a programmer to write programs for a wide variety of computer applications. A programmer must choose a language before writing a program, since each program instruction must conform to the rules and syntax of the selected language.

CONSIDERATIONS

Below are ten questions a programmer can ask to help choose the right language.

1. **How well do I know the language?** Ideally, a programmer must be familiar with the language and should have a working knowledge of its rules and syntax.
2. **What application am I undertaking?** A programmer should use a language that is suitable for the particular application.
3. **Can I use the language with my hardware?** Before selecting a language, a programmer should determine if the language works well with the computer being used.
4. **If I upgrade my hardware or use a different computer, is the language transportable to the new computer?** Programmers should keep in mind the future hardware needs of the organization.
5. **Does the language support structured programming concepts?** Some languages, including COBOL, Pascal, and PL/1, support structured programming concepts better than some others, such as BASIC and FORTRAN.
6. **Is the translating software for the language acceptable?** Most interpreters are interactive, which means they allow a dialog between the user and the software. For novice programmers, this dialog can be beneficial.
7. **How often will this particular application be processed?** Some languages will execute faster than others.
8. **Will I need to make changes to the program?** The amount of time required for modifying a program depends in part on the language being used.
9. **Will changes in hardware technology make this application obsolete?** A programmer should choose a language that is popular among users. Popular languages are typically developed by manufacturers when new hardware technology is developed.
10. **Does the language vendor support, improve, and upgrade the language?** Before choosing a particular language, talk with other users to learn whether or not technical assistance and upgrades of the language are provided by the vendor.

As you can see, choosing a language for a particular application requires careful thought and a thorough knowledge of languages. However, the result is worth the effort. Using an ill-adapted language can result in application programs that are inefficient and time-consuming. Selecting the best language can increase organizational and personal productivity.

If you choose a career in the computer industry, you will probably need to learn one or more third-generation languages. In fact, employers often insist that you learn three or four. If you don't know all the required languages, usually your employer will see that instruction is provided for you, either by another staff member or by an outside trainer.

For those who pursue careers outside of the computer industry, new languages continue to be developed that will suit a variety of users. Just as computer hardware has become more user-friendly in recent years, so have programming languages. You've just seen how user-friendly fifth-generation languages are. The computer industry will continue to develop languages that are easy to learn and use.

Key Terms

Ada
algorithm
application software
assembly languages
BASIC
branching
C
C++
COBOL
coding
commercial software
conditional logic
decision table
desk checking
documentation
flowchart
FORTRAN
general-purpose language
hierarchy plus input-processing-output
    (HIPO) chart
high-level languages
iteration
logic error

machine language
natural languages
nonprocedural languages
object-oriented programming (OOP)
    languages
Pascal
PL/1
procedural language
programmer
programming
programming languages
programs
pseudocode
RPG
run-time error
sequential
software development cycle
special-purpose language
structured programming
syntax
syntax error
user-written software
very high-level languages (4GLs)

Summary

Application software determines the tasks a computer can accomplish. Two kinds are **user-written software** and **commercial software**. User-written software is prepared by the user. Commercial software packages are purchased from a software vendor.

A computer **program** is a set of instructions that direct a computer to perform certain operations. Instructions are expressed by a well-defined set of rules called **syntax**. **Programming** uses a computer language to translate a solution into a computer program. A **programmer** designs, writes, and tests programs that lead to a problem solution.

A **programming language** is a set of rules that provides a way of telling the computer what operations to perform. Each language has its own syntax that dictates the structure of the language and its expressions.

The **software development cycle** involves a set of six sequential steps: defining the problem, planning the solution, coding the program, testing the program, documenting the program, and maintaining the program. **Coding** expresses a problem solution in a programming language. Each language has its own syntax and special words for computer actions.

Frequently used programming tools include **structured programming**, or top-down programming; **flowcharts**; **pseudocode**; **HIPO charts**; and **decision tables**.

Five generations of programming languages have evolved over the years: (1) machine languages, (2) assembly languages, (3) high-level languages, (4) very high-level languages, and (5) natural languages. Machine languages and assembly languages are low-level languages, meaning that they can be executed with little or no translation. **Machine languages** consist of instructions written as a series of binary numbers. **Assembly languages** use abbreviations called *mnemonics* to communicate with a computer.

A **high-level language** is any language that permits a programmer to write instructions in recognizable English words, rather than in machine or assembly language. Most programming applications are created using high-level languages such as BASIC, Pascal, COBOL, FORTRAN, RPG, Ada, C, and PL/1.

In recent years, a new generation of languages, called **very high-level languages** or 4GLs, has emerged. When using a fourth-generation **nonprocedural language**, a programmer needs only to specify what is to be done. These languages include Clarion, Focus, and DataFlex.

An even newer generation of programming languages, called **natural languages**, has been developed. These languages allow a user to access a computer by using conversational language. Additional software developments include **object-oriented programming (OOP)** languages and changes in user interfaces.

14 Easy steps to being a webmaster

STEP 11 LINKS TO OTHER PAGES

One of the truly unique features of the Web that makes it more attractive than, say, the Yellow Pages, is the ability to relate otherwise unavailable information to your page. In this step, we analyze our pages again for what is not there to develop such links.

This step requires "new media" thinking. If you think in traditional paper-bound ways, you will only ask and see what other information about yourself you might provide. In using new media thinking, you will also develop a list of other web sites to provide information about the topic that is of interest to your web page users. Arriving at an optimal linkage strategy requires considerable thought about your goals for your pages, your web page users, and their information interests. If your goal is entertainment or revelations about your personality, you might link to "hot" web sites, such as *the spot* (http://www.the spot.com) which won a Best Site of the Year award in 1995. If your goal is video game programming, you may want to link to a game site or company that you particularly like, for instance, Id Software, Inc. which published Quake and Doom (http://www. idsoftware.com). If your goal is more traditional and serious, you might select sites that add to the usefulness of your pages, such as linking to the companies you have worked for in the past.

Web page links can be compared to index entries in a book—they are only useful if they lead to information that is interesting, relevant, or helpful. Too many links are confusing; too few reduce the usefulness of your pages by depriving web page users of information that adds to their knowledge about the topic area.

This ability to link other pages also has some drawbacks. Poorly selected links that do not add information may confuse users who can not determine why the linkages are there. The new links might alter the way your information is chunked by web page users, causing your pages to appeal to an unintended audience. If you have too many links, web page viewers become overwhelmed by the amount of information and tend to leave the page.

These drawbacks call for careful evaluation of your web pages after you have selected other sites for links. Check that page navigation is intuitive for all links, within and outside of your pages. Check that each set of threads through your pages addresses an information need of one or more of your defined audiences. Check that the web page user will understand, from looking at your pages, all possible destinations, or other actions.

When you have decided your outside links are okay, design them into your pages. You might want to rethink your color choices for links, vlinks, and alinks as discussed in

Step 4. Also, you now have an opportunity to differentiate different types of information from each other a bit more, adding to the overall contrast between different pages. One popular design idea is to define each type of information, or major area of information, in one set of colors that are carried through from one set of pages through an entire thread. This is emotionally comforting to web page users because they know, from the color cues, where they are and how all of the information relates.

Similarly, icons can be reexamined. Consistent use of icons to identify each type of information, or to link the same information among several web pages, provides the same psychological comfort that color choices can.

If you want your web pages to appeal to users in other countries, think about using culturally obvious icons or universal icons to get your meaning across with the icon rather than with words. Is there anyone in the world that does not understand the icons in Figure 11.18? These are universal, not related to a single culture, and were designed to provide understanding of a simple concept without words.

Figure 11.18

Examples of universal icons.

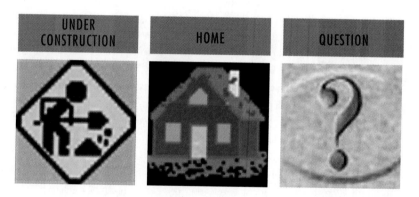

In short, the goal of good link design, and uses of color and icons, is to simplify the structure and content of your pages by providing visual cues that eliminate complexity and uncertainty from understanding and using your pages. Providing color-coded mappings across pages, being consistent in the use of icons and color, and being universal in the choice of icons all go a long way toward simplifying the user's job in understanding and using your web pages.

ASSIGNMENT: Surf the Web, looking for pages you might want to link to your pages. After you have located all of the sites, reevaluate your pages and make sure the linkages add to web page user information and further your page goals. Change your web pages to provide these links and reload your pages to the Web.

Exercises

REVIEW QUESTIONS

1. Explain what a programming language is and why programming languages are important.

2. Name the five generations of programming languages.

3. Explain the main difference between general-purpose and special-purpose languages.

4. Identify several third-generation, high-level programming languages, and explain why these languages are procedural languages.

5. Explain why the BASIC language was developed and why it has become a popular language for use with microcomputers.

6. Explain why COBOL was developed and how it is used.

7. How do fifth-generation languages differ from earlier generations of programming languages? Why are these languages considered to be "natural"?

8. What are some questions a programmer should ask before choosing a particular programming language?

9. Explain why fifth-generation languages are important for people who will pursue careers in fields outside the computer industry.

10. Identify the steps in the software development cycle, and briefly explain what each step involves.

11. Identify and explain some of the programming tools presented in the chapter.

FILL IN THE BLANKS

1. An _____ language is one that allows the user to communicate directly with the computer.

2. A _____ language is one that can be run only on the particular computer for which the program was written.

3. _____ is a high-level language introduced in 1954 by IBM for use in performing scientific, engineering, and mathematical applications.

4. Fourth-generation languages are _____, which means the programmer need only tell the computer what is to be done.

5. An ~~output~~ *algorithm* _____ is a set of rules that, when followed precisely and in sequence, will lead to an accurate problem solution.

6. A symbolic diagram that represents the flow of logic in a computer program is a *flowchart* _____

7. A *decision table* _____ is a programming tool that outlines the set of conditions a computer program might encounter and indicates what processing action should be performed for each action.

8. Two broad categories of applications software are user-written software and *commercial* _____ software.

9. Software *documentation* _____ consists of manuals and tutorials that accompany the applications software package.

10. *Commercial* _____ software encompasses a wide range of software packages that perform specific tasks or functions.

 **MATCHING**

Match each term with its description.

a. user's manual

b. define the problem

c. FORTRAN

d. COBOL

e. C++

f. natural language

g. BASIC

h. general-purpose

i. structured programming

_I_ 1. Dividing program tasks into modules.

_H_ 2. Any programming language used to write a variety of application programs.

_E_ 3. Uses object-oriented procedures.

_F_ 4. Fifth-generation programming language.

_G_ 5. Language developed to teach programming concepts to students.

_D_ 6. Language developed for business applications.

_B_ 7. First step in the problem-solving process.

_C_ 8. Language used mainly for scientific and mathematical applications.

_A_ 9. Contains instructions for using the software.

_E_ 10. Programming language that is procedural and also lends itself to object-oriented programming.

 **ACTIVITIES**

1. With help from your teacher or someone in the computer center at your school, prepare a list of different applications performed on your school's computer(s). Beside each application on your list, write the programming language used for that application.

2. The following languages were among those explained in the chapter:

   BASIC

   COBOL

   FORTRAN

   PL/1

   From the list of languages above, choose the language you believe would be best for each of the following programming applications, and explain why:

   a. A program that computes the net pay for several hundred employees.

   b. A variety of programs that would help you with your class assignments.

   c. A program that computes the area of a circle.

   d. Several programs for both business and scientific applications that must use the same language.

3. Using the appropriate symbols, prepare a flowchart showing all the process steps needed to balance your checkbook. What is the sequence of steps? Are there branches? Are there loops? How many steps are there? Could you program a computer to do this process? Make your flowchart detailed and complete.

Skills for Living

VISIT THE SMITHSONIAN

One of our national treasures in the United States is the Smithsonian Institution. Do you know what it is? Have your been there? The Internet can take you.

In 1996, the Smithsonian Institution celebrated its 150-year anniversary. It is the world's largest museum complex with 16 museums and galleries and the National Zoological Park. Fourteen museums and the National Zoo are in Washington, D.C., and two museums are in New York City.

The Smithsonian is dedicated to public education, national service, and scholarship in the arts, sciences, and history. Its founding mission is to increase and diffuse knowledge through its museums and educational programs.

At any one time, only a small percentage of the Institution's total collection is on display. Expeditions are made to all parts of the world to gather new artifacts and specimens for the museums.

The Smithsonian's annual budget for 1995 was $480 million. More than 25 million people visit its facilities each year. Admission to the museums in Washington, D.C., is free. Hours are 10 a.m. to 5:30 p.m. daily, except Christmas Day. Over 140 million works of art and specimens are available to the Smithsonian. Exhibits in these buildings trace the evolution of mankind, flight and aviation, information technology, the automobile, art, the presidents, etc. Many things that you need to know about the past can be found here.

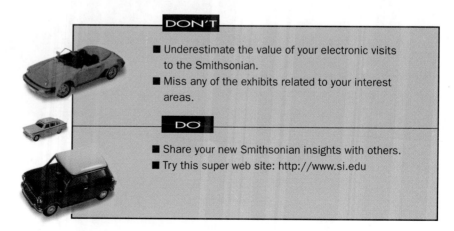

DON'T
- Underestimate the value of your electronic visits to the Smithsonian.
- Miss any of the exhibits related to your interest areas.

DO
- Share your new Smithsonian insights with others.
- Try this super web site: http://www.si.edu

Student Activities

1. Using the Internet, take a tour. Find out about the Smithsonian, the history of the organization, and the complexes themselves. Then, electronically visit two of the museums that are of greatest interest to you. What do they contain? How are they organized? What did you learn? How can you use the Smithsonian in the future? Write up your findings and share your material with your course professor. But also teach the teacher! Share your findings with two other professors at your school who teach the subjects you researched, but may not be aware of how the Internet can help them do research in their field of interest.

2. Review the history of computing. See what information sources you can find at the Smithsonian that help you understand the evolution of computing in our country. Highlight your findings.

3. Now that you have done your project, if you ever go to Washington D.C., you must personally visit these exhibits. Compare your personal visit with your electronic visit. Note the differences.

CHAPTER 12

12

VISUAL SYSTEMS

OBJECTIVES

AFTER STUDYING THIS CHAPTER, YOU SHOULD BE ABLE TO:
1. Explain the need for visualizing information.
2. Explain the do's and don'ts in designing computer-based visual aids.
3. List the traditional types of computer graphics.
4. Explain how presentation graphics can add more information to a presentation.
5. Discuss the role of color in presentations and the emotions particular colors trigger.
6. Explain the different types of design graphics and how they are used.
7. Explain what multimedia is and how it is used.
8. Explain virtual reality and its uses.
9. Identify the different types of computer hardware and software used in visual information systems and discuss how they work.
10. Discuss the role of presenters in visual information systems and how they should prepare for an effective presentation.

CHAPTER OUTLINE

OVERVIEW OF VISUAL DATA
The Benefits of Visual Systems
Classifying Applications

DESIGN PRINCIPLES
Design Objectives
Content
Color

TRADITIONAL COMPUTER GRAPHICS
Line Graphs
Bar Graphs
Pie Charts

PRESENTATION GRAPHICS
Purpose
Delivery Issues
Types of Presentation Graphics

SPECIALIZED HARDWARE DEVICES
Input Technologies
Display Devices

DESIGN GRAPHICS
CAD Systems
CAM Systems

MULTIMEDIA
Computer System Requirements
Benefits and Weaknesses

VIRTUAL REALITY

ADDITIONAL REMARKS

I magine flying off a 100-story skyscraper in New York in a virtual handglider. You pass over every part of the city, diving, turning, and climbing. You almost crash! Luckily, the wind caught you just in time. All of this comes to you compliments of Evans & Sutherland's computer-generated Virtual Glider experience, the perfect location-based entertainment for trade shows, promotions, and other special events.

Or perhaps you prefer shopping. Arthur Andersen & Company, a worldwide accounting and computer consulting company, recently demonstrated a 3-D, Internet web server application called MusicWorld. This software application enables Arthur Andersen's customers to provide virtual, 3-D shopping malls to users on the Internet. The demonstration features audio, animation, and video and provides users with an interactive 3-D environment where they can hear and then buy music and videos.

But, still missing are appeals to our last two senses—smell and taste. Imagine "SurroundSmell" or "TotalTaste." On April 1, 1996 (April Fools Day), Microsoft fooled its one million Microsoft Network users by announcing "Cybersmell." Microsoft said it had found a way to digitize smells and then pass them through the computer's speaker system. Users simply sniffed their speakers to experience the odors of a Thanksgiving turkey dinner, musty tennis shoes, or a summer flower arrangement. At the end of the demonstration, participants were exposed to boisterous laughing and a cartoon on the screen, announcing "April Fool." Perhaps Microsoft or someone else will add these senses to the next generation of computer presentation technologies.

OVERVIEW OF VISUAL DATA

The term *visual information system* covers a large number of applications. **Visual information systems (VISs)** are graphic displays of information using computers. How many VIS examples can you think of? Examples include a single line chart, the construction of complicated engineering designs, and the creation of a computerized reality.

THE BENEFITS OF VISUAL SYSTEMS

These visual decision-making tools transform raw data into its pictorial equivalent. With today's emphasis on the use of teams for projects and problem solving, visual systems can transfer information and insights from one team member to another. Think of this process as a mental brain transplant—with ideas and insights flowing from one human storage location to another. Effective visuals convey the meaning and implications of data and thus improve communication efficiency. This chapter focuses on five common types of visual information systems—traditional numeric graphics, presentation graphics, design graphics, multimedia, and virtual reality (see Figure 12.1)—and the special hardware and software they require.

Five Types of Graphics Applications
Traditional graphics
Presentation graphics
Design graphics
Multimedia
Virtual reality

Figure 12.1

Rapid growth in visual applications has been fueled by rapid increases in hardware and software capabilities. Higher computing speeds, larger computer memories and disk storage, better monitors and printers coupled with more powerful, easy-to-use and less-expensive software have increased performance and lowered prices. Design graphics, including computer-aided design (CAD) and computer-aided manufacturing (CAM), have shown enormous potential. Graphic terminal installations have grown rapidly in the last five years. Almost every organization today uses some type of computer-generated visual aids. Lower prices and user-friendly software in publication graphics have provided almost every personal computer user with the opportunity to design and produce his or her own visual support.

The greatest incentive for visual systems use is the classic statement, "A picture is worth a thousand words." Information is more easily transferred and understood if it can be portrayed in visual or graphic forms rather than in numeric or written formats. The brain processes words serially, or one at a time. However, images and other sensory input are processed in parallel. Many parts of the brain simultaneously analyze different information elements of the image—color, shape, relative size, changes, movement—searching for insights, relationships, emotions, and patterns. This makes visual information transfer more rapid and complete.

Economic incentives also drive the use of visuals. Real dollar savings occur when computers and users create initial designs, slides, overheads, and camera-ready documents for publication. Presentations that used to take several days to complete can now be created in one day. Professional-looking reports are produced in just a few hours. Quicker turnaround times mean higher productivity and lower costs.

Graphics aid in problem solving. Visual representation of data amplifies the informational value. User absorption, interpretation, and implementation are the objectives for a presenter. All of these factors enhance the individual's and organization's decision-making process and competitive advantage. Numerous studies have shown that presentations with visual support are 50 percent more effective than those without. Group meetings are shorter (up to 20 percent, in some cases) and there is a stronger commitment to the group's final decision.

Visual systems also show patterns and relationships. These patterns might include sales trends, customer profiles, new product opportunities, manufacturing changes, and publication processes. Graphics supply **visual early warning systems (VEWSs)** to warn of unanticipated changes in expected data patterns. This approach is called **management by exception**—graphically monitoring a system's performance and acting only when exceptional events occur.

CLASSIFYING APPLICATIONS

It is important that you have a framework for understanding the relationships and differences between the five visual systems. The table below shows the hierarchy and key characteristics of the various techniques.

Characteristics of Visual Information Systems						
The Medium						
Characteristics	**Text**	**Numeric Graphics**	**Presentation Graphics**	**CAD/CAM**	**Multimedia**	**Virtual Reality**
# of dimensions	1	2	2	2 or 3	2 or 3	3
Senses used	Eye	Eye	Eye/Ear	Eye/Ear	Eye/Ear	Eye/Ear/ Touch
Delivery order	Linear	Linear	Random	Random	Random	Random
Data required	Low	Little	Medium	High	High	Highest
Information	Low	Little	Medium	High	High	Highest
Skills required	Low	Little	Medium	High	High	Highest
Development time	Low	Little	Medium	High	High	Highest
Hardware needs	Low	Little	Medium	High	High	Highest
Software needs	Low	Little	Medium	High	High	Highest

These techniques differ based on the human senses they stimulate and the resources they use. First, think of the benefits of a successful application vs. the costs (time, labor, money, equipment, materials) of doing the project. The higher the benefit, the greater the effort permitted. Also, consider the hardware and software you have available and your personal skills and knowledge. It would be difficult to implement a complex multimedia application in a short time, especially if you had no background or equipment. Sometimes, simpler methods will suffice.

As we move up the ladder, each application becomes more powerful than the previous one. Each contains more information, appeals to more of our senses, uses more sophisticated hardware and software, and takes more time to develop. *Delivery order* refers to the ability to change delivery sequence. *Linear* means the material comes in a serial order, one after the other, without the ability to automatically insert or change direction during the delivery.

Random, much like random access in computer memory or hard disk storage, allows the user to move arbitrarily to any place in the order of visuals, based on audience questions or requests. As you review these techniques and try to decide which is appropriate, think of the characteristics you need and the resources you have available to implement your choice. Remember, any of these techniques is usually better than using no visual support at all.

Superstock.

Courtesy of Microsoft Corporation.

Before, students had to wade through piles of books and encyclopedias to get help with homework. They would write down key ideas and hand-draw the visual aids. Text was the primary delivery medium.

Today, by combining multimedia, modems, and on-line user services, students access on-line encyclopedias for help. Material includes voice, video clips, sound, visual aids, and animated diagrams and maps, as well as text. Now the student simply cuts and pastes critical materials (being sure to give reference credit for these pieces).

DESIGN PRINCIPLES

Visuals must have an impact on your intended audience. First, assess your audience or customers. Who are they? What do they want and need from your presentation? Then, determine your agenda. What do you want to accomplish with this visual? What is its objective, its purpose? How does this visual relate to the content and flow of other visuals you plan to use?

DESIGN OBJECTIVES

Audience impressions are built in the first minute of presentation. They are based on dress, posture, and general physical appearance, as well as on presentation content. The way you look is just as important as the way your presentation looks.

Graphic design objectives vary, but the most common objectives include some combination of the following:

- evaluation of historical factors—looking backward
- projecting possible future relationships—the way we think things will be in the future
- monitoring current operations and processes
- transferring insights to others who need to know, a briefing
- marketing or selling—yourself, your product, your understanding, your recommendations

Figure 12.2 shows an example of a poorly-designed graphic. Figure 12.3 shows the same data in a more effective format.

Figure 12.2

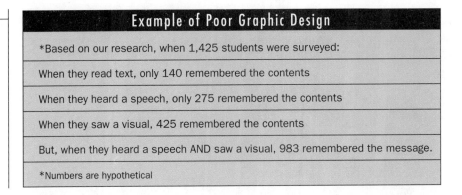

Figure 12.3

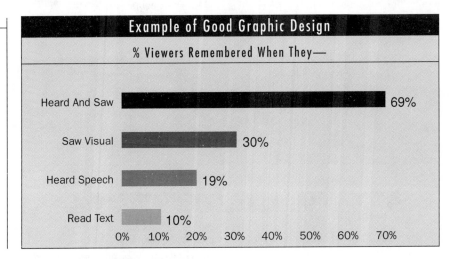

CONTENT

Graphics constitute the form and not the substance of the presenter's message. Your ultimate concern is with the quality of the data behind the visuals and not with the visuals themselves. Guard against **garbage in, garbage out**, or **GIGO**. What was done to the data to transform them into the information you are seeing? Does the visual truly reflect the reality of the situation? Are we correctly interpreting the patterns, trends, and relationships that the graphics seem to suggest? These are the important issues related to designing content. Figure 12.4 lists some basic graphic design guidelines.

COLOR

Psychologists tell us that different colors elicit different emotions from an audience. These feelings stem from cultural influences. Blue represents truth. Yellow represents warmth. Red suggests fire, blood, excitement, and passion. Black is death, grief, and sorrow. Profits are often shown in green (the color of money), while losses are shown in red.

Black and white play special roles in color. To add shade or to darken colors, add black. To add tint or to lighten colors, add white. When you use color in your graphics, consider the psychological values of these colors in the emotional color wheel (see Figure 12.5). Then design those color elements into your visuals for maximum effect.

Figure 12.4

Some Graphic Design Guidelines

Following these guidelines will improve the quality and effectiveness of your visuals.

■ Use white space (blank space) in your visual. It will enhance readability.
■ Use only a few colors. Too many colors detract from the visual.
■ Use the same family of fonts (style of type). You can use different sizes of type to show the relative importance of a topic, such as in an outline. If you use an overhead projector, make text big enough to be read by those in the back of the room.
■ Limit bulleted charts to seven lines or less. Write a dynamic title on the visual to focus reader attention.
■ Don't use more than seven pieces in a pie chart or more than 12 bars in a graph.
■ Don't use passive voice in graphic text.
■ Make your graph clear, concise, and "active."

Figure 12.5

The Emotional Color Wheel

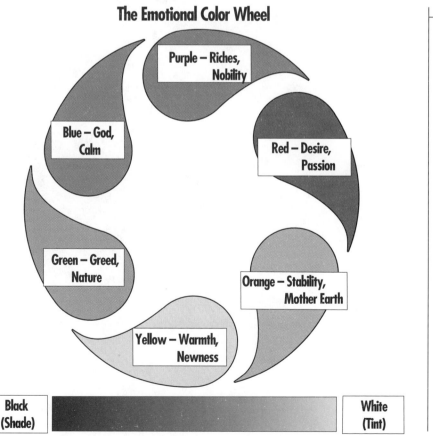

Purple – Riches, Nobility

Blue – God, Calm

Red – Desire, Passion

Green – Greed, Nature

Orange – Stability, Mother Earth

Yellow – Warmth, Newness

Black (Shade)   White (Tint)

TRADITIONAL COMPUTER GRAPHICS

Different types of graphs are used for different purposes. The user must determine the information to be presented and then choose and construct the appropriate type of graph. Spreadsheets are excellent processors for converting table data into information and then into a graphic to display that information. All the current, popular spreadsheet programs: Lotus 1-2-3, Quattro Pro, and Excel, have excellent graphics capabilities. Features include standard graph forms, shading options, font sizes and styles, colors, and clip art. Future improvements will include sound and image animation.

The most common types of presentation graphics used to represent numeric data are line graphs, bar graphs, and pie charts.

LINE GRAPHS

Line graphs show growth or changes in the state of some element over time. Often, there are a large number of observations or data points. The X-axis (the horizontal line) is measured in units of time (days, weeks, years). More than one series can be graphed over the same time frame. A legend or key provides an explanation for each series. A grid is often added to the graph for easy scale reference to the X-axis and Y-axis (the vertical line on the left side of the graph). Line graphs find patterns, relationships, or trends in a data series. Line graphs will show, for example, whether product sales levels are increasing, flat, or decreasing. Line graphs can also show relationships between revenues, cost-of-goods sold, and profit over time. Figure 12.6 shows the format of a line chart.

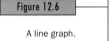

Figure 12.6

A line graph.

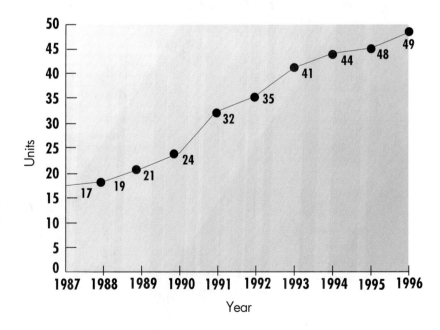

BAR GRAPHS

Bar graphs show size relationships among different series. The bars are discrete measurements assigned to each series. Typically 12 or fewer bars are used in a bar chart. The bars may be filled with patterns or colors to distinguish one series from another.

The relative height of the bar shows magnitude and allows quick visual comparisons among the plotted series. Again, legends and grids are available in spreadsheets for bar graphs. Labels added to the top of each bar help identify its exact value or what it represents. Figure 12.7 shows a bar graph.

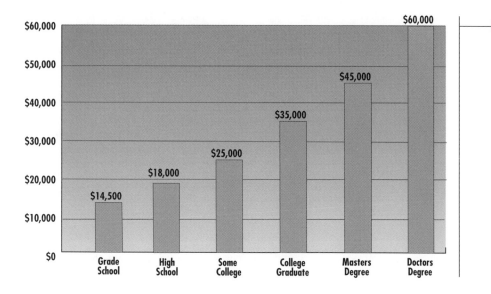

Figure 12.7

A bar graph.

PIE CHARTS

Pie charts compare the relative sizes of parts of a whole at a particular time. A pie chart could show how the U.S. federal government spends its tax revenues. What percentage of your tax dollar goes to defense, social security, or federal administration? The relative size of the wedge reflects the relative size of the expenditure in that area. Shadings may be added to wedges, or one or more wedges may be "exploded," or partially removed from the circle, to emphasize a particular element or issue. Names and values can be attached to each wedge in the pie. Electronic spreadsheets automatically compute the percentage of each wedge in the pie and then draw the wedges to those proportions. Figure 12.8 shows a hypothetical pie chart of government expenses.

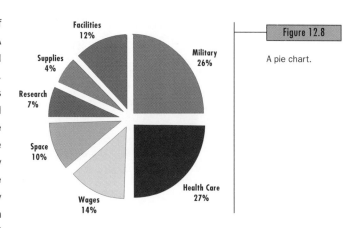

Figure 12.8

A pie chart.

PRESENTATION GRAPHICS

Presentation graphics are visual representations of data or ideas. They are computer-generated visual support systems. Images focus viewer attention on the most significant aspects of a written or oral presentation. These electronic image processors create storable, changeable, reusable, retrievable, and printable documents. Popular graphics software programs include Harvard Graphics, Powerpoint, and Corel Draw. Most spreadsheet programs also have some graphics capabilities. All these programs support **WYSIWYG**—meaning that what you see on the screen is what you get when the final results are printed.

PURPOSE

Why give presentations? We present to inform, influence a decision, or encourage action. Design your presentations with marketing principles in mind. You need to focus on customer needs. What does the customer (audience) need to know? How can you most efficiently communicate your knowledge and insights?

DELIVERY ISSUES

As you prepare your presentation, think about the members of your audience. How old are they? What are their backgrounds? Why are they there? How can you best meet their informational needs?

You should also consider the mechanics of your presentation. How long do you have to speak? How many visuals should you have? A good rule of thumb is one visual for every two-and-a-half minutes of presentation (a ten-minute speech would require four visuals). Finally, plan your presentation ending well. How do you want to leave the audience—with a summary, a call to action, a recommendation, or a final choice?

Think about the delivery environment. How big is the room? How much or how little light does it have? What is the best seating arrangement? What resources will you have—overhead projector and screen, white board, podium, pointer, clock, sound system, handouts, computer support? Always visit the room well ahead of time and test as much of the equipment as you can. Try to eliminate surprises. What will you do if your primary delivery system fails? How will you continue? Build a contingency plan for quick disaster recovery. Figure 12.9 summarizes how you should prepare your visual presentation.

Figure 12.9

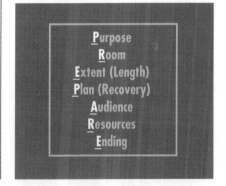

How To PREPARE Your Presentation

Purpose
Room
Extent (Length)
Plan (Recovery)
Audience
Resources
Ending

TYPES OF PRESENTATION GRAPHICS

A *chart* is a visual that highlights key issues or ideas in a presentation. *Bullet charts* define and highlight the sequence of key points to be conveyed.

Clip art is a computerized library of figures, cartoons, and images that can be electronically cut and pasted into a visual. They can be descriptive, serious, or humorous and often add depth and interest to the content of the visual aid. Some clip art software packages contain up to 15,000 images, all stored on a single CD-ROM. You can even find clip art containing animation clips, sounds, and video segments that can be added to your presentation.

Tables are visuals that show numeric relationships between items laid out in rows and columns. Computer spreadsheets are examples of table graphics. Spreadsheet tables can be named, saved, and later retrieved for inclusion in written reports and publications. Figure 12.10 shows how table data can be made more active using a chart format and clip art.

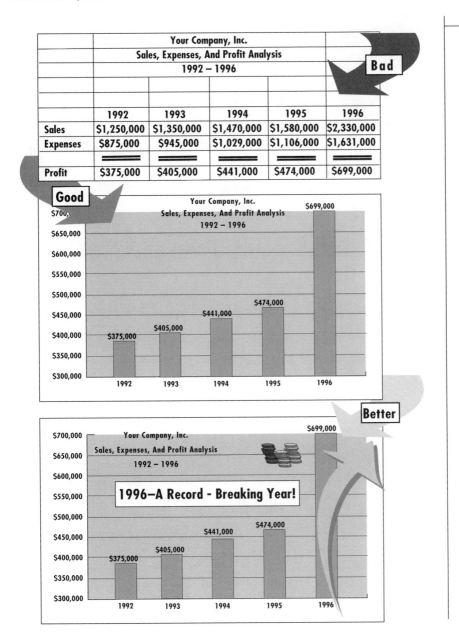

Figure 12.10

Table data within a chart format using clip art.

Schematics are symbolic representations of a flow process or organizational hierarchy. Organization charts, project management diagrams, wiring diagrams, and flowcharts are examples of schematic graphics. They show flow, sequence, activities, levels or hierarchies, and relationships involved in a project or system.

Figure 12.11 shows a schematic chart that depicts levels and relationships in an organization. Remember, each of these forms can be enhanced through the creative use of clip art.

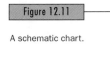

A schematic chart.

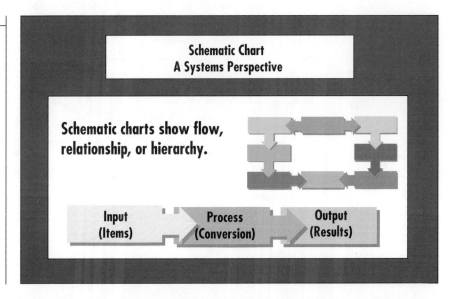

SPECIALIZED HARDWARE DEVICES

When the graphic document is finished, the user must decide how to best display or present his or her document. A number of new input and output graphic support technologies are available to the user. A few of the most common devices are discussed below.

INPUT TECHNOLOGIES

Three popular graphic input technologies include digital cameras, scanners, and video cameras.

Digital Cameras A relatively new input device is a digital camera. A **digital camera** is a small, hand-held computer and camera combination that takes pictures. Smaller models cost $500–$1,500. You can insert the camera photos directly into documents created on both Macintosh and Windows operating systems. You no longer have the expensive hassle of film processing and scanning.

Most digital cameras can use a variety of standard lenses for taking close-up, wide-angle, and telephoto images. They are easy to use and fully automatic. An image file is about one megabyte in size. The camera can store up to 48 images. These cameras are ideal for real estate property listings, insurance claim forms, ID cards, presentations, and image-based databases.

Instead of using film, a digital camera captures color images with a digital sensor and then stores them in the camera's memory. Later, the pictures are downloaded to your computer, where you can use them to increase the effectiveness of letters, proposals, color overheads, and presentations.

Digital cameras offer incredible convenience. There is no film to develop, you can view pictures on a TV or a computer, print multiple copies on your color printer, and even send the photos to others via a modem.

Scanners Text and images on paper can be converted to their electronic equivalent by using a **scanner**. Hand scanners digitize selected segments of a page, and bed scanners (operating much like a copy machine) capture the entire contents of the page.

After an image is scanned, it can be edited using specialized software to change the proportions, colors, or even the content of the image. Care must be taken not to violate publication laws when copyrighted images are scanned.

Video Cameras In shopping malls you often see a merchant in a booth using a video camera to transform images into personalized T-shirts or mugs. Individual frames in the video film can be captured and manipulated. In multimedia applications, entire clips of video film can be stored on CD-ROM, edited, and combined with sound and animation. Figure 12.12 shows examples of digital cameras, scanners, and video cameras.

Figure 12.12

Common graphic input devices.

DISPLAY DEVICES

The most common display devices are color monitors, printers, liquid crystal displays (LCDs), video projectors, and slides.

Color Monitors Most new computer monitors can display graphic images. If the output does not have to be printed and needs to be viewed by one or two people, a color monitor may be adequate. Usually, however, the results must be either printed or shown to groups. Thus, other display options are required.

Printers The most common display device is a printer with graphics capability. Laser printers, with their 300/600/1200 dots-per-inch (dpi) capabilities are very popular. Ink-jet printers, both color and black-and-white, are slower, but less expensive options. Finally, dot-matrix or impact printers are the least expensive, but also generate the lowest quality results. Printer prices range from $200 to $20,000.

Liquid Crystal Displays (LCDs) These flat panel display units attach, via a cable, to a port on the computer and duplicate the monitor's output on-screen. When these display units are placed face down on an overhead projector, the reflected light projects their image onto a large screen. These displays may be in color or in black-and-white. They are ideal for use with small groups that meet in small, darkened rooms. Their prices range from $500 to $5,000.

Video Projectors These projection units mount from 20 feet to 30 feet in front of a screen and receive their input from an output port on the computer. They also replicate the content of the computer monitor, but can project a much larger and clearer screen image and can be used in larger, lighted rooms. Prices range from $2,500 to $10,000.

Photographic Slides It is possible to purchase specialized equipment that captures images on slide film from the monitor screen. Some of the simpler machines use a 35-mm camera to photograph the computer screen, while others electronically capture the image from the computer's video display card and immediately produce a developed slide. Figure 12.13 shows examples of these common graphic display devices.

Figure 12.13

Common graphic display devices.

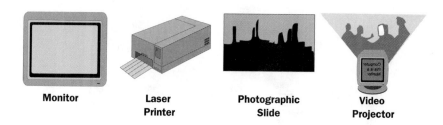

Monitor   **Laser Printer**   **Photographic Slide**   **Video Projector**

DESIGN GRAPHICS

Design graphics is a special family of graphics that includes CAD and CAM—computer-aided design and computer-aided manufacturing.

CAD SYSTEMS

Computer-aided design (CAD) systems create, modify, store, and retrieve technical design drawings. Engineers, scientists, and designers use CAD to develop and test new parts and assemblies. Items are tested for various types of stress. Weaknesses or poor design can easily be modified using three-dimensional graphics.

When a new part is necessary, the designer first searches for similar, computerized designs to modify. Modification of a part saves time and money in the design phase. Engineers estimate that 80 percent of the cost of producing a part is determined by the quality of its design.

CAM SYSTEMS

Computer-aided manufacturing (CAM) involves the conversion of drawings into finished parts using specialized manufacturing machines and process control. When the part is designed, CAM converts these images into machining instructions and process controls that actually machine these parts. Once the individual parts are built, they are assembled. Recent advancements in robotics have even made some simple assembly processes feasible.

FOCUS

The "Paperless Plane"

On April 9, 1994, Boeing Commercial Airline Company unveiled its new 777 passenger jet aircraft. The three-million-part aircraft was assembled electronically on computer before the first rivet was ever driven on the factory floor. Each part was designed and assembled electronically using computerized three-dimensional images.

Courtesy of Boeing.

The 209-foot-long, 20-foot-wide plane has a 200-foot wingspan and can carry between 305 and 440 passengers. The two jet engines are the largest ever produced for a commercial aircraft, generating over 75,000 pounds of thrust at takeoff. The digital graphics system used to design the airliner is called "Catia," which stands for *computer-aided, three-dimensional, interactive application.*

Over 4,000 design engineers combined into 238 design-build teams. Team members submitted their designs through 2,000 CAD and CAM workstations, driven by eight IBM mainframe computers in world-wide locations from Seattle to Kansas to Tokyo. Team members even created "Catia man," a computer-simulated human, to ensure that human mechanics could maneuver through the plane's innards to perform the necessary maintenance and repairs.

The Boeing 777 made its first flight on Sunday, June 11, 1995. Following the flight, the plane was put through the most extensive flight test program ever devised for a commercial airliner. The first 777 delivery was to United Airlines on May 15, 1995.

Boeing anticipates a future airline market environment characterized by greater competition and an aircraft technology focused on delivering increased value, at lower costs to the airlines.

MULTIMEDIA

Multimedia systems combine the elements of sound, color, graphics, animation, and video.

Courtesy of IBM Corporation.

Figure 12.14

Special multimedia authoring systems software such as ASTOUND allows the user to edit images and video clips and create and modify sound.

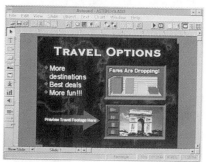

Courtesy of Gold Disk, Inc.

Multimedia presentations represent the next level of visual information systems.

Multimedia consists of electronic presentations created and delivered on computers using two or more media to convey the message. Typical media include text, graphics, 2- and 3-dimensional animation, digital and synthesized audio, and analog video. Multimedia combines the elements of sound, color, graphics, animation, and video into one integrated, seamless delivery. Today, most new computers can process and display multimedia presentations.

The individual media elements must first be acquired, then edited, before they are integrated. Software is available that can edit photos, create and modify sound, or edit video clips. Once individual elements are ready to be combined, specialized **authoring systems software** is used to copy, delete, cut, insert, format, and paste the pieces together (see Figure 12.14).

COMPUTER SYSTEM REQUIREMENTS

Hardware system requirements are higher for multimedia computers. Fast CPU speeds, large RAM memory and disk storage, a color monitor, audio circuit board, a mouse, and CD-ROM player are necessary.

Hardware used to display your presentation to the audience can include the computer monitor itself, an LCD panel combined with an overhead projector, or a three-gun **cathode ray tube (CRT)** projector.

The sound system can include the desktop speakers on the computer, a public address system, or headphones.

Because of their large storage capacity, CD-ROM disks are the primary medium used to store and distribute multimedia. Video media require huge amounts of storage.

The home CD-ROM-based multimedia market is the fastest growing segment of home computing. Market projections estimate this segment will grow at a compound rate of 30 percent through the next few years. By 1997, one-fourth of all U.S. homes will be equipped with CD-ROM capabilities. This situation will create an enormous demand for the products played on these systems. Thirty million CD-ROM products were sold in 1993. By 1997, this number is expected to be 120 million (see Figure 12.15).

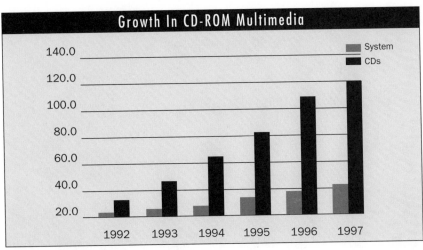

Figure 12.15

Market Size, Dataquest Inc.

BENEFITS AND WEAKNESSES

Multimedia communications increase the richness of content by appealing to more than one sense. They are more effective than just text and numbers and are better than linear media such as videotape. Multimedia is *interactive*—you can branch and move to different locations in the presentation. The presenter has excellent control over the delivery sequence. Basic multimedia is easy and fun to activate. Creation and revision times are quick. Presentation materials are modular and segmented, making them reusable in similar programs. The actual cost of materials is low. As you might expect, computer-based multimedia systems are becoming smaller, more powerful, and less expensive every year.

There are a few weaknesses. Initial costs of the system are relatively high. The user's initial educational requirements and learning curve become a barrier to entry for some, as it requires learning new multimedia terminology, concepts, and tools. Finally, with all these capabilities, there is a tendency to clutter your presentation with different media. Keep it clean and simple—don't distract the audience with the media and have them miss your important message.

VIRTUAL REALITY

Virtual means "being like in effect, but not real"—artificial similarity. Thus **virtual reality (VR)** means artificial reality. Through technology, virtual reality attempts to reproduce elements or characteristics of reality. Think of it as a scientist's three-dimensional laboratory. The user can experience and experiment, but without the negative consequences that might occur in reality. Also, as shown in the table at the beginning of this chapter, think of virtual reality in terms of the number of human senses it employs.

Using special hardware and software, computerized gloves, body suits, and vision glasses, the virtual reality system immerses the participant into an artificial, three-dimensional educational or entertainment experience. Applications of this technology range from video arcade games to complex medical research and space exploration training.

Using special hardware and software, plus vision glasses, the virtual reality system places the participant into an artificial, three-dimensional entertaining experience.

Courtesy of Virtual i-O, Inc., Seattle, WA.

Entertainment applications include flight simulation, aviation dog fights, and hand-to-hand combat. Participants sit in gyrating platforms surrounded by complex, 3-D environments. Movements of the hand, eyes, or the body, are sensed by the computer, and new perspectives and situations are then presented to the user. By reaching out and touching some object in space, another reaction is portrayed.

Research and education are also excellent applications for virtual reality. Hull Medical University in the United Kingdom is using VR to study knee biomechanics. Existing techniques severely limit the study of the complex interactions between bones, muscle tissue, blood, and other support structures. Hull is working on a VR model that integrates all aspects of joint physiology. If successful, it could simulate the impact of various knee operation and physical therapy options.

Research and education are excellent applications for virtual reality such as this simulation that allows surgeons to practice laparoscopic surgery.

Courtesy of High Techsplanations.

COMPUTER CURRENTS

1996 Summer Centennial Olympics in Atlanta: Visualizing Information — A Case Study

The 1996 Olympic Summer Games were the largest sporting event ever held. It was seen live on TV by over half the world's population, 3.5 billion viewers, and over 11 million tickets were sold. A computer infrastructure was built to support 16,500 athletes and officials from 195 countries and 2 million visitors. The system linked 200 locations. It gathered, calculated, timed, measured, and judged performances of 10,000 athletes in 37 sporting events at 27 locations, with up to 22 events running concurrently, and then instantly relayed the results to world media. This was also the first Olympics with its own Internet web page (address: http://www.atlanta.olympic.org).

Six information systems drove the information needs of the Olympics. They included:

System 1. Accreditation: Ensured athletes, media, staff, and officials have appropriate controlled access to sport venues and facilities. Participants wore plastic badges containing digitized images of athletes' handprints for venue access. Biometric scanning and video surveillance added security.

System 2. Info 96: E-mail and information systems for communicating schedules, transportation, and results. This system used a client/server system with 2,000 touchscreen PCs driven by networked AS/400 systems.

System 3. Results Management: Gathered and calculated times, measured and judged performances of 10,000 athletes and 37 sporting events at 27 locations. This system used video signals sent to locations on a fiber optic digital network that broadcasted voice, data, and video.

System 4. Games Management: Dealt with planning, training, purchasing, inventory, warehouse management, sales and order management.

System 5. Telecommunications: Linked organizers, athletes, and attendees through cellular, fiber-optic integrated voice, data, and video methods. The system used existing wireline networks as well as a newly developed wireless system.

System 6. Ticket Sales: Distributed 11 million Olympic tickets in a fair and equitable way. Systems used two IBM System/6000 (RS/6000) servers, 500 terminals, and 300 box office workstations.

See the figure on page 444 for a summary of the six integrated systems.

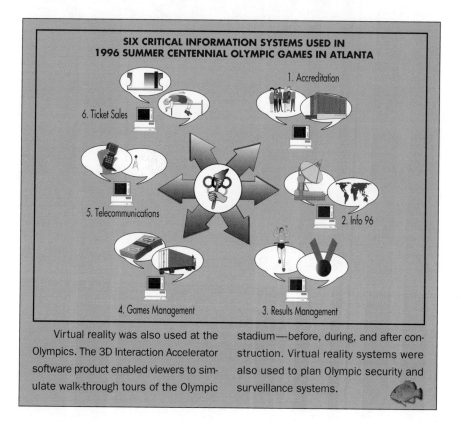

SIX CRITICAL INFORMATION SYSTEMS USED IN
1996 SUMMER CENTENNIAL OLYMPIC GAMES IN ATLANTA

6. Ticket Sales

1. Accreditation

5. Telecommunications

2. Info 96

4. Games Management

3. Results Management

Virtual reality was also used at the Olympics. The 3D Interaction Accelerator software product enabled viewers to simulate walk-through tours of the Olympic stadium—before, during, and after construction. Virtual reality systems were also used to plan Olympic security and surveillance systems.

VR capabilities are being adapted to a wide range of new applications. These include pilot training, workstation graphics, robotics, medical simulations, 3-D animation, and graphic design. All of these VR applications use a 3-D viewing environment for research.

VR is a more evocative tool than multimedia because motion and touch are added to the user's environment. The environment surrounds the user—it's more like everyday life. Due to the complexity and expense of these systems, their applications and availability are currently limited. As costs fall and computing capabilities rise, we will see more users and more applications of VR. In the future, networked virtual reality projects, perhaps delivered through the Internet, could offer a virtual art museum, a virtual grocery store, or a virtual classroom.

ADDITIONAL REMARKS

Data analysis, color, message, medium, computer technologies, audiences, and application are all factors to be considered before an image is constructed. Education and information transfer for problem solving should be the objectives. Designers have a personal responsibility to ensure that their visuals truly represent reality.

Both developers and users of these new technologies must continuously ask questions about the processes used to construct the graphics and the assumptions made to support them. Do the trends and patterns show a true reflection of reality? How should the decision maker interpret and act on the information presented?

Key Terms

authoring systems software

bar graphs

cathode ray tube (CRT)

clip art

computer-aided design (CAD)

computer-aided manufacturing

design graphics

digital camera

display devices

garbage in, garbage out (GIGO)

input technologies

line graphs

liquid crystal display (LCD)

management by exception

multimedia

photographic slide

pie chart

presentation graphics

scanner

schematics

table

video camera

video projector

virtual reality (VR)

visual early warning systems (VEWSs)

visual information systems (VISs)

WYSIWYG

Summary

Visual information systems (VISs) are graphic displays of information using computers.

Graphics supply **visual early warning systems (VEWSs)** to warn of unanticipated changes in expected data patterns. This approach is called **management by exception**—graphically monitoring a system's performance and acting only on the occurrence of exceptional events.

Graphics constitute the form and not the substance of the presenter's message. Be on guard against **garbage in, garbage out (GIGO)**.

Line graphs show growth or changes in the state of some element over time. **Bar graphs** show size relationships between different series. **Pie charts** compare the relative size of parts of a whole at any one point in time.

Presentation graphics are visual representations of data or ideas.

Clip art is a computerized library of figures, cartoons, and images that can be electronically cut and pasted into a visual. **Tables** are visuals that show numeric relationships between items specified in rows and columns. **Schematics** are symbolic representations of a flow process or organizational hierarchy.

Design graphics include CAD and CAM (computer-aided design and computer aided-manufacturing). **Computer-aided design (CAD)** systems create, modify, store, and retrieve technical design drawings. **Computer-aided manufacturing (CAM)** involves conversion of those drawings into finished parts using specialized manufacturing machines and process control.

Multimedia consists of electronic presentations created and delivered on computers using two or more media to convey the message. Display your multimedia presentation using the following hardware: a computer monitor, an LCD panel combined with an overhead projector, or a three-gun **cathode ray tube (CRT)** projector.

Virtual reality (VR) is artificial reality.

14 Easy steps to being a webmaster

STEP 12 | INDEXING WITHIN A DOCUMENT

Sometimes, a web page has to be longer than a single screen or two. Long alphabetical lists, geographic or location lists, time, or other categories can be created to identify the contents by an organizing scheme. Then, the anchor command is used to provide a clickable table of contents to the information on the page. The html code is:

html Command(s)	Text Function
<a href=#refname">hot button text</a>	The anchor command contains the standard hyper reference (href). The href point to the reference name on the same page which is preceded by a pound sign (#).
<a name="refname"></a>	The name command identifies a reference name from an anchor somewhere else on the page. This is an address that is jumped to from the href anchor. This is also called a "head" anchor.

Each classification scheme answers a question—where, what, who, when, or what type. "Where" questions usually can be classified by location. A location may be geographic (e.g., a map), symbolic (e.g., an organization chart), physical (e.g., a manufacturing plant or subway route), or systemic (e.g., the nervous system, the digestive system, etc.). A good organizing scheme for location information is by a map which might then have jump points that move to the descriptive information relating to each point.

Questions relating to "who" and "what" can usually be addressed by creating an alphabetical listing of the information and providing an on-page jump by the beginning letter. Alphabetic classification orders objects by their names. If you look at the cities listing, it frequently uses alphabetic jumps as coded in Figure 12.16 and shown in Figure 12.17 to go to another listing.

Questions relating to "when" identify time classification. If you look at company web pages, many have a history of their products, or major milestones in the company's history.

Figure 12.16

Html code for alphabetic
jumps.

`<a name="top">/a>Press your selection from the list:`
` │<a href="#A">A</a>│<a href="#B">B</a>│<a href="#C">C</a>│<a href="#D">D</a>│`
`<a href="#E">E</a>│<a href="#F">F</a>│<a href="#G">G</a>│<a href="#H">H</a>│`
`<a href="#I">I</a>│<a href="#J">J</a>│<a href="#K">K</a>│<a href="#L">L</a>│`
`<a href="#M">M</a>│<a href="#N">N</a>│<a href="#O">O</a>│<a href="#P">P</a>│`
`<a href="#Q">Q</a>│<a href="#R">R</a>│<a href="#S">S</a>│<a href="#T">T</a>│`
`<a href="#U">U</a>│<a href="#V">V</a>│<a href="#W">W</a>│<a href="#X">X</a>│`
`<a href="#Y">Y</a>│<a href="#Z">Z</a>│`
`<p><hr><p>`
`<a name="A"></a>A Items`
`                  List of A Items`
` <a href="#top">Go to top of page</a>`
`<p><a name="B"></a>B Items`
`                  List of B Items`
` <a href="#top">Go to top of page</a>`

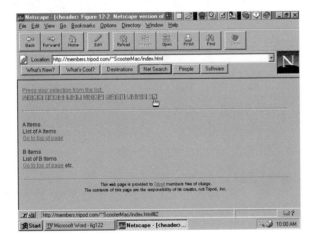

Figure 12.17

Netscape version of
alphabetic jumps.

Well-designed within-page jumps provide for a return to the top of the list from each lower level location. Also, the jump information should be ordered according to the scheme by which they are categorized so that sequential browsing through the page is logical and meaningful.

ASSIGNMENT: Redesign a page(s) using on-page jumps to provide a table of contents. Reload the pages to the Web.

Exercises

REVIEW QUESTIONS

1. List the key benefits of visual data.

2. What are the economic savings related to using electronic presentation media?

3. List the various characteristics of different media.

4. List three graphic design principles.

5. What role does color play in graphic design?

6. Explain what CAD and CAM are and how they are used.

7. What is clip art and how is it used?

8. What is multimedia and what are its benefits?

9. Define *virtual reality*.

FILL IN THE BLANKS

1. _____ information systems are the visual display of information using computers.

2. VEWSs are _____ _____ _____ _____.

3. Different media vary primarily on the number of _____ they appeal to.

4. A _____ chart shows each piece as a percentage of the whole.

5. _____ consists of electronic images that can be pasted into charts and graphs for special effect.

6. An _____ display mounts on an overhead projector and projects a large image of the monitor onto a screen.

7. _____ systems are used to design and engineer parts for future manufacturing.

8. _____ are electronic presentations created and delivered on computers.

MATCHING

Match each term with its description.

a. virtual reality

b. video projector

c. clip art

d. bar chart

e. multimedia

f. graphics

g. CAM

___ 1. Process used to run machines to build individual parts.

___ 2. The glue that holds presentations together.

___ 3. Visual used to show the relationships between different series over time.

___ 4. Images electronically pasted into visuals for special effects.

___ 5. Uses authoring systems to build the final presentation.

___ 6. Is attached to a computer via cable and projects a large image of computer monitor onto a screen.

___ 7. Artificial reality.

ACTIVITIES

1. Find an ad in a newspaper or magazine and perform a review of its contents. What is the key message in the ad? How effectively did the ad transfer this key message to the reader? What graphic design principles were used in the ad? How would you improve the ad?

2. Assume you need to ask your parents for additional money for your education. Design (use pencil and paper) a graphic or visual image that you might use in persuading your parents to lend you the money. Show your image to other members of the class and explain its content to them.

3. A friend at college does not understand computers or how they work. Develop a graphic image or visual to show your friend that explains how these machines operate.

4. Visit a local computer store and ask the salesperson to price a computer with multimedia capabilities for you. Also ask that person to quote a similar computer, but without multimedia capabilities. Then list the benefits and costs associated with the multimedia machine. Discuss your findings with your class and try to come to a decision as to which computer is the better choice for you.

5. Try to find an opportunity in your community to personally experience virtual reality. Check local video arcades, computer stores, or colleges. Report back to your class about what you did and how you now feel about virtual reality.

Skills for Living

SO YOU WANT TO BUY A COMPUTER — WEB SHOPPING FOR A PC

Buying a personal computer can be a harrowing experience. What do I need? What do I need to know? What if I make a mistake? How much do computers cost? Am I getting a good deal? What can it do?

Assume you are going to purchase a personal computer for yourself. Research the resources, opportunities, and materials on the Internet dealing with purchasing a PC—sources, software, types, features, prices, etc. Two major computer options exist—Apple-type systems (approximately 10 percent of the market), and IBM-type systems (approximately 90 percent of the market). For this exercise, assume you are looking for an IBM-type, desktop system. As you go through this exercise, try to collect specific information and prices related to:

Hardware:
1. CPU microprocessor (speed, location in technology cycle)
2. Printer (color, speed, print quality/density, type—ink-jet, laser)
3. Monitor (color, screen size, quality/density)
4. Secondary storage—floppy diskette drive
5. Mouse (features, size, feel)
6. Keyboard (size, number of keys, touch/feel)
7. Hard drive (access speed, storage capability)
8. CD-ROM (access speed, storage density)
9. Power surge protectors
10. Scanner

Communications:
1. Fax/Modem (speed, capabilities)

Software:
1. Operating system (Windows 3.1 or Windows 95)
2. Application programs (word processing, spreadsheet, database)
3. Games
4. Educational references (encyclopedias, medical and travel CDs, etc.)

Support Services:
1. Warranty (coverage, duration, location of service provider)
2. Educational courses
3. System expandability (memory, microprocessor, accessories)
4. Maintenance contract (service beyond warranty period)

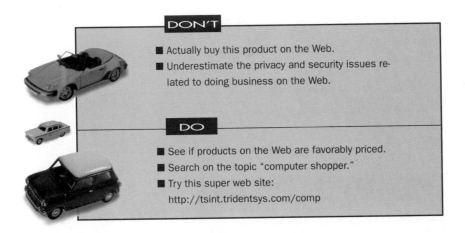

DON'T

■ Actually buy this product on the Web.
■ Underestimate the privacy and security issues related to doing business on the Web.

DO

■ See if products on the Web are favorably priced.
■ Search on the topic "computer shopper."
■ Try this super web site:
http://tsint.tridentsys.com/comp

Student Activities

1. Using the Internet, try to price the following IBM-type PC configuration. Then compare your price and search process with other students. Also price a similar system from a local dealer. Which price is better? What are the benefits of dealing with a local retailer?

New PC Configuration

150MHz Pentium processor	24MB RAM
2000MB hard drive	6X speed CD-ROM drive
28.8 data/14.4 fax modem	1MB video memory
Full motion MPEG video	Mouse
Stereo sound speakers	Phone answering system
Speakerphone	One-year warranty
15" color monitor—.28 dpi,	Color ink-jet printer (6 ppm,
1024 x 768 pixel	4 pp -color)
25 software programs—variety	Total Price: $_____

2. Would you consider this system adequate for your needs? Why or why not?

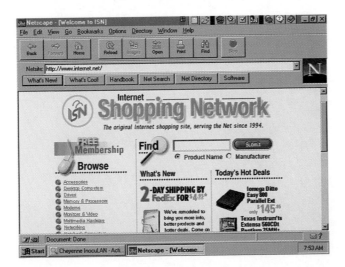

DO THE RIGHT THING

Evolving computer technologies have created a wealth of opportunities. However, some important concerns have also emerged. Issues such as computer crime, the impact of computers on the environment, computer-related health issues, and computers designed to replicate human behavior and human activities have captured our attention. Computer security, privacy, crime, and ethics are largely a matter of common sense, and common sense dictates that good judgment be exercised to protect computers, software, and data. Even the best security measures will not prevent wrongdoing in the computer industry. The behavior of individuals is the ultimate test of a computer system's security.

Courtesy of Apple Computer, Inc.

Spotlights

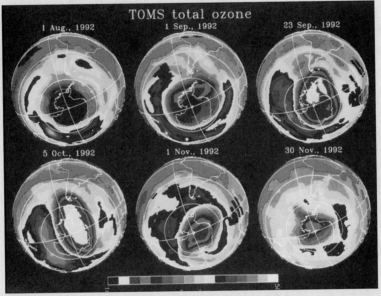

Superstock.

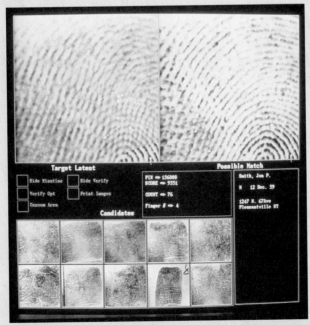

Alan Abramowitz/Tony Stone Worldwide.

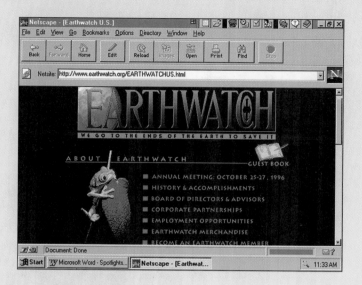

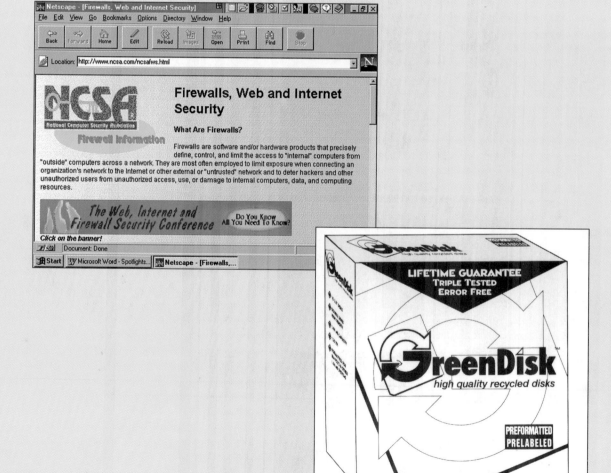

Courtesy of Green Disk, Inc.

Simon Norfolk/Tony Stone Worldwide.

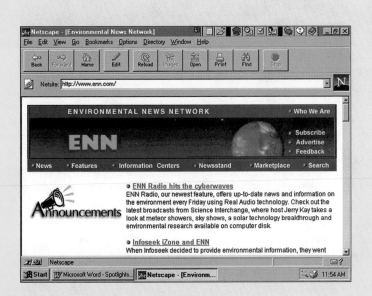

energy ☆

EPA POLLUTION PREVENTER

US EPA.

Courtesy of Hooloen Corporation.

Courtesy of the Software Publishers Association.

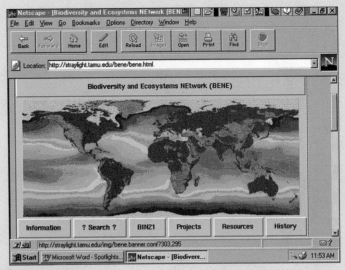

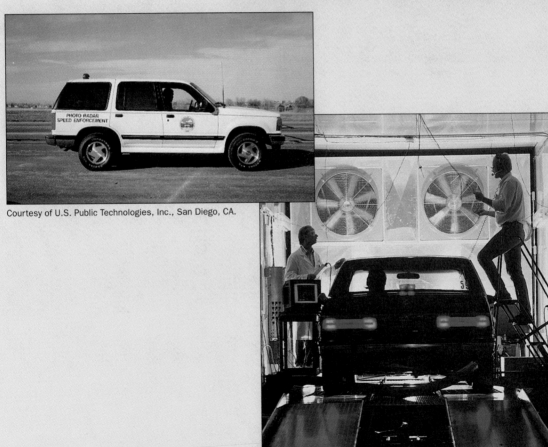

Courtesy of U.S. Public Technologies, Inc., San Diego, CA.

Roger Tully/Tony Stone Wordwide.

Courtesy of Congressman Edward J. Markey.

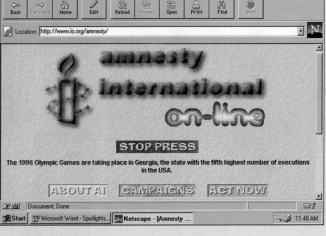

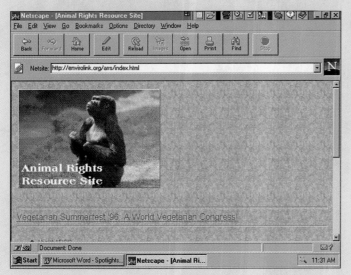

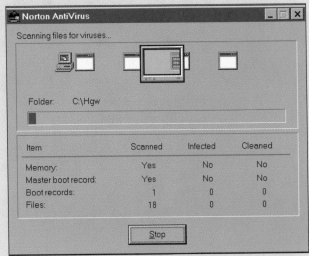

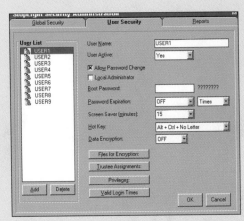

Courtesy of Symantec.

Stoplight® picture courtesy of Safetynet, Inc.

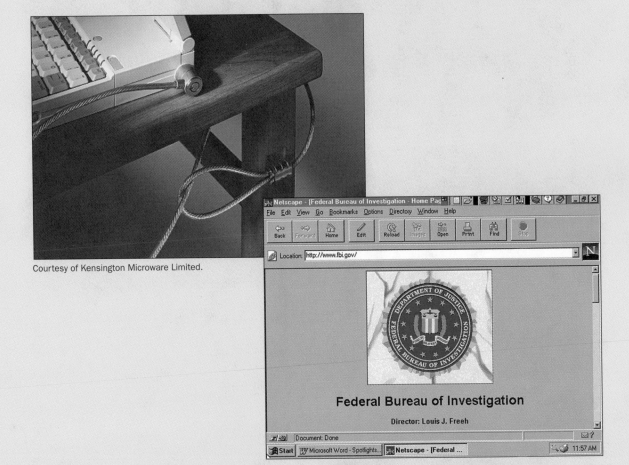

Courtesy of Kensington Microware Limited.

PART FIVE

COMPUTERS AND SOCIETY

Computer technologies have
developed much faster than
our ability to protect them,
and owners and users are
continually seeking ways to
make them secure against
crime. With ongoing advances
in technology, computers will
continue to impact our lives
in the future.

SECURITY, CRIME, AND ETHICS

OBJECTIVES

AFTER STUDYING THIS CHAPTER, YOU SHOULD BE ABLE TO:
1. Explain why computer security is important and why computer facilities and resources need to be protected.
2. Describe why large organizations form computer security groups.
3. Explain what a disaster recovery plan is and how it is valuable in the aftermath of a disaster.
4. Identify specific security measures an organization can take to protect computer resources.
5. Identify specific steps to protect microcomputers.
6. Explain the issues surrounding privacy as they relate to computers and stored information.
7. Identify federal laws intended to protect privacy.
8. Explain the meaning of computer crime and identify some types of crimes.
9. Define *computer hacking* and explain why it is illegal.
10. Explain the meaning and importance of computer ethics.

CHAPTER OUTLINE

PROTECTING INVESTMENTS

SECURITY
Computer Security Groups
Disaster Recovery Plan
Protecting Computer Equipment
Internal Security Measures
Data Security
Protecting Microcomputers

PRIVACY
Issues of Privacy
Privacy Legislation

COMPUTER CRIME
Sabotage
Accounting and Financial Crimes

Theft of Computer Hardware
Theft of Computer Software
Theft of Computer Services
Computer Hacking
Real-Life Computer Crimes
Crime Prevention

ETHICS IN THE COMPUTER FIELD
Software Piracy and Illegal Copying
Employee Loyalty

INTERNET ISSUES
Privacy
Personal Information
Transmission of Pornographic Materials

A FINAL THOUGHT

It's a beautiful day. The sun is shining, the air is clear, the morning rush-hour traffic was light. As you sit down at your desk, coffee cup in hand, life seems very good indeed. A flick of the switch and your computer springs to life. But instead of the usual menu you spent so much time personalizing, you are greeted by a message that says "Your PC is now Stoned." You may feel fine, but your computer is sick—it has a virus.

Though well-known because of a few highly publicized outbreaks, computer viruses are just one of many threats to computer security. One survey showed that 63 percent of American firms with over 200 PCs had suffered at least one viral attack. Given that use of illegally copied software and free software—two major sources of viruses—is much higher in small firms and among private PC users, the total percentage of affected PC users may be much higher.

Viruses vary in the amount of damage they can cause. "Stoned," "Friday the 13th," and many other viruses are relatively harmless unless you have a small hard disk that will rapidly fill up as the virus copies files. Others, with appropriately frightening names such as "Disk Killer" and "Dark Avenger," can wipe out every file on the computer before you can stop them (the mild-sounding and much-publicized "Michelangelo" is such a virus).

Regardless of the degree of damage they do, all viruses pose a threat to the computer world. Just as a biological virus infects a human being, replicates itself, and then is passed on to other humans, so a computer virus infects the computer, replicates itself, infects various files, and gets passed on to other computers when a disk used in an infected computer is inserted into another computer and a program is executed. Once a computer is infected, it can take hours, or even days, to clear a virus out of a computer system (assuming there's anything left to salvage). Thus most computer users—from large companies to private users—now routinely use antivirus utility programs in an attempt to ward off such infections.

While companies take action against these "public domain" viruses, some analysts argue that a far greater threat lies in highly specific viruses created by workers within a company or by outsiders targeting a specific company. Variously described as "attack software," "cruise viruses" (after Cruise missiles), and "stealth viruses" (after the Stealth bomber), these viruses are designed not merely to gratify the egos of the creators, as public domain viruses appear to be, but to take revenge and/or reap a profit. For example, by creating a virus that copies an authorized user's password to a file that the virus creator can read, the creator can then use the password to access files, steal company secrets, or even arrange for transfers of company funds to private bank accounts. All of which is enough to make not only computers, but the managers who rely on them, very ill indeed.

PROTECTING INVESTMENTS

Any computer system, whether mainframe or personal, is an expensive investment that requires protection. Computer resources, including hardware, programs, and data, should be protected from unauthorized access by persons or groups that might damage, alter, or steal these resources.

Historically, computer technologies have developed much faster than has people's ability to protect them. Owners and users are continually seeking ways to make them secure from vandals and intruders. While some intruders are typical criminals, others are not. A company that gains access to a competitor's secret files might not consider what they have done as criminal—nothing tangible was physically removed. A person who buys a single copy of a software program and makes several copies for distribution to others is also committing a crime.

Actions such as these occur frequently. Legislation dealing with computer security, privacy, and crime does provide some protection for computer resources. However, both individuals and organizations can and should take steps to protect their computer resources.

In this chapter, we will look at the problems of security and ethics affecting the use of computers. Although computer resources are sometimes misused by unscrupulous individuals and groups, the rights of private citizens may also be infringed upon. Issues involving computers touch everyone in our society. In 1992, plaintiffs in prosecuted computer crimes claimed losses averaging over $600,000 per case. Billions of dollars per year are being lost through worldwide computer crime. As the industry grows, so will the ability and opportunity to defraud participants.

SECURITY

On August 10, 1984, two people entered a Sperry Computer Corporation plant in Egan, Minnesota. Using hammers, the pair smashed military prototype computers and other equipment before they were confronted by Sperry Corporation employees. Damage was estimated at nearly $65,000.

The Sperry employees immediately notified police, who apprehended the offenders. Neither Sperry officials nor the Federal Bureau of Investigation has been able to determine exactly how the intruders gained entry into the plant, although the use of force has been ruled out. According to one Sperry official, the Egan plant is a secure facility that is protected by fences and guard posts. This true story shows the vulnerability of "secure computer installations." It also shows how quickly damage can be done to hardware, software, and data files.

If a computer facility is to be protected, a carefully planned security program must be implemented and enforced.

Courtesy of IBM Corporation.

The term **computer security** means the physical protection of hardware, software, tape reels, disk packs, source documents, documentation manuals, computer files, and computer programs. Security should never be taken lightly. Computer facilities often represent millions of investment dollars. Perhaps even more important is the value of the programs, data, and information about customers, employees, competitors, and other organizations.

If a computer facility is to be protected, a carefully planned security program must be implemented and enforced. In the next sections, we will examine ways to protect computer facilities from intruders and environmental dangers such as fires, floods, tornados, and earthquakes.

COMPUTER SECURITY GROUPS

A **computer security group** is an internal task force responsible for assuring computer security. In a small organization, this may be one person. In a large organization, this group may consist of several people, at least one of whom should be in a department other than the computer department. The group's mission is to formulate policies and procedures to govern the security of all computer resources. This group decides policies and procedures for all computing tasks, including data input, auditing, handling of checks, and distribution of sensitive reports generated by computer.

DISASTER RECOVERY PLAN

The single most important task of the computer security group is to formulate a **disaster recovery plan** to return the organization to operation quickly should a disaster strike. Although most plans contain elements unique to a particular computer facility, they also include some common provisions.

Disaster recovery plans vary in complexity. Some organizations plan to simply revert to manual operations. Other plans provide for alternate computer facilities at another location. An **alternate computer facility** is a second computer facility that can be used if a disaster destroys the primary installation. Two companies might agree to use the other company's facility if a disaster occurs. In a disaster, computer personnel would simply move to the alternate site and continue their work. Still other organizations, such as government agencies and banks, sometimes form a disaster recovery consortium. A **disaster recovery consortium** is a joint venture in which a group of organizations commit funds, equipment, and personnel toward establishing a separate computer facility. The facility is available to all consortium members if a disaster strikes. The facility is tested routinely but used only in case of an emergency.

There are two types of alternate facilities, or sites. A **hot site** is a fully equipped computer center with hardware, environmental controls, access security, and communications equipment. A **cold site** is an empty facility in which the organization, or group of organizations, can install a complete computer system.

An organization must decide which type of facility best fits its needs. One key factor is cost. A fully equipped alternate facility is extremely expensive. An organization must weigh this cost against the cost of being without a computer system. Having a fully equipped alternate site is like having adequate insurance coverage in the event of a disaster.

A disaster recovery plan must be comprehensive. Below are some issues typically included in the plan:

- **Alternate facilities** Some organizations belong to consortiums that maintain fully equipped backup facilities. Others make provisions for using other organizations' facilities. Each individual organization must decide on its best option.
- **Equipment priorities** A disaster recovery group decides what equipment will be needed and where the equipment can be obtained.
- **Personnel needs** Personnel are notified of their responsibilities in case of a disaster. Personnel routinely practice disaster recovery procedures.
- **Program priorities** The plan includes a list of important programs, files, and locations where backup copies are kept.
- **Handling of programs and output** The plan specifies those programs that are to be run first and a list of those who should receive the output from these programs.

An effective disaster recovery plan must be in writing and have the support of top management. Everyone affected should have a copy of the plan and understand it. If a fast and complete recovery is to be made, every employee must know what to do, how to do it, and when to do it. Computer installations often practice emergency drills without advance notice to employees.

PROTECTING COMPUTER EQUIPMENT

Many organizations go to great lengths to protect their computer hardware and software. Some organizations use special **detection devices** for identification purposes. These detection devices can recognize a person's fingerprints or voice when determining whether the person is authorized to visit the facility. Unauthorized persons are denied entry, and an alarm may be activated to notify security guards of an illegal entry attempt (see Figure 13.1 on page 468). Detection devices are somewhat expensive, and their installation is not always approved. Access can also be limited to authorized personnel with identification badges by requiring that personnel use electronic identification cards to open doors and by using sign-in and sign-out logs to record facility entries and exits. Burglar, fire, and smoke alarms alert personnel of impending dangers.

David Guyen/Science Photo Library/Photo Researchers, Inc.

Courtesy of North American Morpho Systems, Inc.

All company employees are responsible for the physical security of a computer center. The security techniques mentioned above are only as effective as the people that implement them. As long as people are involved with computer-based information systems, it is unlikely that any computer facility will be completely secure.

INTERNAL SECURITY MEASURES

Often security is breached by collusion between two or more employees who have worked together over long periods of time. **Internal security measures** are actions by management to reduce the possibility of this occurrence. Rotating the duties of data processing department personnel, for example, limits the amount of time people work together in the operation of the system. Rotating duties among employees within a certain group (for example, programmers) limits the amount of knowledge a single programmer has about each valuable and classified program. A single programmer who is familiar with an entire payroll program might be more likely to tamper with the program than another programmer who knows only a portion of the program. Also, some organizations have found that periodic rotation of duties among group or team members promotes greater creativity.

Any approach taken to improve security requires careful planning. Usually, more than one procedure, security system, and measure are used to provide maximum security. Once implemented, these mechanisms must be regularly monitored and reviewed to evaluate their effectiveness. Security-conscious managers must implement all company-approved security measures and techniques.

DATA SECURITY

Data security refers to the protection of data from accidental or malicious destruction, disclosure, or modification. To safeguard programs, files, and data, backup magnetic tape and disk media are stored off-site. Also, many organizations have implemented security measures designed to restrict access to computer files containing important data.

There are several ways an organization can protect its data. But, even if all techniques are used at once, there is no guarantee this ensures complete security. Data security measures do, however, serve as a deterrent. The most widely used techniques are explained next.

Computer System Passwords One popular security measure is to issue personal passwords to authorized personnel. A **password** is a special word, code, or symbol that must be typed on a keyboard to gain access to a computer system. Entering a correct password identifies the person as an authorized user.

Because most employees need access to only certain information, some of the more elaborate data protection systems segment information access by passwords. In this way, authorized users can gain access to only the information pertinent to their work.

Courtesy of Optima Shipping Systems, Inc.

Some organizations change passwords periodically. In these cases, the new passwords are issued by management without prior notice. In other organizations, employees are permitted to choose their own passwords. Some of the newer systems require users to change passwords periodically. The justification for changing passwords is that after a long period of time, passwords become known by many people.

Because passwords can be guessed or forgotten, companies are looking for other ways to defend against unauthorized access to their systems. SecurID cards, shown in Figure 13.2, take passwords one step further. These cards contain microprocessors that produce seven-digit passcodes every 60 seconds. These codes are synchronized with a central computer. The authorized user types the code on a keyboard when entry into the system is needed. The cards are gaining in popularity because unlike other types of computer access cards, they do not require a special magnetic strip reader for use. Stock market trading companies are already using SecurID cards and find them successful in thwarting fraud.

Electronic Signatures Many companies are turning to electronic signatures as a means of verifying the identity of those accessing systems and sending electronic messages. Electronic signatures consist of an alphanumeric string that may be as long as 25 characters. The receiving computer performs a series of mathematical operations to ensure the identity of the user. The U.S. Department of Commerce is currently developing a standard for creating digital signatures known as the Digital Signature Algorithm. Already, there is talk of how electronic signatures will be used in the credit card industry to curb fraud and used by the IRS as a means of speeding up the tax return process. One issue that might slow down the application of electronic signatures, however, is the legality of how to enforce electronic commitments.

Data Encryption The process of translating data into secret codes to safeguard them is **data encryption**. Data sent over communication channels can be protected by encrypting the data using special software so that only the person receiving the data are decrypt (or decode) them. The process of unscrambling the data—taking the encrypted data and reconstructing them into the original data—is called *decryption*.

Some organizations encrypt data before they are stored. Then, as the data are retrieved from storage, they are decrypted and put into a meaningful form. Data can be encrypted and/or decrypted by using special hardware or software.

Many organizations use data encryption. Even personal computer users can use encryption software packages to safeguard important files. A typical encryption package offers several security measures, including file encryption, decryption, password protection, and a personal computer system lock.

Figure 13.3

Shredded documents containing important programs, data, or other information can prevent theft or misuse of the programs, data, or information.

Courtesy of Fellowes.

Figure 13.4

Log registers are often used to prevent unauthorized entry into a computer center. Anyone entering the facility must make an entry in the log. For example, some organizations require personnel to record their names, identification numbers, dates and times of entry, and dates and times of exit.

Entry/Exit Log						
Name	I.D. Code	Time In	Date In	Time Out	Date Out
Diego Mercer	8039	9:55	10/9/93	10:23	10/9/93
Jane Wilson	8021	11:15	10/4/93	11:26	10/4/93
Barry Evans	8113	11:40	10/4/93	12:15	10/4/93

Computer Center Waste Discarded paper copies of programs, files, output, and data could easily find their way into the hands of competitors or disgruntled co-workers. Destroy these types of documents by shredding them. A **shredder**, shown in Figure 13.3, is a device that slices the document into thin strips, thereby making the document illegible.

File and Data Access Logs Just as records are kept of those who enter computer rooms and how long they stay, some organizations maintain an ongoing record, called a **log**, that a user must sign to gain access to computer programs and files. An example is shown in Figure 13.4. A computer librarian often keeps the log. A user, seeking to gain access to a program or file, signs the log book and records the date and time of access, and the program or file obtained. When the program or file is returned, a second log entry is made.

Electronic Data Processing (EDP) Audits Large firms often employ financial auditors to periodically review financial documents. Likewise for systems management, special auditing procedures for electronic data processing (EDP) applications are now used by some companies. EDP auditors review computer programs, files, and data. They look at who uses programs, files, and data, and the frequency of usage. If auditors find that an individual accesses certain information often, they may raise questions concerning the frequency of use. Auditors also note any changes made to a program, especially changes that can affect the output.

Careful Screening of Applicants People are often the weakest link in any computer system. Firms hire operators, programmers, and other skilled computer professionals on the assumption that they are honest. While most new employees are honest, some are not.

Job applicants should be carefully screened and references should be obtained from their previous employers. Even if references are obtained, bear in mind that former employers are sometimes reluctant to provide accurate information about former employees for fear of legal reprisals. Nevertheless, employers should carefully scrutinize an applicant's employment history before hiring a new employee.

Software Protection An operating system may include software that restricts access to a computer system. One type of software automatically matches a user identification number to a number assigned to a specific file. If a person attempting to gain access to the file enters the number incorrectly, the computer records the failed access attempt. Then, when an authorized user gains access, the computer displays a message that a particular number was entered by someone attempting to gain access to this file, along with the number of failed attempts.

PROTECTING MICROCOMPUTERS

There is no foolproof method for guaranteeing the security and safety of microcomputers. However, the following steps can be taken to help protect your microcomputer system:

Figure 13.5

Some computer facilities bolt hooks into computer cases and attach cables, securing the system to the workstation and protecting it from theft.

1. **Install a cable lock on the computer.** As shown in Figure 13.5, one end of a cable should be permanently attached to the computer and the other end to a large heavy object, such as a desk.

Courtesy of Kensington Microware Limited.

2. **Do not smoke, eat, or drink near the computer.** A spilled beverage can ruin a computer or other component, such as a keyboard or disk drive.

3. **Place the microcomputer in a safe place away from doors and windows.** Keep in mind that water can destroy electronic devices, including computer systems.

4. **Protect your computer, peripherals, and storage media from damaging extreme temperatures.** Data stored on a diskette cannot be read if the diskette is extremely cold or hot. Hard disk drives will not boot up or rotate in extreme cold.

5. **Keep all computer equipment clean.** Dust particles can cause damage to the system.

6. **Store diskettes in a protective container.** This protects them from dust, smoke particles, and other foreign materials.

Figure 13.6

A surge protector regulates the flow of electricity to computer equipment, protecting it from surges that sometimes occur because of fluctuations in power.

7. **Purchase and use a surge protector with your computer.** A **surge protector**, shown in Figure 13.6, is an electronic device between your computer and its power source (usually plugged into the wall outlet). When a spike or surge of power occurs, as is sometimes the case during electrical storms, the circuit breaker in the surge protector is tripped before the power surge can reach and damage your computer.

Curtis Manufacturing, Inc.

8. **Make backup copies of all important programs, files, and data.** Store the backup copies in a safe place away from the computer. In the case of a fire or other calamity, it is easier to obtain another computer and reload backup files than it is to recreate program and data files that may have taken months to develop.

PRIVACY

How many forms have you filled out in recent years? If you're like most Americans, you've filled out job application forms, loan application forms, college admission forms, magazine subscription forms, merchandise order forms, and many others.

With all of these government agencies, organizations, and private businesses compiling information about your personal matters, you may be concerned about issues of privacy and confidentiality. The term **computer privacy** refers to controlling personal and confidential information and how and when this information is communicated to other parties. Personal information may include, but is not limited to, financial credit, personnel employment records, and federal, state, and local taxes. Privacy of electronic data and information has been a controversial issue since computers first appeared. Once information is stored electronically, there is no guarantee it will remain private or confidential.

Business firms, government agencies, and other organizations often sell or share information. Here's an interesting experiment. The next time you fill out a magazine subscription form, spell your name slightly differently. For example, if your first name is John, spell it "Jon." Then, over the next several weeks, keep track of those pieces of mail you receive on which your first name is spelled "Jon." You will see that companies, agencies, and others distribute mailing lists, some of which include your name and address. Even though laws have been passed to prevent abuses, as long as people are involved with computer-based information systems, there will always be a threat to personal privacy.

ISSUES OF PRIVACY

An individual's right of privacy can be compromised in several areas, including mailing lists, telephone sales messages, and e-mail.

Mailing Lists and Privacy What control, if any, do you have over the information supplied to businesses, government agencies, and other organizations? When you subscribe to a particular magazine, some of the information you provide includes your name, address, and credit card number or a personal check. Did the company erase your credit card number after you charged an item? Probably not. In fact, your credit card number might still be a part of your record in the organization's computer. However, you do have some control over personal information stored in computers. Under federal law, you have a right to see your record and to petition the organization to remove or change any incorrect information. More information about privacy legislation is presented later in this chapter.

Telephone Privacy   Another privacy issue involves organizations leaving computerized sales messages on a person's telephone answering machine. Here's how this system works: before leaving your home or office, you set your telephone recording machine to record incoming calls. While you are away, some organizations use an automatic dial-up program to call area residents. When the computer reaches your on-line telephone message machine, the computerized message is recorded on the tape in your machine. Upon returning, you listen to several lengthy sales messages describing various commercial products or services. Many people believe that these messages represent an invasion of privacy and that legislation is needed to regulate this kind of marketing.

Privacy of Electronic Mail   Another controversial privacy issue involves electronic mail, or e-mail. Until recently, computer users have treated e-mail much as they would telephones. They freely express their thoughts in an uncensored manner, thinking their messages are private. Recent court cases are curbing this practice. Courts are treating recovered e-mail evidence just as they would letters and memos. Many are surprised to find messages they thought were destroyed used in court against them.

Most computer systems save all e-mail messages for several days in order to protect accidental erasure because of system failures. This practice proved costly to one top computer executive whose former employer uncovered e-mail messages supposedly containing company secrets and used this information in a civil case against the executive. Deleting messages doesn't necessarily mean that they are gone forever. Deleting allows computers to overwrite previously protected areas. The computer, however, may not need to make use of that unprotected space for years. Even then, it may only erase part of the information. Programmers know how to uncover these data and are often hired to do just that. Also, some e-mail software makes backups of messages and stores these files under a different file extension.

In order to protect your privacy when using e-mail systems:

- Know every place where e-mail messages could possibly be stored in the computer system.
- Buy commercial software currently available that truly erases files.
- Find out about your company's policy regarding the privacy of e-mail messages.
- Keep in mind that information you provide in e-mail messages can be used as evidence.

PRIVACY LEGISLATION

One of the earliest laws established to regulate privacy was the **Fair Credit Reporting Act** in 1970. This law allows individuals access to their credit records and gives them the right to challenge any data contained therein. All who have been denied credit must be allowed free access to the contents of their credit reports.

The basis for the Fair Credit Reporting Act is that firms often provide credit information to local credit bureaus. In return, contributing businesses are allowed to review a person's credit record with other firms. Prior to the passage of the Fair Credit Reporting Act, many persons seeking credit were turned down because of unfavorable credit information in their records. One result of the act is that people are now permitted to check their own records to ensure that the information is accurate.

COMPUTER CURRENTS

Is Big Brother Watching?

In his now-classic work, *1984*, George Orwell depicted a future society in which the individual's every thought and act were controlled by a pseudo-benevolent government headed by a "Big Brother." This work was science fiction when it was written in 1948. But according to some, Orwell may simply have been a trifle off on the date: the death of privacy is just now arriving.

While Americans have long expressed at least some concern over invasions of their privacy by the government, a 1992 Louis Harris poll showed that, for the first time, a majority of Americans say they are "very concerned" about threats to their personal privacy by not only the government, but also other institutions. Heading the list of these "other institutions" are the marketing firms that sell lists of names.

Despite this concern, laws to prevent such invasions of privacy are rare and largely not enforced. There are no constitutional safeguards of privacy, since no one dreamed that one day computers would enable marketers, private detectives, reporters, or anyone with a bit of computer expertise and minimal scruples to piece together a picture of your private life from computerized information on your mortgage application, driver's license, magazine subscriptions, Ticketmaster purchases, and charitable donations.

Rapid technological advances have stymied legislators' efforts to ensure privacy, as canny operators utilize formerly unheard-of methods to take advantage of loopholes in the laws. Moreover, computerized invasions of privacy are hard to prove without a confession that illegal methods have been used, and those who operate investigative and/or marketing services generally refuse to describe their methods—citing either "trade secrets" or the Fifth Amendment's protection against self-incrimination.

Another change in technology—the widespread use of computers and "e-mail" in business—has also opened the door to "Big Brother" activities by company managers against those who work for them. While federal laws severely restrict the monitoring of e-mail sent over public systems such as CompuServe and MCI Mail, there are currently no restrictions on monitoring of e-mail on company-owned systems. No laws forbid companies from keeping track of what network software and files each user uses and when, and sales of software capable of such tracking are increasing at a rate of 50 percent per year.

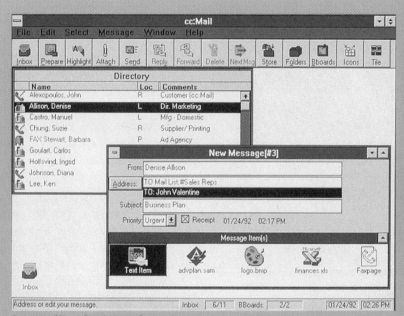

Courtesy of Lotus Development Corporation.

In many cases, the lack of such protection poses no problem. Only about 20 percent of all companies and 30 percent of large companies report monitoring their employees' usage of e-mail and other computer programs. Those that do monitor usually describe such activities as focused on detecting illegal activities such as insider securities trading and drug dealing.

Nevertheless, the potential for trouble increases as more and more companies install computer network systems with monitoring capabilities. A look at some of the e-mail policies in existence also underscores the potential for wholesale monitoring and consequent loss of privacy. For example, one company in St. Louis, Missouri, issued the following e-mail policy: "All computer programs, hardware, and data are the sole property of the company: any use of the computer or applications for other than company and business purposes is expressly prohibited. Contents of e-mail communications will be monitored by our audit department as deemed necessary." Faced with employee protests and subsequent unwillingness to use e-mail, the company revised its policy, but such an attitude is neither unique nor reassuring to critics of corporate monitoring.

Critics of monitoring span the political spectrum, ranging from William F. Buckley to former Senator Paul Simon. Indeed, Simon proposed a Privacy for Consumers and Workers Act that would, among other things, require employers to give employees prior written notice before each monitoring of their e-mail. Although such laws may not stop "Big Brother" cold, they may a least make some companies think twice about monitoring.

Federal laws are not the only way you can protect your privacy while working on a computer. If you are working with sensitive information that you do not wish co-workers to oversee on your computer monitor, you can install a privacy screen that restricts all but a straightforward view of the monitor.

Courtesy of 3M Safety and Security Systems Division.

Another important law, also passed in 1970, is the **Freedom of Information Act**. This law permits all citizens to have access to information about themselves that was collected by federal agencies. While the law was based on good intentions, some agencies are not terribly forthcoming. In some cases individual citizens have been able to gain access to their records only after filing lawsuits.

The most important privacy legislation passed by Congress is the 1974 **Federal Privacy Act**. This legislation was enacted to eliminate secret personal files. The act specifies that individuals and private contractors doing business with the federal government must be allowed to know the contents of their files, how the data are used, and how inaccurate data can be corrected. According to the law, any federal agency must have a justifiable reason for gathering information and maintaining it.

The Federal Privacy Act protects personal privacy at the federal level, but it does

One thing is certain—computer crime is illegal under all existing federal and state laws. A high percentage of computer crimes are so-called "white collar" crimes. It is well documented that computer criminals are mostly young, intelligent, well-educated, and technically competent company employees. Their employment positions range from low to high within the organization.

Four broad categories of computer crime have been identified: (1) sabotage, (2) accounting and financial crimes, (3) theft of computer equipment, and (4) theft of computer services.

not apply to state and local government agencies. Since the enactment of the Privacy Act of 1974, several state and local governments have enacted similar laws.

COMPUTER CRIME

Computer crime can be defined in various ways; it often depends upon whom you ask. Most computer terminology dictionaries often contain at least one, somewhat ambiguous, definition, such as, "a *computer crime* is an intentional act of misusing a computer system." Computer crimes can range from simple fraud schemes to violence. Although using computers to commit unauthorized acts is a crime, legally, the term is not yet well defined.

Congress and many state legislatures are still wrestling with how to define computer crime. In some cases, the term has been changed to "crime *by* computer," because computers do not commit crimes, people do.

SABOTAGE

The deliberate injury to or destruction of computer hardware or software is called **sabotage**. Saboteurs can hit a computer with a blunt object or electronically damage software by a using a magnetic device to erase data stored on magnetic tape or disks. Another form of sabotage is the much-publicized "computer virus." A **virus** is a computer program that alters or destroys programs and data. A virus is spread when a programmer purposely or accidentally transfers the virus to floppy disks or hard disks, or to a computer network, such as an electronic bulletin board. Some viruses can be programmed to remain dormant for a predetermined period of time. During this period, several people may copy the infected floppy disks or hard disks, or save messages (that include the virus program) they obtained from a network bulletin board, thereby spreading the virus. At some future time, the viruses activate themselves and destroy programs and data in the computer systems in which they reside.

Viruses can best be avoided by not copying material on a disk from an unreliable source. Keep backup copies of important programs and data in case a virus makes its way into the computer system.

As discussed in Chapter 8, special utility programs can be purchased that will check for viruses. Such programs are called **vaccines**. Examples of antivirus programs include Norton's AntiVirus (see Figure 13.7) and McAfee. These programs are effective in detecting and in erasing thousands of the most common types of viruses. New upgrade releases of antivirus software should be installed frequently because new viruses are introduced almost every day.

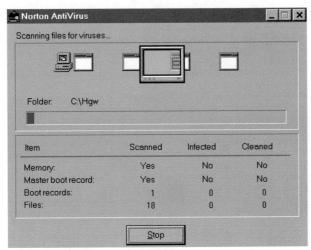

Figure 13.7

Norton's AntiVirus program.

Courtesy of Symantec.

ACCOUNTING AND FINANCIAL CRIMES

Some computer crimes are committed by employees who work in accounting and financial departments. Without adequate safeguards, these areas are ripe for potential misuse or embezzlement of funds.

Millions of dollars are lost to computer criminals each year in the United States. Less than 15 percent of these cases are prosecuted or well-publicized because of the adverse effect this information would have on shareholders and customers of the victimized organizations. Some financial crimes go unpunished because firms prefer to absorb losses rather than be exposed to bad publicity that reveals internal security weaknesses.

Internal financial crimes are also committed by programmers, systems analysts, and other data processing personnel. A programmer working with payroll or accounts payable systems may alter certain program statements to allow the programmer to steal fractions of a penny, which can eventually add up to thousands of dollars. This practice is known as **slicing**. The small amount of money "sliced" is then transferred to another account. The following example illustrates how slicing works.

Suppose you have a balance of $1,000 in a savings account. The bank pays 0.075 percent interest, which is calculated monthly. The formula for calculating your monthly interest is:

$$\$1,000 \times 0.075 \times 0.0833 = \$6.2475$$

Ordinarily, the bank will credit your account for $6.24 in interest. What happens to the remaining 75/100 of a cent? Usually, the bank keeps fractions of a penny. The computer program used to compute interest can be modified so that all fractions of a cent are deposited to a bogus account at the same or another bank. A large bank will process several thousand accounts each month, and the aggregate sum resulting from slicing may amount to huge sums. If the bank processed 100,000 accounts per month, each with a $1,000 balance, the effect of slicing would amount to $750 per month, or $9,000 per year. What would be the impact if the bank held one million accounts?

To help protect against such illegal activity, periodic system audits (discussed earlier) are carried out on all computer-based information systems. A thorough EDP audit should detect illegal activities within the organization. Accounting and financial crimes are among the most costly and potentially damaging of all computer crimes. They are also some of the most difficult to find.

THEFT OF COMPUTER HARDWARE

The theft of computer hardware may involve computers, peripheral devices, and other company property that is stolen or removed from computer-based systems. With the introduction of small, portable microcomputers and minicomputers, the incidence of computer theft has increased. A complete microcomputer system can easily fit into the trunk of a small automobile.

THEFT OF COMPUTER SOFTWARE

Software theft is perhaps the most serious and pervasive computer crime being committed today. Organizations using commercial software have a legal liability to protect that software manufacturer's programs from theft or duplication. Most software is stored on a magnetic storage medium, such as tape, disk, or floppy disk, and can be stolen and then copied for personal use or resale. The pirating and copying of computer software is a big business and one of the computer industry's biggest problems. Theft of software can also be accomplished via remote access to an organization's computer. The theft or copying of computer software is likely to continue to be a serious problem for organizations of all kinds.

THEFT OF COMPUTER SERVICES

All services available to computer users, including processing time and data storage, are called **computer services**. The theft of computer services is a fairly common practice in large organizations. It is especially easy to steal computer time in a time-sharing environment. Although most time-sharing systems require passwords for access to the computer, acquiring a password is relatively easy, especially for one familiar with the computer system. There are several well-documented cases in which computer services have been stolen by both employees and by persons outside the organizations. Also, many cases of computer services theft occur on college and university campuses where students are learning to use computers. Some students are challenged by so-called "secure systems" and try to break system security just to prove that it can be done.

The theft of computer services occurs at all organizational levels. Some organizations allow employees free personal usage of computer facilities at designated times. Other organizations strictly prohibit employees from using the organization's computers at any time.

Theft of computer services can be monitored and controlled by implementing and enforcing strict security measures. However, even with the strictest security measures in place, system security rests mainly on the honesty and integrity of the system users.

COMPUTER HACKING

The illegal entry into computer systems, regardless of the person's motive, is called **computer hacking**. Computer hackers seem to be challenged by the thrill of gaining entry into a computer system. Computer hacking has become widespread in recent years, and it has become a serious problem for organizations and for the computer industry in general. Some hackers seem content merely to view stored information, while others seem intent on altering or destroying stored information. When hackers are caught by the authorities, they are prosecuted.

Although computer crime is widespread, little is known about it, as evidenced by the very few reported cases. Fewer than 2,500 cases of computer crime have been reported in the past 40 years. This number is amazingly small considering the following statistics. In this country alone, there are more than 220,000 computer centers, with approximately 4 million people employed in all areas of computer operations, and almost 30 million microcomputers being used throughout the country. One can only speculate why the number of reported cases is so small. Evidence suggests that most cases of computer crime are not detected and, therefore, go unreported.

The number of reported cases has increased in recent years. Authorities believe this pattern of increasing crime will continue in the future. Reasons for this increase include:

1. More people are now using computers, thereby increasing the number of potential computer criminals.
2. A greater number of computers, including personal computers, are now in use, thereby increasing the potential number of computers available for committing crimes.
3. More data are now being processed by computers, thereby making more information vulnerable to potential criminals.
4. Advancements in technology exceed the development and implementation of security measures. The absence of effective safeguards makes it difficult to protect equipment and software.

REAL-LIFE COMPUTER CRIMES

Although it is not possible to mention all of the known computer crime cases, some cases are particularly noteworthy. Each case that follows represents a particular type of computer crime. Names have been omitted to ensure privacy.

The Attorney and Her Client An attorney was retained to represent a 24-year-old man accused of stealing microcomputers and printers from a university computer lab. After the jury found the man guilty, the judge imposed a fine on the man and sentenced him to 200 hours of community service. At the request of the man's attorney, the judge allowed the man to serve his community service time working as an assistant in his attorney's law office.

As part of his job, the new assistant was required to know the attorney's business account number at a local bank. He used a microcomputer in the attorney's office to transfer almost $90,000 from her business account into his personal account. Only part of the money was recovered.

The University Heist During the late evening hours of May 1, 1996, thieves broke into a computer lab at a state university in North Carolina and stole 32 laptop computers that had been stored in locked cabinets. The value of the computers was $77,291. Six days later, police arrested two men who faced felony charges of larceny and breaking and entering. Both men have confessed to the crimes.

Records revealed that one of the men was a former student of the university. According to the university's director of academic computing, security will be increased at all computer locations on campus. The director stated that plans for extra security inside computer facilities are being developed, particularly where laptop computers are housed.

The National Bank and the Bank Consultant A bank consultant posed as a bank employee and obtained a password that was carelessly taped to the wall above a computer terminal. Using this password, the consultant transferred $12 million into his personal account, withdrew the funds, traveled to Switzerland, and bought diamonds with the money. Soon afterward, he moved to Buffalo. One night after consuming several drinks, he told a friend about his exploits. The friend contacted the FBI. The man was arrested and sentenced to eight years in jail.

The Milwaukee Hackers In 1983, the FBI discovered a group of teenage hackers operating out of Milwaukee. While the evidence is incomplete, it is believed that the group broke into more than 60 business and government computers, including those at Los Alamos National Laboratory and the Sloan-Kettering Memorial Cancer Center in New York.

This case triggered interest in passing federal legislation to outlaw computer hacker activities and to provide stiff sentences for offenders. The irony surrounding this case was that local news media treated the teenagers as computer wizards rather than as criminals.

CRIME PREVENTION

Computer crime prevention requires that steps be taken to prevent computer crimes before they occur. The National Crime Information Center (NCIC) in Washington, D.C., provides information to more than 65,000 federal, state, and local law enforcement agencies.

Courtesy of Bank of America NT & SA.

Courtesy of Intuit, Inc.

Before computers, banking transactions, including deposits and withdrawals, were typically face-to-face transactions between a customer and the teller. Payments for credit accounts were made in a similar manner. Customers would often pay their bills by mail or visit company offices to pay for services such as telephone, electricity, and natural gas. Although these transactions were somewhat time-consuming, they offered a high degree of security for everyone involved in the transaction.

Today, many financial and business transactions are conducted using computers and the Internet with seemingly little concern for security. Some computer security companies have teamed up with credit card companies to provide greater security in the form of digital versions of credit, teller machines, library cards, drivers licenses, or anything else requiring identification. This new technology uses digital IDs containing digital signatures or certificates that identify the card's owner. The signatures are encrypted and work like a key to a safe deposit box. To open a box, two keys are needed—the customer's key, which fits the customer's box, and the bank employee's key, which fits a group of boxes. Information contained on a person's encrypted digital ID is known only to the company with whom the person is conducting business. Without this technology, someone else who might gain access to a user's credit card account number would be able to read or use the account.

The NCIC is a central collection and storage facility for crime data and for information received from all levels of government. Complex statistical models make it possible for the NCIC to plot criminal trends from historical data; to predict, with reasonable accuracy, when and where crimes might occur; and to identify persons who might be involved.

ETHICS IN THE COMPUTER FIELD

The term **computer ethics** refers to a person's conduct and behavior as a computer professional. Ethical standards, however, vary among individuals. A particular action may be considered wrong or unethical by some people, but considered acceptable by others. Differences of opinion concerning acceptable actions have resulted in controversy in the computer industry. As a result, many organizations and firms have taken steps to define acceptable behavioral standards for their employees. Also, several professional computer organizations require that their members agree to prescribed standards of ethical behavior. The Data Processing Management Association International (DPMA) requires that all of its more than 40,000 members sign a written statement that they will abide by the organization's code of ethics before they are approved for membership. Every new member is issued a certificate on which the organization's code of ethics is printed.

Other professional organizations, such as the Association for Computing Machinery (ACM), also have codes of ethics. Members who are found guilty of violating the code may be reprimanded or expelled by the organization.

Professional organizations usually prefer self-regulation. This approach is generally effective. Members regularly receive literature encouraging high ethical standards. Also, members attending professional meetings and conventions often hear papers on the subject of ethics.

Computer ethics extend beyond professional organizations to include everyone who uses computers. Just as you would not steal products from a company, you should not steal or misuse programs or data that belong to others. People who do so are a threat to society.

SOFTWARE PIRACY AND ILLEGAL COPYING

Some of the software people use is free; that is, programmers wrote the software with the intention of making it available to others at no cost. Free software is called **public domain software** or *freeware*. Such software is considered to be in the public domain and, therefore, can be used without violating copyright laws. Some software is distributed for free or with a minimal fee, with the proviso that if the user uses and likes the program, he or she will send a license fee to the programmer or company that developed the software. This kind of software is called **shareware**. However, much of the popular commercial software people use, such as Lotus 1-2-3, QuattroPro, or Microsoft Word, is protected by copyrights that have been granted to the software manufacturers. A **copyright** is the registration of a written expression of a creative idea with the U.S. Copyright Office in Washington, D.C. Software and computer programs have been eligible for copyrighting since 1964. Copyright registration enables individuals to litigate and sue for damages in the event of a violation of the copyright laws.

Legally, copyrighted software can be used only by the person who purchased the software. Most software firms allow (and even recommend) that the purchaser make one backup copy of their software in case the original copy becomes lost or damaged. Although it may be physically possible to make additional copies of copyrighted software, making these additional copies is illegal. The stealing of commercial software, usually by copying it, is called **software piracy**. Offenders can be sued by the software manufacturer.

Each year, billions of dollars in potential sales are lost by software vendors as a result of software piracy. Under no circumstances is it permissible to make duplicate copies of copyrighted software for distribution to another person. Doing so is a violation of federal copyright laws.

EMPLOYEE LOYALTY

Employee loyalty pertains to an employee's obligations to an employer. Employees often have access to confidential information. Employers expect workers not to divulge company secrets or any company-held information to anyone outside the organization.

INTERNET ISSUES

The Internet is still a relatively new resource, but its use is widespread. A number of concerns, problems, and issues are centered around the Internet and its use. Some of these are explained in this section.

PRIVACY

Some users falsely assume that any information transmitted across the Internet is confidential to the sender and receiver. This is not always true. Just as telephone messages and letters can be intercepted by other persons, other Internet users may intercept information you transmit across the Internet and may use the information in a malicious manner. The rule here is to carefully determine what kinds of information to send over the Internet.

PERSONAL INFORMATION

Because information may be intercepted by others, care should be taken when disclosing confidential information to another Internet user. For example, caution should be exercised when divulging credit card identification numbers and bank account information. There have been instances in which credit card numbers were intercepted by people who then used the numbers to order merchandise. In other cases, checking account information was intercepted and used to transfer funds into other accounts. A good practice is to avoid transmitting personal information over the Internet. A safer method is to place orders for merchandise in writing or over the telephone.

TRANSMISSION OF PORNOGRAPHIC MATERIALS

The transmission of pornographic materials, including text, photographs, and images over the Internet is a sensitive issue for many users. Legislation has been introduced in Congress that attempts to ban, or at least restrict, this practice. While some users believe that the transmission of pornographic materials should be banned, others argue that doing so violates the Constitutional guarantee of free speech. The issue is further complicated because the Internet is international. Any legislation that might be enacted by the U.S. Congress would not be enforceable in other countries. While the issue remains unresolved, users should exercise caution. Some information considered acceptable by the Internet user might be considered otherwise by other users. Using good judgment is a basic rule that should always be followed when using the Internet.

A FINAL THOUGHT

Computer security, privacy, crime, and ethics are largely a matter of common sense. As with all valuable possessions, common sense dictates that good judgment be exercised to protect computers, software, and data. For example, you should never give your friends or coworkers your password or access code.

Illegal copies of software is like counterfeiting—instead of copying money, the offender copies intellectual property.

Remember, even the best security measures will not prevent wrongdoing in the computer industry. The behavior of individuals is the ultimate test of a computer system's security.

FOCUS

Talk Is Cheap

About 20 years ago, some clever individuals learned how to use so-called "blue boxes" to illegally make free long-distance telephone calls. The blue boxes produced fake dialing tones in order to initiate calls.

Today, it's beige desktop computers that are causing problems for telephone companies. The "clever individuals" are computer users and, so far, what they're doing is legal.

Using inexpensive software, any computer can bypass the telephone company and send voice messages over the Internet, and do so at a very low cost. Several companies make and sell this Web-phone software, and some software packages are free over the Internet.

Without paying long-distance rates, a user with an Internet account, a sound card, speakers, and a microphone can make calls almost anywhere in the world to another user with the same software.

Although the sound quality is inferior and there are often long delays, more than 20,000 computer users regularly use the Internet for long-distance dialing, according to International Data Corporation, a computer consulting firm. As more software becomes available, the number of users is expected to grow significantly.

Telephone companies want federal authorities to regulate this practice. A group called America's Carriers Telecommunications Association (ACTA) has filed a petition with the Federal Communications Commission (FCC) insisting that Internet telephone services be subject to the same regulations as other long-distance telephone companies. The ACTA wants the FCC to halt the sale of Internet telephone software until a way has been devised to regulate it. The ACTA argues that companies selling the software are selling illegal telecommunications services. ACTA's spokesperson and general counsel, Charles Helein, argues that if Internet telephone service becomes widespread, it will lead to large reductions in the revenues of long-distance telephone companies and an overall decline in the quality of telephone service for all Americans.

ACTA has offered a recommendation that makers of Internet software be regulated as if they were telephone companies. This would mean the software makers would have to file rate plans and bill customers for the time they spent making calls on the Internet.

NetSpeak Corporation, located in Boca Raton, Florida, makes a software called WebPhone that lets one user call another user simply by typing in an e-mail address. NetSpeak's Vice-President of Product Development, Harvey Kaufman, argues that this method of communicating is not going to replace the conventional telephone. Kaufman further argues that Internet telephone products are not compatible. Both users would need the same software package.

Internet telephone products are constrained by the basic design of the Internet. All data going over are divided into tiny digital "packets." Data can travel to their destinations over thousands of different paths, and each packet can take a different path. When all packets reach their destination, the computer uses them to reassemble the message. Because packets may travel over different paths, there are often frequent and lengthy delays. While these delays may be acceptable with electronic mail messages, phone call delays may not be.

Peter Pratt, director of telecommunications at NetSpeak, has a different view of the problem. According to Pratt, voice traffic operates in real time and any delay in the delivery of a message must be minimal before the quality of

© 1996 Netspeak Corporation.

the message is degraded. Pratt doubts that many business customers will trust their important voice communications to the Internet any time soon.

IBM and others are more optimistic. IBM has stated that it will soon introduce its own Internet telephone product and NetscapeCommunications Corporation, which already makes the most popular Internet browser software, says it will include Web-phone software in future releases of its software.

Some of the large long-distance telephone companies are showing little concern. However, ACTA's Helein remains steadfast in his efforts to pressure the FCC into regulating makers of Web-phone software.

Source: *The Boston Globe*, March 10, 1996; "Ringing in the new: 'Net users find long-distance talk is cheap'," by Hiawatha Bray.

Key Terms

alternate computer facility	Fair Credit Reporting Act
cold site	Federal Privacy Act
computer crime	Freedom of Information Act
computer ethics	hot site
computer hacking	internal security measures
computer privacy	log
computer security	password
computer security group	public domain software
computer services	sabotage
copyright	shareware
data encryption	shredder
data security	slicing
detection devices	software piracy
disaster recovery consortium	surge protector
disaster recovery plan	vaccines
employee loyalty	virus

Summary

Four broad issues facing the computer industry, businesses, and other organizations are computer security, privacy, crime, and ethics.

Computer security refers to the physical protection of computer hardware, software, tape reels, disk packs, source documents, documentation manuals, computer files, and computer programs. Many organizations have formed **internal computer security groups** to formulate policies and procedures. A **disaster recovery plan** is a written plan for restoring computing operations back to normal in the event of major damage or destruction. An effective plan should provide for an **alternate computer facility**. A **hot site** is a fully equipped computer center. A **cold site** is an empty facility. A **disaster recovery consortium** is a joint venture in which the member organizations commit funds, equipment, and personnel toward the establishment of a separate computer facility.

Internal security measures protect computer hardware and software. Security measures include **detection devices**, **passwords**, **data encryption**, and **decryption**. Other measures include properly disposing of computer waste, file and data logs, and EDP audits; the separation of employee duties, software and data protection; and the screening of job applicants.

Computer privacy refers to controlling electronic personal and confidential information. The **Fair Credit Reporting Act** gives individuals access to their credit records and the right to challenge any information contained in them. The **Freedom of Information Act** permits citizens to access information collected by federal agencies. The **Federal Privacy Act** bans secret personal files kept by federal agencies.

Four categories of **computer crime** are (1) sabotage, (2) accounting and financial crimes, (3) theft of computer equipment, and (4) theft of computer services.

Sabotage is deliberate injury or destruction to computer hardware or software. A **virus** is a computer program that can alter or destroy programs and data. Computer viruses are spread via contaminated floppy disks, electronic bulletin boards, and computer networks. Special computer programs, called **vaccines**, are available for detecting and curing a virus.

Accounting and financial crimes are frequently committed, resulting in large monetary losses. **Slicing** is the act of transferring fractions of cents into a separate account.

Computer hardware and software theft is a growing problem in our society. **Computer hacking** is the illegal entry into other computer systems, regardless of the motives. One who engages in this practice is known as a computer hacker.

Computer crime prevention involves steps designed to prevent computer crimes before they occur. The **National Crime Information Center (NCIC)** in Washington, D.C., provides information to more than 65,000 law enforcement agencies around the country and uses computers and complex statistical programs to predict the occurrence of crimes.

Computer ethics refers to a person's conduct and behavior as a computer professional. Several professional computer organizations have, and enforce, a strict code of member ethics. **Software piracy** is the illegal copying of copyrighted software. A **copyright** is the legal registration of a person's written products with the U.S. Copyright Office in Washington, D.C. Some software, called **public domain software**, is free for public use. **Shareware** is software that is initially free or low-cost but for which the user should pay a license fee if he or she decides to keep and use the program. **Employee loyalty** pertains to an employee's moral and legal obligations to an employer.

With the increasing popularity of the Internet, some issues have emerged. Some important issues are privacy, the dissemination of personal information, and the transmission of pornographic and offensive materials.

14 Easy steps to being a webmaster

STEP 13 | INTERACTIVE FORMS

CGI is the "common gateway interface" that allows web pages to interact with computer applications that are not directly attached to the Web. One language frequently used to do the background processing is Perl. Others are C, C++, Visual Basic™, and Java™. In this step, we will develop a form for web users to send you comments through a program called *FormMail*. The address of the CGI script for your web site administrator to download for common use is http://worldwidemart.com/scripts.

A **form** is an html command composed of control information and *containers* for information entry by the user. Each html body may have multiple *forms*, each with its own control information. Control information specifies action, method and encoding type. The **action** is a URL of a CGI application to handle the form data. The **method** identifies the means of sending the request as either *get* or *post*; e-mail uses post. We will use the default encode type.

The form body is composed of one or more containers, or *input element*, for user entry of information. Each input element has a name, called the *field*, and the information entered is called the field's *value*. These field-value pairs, along with other control information are inserted within <form> and </form> commands. If a value is defined, it is the default for the field unless the user enters other information. The *input elements* are:⌐

Input Element	Usage
Checkbox	Identifies a yes/no alternative that is independent of other input elements.
Edit box	Identifies user-defined data entry locations. An edit box definition includes name, screen size, and maximum length in characters (maxlength). A default value can be named.
Password	A text box that displays asterisks instead of the actual text entered.
Radio button	Identifies multiple alternatives from which one is selected. Each alternative has a name-value pair in the code.
Reset button	Identifies a button that, when pressed, causes all form controls to be reset to their default states.

Select	Provides a selection box with a list of items displayed as a drop-down list box. May include a size for the number of items visible on the screen. Must include a number of options that identify the list contents. Unless the multiple attribute is specified, a single list selection is allowed.
Submit button	Identifies a button that, when pressed, sends the form to the URL defined in the action attribute of the form statement.
Text area	Identifies a drop-down box area for users to enter multiple lines of text or data. The number of rows and columns specify the size of the box and allowable entry size.
Type=hidden	Identifies an attribute of a field such that the value is not shown on the screen but is available to CGI.

Figure 13.8 is the html for creating a simple form for user feedback. You might customize this wherever "yourname" or "yourhost" appears, or you might create your own. Notice that formatting on the screen is predefined for the body and automatic for the submit/reset buttons. Conventionally, we place user-identification information first, the body of the form next, and the reset and submit buttons at the bottom of the form. Figure 13.9 shows the resulting Netscape screen.

Figure 13.8

General form for
e-mail feedback.

```
<html><title>Please send feedback</title>
<body><form method-post action="http://www.host.edu/cgi-bin/formmail.pl">
<input type=hidden name="recipient" value="yourname@yourhost.edu">
<input type=hidden name="subject" value="Web page feedback">
<input type=hidden name="redirect" value="http://www.yourhost.edu">
<pre>
Name:        <input name="realname" type="text" size="20" maxlength="30"><br>
Email:       <input name="email" type="text" size="20" maxlength="30"><br>
Comments:
<textarea name="comments" rows="10" cols="50">Comments entered
here.</textarea>
<br><br></pre>Enter a single word summary of the pages:<select name="oneword"
size="5">
<option>Awesome<option>Great<option>Average<option>Boring<option>Awful</
select>
<input type="submit" value="send the Feedback">
<input type="reset">
</form></body></html>
```

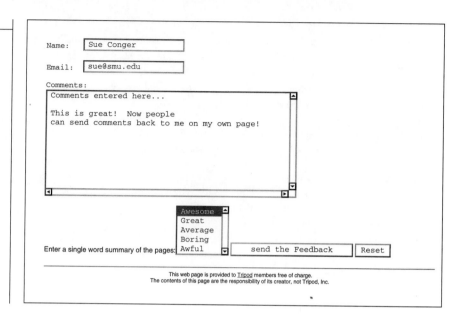

Figure 13.9

Netscape e-mail
feedback screen.

ASSIGNMENT: Create a form for web users to give you comments. Add company name, contact, and e-mail fields for you to contact them. Link it to your web pages and upload it to your site.

Exercises

REVIEW QUESTIONS

1. Why is computer security important, and why do computer facilities and resources need to be protected?

2. Why do many large organizations form security groups to deal with computer security?

3. What is a disaster recovery plan, and of what value is it in dealing with a disaster?

4. Identify some specific security measures an organization can take to protect computer resources.

5. Identify some steps a person can take to protect a microcomputer system.

6. Identify some federal laws that were passed to protect individuals' privacy.

7. Explain the term *computer crime* and identify some specific kinds of computer crimes.

8. What is a computer virus? What is a "vaccine"?

9. What is computer hacking and why is it illegal?

10. Explain the meaning of "computer ethics." Why is this an important issue in the computer field?

FILL IN THE BLANKS

1. An internal task responsible for computer security is called a _____.

2. A _____ plan exists for restoring computer operations in the event of a disaster.

3. A _____ is a joint venture whereby a group of organizations commit funds, equipment, and personnel to the establishment of a separate computer facility.

4. An empty facility or site in which an organization, or group of organizations, can install a complete computer facility is called a _____.

5. The term _____ refers to the protection of data from accidental or malicious destruction, disclosure, or modification.

6. _____ means coding data so that only the person receiving the data can decode them.

7. The term _____ refers to controlling personal and confidential information and controlling how and when the information is communicated to other parties.

8. The _____ Act allows you access to your credit record and gives you the right to challenge any data contained in your record.

9. A computer _____ is a computer program that is a particularly dangerous form of program that alters or destroys programs and data.

10. _____ refers to a person's conduct and behavior as a computer professional.

MATCHING

Match each term with its description.

a. computer security
b. disaster recovery plan
c. hot site
d. computer crime
e. password
f. computer hacking
g. data security
h. DPMA

i. virus
j. vaccine
k. encryption
l. sabotage
m. computer privacy
n. detection device
o. cold site

___ 1. Plan for restoring computing operations back to normal in the event of a disaster.

___ 2. Empty facility in which an organization can install a complete computer facility.

___ 3. Refers to the physical protection of computer hardware, peripherals, and software.

___ 4. Complete backup facility.

___ 5. Can recognize voice or fingerprint.

___ 6. Process of coding data.

___ 7. Special word, code, or symbol used to gain acess to a computer.

___ 8. Protection of data from destruction, disclosure, or modification.

___ 9. Potentially destructive computer program.

___ 10. Computer program that detects and destroys a virus.

___ 11. Intentional act to misuse a computer system.

___ 12. Professional organization that requires members to abide by a code of ethics.

___ 13. Deliberate injury or destruction to computer hardware or software.

___ 14. Illegal entry into computer systems.

___ 15. Refers to controlling personal and confidential information and to how the information is communicated.

 **ACTIVITIES**

1. Visit your school library and browse through several computer magazines and journals. Find and read articles concerning computer security, privacy, crime, and ethics. Prepare a written bibliography of these articles, with a brief summary for each entry.

2. Prepare a list of steps that can be taken in the computer lab at your school to protect computer equipment, including microcomputers. Which steps have been implemented and which have not?

3. What would be the effect if someone gained access to files at the Social Security Administration in Washington, D.C., and erased your record? Make a list of actions you would need to take to convince the Administration that you are a citizen who has already paid money into the Social Security fund.

4. Find and read some articles about hackers who have illegally accessed government computer systems. Do you think the penalties they received were too lenient or too severe? Explain your reasoning.

5. Do you think it should be illegal for magazines to sell your name, address, and telephone number to another company?

6. Assume you recently finished developing a new commercial software package. What measures would you take to prevent illegal copying?

7. Do you think it should be illegal for your employer to examine your e-mail?

Skills for Living

COMPUTER CRIME IN AMERICA

As digital technology has advanced over the last 20 years, people and society have been affected immeasurably. Improvements in computer abilities and capacities are somewhat obvious. However, this restructuring of society also has had disadvantages. Our collective exposure to computer crime increased dramatically. Increased opportunities for the criminal minds also come with the territory. The Web supplies our window to better understand this phenomenon.

The term "computer crime" is not well defined. It does, however, include such areas as electronic intrusions into telephone systems and computer networks, electronic privacy, software piracy, and crimes where the computer plays a major role in committing the offense.

How widespread is computer crime in America? One survey of computer crime in corporate America showed that over 90 percent of the companies surveyed had been victims and a third of the companies said it had happened to them at least 25 times. Common computer crimes included credit fraud, personal use of computers by employees, unauthorized access of computer files, and copying of copyrighted software. Most crime comes from employees, not from outsiders. If you're computer literate, you can commit computer crime. Global estimates of the annual cost of computer crime—over $8 billion!

Some Computer Crime Examples

- A Russian computer hacker in St. Petersburg taps into a New York bank and removes millions.
- A 17-year-old boy in Seattle crashes a local library computer system—twice!
- A California bank cashed a customer's $95,000 junk-mail "Mickey Mouse" check deposited in an automatic teller machine. The customer quickly removed the funds from his account and moved away.
- One of the FBI's most wanted computer criminals had stolen software from cellular-phone companies, caused millions of dollars in damage to computer systems, and even tapped FBI agents' calls.

Today's cybercops are being issued badges, guns, laptops, high-speed modems, cellular phones, and cryptography textbooks in their escalating fight against cybercriminals.

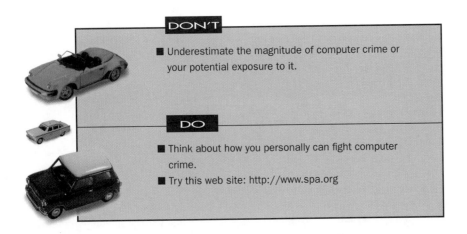

DON'T

■ Underestimate the magnitude of computer crime or your potential exposure to it.

DO

■ Think about how you personally can fight computer crime.
■ Try this web site: http://www.spa.org

Student Activities

1. You are doing a course paper on "Computer Crime in America." Use the Internet to collect data on this topic. What sources did you find, what data did you find, what are the major crimes being committed, and what trends are emerging?

2. The Software Publisher's Association (SPA) is a computer industry organization that focuses on computer crime. Find out what this group does and how. Write up a one-page description of the SPA and its services.

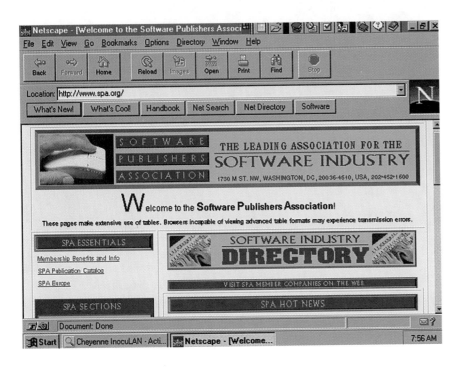

14

OBJECTIVES

AFTER STUDYING THIS CHAPTER, YOU SHOULD BE ABLE TO:

1. Identify and describe the three key building blocks in the national information infrastructure (NII).
2. Discuss the concept and implications of the computer industry's being referred to as the "30/30 industry."
3. Explain what a computer utility is and list its benefits.
4. Define an open system framework and why it is beneficial.
5. Describe what new computer capabilities will be available with the advent of 64-bit microprocessors.
6. List the major career opportunities in the computer field.
7. Identify the major trends in compensation and career growth areas.
8. List the major professional organizations in the computing field.
9. Describe the professional certification programs available in professional computing.
10. Describe an effective job search process and how your academic training and computer skills can help you.

CHAPTER OUTLINE

THE WAVE OF THE FUTURE

A QUICK REVIEW OF THE NII

COMPUTING IN THE NEXT DECADE
   Look for "Computer Utilities"
   Open Systems
   Self-Governance
   More Powerful PCs
   At the Office
   Changes in Society

CAREERS IN THE COMPUTER FIELD
   Evolution of the Information
    Systems Department
   Career Opportunities in an Information
    Systems Department
   Other Computer-Related Career
    Opportunities

COMPENSATION AND GROWTH AREAS

PROFESSIONAL ORGANIZATIONS
   Data Processing Management Association
    (DPMA)
   Association for Computing Machinery (ACM)

PROFESSIONAL CERTIFICATION

THE JOB SEARCH PROCESS
   Be Informed, then Be Prepared
   Planning the Job Search Process
   Using Your Computer in the Job Search
    Process
   Creating a Personal Portfolio

IN CONCLUSION

Previously you learned about computerized kiosks and touchscreens. Chances are you will come in contact with more and more touchscreens in the next few years.

Walk into a new mall and use the touchscreen in the information kiosk. In just three touches, it can help you not only locate a specific store (as well as show you a list of similar stores), but will also "walk" you to it via animate "footsteps" that trace a path from the kiosk to the store.

Next try out the kiosk at the Florsheim shoe store. Touch the screen a few times, run your credit card through the built-in scanner, and your shoes are on their way to your home. Better still, there are no bulky packages to haul around with you for the rest of the day.

In the pharmacy section at the Eckerd Drug outlet in the mall, another kiosk stands ready to supply you with information on a vast range of health care topics, from how to take a particular drug to what kinds of lifestyles appear to be healthiest. In the cosmetics aisle, touch the Clarion screen, and it will tell you the best shades of make-up to use for your coloring.

Also, in Chapter 6, you learned about smart cards, those credit-card-like pieces of plastic that are embedded with a memory chip and microprocessor. These electronic components enable each smart card to store the equivalent of up to 30 typewritten pages of data.

As amazing as these smart cards are, there's an even more amazing storage device in the offing: optical cards. Although optical cards also look like credit cards, they use compact disk technology rather than computer memory chips to store information, and they are thus capable of embedding the equivalent of 2,000 pages of data. For an application such as medical records storage, this expanded capacity makes optical cards the wave of the future for health care. Soon you could be carrying an optical card in your wallet to help physicians and emergency room personnel speed up the process of providing you with medical care.

While smart cards store some health care information—such as a patient's blood type, inoculation records, and health insurance coverage—most people's complete medical records wouldn't fit on a smart card. Visuals such as x-rays and ultrasound pictures take up far too much "room" in digital terms to include even one on a smart card. With optical cards' massive storage capacity, they have plenty of room to include x-rays, electrocardiograms, and other visual information.

At present, the cost of optical card systems is a major deterrent to their use. However, given the trend for computer and electronic equipment prices to fall sharply and rapidly, the price barrier to widespread optical card use may not remain for long.

In the future, technologies such as touchscreens and optical cards will be completely ingrained in your everyday routine. Computer-related jobs of today and tomorrow that support these technologies and how to prepare for them are the focus of this chapter.

THE WAVE OF THE FUTURE

This textbook has been devoted to teaching you about computer information systems and how they are being used by individuals and organizations. With advances in technology and the development of new hardware and software, computers will continue to impact people's lives in many more ways. In this chapter, we will discuss ways that computers might affect your future. We will discuss computer-related career opportunities and identify sources of additional career information. As you read this chapter, you will see that the future of computing offers many exciting and interesting opportunities.

A QUICK REVIEW OF THE NII

In order to understand where we might go in the future, let's review some basic concepts that were presented in Chapter 2.

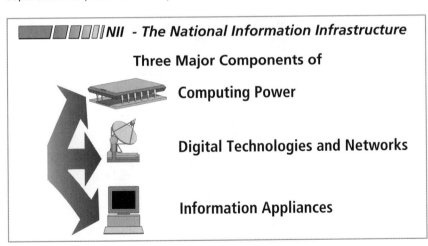

NII - The National Information Infrastructure

Three Major Components of

Computing Power

Digital Technologies and Networks

Information Appliances

Figure 14.1

- The three building blocks of the National Information Infrastructure (NII) are computing power, digital technologies/networks, and personal information appliances (see Figure 14.1).
- For the last ten years, the computing industry has been referred to as the "30/30 industry." Each year computer power gets 30 percent faster and 30 percent less expensive. Prices drop, yet performance improves.
- Connections between computers in the NII will be made through networks sending primarily digital signals. Because normal, voice-grade phone lines cannot handle the data volume required by some of these applications, fiber optic cable and special-purpose digital lines will be installed.

■ Information appliances are personal input/output devices that plug into these networks. Access to networks is through mainframe and personal computers, mobile and stationary telephones, television sets, and special purpose connection devices such as pagers, credit card terminals, or specialized wristwatches.

■ Think of computer applications in terms of two categories. Intra-system computer applications focus on connecting components within an organization's system. Inter-system computer applications connect an organization's system to other systems outside of the organization.

■ Computers and information technologies are enablers. Enablers allow us do work that was not possible before.

With this background, let's look to the future.

Paul Barton/The Stock Market.

Courtesy of Intuit, Inc.

Before computers, money management and bill paying was a time-consuming and tedious process. Records had to be kept for verification and income tax purposes, resulting in massive and unorganized recordkeeping. Long-term investment strategies were difficult to make.

Computers, modems, and software provide relatively painless home banking and personal money management capabilities. Monthly bills can be authorized and then automatically deducted from your checking account. All transactions are stored in organized categories for tax and budgeting purposes. Money management and investement analysis become simpler, more accurate, and more thorough.

COMPUTING IN THE NEXT DECADE

There appears to be no limit for the underlying forces that drive today's computing technology. Most established trends will continue; expansion of processor speeds, storage capacities, communication transfer rates, capabilities, and so on, will continue. The question is then, what new applications will this growth spawn?

Research is under way to develop dense storage capabilities, with hundreds of times greater capacity than the current model's. If successful, the entire Library of Congress book collection (15 million volumes) could be stored on a disk the size of a penny! At the MIT Media Lab, in a project called "Things that Think," scientists are applying technology to inanimate objects. For example, your tennis shoe might contain a microprocessor.

Figure 14.2

Computer Utilities
Self Governance
Open Systems
At The Office
Changes In Society
More Poerful PCs

Suppose you meet another person equipped with the same "Things that Think" unit in her tennis shoe. You shake hands. A low-voltage electrical field transfers your name, employment data, photo image, and even a video clip to the other person's shoe, and vice versa. At the end of the day, you simply download your shoe into your home computer personal database and update your personal contacts list. More importantly, what will the shoe do for your basketball game?

Below are six factors that will likely influence future information technology developments in the next ten years (see Figure 14.2).

LOOK FOR "COMPUTER UTILITIES"

In the 1970's computing was mainframe-based. All work centered around centralized computing power. In the 80's that all changed, via the PC, and we moved to decentralized computing. Now, with the evolution of the NII and connectivity, there is a strong possibility of moving back to centralized computer utilities.

Due to revisions and technological advances, PCs and software are obsolete weeks or months after you purchase them. One way to combat this problem would be to create a centralized computer utility, much like a central utility for water or power. Current client-server systems are the beginnings of centralized computer utility, but they are primarily used for intra-organizational applications. The Internet is the first step toward inter-organizational computing and national computer utilities.

Could we not house the latest versions of hardware capabilities and application software packages on one public, centralized system and then individually use that resource for a small fee? Everyone would have access to the latest and greatest computer capabilities. Capability would not be based on how much you can afford to pay for your own personal hardware and software. Colleges and universities would use the utility in order to no longer have the financial burden of building and maintaining PC labs, continuously replenishing them with the newest hardware and software.

These utilities could be accessed by low-cost, "dumb" terminals that simply send and receive user requests. Complicated processing would occur at the utility. Increased capability, ease of use, and lower costs will fuel the development of utilities.

Some signs of the shift to utilities have already occurred. Microsoft recently reshuffled its products and platforms division. What evolved was a new framework that shifted emphasis away from the Windows 95 operating system and toward efforts to provide new content and tools for the Internet. These new products will extend to other users, creating an open systems (access to all) framework for new products. The company is also developing a new Internet appliance device called a network computer or NC, to be used for remote computing. This inexpensive (less than $500) stripped-down computer will be a specialized personal appliance used almost exclusively for Internet applications.

OPEN SYSTEMS

Computing standards promote efficient computing, but they can also create barriers. Apple Computer built standards for its operating system, but was unwilling to share them with others in the industry. IBM, on the other hand, pursued an open architecture with its PC. As a result, many other manufacturers cloned the IBM system. This encouraged competitors to work efficiently to deliver a high-quality, low-cost product to the market. Currently, IBM-type systems share over 90 percent of the computer market. Open systems strategies created this near-monopoly. **Open systems** are common industry standards and protocols created to support joint development efforts.

Massachusetts congressman Edward J. Markey and Vice President Al Gore were instrumental in requiring manufacturers to place V-chips in all new television sets. The technology allow parental control of TV broadcasts.

Courtesy of Congressman Edward J. Markey.

SELF-GOVERNANCE

Watch for more industry self-governance. Censorship of the Internet is a topic of discussion today. Consumer groups line up on each side of the argument. Finally, the government is forced to enact legislation to control the issue. In the future, we will see all three industries try to develop self-regulating polices to address issues. Special software and programmable chips are being developed for use by parents to monitor and control content of television programs delivered to the home. Privacy and cryptography will grow into major issues. Rating systems are being established for entertainment software.

Again, the consumer and government will drive the changes required, if the industry does not.

MORE POWERFUL PCS

In the next ten years, the entire PC industry will turn to the 64-bit microprocessor. Currently these microprocessors are available at a cost between $7,500 and $2 million. Remember, computing is the "30/30 industry" (30 percent faster and 30 percent less expensive each year). In a few years 64-bit microprocessors will be affordable. Key application areas for the new microprocessors will be processing data-intensive application areas such as virtual reality, multimedia, artificial intelligence, scientific computing, and workgroup collaboration tools (video conferencing, etc.). Currently most hardware and software vendors have plans to adopt this technology.

Intel, Hewlett-Packard, and Digital Equipment Corporation (DEC) either have built or are building such products. DEC now uses this architecture in its current 64-bit Alpha chip. Sun Microsystems Computer Company builds 64-bit workstations for engineers and designers. Microsoft is planning new operating systems that will take advantage of the enhanced power of this chip.

A 64-bit chip is not twice as fast as the current 32-bit chip, but at least ten times faster! This speed increase is due to how the chip accesses main memory. Older technologies accessed 8 to 16 megabytes of main memory. Current 32-bit microprocessor chips can access up to 4.2 gigabytes of main memory. 64-bit machines have virtually no upper limit on the size of main memory access. Thus, huge databases that were originally stored in small segments and read from hard drives can now be completely loaded into primary memory for instantaneous access. No more time-consuming searches and retrievals.

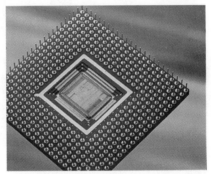

The digital Alpha chip.

Courtesy of Digital Equipment Corporation.

Wall Street uses 64-bit machines to do complex financial stock analyses. NASA combined four 64-bit processors to handle data from deep space exploration and cosmic fossil analysis to evaluate the "Big Bang" theory of how the universe was created. Imagine the new opportunities and products that will be available on the Internet when 64-bit computing becomes generally available. Enterprising students, employees, and employers should be quick to learn and apply computer applications that use this new technology.

AT THE OFFICE

Now and in the future, the goal of organizations is "frictionless business"—minimizing the time, cost, and resources necessary for a project's completion. Ten years ago people used typewriters to develop documents and the U.S. Post Office to deliver them. Today we use programs to integrate word processing, spreadsheets, and graphics into documents and then send them via e-mail.

Office integration will continue to occur, but at higher levels. Networks will connect the office to its environment. Rather than send documents out, we will simply bring people together for an electronic discussion. Participants will share presentations and insights, and a group decision and implementation plan will be formulated. If other data or resources are needed, the Internet can be searched during the meeting for additional information and insights about the topic.

CHANGES IN SOCIETY

For the NII to work, everyone must have access. The NII offers new opportunities for some and a richer life for many. Small companies can compete head-to-head with larger companies. Size and image are hidden via the cloak of communications. Face-to-face office visits are unnecessary. The entire world can participate. The NII can break down some cultural and language differences among nations.

As we rely more and more on these systems, their strength and security must be improved. As with any infrastructure, if it is the backbone, it cannot break without dire consequences. Redundancy, cryptography, and computer crime prevention will be more important in the next ten years.

COMPUTER CURRENTS

Is a Wallet PC in Your Future?

Information appliances are small, specialized, inexpensive devices that link us with our environment. What better information appliance could there be than an electronic wallet or purse? Think of what you carry with you when you leave your home—money, credit cards, business cards, address book, appointment schedule, cellular phone, keys, etc. Can this be automated? Bill Gates, founder and CEO of Microsoft, thinks it can. He envisions a wallet PC in your future.

In his book *The Road Ahead*, Gates suggests this appliance will eliminate the need for a wallet and paper currency. The device, about the size of a regular wallet, will be wireless and connected to stores and banks. Payment will be made by debiting your account. While at meetings, you can receive e-mail, send messages, take notes, check your schedule, make a plane reservation, or order presents for your childrens' birthdays.

The wallet PC is the ultimate traveling companion. In a strange city, you never get lost. The unit can access a global geographical information system, showing your current coordinates and the best route to take to your destination. It can monitor traffic conditions and accept voice commands. It can make reservations at your favorite restaurant. While you are away, it will monitor your home's heating and electrical systems, notify the post office to hold your mail, and pay bills automatically. Should you need help, it will even emit a loud shrill or whistle! What will it cost? That has not yet been determined.

Courtesy of Microsoft Corporation.

CAREERS IN THE COMPUTER FIELD

With technological advancements in areas such as multimedia, virtual reality, artificial intelligence, green computing, and the Internet, it is clear that there are many exciting career opportunities in computer-related fields. In addition, opportunities to find a rewarding career in more traditional computer positions, such as working in an information systems department or selling computer-related products, are also excellent.

EVOLUTION OF THE INFORMATION SYSTEMS DEPARTMENT

How computers are used within a business has changed dramatically over the years. During the late 1950s through the mid 1960s, computers were primarily used in business to process financial information, such as accounts receivable, accounts payable, and payroll. Consequently, computer equipment and staff were usually a part of an accounting department and under the direction of a financial manager such as a controller or a vice president of finance.

In the late 1960s and 70s, the use of computers spread throughout organizations. Management and employees in departments such as marketing and production found ways to increase productivity by using various computer applications. During this time, many companies created separate computer departments. These departments were given titles such as the Department of Information Systems or Computer Information Systems. These departments provided support for users within an organization.

In the 1980s and 90s, the use of microcomputers and advances in communications and software brought computers onto the desktops and into the hands of employees. While most employees continued to depend on the information systems department to provide certain information services (such as maintaining the corporate database), employees became increasingly responsible for providing their own computer solutions. Today, information systems departments continue to service the entire organization and, in addition, usually provide user support and training to meet the computer needs of individual employees.

CAREER OPPORTUNITIES IN AN INFORMATION SYSTEMS DEPARTMENT

The top position within an information systems department is the **vice president of information systems**, sometimes called the **chief information officer (CIO)** or the **director of information systems**. This individual is responsible for the overall operation of the information systems department and usually reports directly to the president of the company (see Figure 14.3).

Reporting to the vice president of information systems are managers responsible for the various areas within an information systems department. These areas include

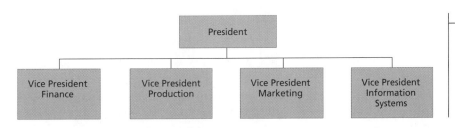

Figure 14.3

Today, information systems departments play a large role in organizations with top management reporting directly to company presidents.

computer operations, systems analysis, application programming, technical support, data communications, and the information center. The table below lists these areas and gives a brief explanation of the main responsibilities in each area.

Groups Within an Informations Systems Department	
Group	**Responsibilities and Duties**
Computer Operations	Has responsibility for the operation and maintenance of the main computer system.
Systems Analysis	Analyzes, designs, and implements computer information systems.
Applications Programming	Writes and maintains computer application programs, such as payroll, inventory, and accounts receivable.
Technical Support	Maintains system software and databases.
Data Communications	Implements and maintains computer networks and communications software.
Information Center	Coordinates computer education and provides support for the users in an organization.

The chart in Figure 14.4 shows the organization of a typical information systems department. Each of the positions shown on the organization chart is discussed in the sections that follow. Be aware that job titles and job descriptions vary among organizations.

Figure 14.4

This organizational chart gives you an idea of how an information systems department might designate job responsibilities amongst employees. Structures vary, however, from organization to organization, depending on their needs.

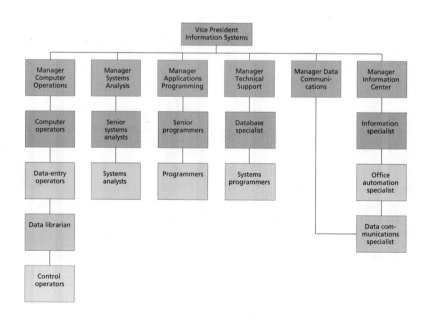

Computer Operations The employees who work in **computer operations** are responsible for the operation and maintenance of the main computer system and for the processing of data on that system to provide information for users throughout an organization. Various computer specialists do their work in or near the computer room where the main computer system is usually housed. Some of these specialists include the manager of computer operations, computer operators, data-entry operators, data librarians, and control specialists.

Systems Analysis
Systems analysis is the art and science of analyzing users' information needs and devising a plan using computer equipment, people, and procedures to meet those needs. Specific activities include gathering and analyzing data about existing systems to determine their effectiveness, recommending changes to existing systems, and designing and implementing new systems. The number of analysts employed by an organization depends on the organization's size and information needs.

Most systems analysts have college degrees and programming and business experience. Also, a systems analyst should have excellent listening and speaking skills in order to establish and maintain a good rapport with users.

Applications Programming
Application programs perform data processing or computational tasks that solve an organization's specific problems. An **applications programmer** takes a system design prepared by a systems analyst and converts it into instructions for a computer to execute. Existing programs being used by an organization often need to be updated. For example, changes in social security (FICA) rates would necessitate changes in a payroll program. This type of program maintenance is often done by applications programmers.

Applications programmers should have a good command of the programming languages in which programs are written and have knowledge of programming methodology. Writing applications programs requires analytical and problem-solving skills. An applications programmer may choose to specialize as a business applications programmer or as a scientific applications programmer. The training and job requirements for these positions are quite different. To become a *business applications programmer*, a college degree is desirable, but not always required. Most employers prefer applicants who have completed courses in computer programming, business, and accounting. Sometimes employees in other areas of an information systems department, such as computer operations, are moved into programming and trained by the company to become programmers. Employers usually require *scientific applications programmers* to have college degrees and advanced course work in mathematics and computer science or engineering.

Technical Support
The **technical support** staff is responsible for system software and database systems support. Large computer installations may employ several technical support specialists, including systems programmers and database specialists.

The **systems programmer** is responsible for maintaining the system software, including the operating system and utility programs, and may also assume some programming responsibility for the database software. These programmers must have an in-depth knowledge of the hardware and system software being used. Employers typically look for applicants with college degrees in computer science and experience in systems programming.

Database specialists design and control the use of an organization's data resources. Responsibilities of the database specialist include developing and maintaining databases, developing database security, maintaining open communications, and assisting users in the effective use of databases. The position of database specialist usually requires a college education with an emphasis on course work in computer science and database design and structure. Many colleges offer courses that prepare students for careers in this field.

Data Communications Data communications systems allow for transfer of data between locations. The responsibility for maintaining these systems falls to **data communications specialists**. Data communications specialists are responsible for developing, implementing, and maintaining communications networks and the software that controls the flow of data among devices in the network.

With the rapid growth of today's network applications, the **network administrator** is among the fastest growing occupations in the computing field. The administrator manages the hardware, software, applications, communication linkages, and personnel elements of the network system. Novell and Microsoft's Windows NT are the two most popular network providers. Because of the importance and high visibility of networks, the network administrator shoulders enormous responsibilities and risks associated with the network's ultimate success or failure. Some colleges are now offering majors with an emphasis in the areas of data communications and network administration.

The Information Center In recent years, organizations haved moved away from centralized processing, where all data processing is done at one location, toward **distributed data processing**, where various users or departments within an organization possess and control their own computer hardware and software. Employees in these departments use their equipment to satisfy much of their own processing requirements. Frequently, these departmental computers are connected through communication lines to the larger centralized computer systems of the corporation. To provide training and support for users in a distributed data processing environment, companies are establishing information centers.

The **information center** consists of specialists who provide educational activities and support services for users. Two specialists commonly found in an information center are an information specialist and an office automation specialist.

Services provided by **information specialists** include conducting educational seminars and workshops, assisting users with the selection and use of microcomputer products, and helping users utilize corporate systems such as databases and e-mail.

An **office automation specialist** assists employees with the selection, installation, and use of office technology products. In addition to assisting with computer products such as microcomputers and software, this specialist is often involved in decisions to upgrade telephone systems and purchase office equipment such as fax machines and copiers.

Information center specialists must have strong backgrounds in microcomputer technology and enjoy working with people. These specialists must strive to stay knowledgeable about the latest products and technology.

OTHER COMPUTER-RELATED CAREER OPPORTUNITIES

In addition to career opportunities available in an information systems department, there are numerous employment opportunities related to computer products and services. Some of these include working for hardware and software vendors or educational institutions.

Hardware Vendors IBM, Apple, Hewlett-Packard, DEC, and other companies manufacture and sell computers and related equipment. These companies, called **hardware vendors**, employ specialists, called **customer representatives**, who call on customers to inform them about their companies' products. Customer representatives act as liaisons between hardware vendors and customers. Customer representatives should have good communication skills and enjoy working with people. Most have college educations with course work in both marketing and computers. Newly hired vendor representatives receive extensive on-the-job training to learn about their companies' products.

Software Vendors Companies that produce and sell software packages are called **software vendors**. These companies hire people with a variety of skills to produce, market, and sell their products, and to provide service to their customers.

Software and hardware come with user's manuals that describe how to install and use the products. **Technical writers** are hired by computer companies to write these manuals. With an increasing emphasis on user-friendliness, manuals need to be well-written and easy to understand. Technical manuals are often written in several different languages.

Education Another area of opportunity is in computer education. There is a growing need for **computer instructors** at all educational levels—elementary school, high school, college, and vocational school. In addition, the microcomputer has spawned a new kind of education in which private companies specialize in training users how to use microcomputer hardware and software. These companies offer one- to three-day training classes on topics such as how to use a specific word processor or spreadsheet package. The classes are taught by people who have an in-depth knowledge of the topic. Anyone who is a good instructor and possesses a thorough knowledge of the subject can teach these classes.

Webmaster As the Internet grows, organizations must learn to use this emerging network as part of their marketing and promotional efforts. People are needed to develop and manage web pages. Much like advertisers, these **Webmasters** combine text, sound, graphics, and video into an appealing and effective promotional medium for use on the Web.

As you can see, there are many excellent opportunities for a career in a computer-related field. With continued advances in technology, new career opportunities will continue to be created. Whether or not you choose a career directly related to computers, it is important to remember that you will probably use computers in whatever career you choose. The effort you make to understand and learn about computers will undoubtedly benefit you, whatever your career choice.

COMPENSATION AND GROWTH AREAS

Want to earn big money in computing? Then you should either go west or become a chief information officer (CIO). Compensation is based on the skills required by the job and the demand in the marketplace for those skills. Figure 14.5 shows the median annual salaries for a variety of information industry job classifications. The figures shown are for 1994, 1995, and estimated for 1996. In general, programmers and systems analysts' salaries have risen, while sales and some specialty area salaries have not.

Figure 14.5

Median Salaries for Information Industry Job Classifications

Job Classification	1994-1996* Median Annual Salary		
	1994	1995	1996
Business Programmer			
Mainframe Systems			
Junior Programmer	$32,000	$34,000	$36,000
Programmer/Analyst	$37,000	$40,000	$43,000
Senior Programmer/Analyst	$42,000	$43,000	$44,000
Midrange Systems			
Junior Programmer	$30,000	$33,000	$36,000
Programmer/Analyst	$35.000	$40,000	$45,000
Senior Programmer Analyst	$40,000	$42,000	$44,000
Microcomputer Systems			
Junior Programmer	$32,000	$35,000	$38,000
Programmer/Analyst	$40,000	$45,000	$50,000
Senior Programmer/Analyst	$45,000	$48,000	$51,000
Business Systems:			
Systems Analyst	$45,000	$49,000	$53,000
Consultant	$46,000	$50,000	$54,000
Specialty Areas:			
Database Analyst	$45,000	$51,000	$57,000
LAN Administrator	$40,000	$40,000	$40,000
End User Support			
PC Support Specialist	$35,000	$35,000	$35,000
PC Analyst	$41,000	$42,000	$43,000
Technical Writing			
Writer	$30,000	$33,000	$36,000
Writer Editor	$38,000	$40,000	$42,000
Systems Management:			
MIS Director/CIO			
Small/Medium Organization	$58,000	$60,000	$62,000
Large Organization	$70,000	$75,000	$80,000
Project Manager	$58,000	$61,000	$64,000
Team Project Leader	$50,000	$50,000	$50,000
Sales:			
Account Representative	$57,000	$55,000	$53,000
Technical Support	$41,000	$39,000	$37,000
Sales Management	$74,000	$75,000	$76,000

*Note: 1996 salaries are only projections.

Source: Source EDP, 1994, 1995 Computer Salary Survey

Compensation packages also vary by region. Figure 14.6 shows how programmers' salaries vary geographically. Salaries in San Francisco are the highest. Florida has the lowest-paid programmers. This disparity may reflect the differences in the cost of living between these two regions.

Figure 14.6

Programmers' Salaries by Geographic Location

1995

Location	Average Annual Salary	% of Average
San Francisco	$ 43,274	115.7%
Los Angeles	$ 42,569	113.8%
Washington, D.C.	$ 39,495	105.6%
New York	$ 38,191	102.1%
Boston	$ 34,955	93.5%
Chicago	$ 33,969	90.8%
Texas	$ 33,406	89.3%
Florida	$ 33,327	89.1%
Overall Average	**$ 37,398**	

Source: Datamation Magazine, October 1, 1995 Salary Survey

Figure 14.7 shows how those same programmer positions are compensated relative to other industry positions. Utilities and financial services rate the highest, while education ranks well below the $36,400 salary median.

Figure 14.7

Programmers' Salaries by Industry

1995

Industry Category	Average Annual Salary	% of Average
Transportation & Utility	$ 41,894	115.1%
Financial Services	$ 41,252	113.3%
Information Systems	$ 38,924	106.9
Medical/Legal	$ 36,514	100.3%
Construction/Mining/Agriculture	$ 36,000	98.9%
Government	$ 35,740	98.2%
Manufacturing	$ 35,503	97.5%
Retail	$ 35,143	96.5%
Other Services	$ 33,187	91.2%
Education	$ 29,840	82.0%
Overall Average	**$ 36,400**	

Source: Datamation Magazine, October 1, 1995 Salary Survey

Once you achieve the level of CIO, salaries mushroom. In 1995, the average CIO base salary in the U.S. was $122,000. A CIO in New York City made $193,000, while a CIO in Florida made about $90,000.

However, there are other important forms of compensation. Bonuses and incentive programs are a large part of IS compensation. These programs, linked to individual and organizational performance, include company stock, lump-sum payments, and travel vacations. As an extreme example of performance-based compensation, a 1995 survey of 35 of the largest companies in the United States (averaging sales of $20 billion) showed their chief executive officers' (CEOs) salaries jumped 23 percent to $4.37 million between 1994 and 1995. Yet, only $1 million was paid in salary. Based on company performance, the average CEO's stock payment was an additional $1.5 million and the average bonus payment was another $1.2 million.

FOCUS

Welcome to Bill's Place

Where does the richest man in the world live? Well, if you are Bill Gates, founder and chairman of Microsoft, you live in a "smart home" on the shores of Lake Washington, near Seattle.

When you enter the home, you are presented with an electronic pin to attach to your clothing. The pin tells the house who and where you are. It also tailors the home's environment to suit your particular needs and interests. If it is dark outside, the pin supplies you with a zone of moving light. Unoccupied rooms are left dark. Your favorite music will follow you as you move from room to room (it also shuts off when you leave a room). Should you receive a phone call while visiting, only the headset nearest you will ring. Favorite films and TV shows follow the guest from room to room.

The home is equipped with a database library of one million still digital images. Guests can call up sunsets, airplanes, ski slopes in the Andes, photos from history, or paintings by their favorite artists, and display them on the nearest closet wall.

The home is built into a hillside and is equipped with 100 microcomputers that drive personalized information systems. It also has an L-shaped swimming pool with an underwater sound system. Parking is adequate with a 20-car garage and room for 100 at the dinner table.

For those who can afford the technology, Gates foresees many new homes equipped with these features in the near future.

Courtesy of Microsoft Corporation.

When it comes time to fill a vacant position, companies would rather pay more for a new employee with a given skill-set than invest the time and effort needed to train current employees. Keeping up with technology changes and knowing how to use them are critical to a successful career.

According to figures from the U.S. **Bureau of Labor Statistics (BLS)**, the fastest growing information systems job classification is systems analyst. In 1992, there were 455,000 analysts. In 2005, that number is projected to be 956,000, a 110 percent increase. This job category is the second fastest-growing of all BLS job classifications, exceeded only by jobs in the field of residential health care, which are predicted to increase by 150 percent.

PROFESSIONAL ORGANIZATIONS

Several professional organizations exist to support professionals in the computer industry. The goals of these organizations include distributing industry-related information and providing training and educational opportunities to help members advance their careers. To achieve these goals, the organizations publish journals and conduct meetings and seminars. Two major organizations are the Data Processing Management Association (DPMA) and the Association for Computing Machinery (ACM).

DATA PROCESSING MANAGEMENT ASSOCIATION (DPMA)

The **Data Processing Management Association (DPMA)** was founded in Chicago in 1951 and was originally chartered as the National Machine Accountants Association. At that time, there were no commercial computers. Members operated and supervised activities associated with early punch-card equipment. The organization's original name was changed to Data Processing Management Association in 1962.

DPMA is an international organization with local chapters throughout the world. Membership extends to people at all levels of computer management. Through its meetings, publications, and programs, DPMA encourages its members to engage in scientific inquiry and share their knowledge with the organization and fellow members. There are several DPMA special interest groups. EDSIG is a group that has a special interest in education. Some local DPMA chapters sponsor student chapters at colleges and universities. Each year, the parent organization presents its "Person of the Year" award to the individual that makes the greatest contribution to the computer profession.

ASSOCIATION FOR COMPUTING MACHINERY (ACM)

The largest mathematical, scientific, and technical society in the computer profession was founded in 1947 as the **Association for Computing Machinery (ACM)**. ACM's charter identifies the association's three main objectives:

- To advance the science and art of information processing, including the study, design, development, construction, and application of modern machinery, computer techniques, and programming software.
- To promote the free exchange of ideas in the field of information processing in a professional manner between specialists and the public.
- To develop and maintain the integrity and competence of individuals engaged in the field of information processing.

Like DPMA, the ACM sponsors and supports special interest groups within its organizations. SIGSMALL is a special interest group for personal computer applications.

PROFESSIONAL CERTIFICATION

Professional certification is a way of recognizing that organization members have attained certain levels of knowledge about their profession. Although no states presently require that computing professionals be certified or licensed, licensing has been proposed by some groups.

The most widely recognized certification program in the computing industry is administered by the **Institute for the Certification of Computing Professionals (ICCP)**. The Institute is sponsored and supported by several professional organizations, including the DPMA. Prior to 1994, the ICCP offered four certification designations. The most well-known of these was the certified data processor (CDP). Other designations were certified computer programmer (CCP) and certified systems professional (CSP). Starting in 1994, all three designations were combined under one standard title, **certified computing professional (CCP)**. A separate designation, that of **associate computing professional (ACP)**, still exists for entry-level personnel.

To become a certified computing professional, candidates must pass both a core examination and an exam in two specialty areas.

Courtesy of the Institute for the Certification of Computing Professionals (ICCP).

To become certified, a CCP candidate must pass a core examination consisting of the following six parts:

1. Human and organization framework
2. Systems concepts
3. Data and information
4. Systems development
5. Technology
6. Associated disciplines

In addition to the core examination, the candidate must choose and pass examinations in two specialty areas. Specialty areas include management, systems analysis, systems design, business applications, languages, communications, and many others.

For ACP certification, the candidate must pass the core examination and one programming language test.

The **certified network administrator (CNA)** certification denotes proficiency in the areas of network products, service, and support. Students take courses in operating systems for networks, networking principles, hardware, systems administration, and installing network applications. Rigorous course testing and performance assessment assure compliance and completion of the educational material and provides employers with some assurance that this person has the knowledge required to successfully manage a network application.

THE JOB SEARCH PROCESS

Finding employment is an exercise in marketing yourself. You are the product and the company is your customer. When looking for a job, you need to plan the process, define the product, find the customer, sell the product, and close the sale.

BE INFORMED, THEN BE PREPARED

The final goal of this book is to inform you about securing a career in computing. Figure 14.8 shows a Gantt chart of the steps in the job acquisition process. This chart also gives guidelines as to when in your education you should begin each step.

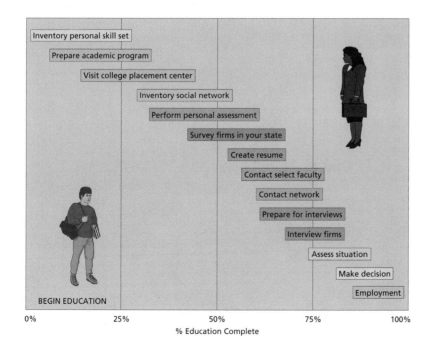

Figure 14.8

Finding a job that is right for you is a complicated task. By investigating options early in your college education, you'll have the groundwork laid for a successful career.

First, realize the work environment is constantly changing. Computers and technology change how work is done and thus redefine the technical skills you need to do the job. Organizations are also social in nature, made up of people joined together in various working relationships. People generally like to work with people they enjoy socially.

Figure 14.9

The new "Inverted" managerial pyramid.

First-Level Employees

Junior-Level Managers

Middle-Managers

Vice-Presidents

Top Management

Today, new management schools of thought such as total quality management, systems reengineering, total customer satisfaction, and employee empowerment, have changed the "boss's" role from that of isolated dictator to coach, mentor, and team leader. These changes create new work environments and social skill requirements for the employee. Presentation skills, listening, leadership, communications, group decision making, and implementation planning are helpful. Now the boss empowers others lower down in the organization and closer to the problem by using a team approach to find creative solutions for critical problems. This reverses traditional roles in the organization and is often referred to as the **upside-down managerial pyramid**. People traditionally at the bottom of the pyramid (but closest to the customer) hold new power and importance in the firm (see Figure 14.9).

Typically there is a high turnover in first professional employment choices for college students (up to 50 percent leave their first "real job" within a year) because of disillusionment and disappointment. Often, the student is unable to integrate personal motives, job requirements, and organizational environments into a successful career choice.

PLANNING THE JOB SEARCH PROCESS

Think of career planning as a five-step puzzle (see Figure 14.10). First, do a critical self-assessment: analyze career concepts, career motives, and personal strengths and weaknesses. What do you like to do and why? What don't you like to do? Second, as early as possible in your college education process, plan your course work and class activities to better prepare for your chosen career track. Use term papers, company

Figure 14.10

Career Planning: A Five-Piece Puzzle

1. You—The Person

Motives
Strengths
Weaknesses
Assessment

4. The Job & Company

Culture Product/
Service Perception
Opportunity

Success
Opportunity
Growth
Fulfilment
Happiness

Academic
Social
Practical

Process
Tools
Alternatives

2. Your Education

3. The Job Search Process

tours, and internships to prepare you for where you want to go. Form a network of people you meet along the way. Gather business cards for future use. Third, think about
how you will do your job search process. Develop tools and strategies for future use.
How will you "sell" yourself? Remember, most students will have three or four careers
during their work life. Fourth, identify organizations, jobs, and even supervisors who
could help you make contacts and launch your career. Fifth, and finally, when you have a
job, it is only the beginning of your career. Plan how you will advance through the organization, gaining valuable skills, experiences, and insights along the way. The table
below shows the ten most marketable skills employers want in their employees.

The 10 Most Marketable Skills
(What the Employer Wants Most)
Skills List
Analytical Skills
Computer Skills
Decision Making
Demonstrated Leadership
Demonstrated Teamwork Abilities
Flexibility
Oral Communications Proficiency/Technical Competence/Intern
Written Communication Skills
Value-Added Marketing

USING YOUR COMPUTER IN THE JOB SEARCH PROCESS

Word processing will become one of your greatest personal productivity tools during the job
search process. First, you will need your word processing skills to develop a resume. A
resume is a major component of your marketing program. Your resume should introduce you
to a potential employer and describe your education, employment history, talents, and
achievements. Second, you will need to write a cover letter to accompany each resume that
you send prospective employers. Finally, you will need to write interview thank you letters as
a follow-up to the interview process. The use of a word processor will allow you to create
professional documents in an efficient manner. Keeping electronic copies of all these documents on a computer system will come in handy. Often, with only minor modifications, a letter used for one purpose can be easily edited and made appropriate for a new opportunity.

It has been estimated that over 80 percent of all jobs are found through networking. Your network consists of all the people you know and includes your family, friends,
professors, other students, and co-workers—anyone you have met or have had contact
with who could help you find a job. To organize this information, develop a spreadsheet
or database containing the names, addresses, phone numbers, and other related information about the people in your network. During your job search, you can use the database to help you contact individuals who might know of job opportunities.

CREATING A PERSONAL PORTFOLIO

A **portfolio** is simply a collection of your best work, bound for display. It is used during an interview to quickly highlight your accomplishments and show a prospective employer examples of your work. The portfolio should look professional. Bound in a spiral or three-ring notebook, the portfolio might include your resume, letters of recommendation, copies of certificates received, samples of your best work, and descriptions of internships or other significant work experience (including color photos). You might want to use desktop publishing or graphics software to incorporate different fonts, page layouts, and clip art in the documents you show.

IN CONCLUSION

Information workers of the future will surely use computers to help them. Smart workers will use computers to increase their personal productivity and leverage their problem-solving abilities. We hope this book will, in some small way, help you achieve both of these goals.

Key Terms

applications programmer

associate computing professional (ACP)

Association for Computing Machinery (ACM)

Bureau of Labor Statistics (BLS)

certified computing professional (CCP)

certified network administrator (CNA)

chief information officer (CIO)

computer instructors

computer operations

computer utilities

customer representatives

data communications specialists

Data Processing Management
    Association (DPMA)

database specialists

director of management information systems

distributed data processing

enablers

hardware vendors

information appliances

information center

information specialists

Institute for the Certification of Com-
    puter Professionals (ICCP)

network administrator

office automation specialist

open systems

portfolio

software vendors

systems analysts

systems programmer

technical support

technical writers

upside-down managerial pyramid

vice president of information systems

Webmaster

Summary

The three building blocks of the national information infrastructure (NII) are computing power, digital technologies/networks, and personal information appliances.

Intra-system computer applications focus on connecting various internal components of an organization. *Inter-system computer applications* connect an organization's system to systems outside the organization.

An information systems department provides computing services for an entire organization and is under the direction of a senior officer called the **vice president of information systems**, **chief information officer (CIO)**, or **director of management information systems**.

The employees in **computer operations** are responsible for the operation and maintenance of the main computer system. **Systems analysts** analyze, design, and implement information systems. **Applications programmers** take a system design prepared by a systems analyst and convert it into computer instructions. **Technical support** is responsible for system software and database systems. The **systems programmers** are responsible for maintaining system software, including operating systems. **Database specialists** are responsible for development, maintenance, and security of databases. **Data communications specialists** develop, implement, and maintain computer network and communications software. The **network administrator** manages the hardware, software, applications, communication linkages, and personnel elements of the network system.

Distributed data processing has contributed to the need for **information centers**. **Information specialists** provide computer support for users, and office **automation specialists** assist users with office technology.

There are many other computer-related career opportunities. **Hardware vendors** hire **customer representatives**, who call on customers to tell them about their companies' equipment. **Software vendors** are companies that produce and sell software packages. Both hardware and software vendors employ **technical writers** to write user's manuals and other types of documentation. **Computer instructors** are needed at all educational levels to teach computer classes.

Several organizations exist for computer professionals. The **Data Processing Management Association (DPMA)** and **Association for Computing Machinery (ACM)** are the most widely known.

The **certified computing professional (CCP)** designation indicates that a computing professional has passed an examination requiring an in-depth knowledge in information systems.

The **certified network administrator (CNA)** designation indicates proficiency in the areas of network products, service, and support.

Begin the search for employment before graduation and prepare a package of materials, or a portfolio, that you can use during interviews. Computers can help you in many ways during the job search process.

14 Easy steps to being a webmaster

STEP 14 | JAVA

One of the most popular and fast-growing usage tools for the Web is JavaScript™. It is a customized language jointly developed by Netscape and Sun Microsystems. JavaScript allows the incorporation of small computer programs, called applets, in web pages. JavaScript requires Netscape 2.0 or higher and has some bugs, so examples provided here should work, but cannot be guaranteed for all environments (for instance, Netscape 2.0 on Windows 3.1 may have some problems with these scripts). The JavaScript code basics are below.

Code	Meaning
<script language= "JavaScript"> </script>	Script beginning and end.
<! --	*script code*
//-->	The *script code* is imbedded in script commands above. The first line identifies the code as a comment to non-JavaScript browsers. The second line, *script code*, is replaced with the code you program. The last line is an end-comment to non-JavaScript browsers and a close-script command to JavaScript browsers.
<body onload= "*script method()*"">	The onload subcommand calls a JavaScript by its name to begin processing when the page is loaded. *Script method()* identifies the code within script commands.
<body onunload= "*script method()*"">	The "onunload" calls a script when the page is unloading from the viewer's display.

Figure 14.11 is a script that is executed when it is encountered by the html page load routine. In Step 5, we recommended that each page have the date of last update on it. Figure 14.11 uses JavaScript to do this automatically. The date of last change for the document (document.lastModified) is placed within the words as, for example: Last updated on July 26, 1996. This means that you, the programmer, never have to worry about updating this information because the computer does it automatically. The most efficient way to use this code is to copy the short script into every html page. This type of JavaScript program, or *method*, uses system resources to display this information. Notice that upper and lower case is important within the script commands.

```
<html><body>
...
<script>
<!--
document.write("Last updated on "+document.lastModified+".")
//-->
</script></body></html>
```

Figure 14.11

JavaScript for document version.

The script in Figure 14.12 shows a banner message that flashes across the screen. You can customize the message by changing the words in quotes that are assigned to *msg*. The information in *msg*, *delay*, and *timerId* are all variables. The *value* of *delay*, for instance, is set at 100 milliseconds. Counting in JavaScript begins at zero. The *msg=* command takes all of the characters beginning at the second and adds the first character at the back. So, the first flash of the message is: "Hello from me to you. . .". The second is "ello from me to you. . .H", and the third is "llo from me to you. . .He", and so on. The message looks like it is moving off the screen on the left side and back onto the screen on the right side. The timer is used to say how often to *move* the letters.

```
<html><head><title>Figure 14-2. Message Scroll</title>
<script language="JavaScript">
<!--
var msg="Hello from me to you..."
var delay=100                    //To speed scrolling, reduce the
                                    number.
var timerId                      //Note the Capital 'I'
function scrollmsg() {
        window.status=msg
        msg=msg.substring(1,msg.length)+msg.substring(0,1)
//      The above line moved the current 1st character to the end
        of the message.
timerId=setTimeout("scrollmsg()",delay)
//      The above line sets up the display to be continuous
}//-->
</script></head><body onload="scrollMsg()">
...
</body></html>
```

Figure 14.12

JavaScript scrolling banner.

Now that you have completed these steps, you are truly on the way to becoming a web master. Congratulations!

ASSIGNMENT: Visit a Java applet site at http://www.javasoft.com, http://www.applets.com, or http://www.teamjava.com/links, and add a link to one of them in one of your pages. Or, modify one of the JavaScript applets provided here and add it to one of your pages.

Exercises

REVIEW QUESTIONS

1. What is a computer utility?

2. What characterizes an open system?

3. What new computing capabilities become possible with a 64-bit microprocessor?

4. Name as many job titles as you can in an information systems department and explain the kind of work performed by each.

5. Identify some specific career opportunities with companies that provide computer products and services.

6. What factors affect compensation in the information systems industry?

7. Identify the certification programs available for computer professionals.

8. List the five steps in the career planning process.

9. What should be included in your portfolio?

FILL IN THE BLANKS

1. The computer industry is often referred to as the _____ industry.

2. When a technology allows us to do activities we have not been able to do before, this technology is said to _____ us.

3. _____ systems are designed to be shared by other developers and competing users.

4. Business becomes _____ when a minimum amount of time, cost, and resources are necessary for a project's completion.

5. The main tasks of the _____ is to analyze, design, and implement information systems.

6. A(n) _____ must be able to take a system design prepared by a systems analyst and convert it into instructions for the computer to execute.

7. In large organizations, the _____ is responsible for developing and maintaining databases, developing database security measures, maintaining open communications, and assisting users in the effective use of databases.

8. According to the Bureau of Labor Statistics, the fastest growing information systems job classification is the _____ _____

9. A _____ is an excellent tool to take on a job interview to show the quality of your work.

 **MATCHING**

Match each term with its description.

a. DPMA
b. 64-bit microprocessor
c. type of industry
d. systems programmer
e. webmaster

f. computer instructor
g. systems analyst
h. database specialist
i. portfolio
j. CCP

___ 1. Instructs students in the use of computer hardware and software.

___ 2. Professional computing organization.

___ 3. Professional computing certification earned by passing an examination.

___ 4. Responsible for system software.

___ 5. Responsible for managing the organization's connection to the Internet.

___ 6. Package of your materials that you can use during an interview.

___ 7. Analyzes, designs, and implements information systems.

___ 8. Responsible for development, maintenance, and security of databases.

___ 9. Estimated to be 100 times faster than the current processing chip used in most microcomputers.

___ 10. Affects the median annual salary level for a programmer.

 ACTIVITIES

1. Describe the ideal job for you in the information systems industry. What are its characteristics, and how do these characteristics match your personality and interests?

2. List some new career opportunities that you believe will emerge over the next ten years. Why will these opportunities arise?

3. Explain the rationale for the statement, "In the next five years, almost everyone seeking employment will need to know about computers." Give reasons why you agree or disagree with this statement.

4. Prepare a one-page resume for yourself. Identify three concrete ways your presence would benefit the organization.

Skills for Living

As college professors, the authors observe many student successes and failures as they pursue careers and employment opportunities upon graduation. Your education is an investment of time, energy, and money. Professional employment, fair compensation, and your career are your returns on that investment. Employment statistics show that college graduates enjoy higher salaries and more rapid advancement than non-graduates. View your job search and career planning as an ongoing, life-long process.

Remember that the career field has changed drastically in the last ten years. Experts say today's typical college graduate will have four careers during his or her work life. How do you prepare yourself for four careers? Anticipate change and be ready to make those career changes.

Historically students have used a number of resources to help them through this process. Professors, friends, and the college or university were used most often. These are still very helpful sources. But, with today's stiff employment competition and employers looking for the best employee for their investment, students must use every resource available. Today, the World Wide Web offers a new and dynamic addition to traditional resources. These sources include descriptions of various types of jobs and careers, what those jobs currently pay per year, what types of education they require, and the future outlook for those jobs.

Now we ask you to visit the Web and try these services.

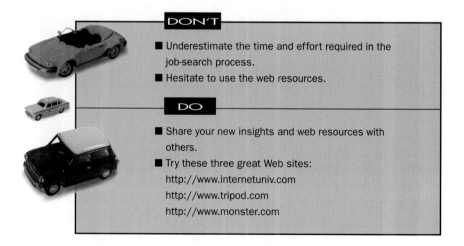

DON'T
- Underestimate the time and effort required in the job-search process.
- Hesitate to use the web resources.

DO
- Share your new insights and web resources with others.
- Try these three great Web sites:
  http://www.internetuniv.com
  http://www.tripod.com
  http://www.monster.com

STUDENT ACTIVITIES

1. For this final exercise, research the future opportunities for two first-level, professional positions. First, look at the systems analyst position. What does this job require? What are the academic skills and concepts required? What previous work experience is helpful? What is the job description? What does the future hold for this position? Then, based on these insights, try to identify the typical career path a person with this job might take. How long would each job normally last before a promotion to the next level? How successful do you think you would be in this career path?

2. For the second activity, pick a career and starting position that currently appeals to you and do the same review as discussed above. What would be a good starting position in that career? What are the opportunities, requirements, etc? What might be a typical career path in that field? Now that you have done this research, how interested are you in this career? How successful would you be?

3. Finally, for both these careers, how can your current college academic program best help you prepare for positions and a career in that field? What courses, work experiences, and internships are available? How would you prepare to interview for a starting position in that career?

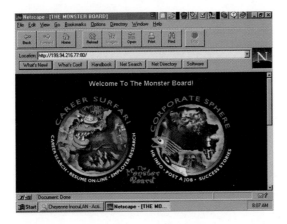

INDEX

D

J

K